Sacha Runa

SACHA RUNA

Ethnicity and Adaptation of Ecuadorian Jungle Quichua

NORMAN E. WHITTEN, JR.

with the assistance of
Marcelo F. Naranjo   Marcelo Santi Simbaña
Dorothea S. Whitten

UNIVERSITY OF ILLINOIS PRESS

Urbana   Chicago   London

© 1976 by Norman E. Whitten, Jr.
Manufactured in the United States of America

Library of Congress Cataloging in Publication Data

Whitten, Norman E., Jr.
  Sacha Runa.

  Bibliography: p.
  Includes index.
  1. Canelos Indians. 2.   Indians of South America—
Ecuador—Government relations. I.   Title.
F3722.1.C23W47   986.6'4'00498   75-28350
ISBN 0-252-00553-8

Al compadre Marcelo Santi Simbaña, a la comadre Faviola Vargas Aranda de Santi, al ahijado Orlando Victor—*sinchi yachaj runa, ñuca llullucu marcashca*—a los otros miembros de su *huasi, llacta,* y *ayllu,* y a todos los otros participantes en su cultura, dedico este libro.

CAUSANGUICHI ALLI RUNAGUNA
SACHA RUNA CAUSAN

Contents

Illustrations

MAPS

DIAGRAMS

Acknowledgments

My basic purpose in writing *Sacha Runa* is to present the rich integration of a particular set of Jungle Quichua lifeways existing in a dynamic moment of time in some areas of eastern Ecuador. Processes of nationalization and modernization are now well under way there, and the Jungle Quichua are ready to participate in certain types of national consolidation of their rugged jungle domain. They want to bring their knowledge of the vast, complex Amazonian ecosystem to bear on matters of critical national and international concern. At the same time, they want to maintain creative, logical, adaptive systems of relations inherent in their culture, and they express a desire to inform a literate world of this.

This book is the direct result of support received by the National Science Foundation, Grant No. GS-2999, between 1970 and 1975. NSF supported the preliminary field work in 1970 and 1971, and provided most of the finances needed for field research expenses of Dorothea Whitten, Marcelo Naranjo, and me, and for an applied program of medical care delivery in 1972–73. In addition, this grant established the basis for the necessary library and archival work, analysis, and writing at the University of Illinois by freeing the principal investigator from teaching obligations during fall semester, 1973. Without such support, publication of *Sacha Runa* would undoubtedly have been delayed for years. We are especially indebted to the two former directors of the NSF Anthropology Section, Richard Lieban and John Cornell, and to the present director, Iwao Ishino, for the clear, consistent, and efficient communications which facilitated all of our planning, and allowed us to proceed with the necessary work without undue strain, even as conditions changed.

The proposal itself was developed on the basis of research supported by the Committee on Latin American Studies, Washington University, St. Louis, and NIMH Grant No. PO1 MH 15567-01. Additional funds from the Research Board and Center for International Comparative Studies (CICS) of the University of Illinois, Urbana, provided research and training experiences for several graduate students. The Archives of Traditional Music, Indiana University, supplied extra cassettes and advice. The Appendix briefly documents the development of the project, describes the ways by which data were obtained, and indicates the role of each person who participated—Cynthia Gillette, Michael Waag, Margarita Wurfl, Nicanor Jácome, J. Peter Ekstrom, and Theodore Macdonald. It also sets forth some of the pivotal ways by which Dorothea S. Whitten, Marcelo Naranjo, and Marcelo Santi Simbaña contributed to almost every phase of research, and to the preparation of the manuscript for this book.

In Ecuador we were sponsored in 1968 by the Casa de la Cultura Ecuatoriana. From 1969 to the present we have worked under the auspices of the Instituto Nacional de Antropología e Historia (I.N.A.H.), with the approval and consent of the Casa de la Cultura Ecuatoriana. We must acknowledge our continuing debt to the I.N.A.H. director, Hernán Crespo Toral, for his creative and constructive help in virtually every stage of our continuing research in Ecuador.

I am also grateful to Carolyn Orr of the Summer Institute of Linguistics (S.I.L.) field staff in Ecuador, and to Udo Oberem, Seminar für Völkerkunde, Universität Bonn, for their technical help, advice, and encouragement. Both of them commented on some of the results of our field work, and provided very helpful supporting information. Udo Oberem also kindly sent to me documentation of early juro-political moves on the part of native peoples near Puyo, photographic documentation from his field research in 1955, and prepared a paper on that work as well. Louisa Stark provided fresh data and analytical acuity on Jungle Quichua dialects, and reviewed Chapter 1.

In eastern Ecuador many people helped this research along. As will become apparent in the body of the text, native people near Puyo must adapt to series of imposed constraints emanating from national and local processes of modernization and economic development. In spite of our interest in native adaptation, and our help to many native peoples, most of the non-native people of Puyo and other small colonist settlements were open, friendly, and in some cases overtly supportive of applied and academic endeavors. We wish to extend our gratitude to the non-native people of Puyo, Tarqui, and Madre Tierra.

Within Puyo itself we owe a particular debt of gratitude to Joe Brenner of the Turingia Tropical Gardens. He has taken a special interest in the ethnography since its inception in 1968, and has contributed in multiple ways to the project's development and completion. His friendship and creative response to our many requests for use of his facilities exceeded all normal expectations of collegial aid. We also wish to thank Sister Francesca Cabrini, O.P., Sister Reginald Marie, O.P., and Sister Rosario Marie, O.P., of Puyo, and Dr. Wallace Swanson, of Shell, for sharing information and for their technical support in our applied program of medical care delivery, and Absolom Guevara for his collaboration in the museum project.

Father Raoul Maldonaldo provided helpful information and hospitality to me, in Paca Yacu and Canelos, and gave me access to materials in the Canelos archives. Rudi Masaquisa and Francisca de Masaquisa always made traveling between the Andes and tropical lowlands pleasant through their hospitality in Salasaca. They also gave us a great deal of encouragement, and suggested many interesting relationships between Lowland and Andean Quichua symbolism, as well as other interrelationships of Andean and Lowland peoples.

The personnel of Western Geophysical Company of America, working as an exploration company for Anglo-Ecuadorian Oilfields, Ltd., provided facilities and transportation on many occasions. I am especially grateful to William G. Quirk, G. Thomas Walker, Douglas Newman, and the late Frank Freedman of Western for their interest in the project, and for their willingness not only to open facilities to me, but also to provide maps and technical information on geological and geographical aspects of the area of my concern. Art Lusier of Americana Airlines, Fred Engelmann of ATESA Airlines, Walter Snyder and Larry Peterson of Ecuavia Helicopter Service provided considerable technical support leading to more efficient travel plans, and got me into (and out of) many areas essential to the project.

In addition to the obvious aid extended by other participants in the project, documented in greater detail in the Appendix, it is essential that a few very special debts be acknowledged here. In her M.A. field work and thesis Cynthia Gillette anticipated many of the concerns to which this research turned; we are especially grateful for her insights into colonization and change in the Ecuadorian Oriente, and for help in initially forming the perspective leading to the research. Theodore Macdonald contributed to many phases of the work, not only by creatively and competently carrying through many facets of archival and preliminary field research, but by frequently suggesting syntheses between diachronic and synchronic processes through provocative application of theory to collected data. Marcelo Naranjo worked with us through part of 1970, through almost the entire field work in 1972-73, and manifested an indefatigable drive to pull together our field data within a historical and comparative framework, and to apply the synthesis to issues of contemporary Ecuadorian juro-political relevance. Dorothea S. Whitten developed and directed a program of medical care delivery while at the same time undertaking participant field research and a study of Puyo modernization. In addition to this, she read each draft of each chapter, in some cases reworking sections until both of us were satisfied that the prose actually said and implied what our data and synthesis indicated should be stated.

Many anthropologists have contributed to the development of this project through their publications and deep sensitivity to native South American lifeways. I have been especially influenced by the work of

Napoleon Chagnon, Irving Goldman, Michael J. Harner, Kenneth Ken-
singer, Claude Lévi-Strauss, David Maybury-Lewis, Curt Nimuendajú,
Gerardo Reichel-Dolmatoff, and Terrence Turner. Robert Braun, Michael
J. Harner, Roswith Hartmann, James Lemke, Udo Oberem, Gary Urton,
Katherine Wagner, and Sandra Weber read sections of original drafts of
some chapters and offered suggestions. Theodore Macdonald commented
on an earlier version of the first six chapters, and Marcelo Naranjo reviewed
the first eight. Joe Brenner and Joseph B. Casagrande also read and
commented on the entire manuscript and discussed many sections with
me. Mary W. Helms provided a splendid critique of the work, which led to
the final revision. All of these scholars are, of course, absolved from any
responsibility for shortcomings.

Darlene Graves worked as secretary to the project from the end of the
first summer's field work, 1970, until late summer, 1974. She not only
typed all material involved in proposals and manuscript drafts, but also
handled all correspondence between field workers and those working in
Urbana and elsewhere. Without her careful, diligent, dedicated support
we would all probably be lost in a sea of uncoordinated papers, notes, and
miscommunications. Dorothy Osborne of the Center for Latin American
and Caribbean Studies, University of Illinois, completed the work of typing
in the preparation of the final draft. David Minor prepared all of the
photographs from color slides, and made the pictures of the ceramic
figurines from the author's collection. The maps, diagrams, and sketches
were prepared by Sally McBrearty. Both have taken considerable pains to
help illustrate aspects of life and concepts pertaining to the Jungle
Quichua. Elizabeth G. Dulany, University of Illinois Press, devoted much
time and effort to the final editing prior to publication. Criticisms
pertaining to any aspect of this work are attributable only to me, not to
those who have so generously aided in the undertaking.

The people who contributed most to this study are the Jungle Quichua
inhabiting areas ranging from the east Ecuadorian towns to the farthest
refuge areas in one of the world's most rugged rainforest zones. I have not
given identifying maximal clan names in this book, nor have I indicated
recent changes to Spanish surnames, simply offering to scholars what I
trust are adequate generalizations, without including the information
sought by those bent on ethnocide. Each of the names mentioned below is a
common one in the Canelos Quichua culture area. The individuals
themselves know whom I am designating, but there is no identifying, or
organizing, series of places to aid the reader. I have also not identified the
site of Puma Llacta, where we resided in 1972–73 (see Appendix for
discussion of our dual residence pattern).

In one way or another, all of the following native people furthered our research, although in no way should any one of them, or any grouping of them, or the total aggregate of them, be held accountable for my errors in fact, for my generalizations, for my ideas about process, structure, or national intent: Venancio Vargas, Eliseo Aranda, Josefina Aranda, Reinaldo Huatatuca, Aurelio Huatatuca, César Mucushihua, Cecilia Vargas, Camilo Santi Vargas, Delfina Maianchi, Tomás Maianchi, Teofilo Santi, Nelson Santi, Rosa Santi, Victoria Santi, Marcelo Santi Maianchi, Gloria Santi, Basilio Álvarez, Beatriz Santi, Marta Vargas, Leandro Santi, Herminia Cariajano, Eularia Vargas, Manuel Aranda, Andrea Canelos, Apacha Vargas, Severo Vargas, Juana Vargas, Atahualpa Vargas, Baltazar Vargas, Teresa Dahua, Adolfo Chango, Miguel Vargas, Corapicación Aranda, Pastora Vargas, Segundo Santi, Atanacio Vargas, Tito Vargas, Gilberto Tapuy, Faviola Vargas, Luis Vargas, Estela Dahua, Fernando Vargas, Saraita Vargas, Eva Vargas, Rosenda Vargas, Eliseo Vargas, Manuel Vargas, Guillermo Santi, Rebeca Machoa, Eusebia Aranda, Alicia Canelos, Luis Aranda, Gustavo Vásquez, Corina Santi, César Vásquez, Rafael Santi, Lucinda Vargas, Samuel Isamil Vargas, Alejo Vargas, Dina Illanes, Rubén Santi, René Santi, Yolanda Imunda, Julian Santi, María Aguinda, Jorge Aguinda, Antonia Aguinda, Leonardo Santi, Gladys Salazar, Domingo Salazar, María Grefa, Asensiona Canelos, Manuel Vargas, Juan Vargas, Victor Machoa, Solis Grefa, Domingo Grefa, Oscar Huatatuca, Honorio Santi, Turibio Santi, Rosalina Machoa, Enrique Moya, Rebeca Calle Vargas, Juan Vargas.

In addition to these people, and to many others—especially the children—who are not named, the following group taught us more about the dynamics of social life, culture, and basic humanity than we can possibly express. To Marcelo Santi Simbaña, Faviola Vargas Aranda, Bolívar Santi, Clemencia Vargas, Virgilio Santi, José Abraham Chango, Clara Santi, Juana Chango, Alberto Chango, Teresa Santi, Reinaldo Chango, Pastora Vargas, Alfonso Chango, Gregorio Chango, Luis Vargas Canelos, Celia Santi, Gonzalo Vargas, Olimpia Santi, Elsa Vargas, Venancio Vargas, Anselmo Vargas, Camilo Santi Simbaña, Soledad Vargas, Segundo Vargas, Balvina Santi, Dario Machoa, Adelaida Santi, Juan Machoa, and Matilde Collahuaso goes our deepest sense of gratitude, not only for their aid in this research, but for the fundamental friendship and sense of community with which they encompassed us in the general vicinity of Puyo and Puma Llacta.

N. E. WHITTEN, JR.
Urbana, Illinois
February, 1975

Orthography

Jungle Quichua in Ecuador is now a written language based on Spanish orthography. With the exceptions noted below, this orthography follows that of Orr and Wrisley (1965).

VOWELS

a   Spanish *a*
i   Ranges from Spanish *i* to Spanish *e*
u   Ranges from Spanish *u* to Spanish *o*

CONSONANTS

b   English *b*
c   Unaspirated *k*
ch Unaspirated *ch*, voiced after nasals to give French *je* sound[1]
d   English *d*
g   English *g*, written *gu* before *i*
hu English *w*[2]
j   English *h*,[3] a fricativized *k* (voiceless velar fricative) sound when terminal
l   Spanish *l*
ll Spanish *ll*
m   English *m*
n   English *n*
ñ   Spanish *ñ*
p   Spanish *p*
qu Unaspirated *k* before *i*[4]
r   Spanish *r*
s   English *s*
sh English *sh*
t   Spanish *t*
ts Similar to English *ts* as in ha*ts*, but heavily aspirated and sometimes voiced
y   English *y*

Here and there I deviate from this orthography in cases where pronunciation of loan words from Spanish is rendered much more clearly in Spanish orthography. This usually only involves use of the Spanish vowels *e* and *o* as in *jistero*, from the Spanish *fiestero* (ceremonial participant). Some place names that have Spanish spellings (e.g. Puyo Pungo instead of Puyupungu) also necessitate deviation from the orthography. Jívaro orthography follows that given by Harner (1972); Achuara orthography is not phonemicized, and is based on roughly English equivalents.

NOTES

1. I am simplifying the Orr and Wrisley "Quichua Alphabet" here by grouping the allophones of the /zh/ phoneme under the /ch/ grapheme. For example, Orr and Wrisley's *punzha*, day, is here written *puncha*, and pronounced approximately as *punja*. This simplification is useful only with the Canelos Quichua, and must not be applied to speakers of other Jungle Quichua dialects.

2. English readers must be very careful to "think" *w* here, so that *huasi*, house, is pronounced *wasi*.

3. Again, English readers must be careful to pronounce this sound as in Spanish. *Jauya*, for example, sounds much like English "how ya."

4. Here again, English readers must "think" of a *k* sound so that *Quichua* is pronounced *keéchua*.

Sacha Runa

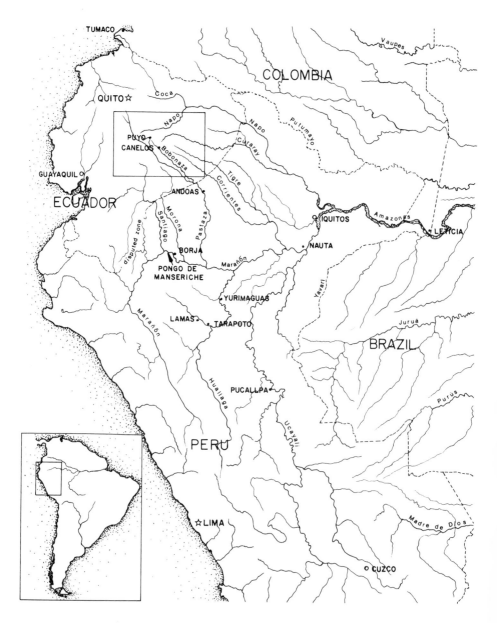

Western South America

CHAPTER

1
Introduction

Just east of the Andes, in clear view of spectacular snow-capped peaks, live two of the largest concentrations of tropical forest Indians in central Ecuador. Both speak Quichua,[1] a language long associated with Incaic expansion in the highlands and well known as a lower-class rural, "Indian" means of communication in contemporary sierran Ecuador.

These Jungle Quichua live near the towns of Puyo and Tena, each the capital of a province, Pastaza and Napo. The policy of the contemporary Ecuadorian military government is to destroy their way of life. Those near Puyo and Tena bear the brunt of this national anti-native policy, and carry their ecological, social, and ideological resources into the very teeth of the expanding "national culture."[2] By elaborating and adjusting their system of tropical forest culture to the dynamics of national expansion, Jungle Quichua peoples continuously create a core ethnicity with expanding boundaries.

This book is about the indigenous people—*Runa*—who live near Puyo, the most dynamic town in eastern Ecuador. It is about their high jungle—*sacha*—and, especially, the culture area which runs eastward through an increasingly low rainforest, providing the Puyo Runa with meaningful and resourceful bases for coping with nationally sponsored anti-native colonists from other parts of the republic. All native Quichua speakers refer to themselves as *Runa* (*runa shimi*, human speech). I shall use "Canelos Quichua" to refer to the people participating in the culture which will be presented in this book. The Puyo Runa, then, are a territorial grouping of Canelos Quichua culture.

INDIGENOUS LANGUAGE, CULTURE, AND TERRITORY

Canelos Quichua culture differs from that of the people dominating the native culture of Tena, known as the "Quijos" (Oberem 1971, 1974) or "Quijos Quichua" (Whitten 1975). In spite of their proximity to the Andes,

3

Puyo, 1973.

and their language, the Canelos Quichua have a fundamentally tropical
forest way of life, which they have applied to Andean foothills and montaña
existence in some instances.

Nationally, the overwhelming majority of native peoples of the Oriente,
as all territory east of the Ecuadorian Andes is called, are classed as either
Jívaro or Quichua, and the contrast is widely thought to designate very
different cultures. In the Oriente there are two known, contemporary
Jivaroan dialects called, among other things, "Jívaro proper" and "Achuara
Jivaroan." The former people are so named by the anthropologist Michael
J. Harner (1972), who has clarified their particular lifeways and ecological
adaptation. They refer to themselves as *Shuara* (sometimes written *Shuar*,
as the final *a* is silent). The word means essentially "native people"
including Quichua speakers. Speakers of the other Jivaroan dialect group,
who share other cultural characteristics and about whom far less is known,
call their language *Achuara* or *Achual.*

But the dialects spoken tell only part of a story, for some of the Achuara
speakers north of the Pastaza River are politically estranged from eastern
Achuara groups, and a few are allied with the Jívaro proper. Such Achuara
often give their cultural or political identity to outsiders as simply *Shuara,*
which, translated as *Jívaro,* gives the false impression of cultural similarity
between two different Jivaroan peoples. I have dwelt a bit on this Jivaroan[3]
distinction because the Canelos Quichua have been considerably influenced by the Achuara Jivaroans, and many of the Achuara Jivaroans,
hereafter referred to simply as "Achuara," are bilingual in Quichua and
Achuara.

Ecuadorians are somewhat ambivalent about Jivaroans. On the one hand, there is a certain pride that fierce and until recently completely unconquered tribal peoples lived their head-taking ways in the rugged jungle terrain. On the other hand, there is a national shame that the land of Jivaroan insolence is as yet unconquered, and the conquest, as it grinds on, depends nearly totally on foreign-made planes and equipment borne mostly by missionaries, oil searchers, and the military. Ecuadorians are not ambivalent about Quichua speakers, who are generally regarded with contempt (Casagrande 1974), and most certainly so when contrasted with the Jivaroans.

The Jungle Quichua of the central Oriente, which includes the provinces of Pastaza in the south and Napo in the north, have been linguistically classified into three major dialect segments (Orr and Wrisley 1965). The southern dialect is spoken by the Canelos Quichua, the northwestern by the Quijos Quichua, and the northeastern may or may not represent peoples with separable cultural characteristics.[4] The Quijos Quichua, also sometimes pejoratively known as *Yumbos* (see Porras 1955, 1974:164–175), seem to have a montaña cultural hearth and have moved eastward at various times as tropical forest Indians were pushed back, enslaved, or obliterated by disease (see, e.g., Oberem 1971). The Quijos Quichua have been particularly oppressed by church and hacienda serfdom within the last 200 years and seem to have a history quite different from the Canelos Quichua. This book will not deal with the cultural characteristics of the Quijos Quichua, nor will it deal with those Napo Quichua speakers who extend eastward to Iquitos, Peru.

The Canelos Quichua are contemporary Jungle Quichua whose lifeways comprise the basis for this book. They are so named because of the historical importance of the Catholic mission of Canelos, because of the trade nexus in the Canelos area (Oberem 1966/67), and because the "Canelos [or "Canelo"] Indians" have been recorded by other ethnographers as a distinct "tribe" or Jivaroan variant (see especially Karsten 1935). Many writers lump Canelos Quichua speakers together with the Quijos (e.g. Ferdon 1950) as presumed bearers of a common culture. Although Quijos penetration exists, the Canelos Quichua are seen here as culture bearers from the east and southeast, probably from areas drained by the Curaray, Tigre, Pastaza, Marañón, and Huallaga rivers. The contemporary Canelos Quichua represent a rich, dynamic culture which is today territorially specific, although outwardly ramifying into other culture areas; the elements themselves are widely shared with the peoples mentioned above, and throughout Amazonia and the Andes.

We have thus far noted four cultural sets—Achuara Jivaroan, Jívaro proper, Quijos Quichua, and Canelos Quichua—all of which contain

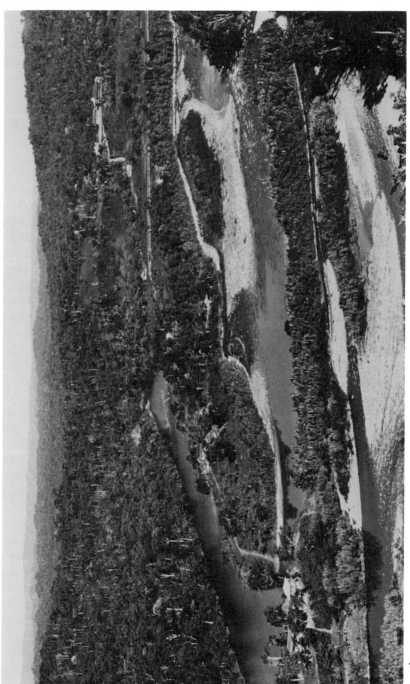

Canelos, 1973.

members who occupy specified territories in the Ecuadorian Oriente. Intermarriages occur, and political alliances weave in and out of the established, but always flexible, territorial divisions.

Another language family—Zaparoan—was once prominent in the territory of the Canelos Quichua, and some speakers still live there. The language is still "isolated," which means that it has not been classified by linguists, on linguistic grounds, as belonging to a family larger than that of obviously Zaparoan affiliation (Andoa [Shimigae], Iquitos, Arabela, and perhaps Candoshi—Anderson and Wise 1963, Eastman and Eastman 1963, Wise and Shell 1972). Zaparoan speakers have been labeled by dozens of names (see, e.g., Loukotka 1968:159–160, Steward 1948:628–639). The term itself may derive from *zapára*—a hexogonal-weave basket, with lid, enclosing broadleaves to make a waterproof back pack—which is manufactured and used by Jivaroans, Quichua speakers and Zaparoans alike. There are two identified dialects of Zaparoan in the contemporary Oriente (Stark, personal communication).

Zaparoan speakers ranged widely through eastern Ecuador and Peru in historic times, and inhabited the areas of the Canelos Quichua and the Quijos Quichua. They apparently suffered massive (60–100 percent) annihilation due to disease and enslavement during the sixteenth through eighteenth centuries (Sweet 1969) and thereafter began to live in settlements on affluents of the major rivers, sharing their hunting, fishing, and swidden horticulture territory with Achuara Jivaroans.

The Canelos Quichua seem to have formed from a basic merger of Achuara and Zaparoan peoples, the culture being spread by Quichua speakers (see, e.g., Oberem 1974, n.d.). Unfortunately, we have no descriptions of cultural or social patterns in this zone prior to around the mid-nineteenth century (Simson 1886, Villavicencio 1858, Magalli de Pred 1890, Valladares 1912). Oberem (1966/67, 1974, n.d.) argues persuasively, on the basis of an exhaustive search of available materials, that the Canelos Quichua represent an emergent culture formed out of "early" colonial experiences: "The Canelo are exceptional in being a group formed during the Colonial period consisting both biologically and culturally of a mixture of the original inhabitants of the northern Bobonaza area: Highland Indians; Quijo; Záparo and Jíbaro. Today the Canelo are distinct from their neighbors even linguistically, since they speak Quechua, and are well aware of their homogeneity" (Oberem 1974:347). The problem of establishing any baseline lies in the concept of, and historical documentation for, "formation" (Naranjo 1974). The Canelos Quichua may well have "formed" out of an Achuara-Zaparoan merger, and expanded the emergent culture through increased use of the Quichua language. The process is apparent in recent history, and extends back in time to "early colonial"—presumably at least to the seventeenth century. In short, we are confronted with a

perpetuative formative process. Travelers, explorers, and missionaries in
this zone seem repeatedly to encounter Canelos Quichua forming out of
Zaparoan and Jivaroan intermarriages and alliances, with a mediating
Quichua language borne by people in contact with distant sources of valued
goods. In the colonial era these goods consisted especially of steel tools
(Oberem 1974, Naranjo 1974).

Existing evidence for the formation of Canelos Quichua culture, then,
cannot be taken as indicative of any original baseline for three reasons: first,
we have no cultural factors with which to work in the establishment of such
a base; second, the paucity of ethnographic descriptions of Achuara and
Zaparoan culture prohibit reasoning by analogy and reconstruction; third,
evidence first appearing in the colonial era through materials from travelers
is inadequate to demonstrate a colonial emergence of culture. Achuara-
Zaparoan (and other prehistoric culture) interchange, intermarriage, and
syncretism could easily pre-date descriptions by colonial writers and
visitors. We simply do not know what the bases for the expansion of
Canelos Quichua culture within, or prior to, the colonial era were, though
re-expansion within the past 100 years can (and will) be documented.

In this book use of the terms "Achuara" and "Zaparoan" are quite loosely
applied to refer to languages or language dialects. My basic source stems
from elicited information given by contemporary old bilingual native
peoples, themselves concerned with indigenous classification of "other
native peoples" sharing a common stipulated descent system and territory.
For example, I tentatively accept contemporary Canelos Quichua and
western Achuara informants' reconstructive statements that the "Canelo"
or "Penday" Jivaroan (Loukotka 1968:158) once spoken near Canelos, but
replaced by Quichua, was "Achuara."

In the central Oriente of Ecuador remarkable adaptability and transformation of cultural system and core ethnicity exist. The markers of a culture
area in no way prohibit specific individuals from crossing the boundaries,
provided that the appropriate transformations in identity portrayal and in
cultural makeup are acceptably enacted. For example, there are Jívaro
proper and Quijos Quichua culture bearers living by intermarriage among
the Canelos Quichua, but such penetration in the culture area is absorbed
and reconfigured into the Canelos Quichua way, just as the Canelos
Quichua peoples who out-marry into Jívaro proper, Achuara, or Quijos
Quichua zones submerge the Canelos Quichua way.[5]

NON-INDIGENOUS TERRITORY AND INDIGENOUS ETHNOHISTORY

The eastern zones of the contemporary territory of the Canelos Quichua
were part of the mission of Maynas (Mainas) from the sixteenth to the early
nineteenth century. This Jesuit mission was centrally located in Borja, in

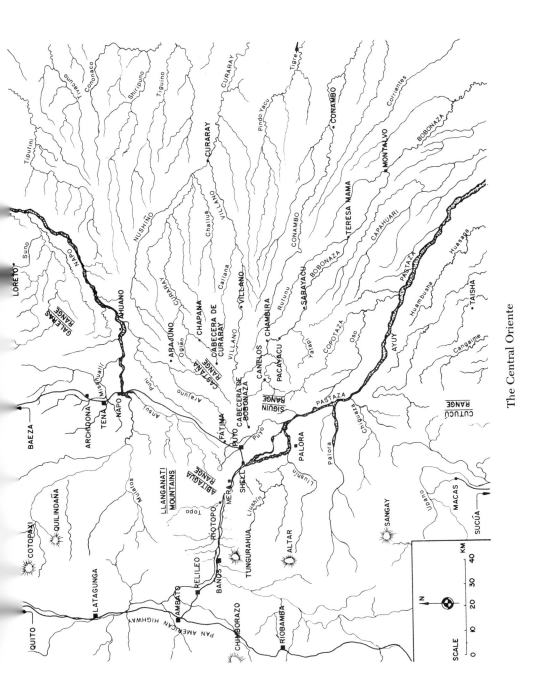

The Central Oriente

what is now eastern Peru. The western area, from Canelos to Río Topo, was part of the Dominican mission of Canelos at this time, with headquarters moving from near Puyo in the late sixteenth century to near the present site of Canelos by the seventeenth century. In 1803 Franciscans gained control of the Canelos mission, while Jesuits maintained their dominion over the adjoining mission of Gayes just to the east (González Suárez 1970:201). The central area for dispersal of priests and services for the latter came upriver from Borja (see, e.g., Stirling 1938:24); the former was dependent upon Quito.

Contact with outsiders prior to the mid-nineteenth century was sporadic but profoundly destructive. Intruders from all parts of the world extracted gold, furs, spices, medicines, rubber, and slaves. They brought steel tools, firearms, powder, shot, beads, disease, as well as concepts of perpetual service to priests, practices reflecting ideas about linguistic and racial inferiority, and an alien, Western god. Cataclysmic population destruction of from 50 to 100 percent of various peoples resulted as measles, smallpox, chicken pox, and malaria repeatedly took their awful toll (Sweet 1969:103).

By the mid-nineteenth century Canelos was a canton of the Ecuadorian Oriente, with a political lieutenant appointed by the governor of Quijos, the northern Oriente province. The boundaries were demarcated as the western slopes of the Abitagua range of Andean foothills, the left bank of the Pastaza River to its mouth in the south, and vague designations made according to shifting locations of reputedly Zaparoan groups in the north and east. Canelos proper was the canton head, with two downriver hamlets, Paca Yacu and Sara Yacu, on the Bobonaza River, as the only other civil administrative sites (Villavicencio 1858:411, Valladares 1912). The Canelos Quichua area by this time was characterized by trade with Andean peoples, the basic products being gold, panned by the native peoples (Spruce 1908:125 ff.), and cinnamon and honey, also collected by natives (Naranjo 1974).

The Canelos Quichua themselves traded with Andean merchants coming to their territory (Spruce 1908:350–351), and with the Quijos in the north, whom they visited and who sometimes came to them. They also carried gold, honey, and cinnamon westward to trade centers at contemporary Puyo, Mera, Baños, Pelileo, and Ambato (Oberem 1966/67, 1974; Villavicencio 1858:411–418).

Not long after the establishment of civil administration in the Canelos area the Dominicans from the archdiocese of Quito relocated a specific mission site somewhere between contemporary Puyo and Canelos, officially lost it again briefly to the Jesuits in 1869, and then reincorporated it as the archdiocese of Canelos in 1887 (Marin 1927:5), this time including the mission of Gayes. The present site of Canelos became the Dominican headquarters of the archdiocese.[6]

CULTURAL MARKERS OF THE CANELOS QUICHUA

The contemporary Canelos Quichua *refer* to themselves, in Quichua, as *Runa*, person, indigenous person. Among themselves they also use the term *alaj*, my mythic brother, to *address* those men who come from the Bobonaza or Curaray drainages. The derivation of the term *alaj* comes from a myth segment in which two brothers become separated from one another. The older in search of the younger wanders in the forest and, in hunger, begins to break off a piece of tree mushroom, *ala*. As he pinches the mushroom it cries out and turns into the lost brother. The *ala* notion (discussed at greater length in Chapters 2 and 7) is crucial in defining a basic level of male self-identification of the Canelos Quichua. Many ancient men had the ability to send their souls, *aya*, into special rocks or logs when their bodies died, from whence mushrooms would emerge to await wandering male Runas who, in hunger, would pinch the mushrooms and awaken the ancient Runas. An interplay between the need to wander, to be on the edge of destruction due to war and illness, and the ability to awaken ancient souls and effect a resuscitation of population and culture (the ancient souls regenerated ancient knowledge) is bound up in the concept of alaj (the *j* is possessive).

Male continuity is closely tied to the concept of soul master spirit, *Amasanga*. As long as Amasanga lives, and as long as mushrooms grow out of trees and rocks, the Canelos Quichua men believe they will survive, even if there are no corporeal representatives through the immediate centuries. Significantly, this is the ethnic term (*Amasanka*) by which Zaparoan speakers in the Montalvo area refer to the Canelos Quichua (Stark, personal communication). Female continuity is part of a complex structure involving Amasanga's wife, *Nunghui*,[7] and the pottery tradition transmitted from older women to younger women. From the female standpoint the culture will live as long as the rock- and clay-dye soul designs endure. The union of man and woman constitutes a very special *huasi*, household unit, among the Canelos Quichua, through which cultural perpetuity is transmitted to future generations.

The kinship system, *ayllu*, of the Canelos Quichua is seen by them as descending from ancient times to the intermarried ancestors of the contemporary elders. The interpenetration of ancestor souls, and souls acquired in a process of male shamanistic power quests, also seems characteristic of the Canelos Quichua, though also structurally similar to the Achuara, Jívaro proper, and perhaps Quijos Quichua.

In the area of ritual, too, the culture has specific patterns of performance which relate directly to kinship, mythology, and aspects of pottery design, and seem to distinguish Canelos Quichua culture as well integrated with definable characteristics.

CONTEMPORARY CANELOS QUICHUA TERRITORIALITY

The contemporary culture area is bordered in the west by the Andean escarpment, in the north by the Villano and Curaray rivers, in the east more vaguely by the Peruvian border or the viscissitudes of contemporary movements of northwestern Peruvian peoples, and in the southeast by Achuara Jivaroans of the Copotaza and Capahuari rivers, and the Jívaro proper on the right bank of the Pastaza.

Participants in Canelos Quichua culture clearly state their segmentation of ethnic categories and territories. They seldom refer to their own dialect group except by implicit contrast, using the following distinctions. In the west—the Andes—there are two "territories": *Runa Llacta* and *Ahua Llacta*. The former is "indigenous territory" but is also used around Puyo to refer to highland Indian territory—regarded as all of the Andes. The latter term, literally "highland," refers to all non-Indian Ecuadorians and is used as a polite synonym for the Spanish *blanco* (white). The Puyo Runa also use the Spanish term *gente* (person) for themselves, and specifically contrast *gente* with *blanco* for all purposes. Today, around Puyo, *blanco* has become synonymous with *mestizo*, and both are labeled *mashca pupu*,[8] barley-gut national intruder, by the Puyo Runa.

To the north-northwest two territories of Quichua which correspond to the Orr and Wrisley (1965) dialect areas are called by the Canelos Quichua *Alchiruna* [Spanish *Archidona*] *Llacta* (the Quijos) and *Napo Llacta* (which includes such settlements as Tena, Arajuno, and Santa Clara). Sometimes *Ansuj Llacta* is added to indicate settlements of Quichua speakers along the Ansuj (Anzu) River, southwest of the Napo. To the north-northeast and south-southeast lies *Auca Llacta*, heathen territory. In the north this includes the *Cushmas* (Cofán, Tetéte, Secoya, Siona), who are but dimly known by reputation, and the hostile *Huarani* (called *Llushti Auca*, naked heathen, or *Tahuashiri*, ridge people, in Quichua). On the Curaray River, and recently along the Bobonaza, distinctions are made between the Huarani or "true" Llushti Auca, to the west, now fanning out from the Curaray River above the mouth of the Villano River and from the Nushiño River, and the Awishiri (Tahuashiri) Auca to the east, who now live between the Cononaco and Tivacuna rivers. The Quichua legendary *Puca* or *Manduru Chaqui Auca*, red- or achiote-foot heathen, of the Tiputini drainage are said to constitute a third division, and the Canelos Quichua insist that these unknown people speak another language, which some relate to old *Gaye* or *Gae* (Zaparoan), and use bows and arrows. Some workers for oil-exploration groups also claim to have seen a native group with the lower parts of their legs painted red using bows and arrows. Also belonging to Auca Llacta in the north are Zaparoan speakers, most of whom are bilingual in Jungle Quichua and many of whom are trilingual in Spanish as well. Northern Achuara from the Corrientes and Conambo river systems are also part of the Canelos Quichua concept of Auca Llacta (Tessman 1930, Steward 1948, Steward & Métraux 1948, Ferdon 1950, and Oberem 1966/67:71 give data supporting these Canelos Quichua distinctions).

Contemporary Canelos Quichua often include the *Andoa Runa*, from the Peruvian site of Andoas Nuevo near the Ecuadorian border, as the easternmost members of their culture area. Within the last twenty-five years the Andoa Runa, mainly Zaparoan speakers, some married to Achuara, have completely taken over Quichua as their language (Orr, personal communication). Nevertheless, they seem culturally part of the Canelos Quichua system, giving contemporary weight to the basic Achuara-Zaparoan merger as fundamental to the culture area. Beyond Andoas Nuevo live other "Auca": the Murato (often called *Mulato*) and Shapra Candoshi (often called *Canduishuar*); and beyond, in Marañón River territory, fierce Zaparoans or Jivaroans sometimes called *Mainu Shuara*, enemy Jívaro proper (known as *Huambishuara* or *Huambisa Shuara*), and Achuara in various areas. Friendly Cocama, called *Yajocha*, live on the Tigre River, and other Zaparoans with bows and arrows, thought to be related to the Puca Chaqui Auca, are said to inhabit the interfluvial zones near the Peruvian border (possibly westward-moving Arabela).

Within Ecuador the Canelos Quichua designate large Runa territories in their culture area by mission, administrative, or trade center. The Dominican order has established a cabildo system within each major territory. Four to six native officials are named by the priest each year to serve as middlemen between visiting or resident clergy and the people. The number of officials varies from four to six according to population, recorded church marriages, and size of the annual or biannual ceremony. A *vara* (staff of authority or clerical prestige) is given to each *varayo* (official; *varayuj* in Quichua). Among the Puyo Runa the cabildo has become a *directiva* (governing board), under the direction of the national *Ministerio de Previsión Social* (Ministry of Social Security), with these officers: president, vice-president, secretary, treasurer, and lawyer (*síndico*). The staffs of authority in the Puyo area have been reclaimed by the church.

Perhaps 10,000 Canelos Quichua inhabit the culture area of our concern, a large jungle territory which would seem adequate for idyllic subsistence existence, without concern for land disputes or territorial hierarchies. However, dependence on trade for some goods, especially salt and steel machetes, together with political asylum from vengeance killing, provided by the mission site or by a concentrated population there, conditions a system of territoriality where land disputes over access to strategic resources are important dynamics in the cultural ecology. A sporadic, non-seasonal sequence of population concentration and deconcentration around the mission site or trade-administrative center coincides with an expanding population. Residence in such centers is more desirable when exchangeable goods are available and less desirable when they are scarce.

Outward expansion of people in a given territory inevitably involves them with people of another territory, and inward movement toward their central locus inevitably intensifies interactions contributing to alliances and oppositions of the territorial groupings. A subdivision, *llacta*, of the territorial grouping consists of a defensible swidden horticultural zone utilized by an intermarried segment of a wide-flung kinship network. But before discussing the Canelos Quichua social order, itself the subject of later chapters, let us set forth the major divisions, which I call the "Runa territories." From west to east, with the Bobonaza River as the world's most crooked line, the major "people" are as follows.

Runa Territories

Puyo Runa (fog people, sometimes *Pinduj Runa*, river-cane people—named after the Puyo and Pinduj [now Pindo] rivers, which circle Puyo and flow into the Pastaza) includes all people from the Pindo and Puyo rivers south to the Pastaza River, north on either side of the Puyo-Napo road for a few kilometers, and northeast to Cabecera de Bobonaza. *Canelos Runa* includes people from east of Cabecera de Bobonaza to Canelos, and from Canelos north to the headwaters of the Villano and Curaray rivers, east to Chambira, and south to the headwaters of the Copotaza River. *Paca Yacu Runa* (guama river people—named after the Pacai River, which enters the Bobonaza there) includes all people around the settlement of Paca Yacu north to Villano, where mixture with Quijos Quichua defines another settlement ranging from Villano to Huito. *Sara Yacu Runa* (corn river people—named after the Sara Yacu River, which enters the Bobonaza) includes all people there south to the Capahuari River, north to the Conambo River, and east on the Bobonaza River to Teresa Mama. The *Montalvo Runa*, sometimes *Juanjiri Runa*, includes those in the territory north to the Conambo River, east to Peru, and south toward the Capahuari River. The latter Runa territory also includes Achuara and Jívaro proper who do not speak Quichua (Pedro Porras, personal communication).

These are the five Runa territories of the Río Bobonaza, the contemporary heart of Canelos Quichua culture. There is another Runa territory—the *Curari Runa*—long a northern extension of the Canelos Quichua on the right bank of the Curaray River, extending west, south, and east, but never north into Huarani Auca territory. At the headwaters of the Curaray River there is a mixed Quijos-Canelos settlement called Chapana (from *Chapan Auca*, Auca ambush) and near Puyo another such mixed settlement-

The Bobonaza River at Sara Yacu, 1973.

territory, now legally formed into a *comuna* called San Ramón. The people from the zone are also referred to as *Jatun Paccha Runa*, high waterfall people.

Each of the six basic Runa territories—Puyo, Canelos, Paca Yacu, Sara Yacu, Montalvo, and Curaray (*Curari*) is subdivided into llactas which have recognized living or dead founders and consist of intermarried clan, *ayllu*, segments which trek periodically to identified zones, where they encounter other people from other Runa territories similarly engaged. I see the Sara Yacu–Canelos zone as the contemporary cultural hearth of the Canelos Quichua culture, but the greatest population concentration now fighting the grim battle for ethnic survival is between the Puyo-Pindo and Pastaza rivers. Many people in the Puyo area see their cultural origin as somewhere around contemporary Yurimaguas, in Peru, others identify zones between Puyo and Canelos, the Villano-Curaray-Conambo drainages, and the Corriente-Pindo-Tigre drainages as the ancient feeder zones for the contemporary people.

Because of the designation of Canelos as the stereotypic center of southern Quichua culture, and because the people of this zone have so frequently been designated as the "Canelos tribe" in the literature, I have chosen to use the phrase "Canelos Quichua." The reader is warned, however, that the Dominican and administrative site of Canelos proper is characterized by *more intrusion* from Quijos Quichua and Highland Quichua than any other area of Canelos Quichua territory, including Puyo (González Suárez 1970:202–203, Tobar Donoso 1960:130–131, Oberem 1974:347, Naranjo 1974).

Marriage between Canelos Quichua and Achuara has been recorded by evangelical Catholic friars for the past 200 years, in all of the mission sites discussed above. "Záparo"–"Jívaro" (usually Achuara) marriages, with Canelos Quichua ritual sponsors (Catholic *padrinos-madrinas*), are also common in the existing Dominican archives. In Puyo, Canelos, and Montalvo, marriage with the Jívaro proper has also taken place, to a more limited extent. The Canelos Quichua have virtually absorbed the Zaparoan speakers in the last fifty years, and marriage with highland Indians, occasionally with highland whites, and with Quichua-speaking Indians from both northern dialects of Jungle Quichua takes place. Nonetheless, the Canelos Quichua aggressively assert cultural commonality to characterize themselves as a distinct people, and manifest their distinctive cultural markers through their pottery tradition, soul acquisition, ceremonial structure, and in many other features discussed in ensuing chapters.

ETHNOGRAPHIC SYNOPSIS

Economically, the staple of Canelos Quichua life is manioc (Spanish *yuca*, Quichua *lumu*). A *chagra*, cleared field for swidden cultivation, covers from one to two hectares. Land is cleared with axe and machete by a man, his wife, sons, and sons-in-law, more often than not without help of kinsmen or friends, although a *minga*, reciprocal labor exchange, may take place. Men plant plantains, bananas, maize, and naranjilla (*Solanum quitoense* and other species). Women plant manioc and other root crops, keep the chagra clean, harvest tubers, carry them to the house, prepare them, and serve them as food and drink. Palms, taro, yautia, jicama, and a wide variety of fruits, peppers, tomatoes, and herbs are grown in kitchen gardens in back of the house as well as on the chagra. Near Puyo the naranjilla is grown as a cash crop; otherwise, the Canelos Quichua have few current crops of cash value, even though the Puyo Runa are ringed on their western and northern flanks by sugar and tea plantations.

Manioc beer, called *chicha* in Spanish and trade Quichua but *asua* in Quichua, of very low alcoholic content (more of a gruel), is a staple of life, and the making and serving of chicha constitutes a focal point of symbolic interaction within the household. The masticated manioc is stored in a large pottery jar, called *tinaja* in Spanish and trade Quichua and *asua churana manga*, "dressed" or painted chicha pot, in Quichua; it is served in a thin, finely decorated bowl, *mucahua*. All pottery is made by coiling.

Women make their own serving bowls and storage jars and guard small secrets pertaining to color, design, and ways to produce the thinnest possible sides and rims. Knowledge and techniques are passed from mother to daughter or from mother to son's wife. The pottery is fired without a kiln. This is the finest pottery made today in the Ecuadorian Oriente, and one of the finest in the Central, Northwest, and Upper Amazon. Most, if not all, pottery sold in the Ecuadorian highlands as "Jívaro pottery" comes from the Canelos Quichua. Indeed, some of the Jívaro proper marry Canelos Quichua women and bring them to their own houses in order to enjoy Canelos Quichua pottery and the associated female knowledge of ancient souls. A black pottery cooking pot, *yanuna manga*, and eating dish, *callana*, are also made, sometimes with thumbnail decoration called *sarpa manga*.

Fine decorated pottery for intra-household use is dwindling, though not disappearing, with the introduction of aluminum pots and pans, but the black pottery is rapidly disappearing. People buy the new goods, or trade other things to obtain them, but they maintain at least one or two tinajas for chicha storage, and at least one mucahua for serving.

Several fish poisons, such as barbasco (*Lonchocarpus* species), are grown in the chagra to be used during relatively dry times of the year, when the rivers and streams run especially low and clear. Hallucinogens such as *ayahuasca* (at least three *Banisteriopsis* species) and *huanduj* (several *Datura* species), are grown, together with *huayusa* (*Ilex* species), tobacco, and a large variety of *jambi*, medicinal, and *supai*, spirit, herbs, shrubs, vines, and trees.

Men fish with spears, traps, weirs, lines, and nets, and hunt with blowguns and poison darts, muzzle-loading shotguns, and traps. Although many of the Canelos Quichua men make curare poison (also *jambi*), using some forty or more plant and other substances, more powerful curare for the blowgun darts comes along trade networks originating in the east and southeast. Peruvian Achuara bring poison to Conambo, Montalvo, Copotaza, and Sara Yacu, and Copotaza Achuara and Conambo Achuara carry it on westward. Muzzle-loading shotguns are also used for small game, and cartridge guns are becoming available. Once or twice a year a long trek, *purina*, to gather turtle eggs, to hunt for large quantities of meat, to catch and dry large fish, to keep a distant chagra, and to trade for the appropriate black, red, and white clays for pottery decoration is made by a family, sometimes by itself, sometimes with a larger kinship or settlement group.

Travel is frequent among the Canelos Quichua, and it is usually by foot. The rivers are too rapid and unpredictable in depth (sometimes flooded, sometimes quite low) to provide stable avenues for transportation on the Pastaza east to Ayuy, or the Bobonaza east to Canelos. The Curaray itself meanders so much that it is about as efficient to travel on foot from one point to another as to make one oxbow turn after another by canoe. Nevertheless, canoes are used when heavy cargo is to be moved, and the Canelos Quichua are excellent canoe makers and superior boatsmen.

The nuclear family is a very tightly knit unit with man and woman sharing equally in decision making, in spatial mobility, in upward socioeconomic mobility in some cases. Residence is ideally in the area of a wife's father, for one year, then in the vicinity of the husband's father, but much variation exists. There is no term for this unit except the Quichua term *huasi*, house or household. The huasi symbolizes a microcosm of the combined concepts of the universe brought to the unit by the man and woman founders.

Long before dawn husband and wife share information from their dreams, seeking more visionary symbolism to combine with their technical knowledge. Around 4:00 A.M. the Runa day begins with women bringing water, cutting firewood, preparing chicha and food for the household members. Men, in turn, may hunt or fish for a couple of hours before daybreak or work on some craft. Soon after dawn one of the two daily meals is eaten, and the couple most typically goes to the chagra for the day between 7:00 and 8:00 A.M., returning between 3:00 and 6:00 P.M. for their second, final meal. Chicha sustains them during the approximately ten-hour day.

Although information often enters the huasi from outside sources— radios, traveling peoples, news picked up by children during the day while the parents are at work—such information is usually reflected upon and slept on until the pre-dawn hours. Then, when it seems important, the news is transmitted by individuals from household to household during the pre-dawn period of chicha drinking and vision-knowledge regulating.

The maximal kinship grouping, and segments of this grouping, are referred to as *ayllu*. The ayllu, as maximal clan, is a stipulated descent system from a common animal ancestor, often a variety of cougar or jaguar. Each ayllu is today identified with a set of surnames, and extends through much of Canelos Quichua territory and on into other culture areas as well. Segments of these maximal referential systems are constructed by men and women who formally reckon their position according to certain ground rules. Each man derives a position in an ayllu segment by reference to a sequence of ties going from his father to his father's father to his father's father's wife. A woman reckons her primary position by reference to a sequence of ties going from her mother to her mother's mother to her mother's mother's husband. Segmental clans emerge from ayllu structure and are linked to one another in several ways.

These segmental clans are built around the core of tightly knit stem kindreds, the members of which reckon ties from old, founding shamans.

Members of a stem kindred may refer to their localized relatives as *ñuca ayllu*, my ayllu, or *ñucanchi ayllu*, our ayllu, but because of the intertwining of clan membership through marriage with other clan segments within a territory, intermarried, residential relatives often refer to their common membership by the term for a territorial subdivision, *llacta*.

Each ayllu (maximal, territorial, segmental) maintains its special culture, transmitted to intimate residential in-laws. In this transmission special concentrations of knowledge or culture concatenate within the actual subdivisional residential systems of the Runa territory. These ayllu units—many of which span two or three llactas—expand and contract with the purina (trek) system, as well as segment within a given llacta system. Such fissioning produces clans which ramify throughout a territory and across territorial boundaries. In this way shared knowledge embedded in the dispersed, maximal ayllu of antiquity is maintained through conflict and competition in the llacta system, and transferred repeatedly across ayllu and territorial boundaries. Ayllu members maintain their special descent ideology through visionary experience, through mythology, and through actual travel. They can reactivate the maximal ayllu concept after many generations through the stipulated system of shared descent from a common animal ancestor, and through shared possession of the linked souls of the deceased.

In ascending order of kin and neighbor units, a child is born into a huasi, of which the woman's cultural maintenance through pottery tradition and the man's maintenance through soul acquisition assure each newborn a place in a maximal clan extending into ancient times. The huasi itself exists within a llacta which was established by a founder in alliance with other founders of ayllu segments. These minimal segmental ayllus within a llacta (or between adjacent llactas) are stem kindreds (Davenport 1959:565, Goodenough 1962:10–11 ["nodal kindred"], Whitten 1965:156–159). Beyond the stem kindred is the extended clan, which includes localized and dispersed kinsmen within and beyond a Runa territory. And beyond the extended clan is the maximal clan, the everlasting system of stipulated descent into mythic time and structure.

A developmental sequence exists which ties male hausi, ayllu, and llacta founders to the knowledge of mythical times. On marriage a male must, by taking huanduj, converse with the soul master spirit, Amasanga, and have the soul master cure him of *supai biruti*, spirit darts, sent by jealous suitors of his wife. Also, the bride must visit the wife of Amasanga, Nunghuí, to get her sacred stones and knowledge to make the manioc grow. If a man wishes to head a stem kindred he must, through a long period of time, acquire the status of *yachaj*, shaman, becoming both curer and potential mystical

killer. If he ever seeks to found a llacta he must make pacts with the various
supai and *aya*, spirits and souls, of the territory, through which process he
potentially becomes a *bancu*, seat, for the spirits and souls. He usually does
not serve as bancu, however, because retaliation for the evil done by the
spirits and souls through the bancu leads many people to attempt to
eliminate the bancu's social capital—his family, neighbors, friends—
usually by sorcery.

As the process of making pacts with spirits and acquiring souls goes on,
something else also occurs due to the constant outward movement of
affinally related clan segments, and territorial consolidation by remaining
members of clan segments: certain extended clans gain ascendancy within a
territory. Such clans are often identified with a given area. Terms such as
Puyo Runa, Canelos Runa, Sara Yacu Runa, etc. then take on another
meaning, for not only do the territories exist as interrelated and intermarried clan segments, but certain clans come to dominate, and knowledge of
the Runa territory suggests the dominant clans. Segments of other clans do
cut through these territorial boundaries, however, as do alliances formed
through intermarriage. Such crosscutting of the circumscribed territorial
clans suggests evolutionary potential toward an ethnic state of the Canelos
Quichua. Such development, however, is today confined and disrupted by
frontier politics of mission and nation-state controls.

QUICHUA ORIGINS: UNRESOLVED ETHNOLINGUISTIC ISSUES

Before proceeding with the description and analysis of the Canelos
Quichua let us turn briefly to the language itself. Ecuadorian Quichua
belongs to the major Quechua group called "Quechua A" (Parker 1969:7;
"Quechua II" of Torero 1965, 1972) which is borne by speakers who
separated from the "Quechua B" group of northern Peru around 800 A.D.,
and is the language grouping of the people who lived around Cusco, Peru,
in the fifteenth century. Incaic imperialist expansion extended this
language south into Bolivia and north into Ecuador. Louisa Stark (1973) has
recently classified Ecuadorian Quichua dialects into two groups:
"Ecuatoriano A" and "Ecuatoriano B." The former is represented today by
many dialects spoken in the central highlands of Ecuador; the latter
contains less diversity and is more widely distributed in the Ecuadorian
Andes and in the Oriente. It is significant for our work that Ecuatoriano A is
regarded as containing ancient forms of Proto-Quechua which pre-date the
800 A.D. reconstruction for northern Peru, while Ecuatoriano B more
closely approximates that of Cusco Quechua of the fifteenth century (Stark
1973:11).

Stark goes on to suggest an Ecuadorian Oriente origin for the emergence of Ecuatoriano A prior to 600 A.D., a spread westward and southward, establishment in northern Peru, and eventually a reintroduction as a lingua franca, in Ecuatoriano B form, with the Incas. What remains to be understood is the possible development and perhaps diverse routes of dispersion of Ecuatoriano B in lowland and highland Ecuador before, during, and after the Incaic and Spanish conquests. The serious study of Ecuadorian Quichua is on the verge of clarifying many issues revolving around the spread of this ancient language, which became a lingua franca for Incaic expansion and later for Spanish expansion as well.

There is no question but that Catholic missions, always understaffed in a vast, unfamiliar, rugged jungle territory of warring peoples, established small sites and endeavored to spread Quichua from the sixteenth century on to the present. But for the area of our concern it does not seem *sufficient* to claim, as the Catholic Church does, that such missions caused the language to become dominant. There is today, and apparently has been for centuries, a coherent jungle trade Quichua which allows speakers of various jungle and highland dialects to communicate with one another and which can be picked up without great difficulty, in pidgin form, by Jivaroans, Zaparoans, Panoans, and others (Uriarte 1952:76–77). But a pidgin trade language, even with some perfection and creolization around mission bases, is probably also inadequate to claim as the origin for what is currently represented by a clear-cut set of mutually intelligible dialects.

Many people in the Puyo area insist that a former home was in the east and southeast, and even in the westernmost zone of the Puyo Runa their orientation toward necessary jungle products—*chambira*-palm fiber for fishnets and net bags, chicle for stone-sinker coating, stones, clays, and rubber sap for pottery manufacture, genipa for face painting—is eastward, even where substitutes are readily available from the nearby Andes. We must consider the possibility of an ancient, Andean-lowland pre-Incaic, early Quichua language family to have ranged from the semi-Andean warm-valley Quichua living north of Cusco in the early fifteenth century (Rowe 1946:189; see also Savoy 1970:169–172, Orr and Longacre 1968:546, and Lathrap 1970:171–179) northwest to Yurimaguas (see Tessmann 1930:219, 234, Uriarte 1952:76–77, Steward and Métraux 1948:598–599). The lowland and montaña bearers of the language were by this period probably surrounded by speakers of other languages and dialects, and separated from one another long before the Incaic expansion. Under such circumstances bilingualism, or multi-lingualism, may well have become a basic adaptation of Lowland Quichua speakers.

Quichua was not the lingua franca in highland Ecuador prior to its forced spread by the Incas. In southern Ecuador the Palta spoke Jivaroan. Farther north the Cañari spoke another language which may or may not have been related to Jivaroan, and continuing north languages such as Puruhá, Panzaleo, Quito, and Caranquis may have been related to languages of the Quijos in the east, and to languages such as Manta, Esmeralda, and Cayapa on the central to north coast (Jijón y Caamaño 1951, Murra 1946). Karsten (1935:2–3) suggests Jivaroan habitation of the south central highlands and south coast to around the mid-sixteenth century, when the Inca conquest destroyed them.

A legend, which the Puyo Runa tell as they watch a red sunset, is that the sun is eating the blood of fallen Jivaroans, in the face of Inca Atahualpa's conquest. Prior to Incaic rule, Jivaroan languages undoubtedly served as an important source of communication for trade between lowland and highland peoples, in south and east central Ecuador, on both sides of the Andes (and perhaps beyond through the Guayas basin to sea-traveling peoples). Jivaroan dialects—Palta, Jívaro, Achuara, Huambisa, Aguaruna—are mutually intelligible (Wise and Shell 1971), and apparently once extended from Upper Amazonia over the Andes, perhaps to the Guayas basin or to the Pacific Ocean. With the demise of this language in the sierra, and its replacement with Quichua throughout Andean Ecuador, good reason for the expansive spread of Quichua in the adjacent tropical forest and montaña becomes apparent: Quichua replaced Jivaroan and other languages such as Quijos and Zaparoan as the language used to maintain trade relationships. Of course this reasoning cannot tell us where Quichua originally came from.

Penetration of the Quichua language into Canelos in the mid-seventeenth century occurred (Oberem 1971:37) when 150 Quijos Quichua from Napo fled hacienda oppression, but this does not explain why it should have spread eastward, or become dominant, except as a convenient highland-lowland lingua franca after the south highland and south central montaña demise of Jivaroan. Nor does such a documented spread of Quichua speakers imply any "beginning" of the *spread* of the Quichua language in this area. The reader must bear in mind that many indigenous peoples of Amazonia have long been bilingual in native languages (see, e.g., Sorensen 1967, 1973). The learning, spreading, and elaborating of trade languages does not necessarily suggest linguistic replacement, even when we know that a language is spreading in an area. I am talking about dominance of the Quichua language, which became clearly identified with a culture area by the mid-nineteenth century. But it must be remembered that many contemporary Canelos Quichua speakers continue to maintain another language.

The following simplified scheme of ethnic-linguistic relationships is postulated to guide further archival research and to clarify relationships in the culture area considered. It will have to suffice until archaeology and linguistic reconstruction clarify some lingering ethnohistorical issues. By the time of the Incaic conquest of Ecuador, the area east of Baños, in central Ecuador, represented a narrow, spectacular transition zone between the high Andes, montaña, and the very hilly jungle to the east. South of the Llanganati Mountains this area was occupied by both Achuara and Jívaro proper, warring and feuding with each other, among themselves, and perhaps with the "Huamboyas" (Monteros 1937:167–168) to control the montaña territory of the trade routes. North of Baños, along the eastern slopes of the Llanganati Mountains, lived other peoples speaking other languages such as Quijos. As the Jivaroan language began to disappear in the sierra and Incaic control was extended west of Baños, Quichua became the dominant lingua franca of the sierra. Sierran mission, Highland Quichua, and Quijos penetration brought Quichua to the Puyo-Canelos area by the seventeenth century, but still farther east-southeast the language already existed.

The existence of a new trade language in the sierra, a need for a "mixed" ethnic culture to buffer and cover warring Zaparoans, Jivaroans, and probably Tupians, and sporadic entry from the east, southeast, and west of more Quichua speakers gave the Quichua language an adaptive advantage earlier enjoyed by Jivaroan. In an area where bilingualism was common, and where war and trade complemented one another, the existence of an ancient stock plus new reasons for learning the language contributed to its ascendancy to dominance over the past two centuries.

By adopting Quichua as the lingua franca the Canelos Quichua were able to maintain and transform their distinctive cultural characteristics and adaptive strategies in the face of expanding nation states and new "frontier" conditions brought to them. They also gained certain trade advantages over the Jívaro proper, and came to occupy central positions between the Quijos and their southern neighbors (see Oberem 1966/67:243–255).[9]

CONTINUITY AND CHANGE

The first part of this book, "Canelos Quichua Culture and Continuity," seeks to portray these lifeways as they exist today in many areas, in spite of, or even in the face of, current obliteration and confinement policies of the Ecuadorian government. An academic rationale for such portrayal of enduring structure is provided by Claude Lévi-Strauss (1963:95–96): " . . . as soon as the various aspects of social life . . . are expressed as relationships, anthropology will become a general theory of relationships. Then it will be possible to analyze societies in terms of the differential features characteristic of the systems of relationships which define them." This approach makes

Unloading fibers for brooms at Cabecera de Bobonaza. The fibers are then carried to Puyo to be sold.

Purchasing goods in Puyo.

The road to Puyo, 1973.

Puyo, 1971.

an assumption well articulated by David Maybury-Lewis (1974:ii) in his
exhaustive treatment of Akwẽ-Shavante social relations:

> A structural analysis deals first with the cultural categories in terms of which
> a given people organize their own experience. It then seeks to relate the rules
> of their society and the patterns of action observable within it to these ideas.
> Above all it seeks to determine what are the principles underlying this
> aggregate of ideas, rules and actions and relate them to each other in such a
> way as to show the crucial relationships in the society studied. . . . *The only
> necessary assumption it makes is that there is at any given moment a systematic
> aspect to any culture which is worth studying* [emphasis added].

The Canelos Quichua "think structurally." Time and time again when we
thought we understood the adaptive dimension of a particular aspect of
social life, our friends would gently, insidiously, but persuasively point out
that our interpretation was all right "for now" (Spanish *para ahora*,
Quichua *cunalla*), but then demonstrate or assert the "antiquity" (Spanish
antiguo, Quichua *rucuguna*) involved, whether of naming principle, ritual
item, kin term, or way of sharpening a stick. The Canelos Quichua perceive
their system as one of transformable relationships, the relations being
discerned in specifiable contexts, and the transformations occurring
according to postulated enduring principles in the face of changing
contingencies and constraints. Part I deals with the culture of the Canelos
Quichua as a system worth understanding in its own right, through its own
system of relationships, within its own ecology.

   In the next five chapters I set forth pivotal aspects of Canelos Quichua
culture and society. I try to portray the continuities that give the Canelos
Quichua a reason to live on in the face of chaos. Toward that end I begin with
the world view of the *Sacha Runa*, sketching a biosphere of souls, spirits,
symbolism, and cosmology. Then I move briefly to time structure, origin
myth and mythic structure, soul acquisition, and temporal-social regulation through marriage. Chapter 3 deals with the cultural complex bound to
the huasi—including household symbolism and continuity—and introduces the basic economics of Canelos Quichua life. I then discuss Nunghuí
and pottery tradition as female continuity and Amasanga and soul
acquisition as male continuity, both continuities being embedded and
regenerated in the household micro-universe, which I treat as an invariant
structure. In Chapter 4 I introduce a second invariant structure, the
maximal clan—the ayllu in its mythic and cognitive dimensions—and go on
to organizational variance of ayllu segmentation, marriage, and territoriality. Chapter 5 considers the dynamics of shamanism and ayllu regulation,
and Chapter 6 focuses directly on processual ritual structure which
merges spirit and Runa domains.

During this discussion of Canelos Quichua culture I shall, from time to time, indicate points of continuous articulation between the system of relationships and the changing parameters brought about by escalating contact with other peoples and new technologies. By the time that Chapter 6, "Ritual Structure," is concluded, it will be clear that there are points of articulation with the outer world at every level of ecology, social organization, and ideology. And it will be equally clear that the Canelos Quichua system is also articulated to other native cultures.

Part II, "Puyo Runa Adaptation and Change," seeks to document adaptive *versatility* of the Puyo Runa in the face of changing environmental circumstances. This section discusses the means by which they bring their cultural and material resources to bear on changing conditions and at the same time maintain a meaningful existence in the face of inconsistent, chaotic, and destructive national policies. It also continues to build on the analysis and description presented in Part I to illustrate the layers of cultural patterning and identity structures created out of a transformable set of lifeways which extend through a diverse ecosystem ranging from the most urbanized to the least accessible regions of the central Ecuadorian Oriente.

All native peoples in contemporary Amazonia challenge the virtuosity of national bureaucracy. And when, in cases such as that presented by rapid expansion of the Puyo Runa, *cultural integrity and social integration are maintained by people in the process of rapid change and population expansion,* the validity of policies which assert a unified "national culture" for all peoples within consolidated state boundaries is doubly challenged. In the mid-twentieth century Ecuadorian Amazonia became regarded as a last frontier to be conquered. Aid for conquest and colonization came from the most industrialized nations and, though much of the frontier has thus far remained beyond the pale of national control, dependency on technology imported from the outside has enormously increased.

In 1968 an oil boom struck northern Ecuador, and by 1970 the technological might of North American oil exploration blanketed Canelos Quichua territory, and then suddenly withdrew in 1973. The crest and wake of oil exploration and its technological paraphernalia—roads, helicopters, planes, airstrips, radios, base camps—allowed the Ecuadorian bureaucracy to modernize into its contemporary military dictatorship, and to begin a plan of native destruction and national expansion through conquest of its Amazonian forests and suppression of native residents (see, e.g., Robinson 1971).

The Canelos Quichua have seen examples of North American technology, and they know that non-Indian nationals are free to participate in its acquisition, including the means by which to turn machinery to useful, needed tasks. They know that they are excluded from such a learning process, and that further incorporation into national life will place them in a position of poverty and ignorance. They stand to lose their subsistence base, and they have no viable economic alternatives within national political economy. Their culture is rich and their knowledge profound; the general motivation is for rapid change without alteration of ethnic identity. Here they clash totally with the national military outlook, which seems to regard poverty and ignorance as a necessary transition point for becoming a national mestizo.

The clash itself exists at all levels of ecology, society, and ideology, and establishes its own system of articulation to national culture, one juxtaposed upon that created by the continuous adjustment of Canelos Quichua culture to the outer world. Part II is designed to portray the *continuing ethnic adaptation* of the Puyo Runa, not only in terms of their survival strategies, but also in terms of their accumulating ethnic glosses, which contain reversals of national stereotypes as well as a reintegration of the stereotypes into their adapting culture—itself made up of a system of transformable relationships.

Chapter 7 describes a cultural ecological baseline of Puyo by focusing on the Pivotal role the bilingual Jivaroan-Quichua people of this zone came to play in twentieth-century Canelos Quichua cultural expansion during a time when most native peoples of Amazonia were being ravaged by the rubber boom. It also explores more thoroughly points of articulation in ritual structure through which ideological adaptation to an expanding "purchase society" (Helms 1969, 1971) in a frontier cultural ecology took place. In Chapter 8 I examine the adaptive dynamics of Puyo Runa life from 1930 to the present, including in the forces affecting them such events as early petroleum exploration, World War II, the Peruvian invasion of Ecuador, colonization and urbanization of Puyo, and the east Ecuadorian oil boom of the late 1960s and early 1970s. Chapter 9 deals with the complementarity and paradox of ethnocide from the national perspective, and ethnogenesis from the native point of view.

Throughout this book I maintain a perspective that cultural continuity and change can be handled within a unified frame of reference. Wherever possible I seek to submerge lists of references, technical arguments, and complications which will detract from the utility of a work directed toward a full understanding of how participants in one Jungle Quichua culture endeavor to maintain ethnic integrity, expand their culture, increase their population, and at the same time find a new position in a disappearing frontier.

NOTES

1. This spelling is the standard Ecuadorian one, although some intellectuals in that country are beginning to write *Quechua* and to use that pronunciation as well. The best dictionary for Ecuadorian Jungle Quichua is Orr and Wrisley (1965). For a technical discussion of Jungle Quichua phonology see Orr (1962). In Peru and Bolivia the language is generally given as *Quechua* and in Colombia it is often called *Ingano* or *Inga*. The language itself is one of the most important in the Americas in terms of contemporary native speakers. Bills, Vallejo, and Troike (1969) give a conservative estimate of between five and seven million speakers. In the fourteenth through mid-sixteenth centuries the language was spread by the Incas up and down the Andes, north into Ecuador, and south into Bolivia and Chile (Torero 1972). This expanding nation imposed hegemony and a lingua franca over dozens of different languages and dialects (see, e.g., Row 1946). The Spanish took up the expansion of Incaic Quechua, helping to spread it to Argentina and into various jungle areas of Ecuador and Peru. But there is good evidence that Quichua existed in Ecuador prior to the Incaic conquest (Orr and Longacre 1968:546, Guevara 1972:17, Stark 1973).

One final note on Ecuadorian Jungle Quichua in terms of the broad field of native American languages is appropriate. The recent attempt by Summer Institute of Linguistics professionals (Matteson *et al.* 1972) to begin to draw together proto languages, and even to suggest directions to be taken toward Proto-Amerindian (Matteson 1972:21–92), underscores the vigor with which current work in South American languages is being sporadically undertaken. It appears that, in the next decade or so, real classificatory order suggesting linguistic relationships among contemporary peoples will emerge. But our present state of knowledge suggests caution. Reconstruction and classification are still inadequate to manipulate data pertaining to dialect in such a manner as to draw clear historical inferences (Orr and Longacre 1968, Stark, personal communication). The Matteson reconstruction used Jungle Quichua from Puyo Pungo, a mixed Quijos–Canelos Quichua settlement in daily contact with Jívaro proper, as one of four bases (Matteson 1972:24) for reconstructing the overall Quechua language, which was then reconstructed to a general Amerindian superstock.

2. The process of creating a "national culture" (*cultura nacional*) through military bureaucracies dominated much of the publicized ideology of the presidential decrees from around September, 1972, to the present time. The text of the "Law of National Culture," published in *El Comercio*, Feb. 24, 1973, is illustrative. A National Cultural Council (*Consejo Nacional de la Cultura*) having been established, it was charged with "a) Planning the cultural politics of the country; b) Coordinating the cultural action so as to incorporate distinct regions of the country into the national culture." The idea of a "national culture" merged with that of "cultural politics" (*política cultural*) by early 1973 as the National Revolutionary Government (*Gobierno Nacionalista Revolucionario del Ecuador*) began to decree the cultural basis upon which development would occur. Those who fall outside of the national culture may be accused of engaging in political activities directed against the new cultural revolution (see Whitten 1975).

3. Ethnic definitions in native terms are more complicated than presented in the above text, especially as regards Jivaroan and Quichua interchange when they intermingle, intermarry, and intertwine definitions of one another. Harner (1962:258) differentiates the Jívaro proper as the *Untsuri Shuara*, "numerous Indians," because it is "the designation applied to this tribe by its close eastern Jivaroan neighbor, the Achuara tribe. . . ." The Achuara that I know—those who intermarry with the Canelos Quichua—pronounce *Untsuri* as *Anzorí Shuara*, but more commonly use the term *Nucap* (silent *p*) *Shuara* to refer to the Jívaro proper who have expanded in the past century around the Chiguaza River, and by extension may employ these two terms in the sense of "numerous Indians" to refer to the other

Jívaro proper. They insist that the Jívaro proper use the term *untsuri* for themselves. (That *untsuri* and *anzorí* are close cognates is obvious from immediate inspection.) Often the Jívaro proper living near Puyo use the phrase *tsumú Shuara* to refer to "downriver" Shuara, and give synonyms of "Achuara" and "strange Shuara" for the term *tsumú*, which contrasts with *yakíia*, "upriver" or "high-ground" Shuara. In such contrasts they call themselves Yakíia, as distinct from the Tsumú. Harner (1972:12–16) provides further clarifications from the Jívaro proper.

Some Jívaro proper living near Puyo insist that the term *achuara* derives from the name of a particular palm tree, *achu*, and that *any* Indians living in a lowland area with abundant palms would be known as Achuara. Finally, many Jungle Quichua of Quijos and Canelos cultures now employ the term *Shihuara* as synonymous with *Auca* and *Jívaro*, grouping together all non-Quichua speakers including the Awishiri and Zaparoans.

Although *Jívaro* is pejorative when used by an Ecuadorian Spanish speaker, I have chosen to employ it in this book for two reasons. First, the Jívaro are well identified in anthropological literature, and Harner's recent work clarifies their cultural ways within a particular area, which we contrast with the Canelos Quichua and Achuara. Second, the term *Shuara* has assumed a national meaning in Ecuador, where, lumped together with Achuara and sometimes with Canelos Quichua and Zaparoan, it has acquired the pejorative connotations of *Jívaro*.

4. Orr and Wrisley (1965:iii) label these dialects differently. They refer to the Canelos dialect as "Bobonaza" after the Bobonaza River, the Quijos dialect as "Tena" after the town of Tena, and the Napo dialect as "Limoncocha" after the Summer Institute of Linguistics base there. One of the most pressing tasks that confronts us in the study of Jungle Quichua is to see just how far these three Ecuadorian dialects extend in geocultural distribution. We must learn what the relationships are between Ecuadorian Jungle Quichua and Jungle Peruvian dialects, known to have a considerable time depth, if we are ever to place Ecuadorian Jungle Quichua in proper perspective. For example, using the excellent ethnic map in Girard (1958:8) as a guide, we find one Jungle Quichua in the area between Chachapoyas and Yurimaguas, and another at the mouth of the Corrientes and Tigre rivers. I speculate that these dialects should resemble that of the Canelos Quichua, for this is the region from which the Canelos Quichua say they came, and where, historically, they traded through hostile territories to obtain salt. The Quichua spoken around contemporary Iquitos, Peru, should fit that of the Napo dialect, and both of these should differentiate from that of the Quijos Quichua.

5. Some note on cultural roots should be made by considering possible, if premature, reconstruction through the media of ceramics and linguistics. Canelos Quichua, Zaparoan, and Achuara pottery traditions that I have seen are nearly identical, and the description of Omagua-Cocama (Tupian) pottery in Métraux (1948:695–696) states their stylistic features almost exactly. It would seem that the tradition was once widely shared in Central and Upper Amazonia. Today this pottery style is one of the clear markers of the Canelos Quichua, representing a deep cultural complex shared to some extent with Zaparoan and Achuara traditions, and distinct from Jívaro proper and Quijos traditions. Non-Quichua linguistic possibilities for a Canelos Quichua baseline are diverse. It seems to me that speculation on such an "origin" prior to a clear classification of such languages as Kahuapana, Munichi, Cholona, and Mayna "stocks" (Loukotka 1968:153–156, Steward 1948:598–601, Wise and Shell 1971) to determine their location in (or out of) the Andean-Equatorial language family (Greenberg 1960), which supposedly (but not definitively, and perhaps erroneously) spans Quichua-Jivaroan-Zaparoan-Chebaroan, is essential. When we are clear on the linguistic relationships (or lack of them) within this heretofore confusing melange of language-tribal groups we may be in a much better position to make sense out of the Canelos Quichua cultural endurance than at present.

6. Chapter 7, "Puyo Runa Baseline," discusses aspects of depopulation and gives the pivotal references for more data on the Maynas and Canelos missions.

7. *Nunghui* (Nungwí) is the Canelos Quichua pronunciation of the Jívaro proper earth mother, *Nuŋuí* (Harner 1972:71–76), about whom Karsten (1935:125) also wrote, lumping both Jívaro proper and Canelos Quichua beliefs and practices together. His spelling was *Nungüi*.

8. *Mashca* derives from *máchica*, a staple Ecuadorian sierra barley mash which is sold as a fine, dull gray flour. Lower-class highlanders, in particular, carry a bag of such flour on long trips, mixing a bite at a time with water, and chewing as long as possible for sustenance in the absence of other food. *Pupu* literally means "belly button" or umbilicus but also refers to the part of the stomach (*shungu,* which includes the throat and heart) where food is stored and digested.

9. Historical research leading to these conclusions and perhaps cavalier generalizations began in 1970. Margarita Wurfl, Theodore Macdonald, and Marcelo Naranjo have contributed greatly to the task of ethnohistoric reconstruction. Among other things, such research demanded a complete reading of approximately 400 issues of *El Oriente Dominicano* (published in Quito since 1927 by the Dominican mission of Canelos) by Theodore Macdonald and Marcelo Naranjo. Because of the amount of documentation involved in reconstruction and "proving" our various assertions, and because much work needs to be done with other materials gathered, we have decided to publish the historical reconstruction, and detailed references, separately.

I

Canelos Quichua Culture and Continuity

CHAPTER

2

Sacha Runa Biosphere

The rainforest and its ubiquitous rivers are never quiet, never still. Sounds of buzzing insects, singing and screeching birds, whistling and coughing animals concatenate in infinite ways to produce multiple systems which the uninformed perceives as "noise." Plants grow so rapidly that a given section of forest appears quite different from one week to the next, unless the real botanical dynamics are taken into account. Heavy rainfall creates its own noise system, which changes from the roar above as the broadleaves take the first brunt to various sorts of drippings and spout-like pourings under the canopy. River courses, depths, appearances, and sounds are forever changing as they rise, swell, reach strange peaks of blended resonance according to the eternal variety of lowland and Andean rainfall, and in the amount of tumbling pebbles and alluvium carried.

People structure these natural dynamics in order to cope with the biosphere. They do so through observation, understanding, and classification. The more one knows about each aspect of the continuous motion and sound, the richer the process of life-in-creation becomes. The ability to understand life's processes, to become integrated with them as an intellectual, questing, creative human is the primary meaning of *Sacha Runa*—jungle person, knowledgeable (*ricsina*) person.[1] The structure of the biosphere generated by Runa-induced realities defines a particular meaning system which integrates earth, jungle, water with underworld and sky. The meaning system, in turn, provides a rich set of relationships—a cultural basis—for every individual's search for personal knowledge, strength, and competence.

The jungle of the Canelos Quichua exists on an east-west axis, an invariant directional system established by the rise of *Indi*, the sun. He appears downriver, *urai*, at 6:00 A.M. and moves steadily upriver, *janaj*,[2] until 6:00 P.M., when he retires, exhausted, over the Andes and begins his descent ever downward to light the underworld and to gain strength for the next forest-world day. From western to eastern points of the equatorial axis

35

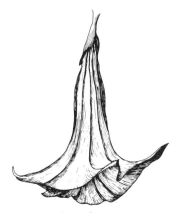

huanduj sisa

the jungle changes from the 3,000-foot forest of hills and 1,000-foot depressions of the Puyo Runa to the high-canopy, 1,000-foot or less Amazonian ecosystem of the Montalvo Runa. Small mountains and large hills, ledges, depressions, and miles of ridges rise upward throughout the territory; thousands of fast-moving rocky streams cut between this high terrain while two serpentine rivers, the Bobonaza and the Curaray, carry alluvium eastward.

Wet, slippery soil, *allpa,* ranging from black and brown loam to red, yellow, and white clay, provides not only a floor for the rainforest, but is also the medium for fantastic displays of flowers in and on the edge of the jungle. Sometimes, for example, along the banks of the Puyo River, a thousand or more of the *huanduj sisa,* Datura flower, open almost at once, sending their trumpet blossoms down over the water; the bees and other small creatures buzz in and out of them, creating a drone-like sound-vision system which stirs the forest even more. Hundreds of birds sing and screech, the loudest and perhaps most striking of which is the toucan, *sicuanga*—embodying and epitomizing the four Canelos Quichua basic colors, black, white, red, yellow—which is seen either flying like a lance or bounding like a dancer. Jaguar, ocelot, cougar, all called *puma,* and tapir, *sacha huagra,* jungle cattle—together with peccary, agouti, paca, deer, and monkey—range throughout, and provide sources for endless observation to those in search of knowledge, as well as ready sources of pelts and meat.

Water itself, *yacu,* is as dominant an element as the forest. Yacu refers to small and large rivers, in distinction to *tamia,* rain, and *cucha,* lagoon. The downriver waters, from Sara Yacu to Montalvo on the Bobonaza River, and from Curaray eastward on the Curaray, are the home of inland sea creatures: porpoises, giant otters, rays, occasional sharks, electric eels, and catfish weighing up to 300 pounds. Catfish can be found upriver to Canelos on the Bobonaza, the upper Copotaza River, and sometimes on affluents of the Pastaza to the Llushín River. But smaller tropical fish, many popular in North American aquariums, make up an important source of food in the higher elevations. A two- to six-pound sucker-mouth carp-like fish, *challua*,[3] runs upriver throughout the territory. Caymans are found in lagoons, swamps, and rivers, and anacondas range from the tiny streams to the larger rivers. Everywhere water rushes on, usually eastward, and the western-zone rivers are particularly full of cataracts, rapids, whirlpools, and small waterfalls.

BASIC FOREST, WATER, AND SOIL SYMBOLISM

The contrast between forest and water is fundamental to the Canelos Quichua world view. This and other contrasts establish a system of domains—fields or sectors of biosphere activity—with postulated interrelated and interpenetrating sentient spirit foci. The people are of the forest—Sacha Runa—but dependent on water and therefore on the water spirit people—*Yacu Supai Runa*—of which the most important manifestation is the boa or anaconda, *amarun*.

Souls, *aya*, and spirits, *supai*,[4] are everywhere in the forest. The soul master of the forest is Amasanga; he is the spirit who knows most about everything in the forest, and who oversees soul movement during Runa dreams and visions. He is male, *cari*, and wears a cloak of beautiful "black," *yana*. This is not the dull black of mourning drab, but rather the iridescent black of tropical bird feathers that ranges to brilliant blues and shimmering greens. His stool, *bancu*, is a greenish-brown lizard with red throat, *sacha runa*, another lizard known as *jayambi*, or the land tortoise, *yahuati*. Amasanga appears at times at dusk, as he moves into a tree for the night. He is one and many—there is no contradiction—just as a Runa is one, an individual, but *of* other people and sharing the forest domain with others of common descent. His animal manifestation, the living embodiment of his continuing aya, is the great black jaguar, *Jatun yana puma* or *huagra puma*.

The Canelos Quichua not only live in and off the forest, they also remove sections of it and plant their own crops—especially manioc. The wife of Amasanga, often called Nunghuí but also *Chagra mama*, garden giver, or *Manga allpa mama*, pottery-clay giver, is the spirit master of the soil, the crops that produce food under the soil, and the clay from which pottery is made. Where Amasanga may be thought of as the trunk of life, using a tree as our analogy, Nunghuí represents the roots. Her manifestation is a harmless brown snake. Nunghuí's dress is also shimmering or iridescent black.

She appears to women, before dawn, in the chagra. They may see her there
by being present, or they may see her in their dreams before they awaken.

Both Amasanga and Nunghuí are *huanduj manda,* "of" or "from" *Datura*
(Solanaceae *Brugmansia* species); they are *huanduj supai,* Datura spirits.
They confer knowledge, respectively, on men and women. They sometimes do this directly, when the seeker takes a brew prepared from the
huanduj stem to induce visions, but they sometimes confer knowledge by
mediation with the underworld people, called *ucupachama* or *ucupacha
manda.* [5] Before considering this process, let us complete our contrast between sacha and yacu, each the environment of a contrasted cultural domain.

Sungui is master of water spirits; he is *Yacu supai runa* and his wife is
Yacu supai huarmi, water spirit's woman, or *Yacu mama,* the continuity of
water life.[6] Sungui, whether male or female manifestation, is dressed in a
beautiful multicolor cloak representing the spectrum of the rainbow, with
red predominant. He sits on a bancu which is either the cayman, *apamama,*
or the large water turtle, *charapa.* Sungui's animal manifestation is the
giant anaconda, which he uses as a canoe when traveling beneath the
surface of a river, and which itself spans the forest domain as a rainbow.
Water anacondas and land or tree boas are classed as the same creature
—amarun—by the Canelos Quichua; and all amarun symbolism spans or
links the forest and water domains of Amasanga and Sungui. In fact,
Amasanga wears a crown made from the boa's (or another snake's) skin, and
himself travels at times on a boa, not under the water's surface but on it.

Amasanga and Sungui long ago made a pact with one another to respect
their mutual domains, just as the jaguar and anaconda maintain mutual
respect. Women gain access to this pact through the mediation of Nunghuí,
and through the medium of clay, which is found both under the humus of
the forest floor and in river beds. Rain is of the water domain and nearly
omniscient evidence of Sungui's power in the world. But Amasanga
controls the weather, keeping the water domain in tenuous check as it
moves over the land, producing mud and mire. Thunder and lightning,
rayu, are Amasanga manifestations, and the rainbow, *sinchi amarun,*
powerful anaconda, is a Sungui manifestation.

The contrast between black (as a blue-black continuum) and multicolor
with predominant red is very important to the Canelos Quichua. Meat,
aicha, is prepared in black cooking ware and served with grated plantain,
palanda, in black bowls. Chicha, a merger of food and water, is brewed in
multicolor storage jars and served in delicate multicolor drinking bowls.

Hunting for food and growing plantains and corn are male tasks,
overseen by Amasanga. Growing manioc and other root crops and making
and serving chicha are strictly women's jobs, overseen by both Manga allpa

mama (Nunghuí) and Yacu mama (Sungui huarmi). Manioc grows in soil (allpa), yields its food substance within the soil, and is served as both food and drink; each manioc clone renders large tubers, which are eaten on plantain leaves, and smaller ones, which are used to produce chicha. Pottery clay (also allpa) is dug from special pits on river banks or from areas where underground streams or brooks exist. Women make all pottery from clay and carry all water from the river. They plant, tend, harvest, and carry the manioc to the house, where they peel it and then lug it to a stream, wash it, and return to the house to prepare it. The intra-household symbolism involved in this complex interplay of contrastive but interpenetrating domains will be discussed more extensively in the next chapter on the huasi.

All fish are classed with animal meat. All forest meat is *sacha aicha*, and all water meat or fish is *yacu aicha*. Men invade the water domain for fish,[7] and the fish are cooked and served in black ware. In fishing, Runa cross territories, so to speak, with the amarun, which also hunts on land. Although ordinary men seek contact with Amasanga, they avoid contact with Sungui, for the female form of this spirit can easily lure them under the waters and keep them forever enchanted there as fish.

A whirlpool, *cutana*, is the direct entrance to Sungui's domain, and through this under-river domain on down to the underworld in a *yacu cuta*, underground river. Each whirlpool is thought to be inhabited by a giant anaconda capable of overturning a canoe and drowning the water-traveling Runa.

When men encounter boas in the forest they kill them, for they know the boa is hunting people, and when the giant anaconda encounters men fishing in its territory it kills them, for it believes that men are hunting it. The most dangerous amarun is the *turu amarun*, mud boa; this is the rainbow-red boa which spans soil, river, and rain, and is primarily oriented toward hunting and eating the Runa.

The white or gray color of the sky lights at night, and the useless wet chapaj (mire) clay below the soil and below the river may, in some contexts, symbolize a fading of the rainbow and a lightening of black. As brilliant, shiny, iridescent black and multicolor rainbow represent different forms of life force, white seems to represent death. The contrast between life and death contains many transformations in Canelos Quichua cosmogony. As living beings and spirits lose their souls on death, the lost souls continue in forest or river; in similar manner the dead body itself, *huanushca*, continues to exist as a dead soul, separate from the living soul escaping the body. Death and life represent different dimensions of the various domains. The turu amarun, mentioned above, is especially dangerous because it spans dimensions of death and life, in mud, clay, water, jungle, and sky. Beginning in the white powerful bottom of a special lagoon, called *tsalamanga*, palid bowl, it comes up through the water domain with its rainbow colors, exuding red symbolizing blood, and enters the forest domain, turning black when it wants to eat people.

The serpentine climbing vine called *ayahuasca*, soul vine, provides special linkages between humans and spirits through their mutual souls.[8] The Canelos Quichua use a brew made from this soul vine to enter forest, soil, water, sky, and, to some extent, underworld domains, and to bring the spirits of known and unknown domains to them. Ayahuasca, and other named vines mentioned below, are *Banisteriopsis* species—botanical substances which contain strong but manageable psychotropic properties. These species of woody vine are postulated as sentient entities, and certain qualities are attributed to them. The crucial ayahuasca supai is *Ayahuasca mama*. She is a beautiful young woman, *alli huarmi*, who is usually not seen but whose presence is felt after ingestion of the drink made from actual vine sections, called *ayahuasca huahua*, soul vine children. The Canelos Quichua harvest these vines in wild form and cultivate them as well. Another *Banisteriopsis* species, *mucu huasca*, knotty vine, is conceptualized as being the male, or husband, component of Ayahuasca mama continuity.

Yaji,[9] *Yaji mama*, or *Amarun yaji* is either another *Banisteriopsis* species (perhaps *Banisteriopsis Rusbyana*—Schultes 1972:36–38) or *Psychotria* (Schultes 1972:45–46). It is harvested in a wild state, or cultivated to obtain the leaves used to make the chemical bonds which result in clear visions. Where Ayahuasca mama gives the feeling, through her ayahuasca huahua, and suggests the way to visionary clarity, Yaji, who has neither husband nor children—a *huaccha huarmi*—is needed to synthesize feeling and spirit presence with *actual vision*. Ayahuasca mama can make the earth shake, and bring the sound of a waterfall tumbling over the house of the user, thereby invoking forces from the domains of Amasanga, Nunghuí, and Sungui. But the clarity of *sight*, which men must have to see the visions of the spirit world, especially the primary ones of a pair of jaguars and a pair of anacondas, is brought by the leaves of Yaji. The visionary brew cooked by a man must contain the vine of continuity through Ayahuasca mama's children, and the leaves of the present "orphan," or single woman, capable of "seeing" that which is brought to the taker. The concept *huaccha* is important in the Canelos Quichua world view, as it relates the continuity of descent—the ayllu, including its ancient souls—with the individual Runa with special personality and substance. An individual does the "seeing" but the soul vine brings the vision. The lone Yaji creates the vision brought by Ayahuasca mama's continuity. There is even more to this complex relationship (discussed in Chapter 5), for after a man receives a vision his wife must clarify it through the mediation of tobacco.

Hills, *urcu*, with their own jungles and rivers rise up toward the sky world, and through their caves penetrate downward into the underworld. Specific populations of Amasangas live under hills in territorial groupings; some even live in great cities. There, too, live the black jaguars, great caymans, and boas; monkey troops are thought to abound in some of the imagined and real caves. Another supai, called *Juri juri* (or *Allpa supai*, or *Urcu supai*) lives there too. This is a small though dangerous brown furry monster who has a special relationship with monkeys. Some say that the Juri juri is the master of monkeys; others disagree. Some say it always lives nearby, under all the hills; others place it at a distance, on hilltops that are dangerous because they abut with other territories. Everyone agrees that it has two faces, and that each face is both male and female. It eats monkeys with its front face, and people with the one in the back.

Understanding of the Juri juri involves us in another concept, that of the monkey people, *Machin Runa*. All monkeys are thought to have human souls. Any outside man *accepted* into Canelos Quichua culture, whether by marriage or not, is regarded as having an ancient monkey soul. When Canelos Quichua hunting groups go off to special territories to hunt monkeys (and other animals), they live in fear of a Juri juri attack. If they hear this two-faced people eater in the night they immediately flee the territory. Conquest of hunting territories and their conversion into residential locations by Runa groups involve the shamanistic driving out, and making a pact with, the resident Juri juri. The Juri juri is both a link between territories and a representation of the dangers which such linkage with other people in other territories involves.

To recapitulate the supais of forest, soil, and water, we have discussed the following: *Amasanga* (forest soul master), *Nunghui*, his wife (pottery clay–crop soil master and root-crop giver), *Sungui* or *Yacu mama* (water spirit master), *Ayahuasca mama* (vision master), *Yaji* (vision maker), and *Juri juri* (acceptable foreign people's soul master). All animals, living things, and spirits have souls, and some creatures that appear to be normal animals are actually spirits in animal form. In addition, some spirits take on other forms and appear as monstrous fear-creatures, enchanters, or beautiful women and men who attempt to lure humans away to live with them.

Huanushca runa, dead people, live a parallel existence in all domains. They represent a separate dimension of the universe, one which sometimes penetrates the living dimension. Walking along a trail early in the night one may encounter a specter soul standing quietly, dressed all in white. If the walking Runa has gained knowledge of ancient souls from Amasanga by taking Datura, then he knows something of the ancient soul specter, and why he is standing by a trail. He immediately says, "Grandfathers, don't frighten me, I am 'orphan' " (*huaccha mani*).[10] The ancient soul, long ago connected to an ayllu, can enter a lone individual (huaccha) without difficulty, and stay with him as a spirit helper.

ROCKS: TRANSFORMATIONAL SUBSTANCES

A rock or a stone, *rumi*, is regarded as a transformational substance. Just as ayahuasca and huanduj provide domain-spanning visions of other realities, rocks and stones bottle up and release animistic substances which provide the transformations between statics and dynamics, between continuity and change. A stone which has been polished, by ancient peoples or by water action in a river, contains a soul, and is accordingly called *aya rumi*, soul stone. An aya rumi is like a flower bud, a hard, silent enclosure which, when opening, brings to itself insects and birds with their continuous noise and motion. The aya rumi may change itself into a large toad with a poisonous spine, *tulumba*. The tulumba sings an owl-like song every evening, bringing constant reinforcement to the concept of the ubiquity of souls.

All stones have the power to contain ancient souls, and the link between large enduring rocks and tree trunks that span centuries is readily made by the Canelos Quichua. Sometimes Nunghuí and Amasanga together are known as *rucu chitus*, an ancient, permanently rooted, tree trunk. Rocks with petroglyphs, which are fairly rare but do exist in Canelos Quichua territory, are called by the same name. When such carved rocks are discovered, women study the designs very intensively. In their dreams, and through huanduj trances with the Manga allpa mama, they intensify the symbolism and understanding of such study so that they can replicate such ancient soul carvings in contemporary pottery design. The Chagra mama also gives stones to women. Among the Canelos Quichua these are black, and come from the "stomach," *shungu*, of the peccary, *lumucuchi*, manioc pig. Such a stone is called *Lumu mama*, manioc mother. Women use these stones to maintain contact with Nunghuí, to take their songs to her, to protect the chagra against marauding animals, and to make the manioc grow.

Men, by contrast, acquire stones from Amasanga to attract animals, to understand their ways, and to have good fortune in hunting. They also find stones with special souls and spirits inside, some of which they keep for hunting and other magical skills, and some of which—those "too hot to handle"—they pass on to more skilled and powerful shamans. Men use an aya rumi in making a drum, too, and with it convert monkey skin to resonating membrane which, when a snare is attached, buzzes out the song of an ancient or distant human soul, and sometimes of a spirit soul, as the man beats it on the opposite, peccary-skin, side.

Any excavation in the ground is an exciting business, because old polished stone hatchets, shamans' stones, stone mortars and pestles for grinding capsicum, and the rocks and hard clays used by the ancient Runa ancestors are bound to turn up. The finder is quite lucky, for such "hard evidence" of antiquity links him with ancestral, territorial, souls.

Stones, as transformational substances, are especially important in the pottery tradition. All of the colors used in the pottery are derived from either clay or rock. The Canelos Quichua make the distinction between these two substances, allpa and rumi, in terms of color *change*. For example, a white clay which, when fired, turns to black on the pot or bowl is classed as rumi, while a white clay which remains white when fired is allpa. A polished stone is also used to burnish the mucahua before the final decoration is made. It, too, is an aya rumi, one which Manga allpa mama provides to impart her continuity into the woman's decorations on the drinking bowls and storage jars.

Stones move all over the Canelos Quichua territory, and beyond into the zones of all other indigenous people of Ecuador, as far as I can determine. They are traded, bought and sold, and create local male-female linkages in dispersed male trade networks. Women who want special stones with which to paint pottery ask men on hunting trips to negotiate such a transaction. A man may have to give up a special shaman's stone to acquire the proper substance for his wife's, and hence his, household continuity through pottery design.

A special historical meaning is given to stones by the Canelos Quichua. They say they used them as important weapons in maintaining, and expanding, their territory. The basic strategy was to establish a camp, or small settlement, on the edge of the territory of another group of Indians—Jívaro proper, Zaparoan, or Huarani Auca—using a clear stream with hundreds of one- to two-pound pebbles as their location. They would quickly collect the pebbles and hide in the forest, allowing the enemy to attack and destroy their temporary settlement. Then the enemy would be ambushed and stoned in the river on their return. In such a story it is often said, especially at Canelos, that the spirits of the stones became Runa and helped in the fight.[11]

Finally, large stones serve as boundary markers and history markers for the Canelos Quichua. Territoriality is frequently demarcated by a boulder with a depression in it. Here a founder of a territory is said to have made the depression by blowing a spirit dart into the stone; then he drank huanduj

from the depression, and either made pacts with the territorial spirits or
drove them from the region.

THE SKY AND THE UNDERWORLD

The transition from earth to sky is a continuous one for the Canelos
Quichua. As fog, *puyu*, swirls and rises, it carries aspects of earth life
upward toward the sky, and also to the rivers. Aspects of sky life and river
life are carried downward by rain, *tamia*. There are many possibilities for
metaphor based on movements of celestial bodies which, as mythical
systems, can be applied, in context, to virtually any event. White clouds
are regarded as high fog, and long, dark clouds streaking across dawn and
dusk skys, or seen on bright moonlit nights, are regarded as high
river—*jatun yacu*. Parakeets, *ucupachama manda huichu*, come and go
between earth, sky, and underworld, carrying songs and mediating between the souls of spirits and souls of humans. Women, mediators between
soil and water, are able to send human and spirit songs upward through
fog or by parakeets to the sky rivers, and along these rivers to their destina-
tions. Such songs are sung to absentee men to give them comfort or do
them harm.

Amasanga, as we previously mentioned, controls the weather. His very
special Datura is *rayu huanduj*, lightning Datura. All men have the power
to blow away rain clouds, especially if they use tobacco smoke, and both
men and women have the ability to bring rain by using an unidentified
substance known as *piri piri*, and bathing with this substance in a river or
stream. But too much control of rainfall in a local area causes enormous
disturbance elsewhere, and an ever-present fear of the Canelos Quichua is
a system out of control where rain, flood, and earthquake combine to send
them eastward on the crest of a muddy, rampaging river-sea.

Beyond the four cardinal points—upriver, downriver, and either side,
chimbajta—there are two other basic directions—straight up, *cusca*, and
straight down, *ucumu*. The center of the sky is "straight up." The most
acceptable Jungle Quichua term for what we call sky is simply *jahuama*,
from *jahua* or *ahua*, high. The sky is also called *silui* or (plural) *siluguna*.
Sky and earth domains join at cardinal points of the horizon.

Indi, the sun, is yellow, and he symbolizes light and warmth; he is
regarded as a predictable sky Runa. Two other predictable sky Runa (when
they are in their own sky domain) are the morning star, *Cuillur*, who
appears in the east, and the evening star, *Docero*, who appears in the
west.[12] Both of these sky Runa are positioned near the earth since they are
just above the east-west cardinal axis. When they descend to earth they
become completely unpredictable and generate variety and transformation

in mythic structure. There are many stories about these star Runa, and about the sun; they are often used in Runa metaphor as people. The rest of the stars are also regarded as Runa with their own system of directionality, determined by the movements of the moon. The Milky Way is their fog, and the dark streaky clouds their rivers. Every celestial body is regarded as a night sun, *tuta indi;* though stars are white, in this sky context they symbolize life, an extension of the sun's yellow.

The most important celestial body is the moon, *Quilla,* for he links predictability with unpredictability, and provides a charter of Canelos Quichua continuity through original incest. Both phase and directionality are important in conceptualizing the moon. The "new," "green," "unripe" moon, *llullu Quilla,* is feminine but prepubescent. It cannot have children or make chicha or pottery. Only when the moon is "ripe," *pucushca Quilla,* from half to three-quarters full, is it regarded as adult male, ready to perform its various mythical sexual relationships, including incest (discussed below). Because the moon does not rise at the same time or in the same place, a second set of concepts related to positioning are applied to Canelos Quichua cosmology. The moon is strongest when it is eastward, southward, or northward, and weakest when it is westward. Stated another way, I think it safe to say that it is at its metaphorical best when it is strongly masculine in either the clear female sector, east, or potential female sector, north, or south, or when it is cusca—straight up—in the dimension which cuts through the center of a circle drawn around the perimeter of the cardinal points. It is at its metaphorical worst when it is a weak male in the west, the undisputed male sector.

Eventually, in its movement across the heavens, Quilla enters into the sun's special place over the Andes—*Indiaycushca*—and passes on down into the underworld. Weakness and fatigue overtake both Quilla and Indi as they move to the Andes at the end of a visible tour.

The underworld, *ucupachama,* is thought to be inhabited by small Runa and animals, just as this world is. But these Runa, the *ucupachama manda* (manda = of, from) are very powerful shamans, and they forever question the sincerity of the Canelos Quichua Runa. Their world is also divided into day, *puncha,* and night, *tuta,* but the times are reversed, for when there is night on earth, Indi is bringing yellow warmth to the underworld, and when it is day on earth the stars, and often the moon, are bringing their night sun to the underworld. Directions, too, are reversed in the underworld. Again, Quilla is anomalous, for he may be above the earth during the day, and also in the underworld during its day.

To call a visitor from the underworld it is necessary to take huanduj, have a satisfactory visionary experience in a trance state, and convince the huanduj supai—Amasanga—of personal sincerity. Then the Amasanga can

call up an ucupachama shaman, a small but all-knowing yachaj, and that
shaman can grant special powers, after he himself determines the Runa
sincerity. These journeys into other worlds, and the calling of other
shamans into the Runa world, are filled with danger, but the Canelos
Quichua find danger an exciting challenge to which to respond, for in
successfully meeting challenges of the unknown, knowledge and power are
acquired and subsequently integrated into *yacha*, a continuous process of
learning.

TIME STRUCTURE

Considering time as a linear sequence the Canelos Quichua make a basic
contrast between present, *cunan*, and ancient, *callari*, which derives from
callarina, beginning. The concept of "present" is modified according to the
speaker's age, knowledge, and sex and is always considered in the plural,
for there are as many "now times" as there are people in specific localities
with specific histories. There are no present times, in the abstract, which
do not involve some aspect of continuity with the past. Even though people
are *from* the present, *cunan manda*, and live in the immediate present,
cunalla, they nonetheless insist that *rucuguna*, old (plural), is an appropriate suffix to *all* time concepts. Today's people look toward the future, but
strive to remember and transmit what they know of their continuity with
the past. The elderly with direct knowledge of the past live in *cunan manda
rucuguna*, from the old present, which extends back to the end of the
memories of the oldest living men and women, all of whom were either
founders of a llacta and segment of a clan, or are living in a llacta or segment
of a clan founded by a "brother."

Continuity with the past is also given in specifically male or female
terms. This is done when men talk of *apayaya rucuguna*, times of the
grandfathers, and women talk of *apamama rucuguna*, times of the grandmothers. The concepts of apayaya and apamama are crucial for the Canelos
Quichua, because people in the present time are in the process of gaining
their knowledge from grandmothers and grandfathers, and seek to marry
so as to maintain continuity from past to present, and on to future generations.[13]

It is said in Puyo Runa legend that, in Ancient Times, *callari rucuguna*,
ancestors of the contemporary people were human, as the people are now,
but far more knowledgeable. Before the coming of steel and disease
ancestors of the contemporary Canelos Quichua cleared their fields with
palmwood (Spanish *chonta*, Quichua *chunda* or *taraputu*) or bamboo
machetes, fought with chonta macanas, hunted with lances, and cleared
heavy timber with stone axes. According to the Puyo Runa, Puyo was

inhabited by thousands of Indians. But the Spanish came and everyone died. With the death of the ancient Puyo Runa knowledge declined. It did not disappear, but without the ancient people around to study the natural order and transmit such knowledge from generation to generation, new techniques of acquisition had to be devised. Almost everyone died in the Canelos zone, and in Sara Yacu too. But more people came upriver from Peru and began to repopulate the Bobonaza, initiating great wars into which the Spanish again intruded. The inevitable discussion of near total destruction between Ancient Times and Times of the Grandparents suggests the category Times of Destruction, even though we have no common Quichua phrase for this.

The Puyo Runa often invoke an intermediate period between Ancient Times and Times of the Grandparents, called *alfaro rucuguna*, Republican Times. This is always described as a continuity of destruction, depopulation, and the loss of knowledge. But out of this period emerged the time period of the contemporary elders. Wars then occurred between the Zaparoan Gayes who attacked the Canelos Runa, and between the Canelos Runa and the Jivaroans from the area of the Chiguaza and Palora rivers. According to the Puyo Runa the *Tahuashiri* were friendly during Ancient Times, and did not begin to spear outsiders (as they did until very recently) until their near destruction in Republican Times. The age of the *caucheros*, or rubber exploiters, falls into Republican Times, and can easily be dated as the turn of the twentieth century. By this time the population of the Bobonaza drainage was building up again, but new slave raids and wars occurred. Specifically, people referred to as *Mainu* (Mayna), *Mulato* (Murato Candoshi), and *Canduishuar* (Shapra Candoshi) invaded the Bobonaza and Pastaza, and some groups of Achuara and Jívaro proper allied with one another against these upriver mauraders. People known as *Llamistas* also entered from the area around Yurimaguas, Peru, but they returned there. Havoc reigned, knowledge was lost, but the Canelos Quichua endured, and once again, in Times of the Grandparents, began to resettle their territory.

During Ancient Times full knowledge of the spirits of huanduj and ayahuasca existed. The ancients entered all domains without fear of soul theft, soul loss, death, or enchantment, and communicated directly with Sungui and Amasanga. There was never a question as to who, or what, caused illness and death, and the ancients had full command of remedies for illness, and could retaliate rapidly if one caused the death of another. Some say that during the time of the ancient people Sungui, Amasanga, Nunghuí, Juri juri, Ayahuasca mama, and Yaji mama lived, as people or as spirits, side by side with all the ancient Runa.

The basic importance of the contemporary concept of linear time structure is the belief that knowledge was lost between Ancient Times and Times of the Grandparents. For this reason I include Times of Destruction as a Canelos Quichua temporal construct. But the loss of knowledge is potentially retrievable from ancient souls and spirits, through night dreams, by observations in the forest, through participation in the ways of the Sacha Runa.

Linear time structure can be summarized as follows, beginning with the Ancient Times:

Ancient Times

↓

Times of Destruction

↓

Times of the Grandparents

↓

Present Times

The basic contrast is between ancient, or beginning, callari rucuguna—Ancient Times—and present, with continuity with the past, cunan rucuguna. There are two means of maintaining continuity with the linear past, each important in gaining an appreciation of the world view of the Canelos Quichua. The first is that represented by the bottom arrow: direct inheritance of knowledge and soul substance from Times of the Grandparents to the present. The second form of continuity is in the acquisition of ancient souls from Ancient Times. The ancient peoples themselves acquired souls from the animals before creation; when the ancient peoples died these souls lived on.

Mythic Time

In the time of *unai*, a long time ago, before the beginning, the world was not divided into domains as it is today; rather, there was integration of all the life forces. The underworld people lived on the earth with all of the birds and animals, which were human at that time. All the celestial bodies also lived on the earth, "as people" (Spanish *como gente*, Quichua *runa sami*), and sky-earth-underearth were unified; all beings could pass from one to the other. Work was almost nonexistent, for the animals knew how to fell trees with a special *pinduj*-cane lance, *huachi*, and to make easy climbs into the sky with the same kind of lance. This is what I shall call "mythic time"; it is not linear, but transformational and always in existence. Contemporary Canelos Quichua maintain a mythic structure which relates events in mythic time to the times of the ancient people. During mythic

Cucha pillan.

time, the human ancestors of contemporary Runa crawled on their hands and knees, for they were *llullucu*, unripe, weak, unknowledgeable babies. Animals imparted knowledge by example, not by formal instruction. As the ancient Runa babies of mythic time learned, they began to grow, and as they grew they made mistakes, for which they dearly paid, often with their lives. But many of their experiences with near disaster were overturned, and the ancient Runa triumphed, became fully human, and began a quest for knowledge which resulted in the imposition of structure in the biosphere. The following brief story illustrates such a learning process.

THE CAYU OF THE HUATSALALA

Long ago, before creation, when animals were human and people were still growing from the babies which they used to be, there was a man hunting near a *huatsalala.* A huatsalala is a term used by the people who lived in Ancient Times, after creation, to refer to a very special, enchanted, lagoon. A *cayu supai*, which is a people-eating seven-headed boa shaped like an oblong bowl, lives in the huatsalala, and is surrounded by sharks.

The hunter was in the vicinity of the enchanted lagoon when he spotted a baby giant anteater called *cucha pillan*, lagoon anteater. He sat his muzzle-loading shotgun down and went to capture it. He wanted to take it home to keep as a pet, and to play with. What a child this hunter; no adult Runa would keep a giant anteater in the house!

The mother of the baby came, reared up in front of him, and hit him, *whack*—he fell, unconscious. The mother anteater trussed up the Runa with arms and legs tied behind him so that he could not stand. He could only roll back and forth. Then she put balsa plugs in his ears, eyes, nostrils, and mouth—seven plugs; and then she put one in his penis and the final one up his anus.

Then she picked the man up and carried him to the enchanted lagoon. She put the man down, turned from him, and reared up over the edge of the lagoon with arms outspread to call the cayu. *Grrrrr*, she said. The sharks came ahead of the cayu, and while the anteater was watching them approach, the man, trussed up though he was, kicked the anteater into the lagoon. *Splash!* she went; the sharks tore into her and ate everything except the white liver, which rose to the surface and floated away.

This short account is one of hundreds. It is a segment of a seemingly never-ending narration of life in mythic time that can carry various messages and be invoked in different contexts. Learning was important in the telling of this segment. The people relating this were letting me know that even though the "man" was hunting with a sophisticated weapon not available in Ancient Times he was still a child, for he acted like a child in trying to capture an animal that an adult would not capture. But the giant anteater, for all its intelligence, underestimated the maturing Runa, and thereby paid with its life.

Early in the narrative the speaker lets us know that the event took place before creation, but that the old term for the huatsalala and its full meaning were known by the ancients, who were fully adult because they knew everything about mythic structure in mythic time, and about their biosphere, which was later mutilated and partially destroyed by outside intrusion.

Cultural continuity for the Canelos Quichua involves not only acquisition of grandparental and ancient souls, but also acquisition of knowledge of mythic thought and structure, through the repertory of tales of never-ending events in mythic time, and through understanding the metaphor, inner meanings, connotations, extensions, analogies, and transformation of events and relationships in mythic time and structure. It is best to think of mythic time as existing just beyond, outside of, the linear sequence of time from the ancients to the present. Mythic time or structure can be entered by song, by night dreams, by graphic design, and by ceremony.

MYTHIC STRUCTURE

Imagine a world as rich as the contemporary one but where all celestial bodies, animals, fish, reptiles, and many plants are human, and interact in all the different sorts of ways in which people do today. Imagine also that linear sequences, such as aging, and cyclical ones, such as those created by the changing of night into day, do not exist. The world is as rich and as varied as a mind in intersubjective interaction with other minds can make it. What emerges from such a world are certain relational systems which allow people to transcend domains through the use of metaphor, and certain postulated sequential or transformational events to which people can orient their narrative, dream, and thought in seeking vision, knowledge, and understanding.[14]

My purpose here is to indicate a very few relationships and events which we shall have to consider in various parts of this book, moving deeper and deeper as more information is presented. It seems advisable to begin with Quilla, for he represents a sentient being less predictable than any other, and presents us with a particular sort of origin story. The moon in his most virile, irascible form had sexual intercourse with his bird sister, *Jilucu*,[15] and out of this union came the stars, as people. Jilucu had never seen her lover, for he always came to her bed at night. One night during her pregnancy she smeared or painted genipa juice on his face, telling him it would make him feel fresh and good (it is an astringent). By morning the black color had emerged, and Jilucu saw that her lover was the moon. The stars, as people, cried and cried when they saw the moon's spotted face, for they recognized the shame of incest. They now saw that they were descended from an incestuous brother-sister union. They too put *huiduj*, the black juice of the genipa seed, on their faces. They cried as the collective sister of the moon, because huiduj, along with *manduru*, the red achiote, are both "sisters"[16] of the moon. As they cried their black tears fell to the earth and seeded the huiduj tree.

Such collective crying produced the fearsome merger of rain, earthquake, and flood. The rivers swelled, volcanoes erupted, new high hills appeared, and the earth shook. The earth people were caught up in a great river which swept them eastward into the sea. Out of this river came the sun, who ascended to the sky to begin his regular course, and to bring an orderly east-west axis to the earth-world. Also, night and day developed, and the night lost much of its light because the moon and stars lost some of their power due to the incestuous relationship between Quilla and Jilucu.

The Runa became separated from one another and had to wander back

Ala.

westward, looking for people like themselves and having thousands of
adventures, through which they learned individually and which today
make up an enormous corpus of mythical knowledge. During the return
wandering the Runa had no manioc to eat, and they had to fight and kill
animals with chonta sticks. They ate tree mushrooms and lichens, *ala*, and a
species of *Araceae* called *laglia tupi*. Eventually they found their way back
upstream to the hills where it was safe for manioc chagras. They recognized
the chagras by the huayusa growing there. They fought with other animal
people over possession of the territories.

In telling stories about such wandering, concepts of the "creation" of
men and women are discussed. The stars are human, and from a female
perspective they are white grubs or botfly larvae; from a male perspective
they are mushrooms. In the creation of women two shooting stars come to
earth in the form of white grubs. They live in logs, or in the earth, but they
are of the sky. Usually the sisters come to two brothers on a river bank; one
is rejected by one brother, who ascends to heaven, but the second turns
into a beautiful woman and becomes the wife of the second brother.

Throughout myths concepts of "brotherhood" are dealt with, as are concepts of husband-wife, wife and brother's wife, and the relationship of the living with important soul-conferring animal ancestors, notably the jaguar for men and the cayman for women. *Pairs* of animal-humans make up most of the characters, the duality signifying, inter alia, simultaneous participation in animal and human worlds, or in any two domains.

I noted in the first chapter that the concept *alaj* derives from a myth segment dealing, in various ways, with older brother–younger brother authority and tension.

An older and younger brother were stuck on a great rock in the middle of a mighty river. The older brother called to a giant cayman, "Come Apamama [Grandmother], take us across." He told the younger brother to go first, but the younger brother, who always argued, said, "No, you go first, older brother"; so the older brother did, keeping his eyes closed all the way, and arrived on the bank. But on the next trip the younger brother did not keep his eyes closed; he fell into the water and was swept away. The older brother searched and searched, and had many other adventures. Eventually, heading upriver and very hungry, he reached out to pinch a mushroom, *ala,* which was growing out of the large, red trunk of a *Mindal* tree, and the mushroom cried out, "Ouch, my mythic brother, don't pinch me, real brother,"[17] and turned into the younger brother.

This is the derivation of the term which the Canelos Quichua men use in addressing each other. They usually say *alaj,* my brother, but they sometimes say *alajma* or *alama,* using the *ma* emphasis form.

In this brief myth segment we noted the role of the cayman, addressed as "Apamama"—Grandmother. Another myth segment deals with the relationship of two brothers to the great cayman, and suggests an aspect of social relationship as well.

An older and a younger brother were trying to cross a great lagoon on top of a high hill. The older brother cried out "Apamama, Apamama, carry us across," and a giant cayman came. The older brother told the younger to go first, but as usual he refused, so the older went across, with eyes closed. Then the cayman made the return voyage for the younger. But just before landing on the shore the younger brother opened his eyes, saw the great cayman instead of a canoe, and shouted to be let off. The cayman turned; *crunch!* she snapped off his right leg. (This was terrible because a person's soul is in his right shinbone!) The brother was now without a leg, so he could not walk, and without a soul, which had been stolen by the cayman. The older brother fought back; he got five white termites and threw them into the lagoon, where they proceeded to drink up the water. Caymans appeared from all over and the Runa killed them. Finally, in fear of losing their entire population, one giant cayman pointed to the guilty cayman, with the younger brother's leg-soul, and the Runa killed it. The younger brother put his leg back on, and off they went again.

Pottery representation of an ala growing out of a tree.

The back of the same piece of pottery.

Ruya lagartu.

Among other things this myth segment asserts that the cayman is a crucial vehicle of transmission in the water domain, but that dangers are always present there. It also asserts that, even if the apamama gets the soul of a man, the man has ways of retaliating and regaining it. The two brothers are frequently represented in myth as Cuillur and Docero, star brothers who represent continuity on the east-west sky axis, but also represent opposite sides of the sky universe and reverse episodes in the transition from day to night. In such stories Cuillur is usually the older brother.

The apamama itself is created, or regenerated, in another myth segment, by the two star brothers.

> Cuillur and Docero set out to make a canoe. To fell a tree they used huachi spears made from the pinduj, or river cane. Cuillur, the older, told the younger to throw his spear at the lower trunk of the tree, where the stern would be; but the younger said "No," and threw the spear upward, to where the prow would be cut; he missed. The older brother threw his spear down into the trunk, where the stern would be cut, and the tree fell and became a cayman canoe called *yacu apamama* or *ruya lagartu*.

Most apamama stories begin with the actions of the two brothers, but puma stories usually begin with the wandering of a pregnant woman.

> A pregnant woman was in the jungle and a great black jaguar was hungry so he grabbed the woman and put her under a mountain of corn. Other jaguars and cougars entered carrying people and began to divide up the kill. They leaped and leaped at the woman but could not reach her. Eventually the ancient jaguar, apayaya, took the child of the woman [often twins], placed it in a tinaja with cotton, capped it well, and the child grew in there, eventually becoming an apayaya puma—a veritable grandfather jaguar. He became a brother of other Runa, and went off to kill the original animal jaguar with a macana. He learned where to find the ancient jaguar (who earlier had captured his mother) from the jaguar and cougar youths. He found the old jaguar, killed

it, and became master of the animal domain as jaguar man; the surviving
animal jaguars became his uncles.

It is at this point in myth telling, with the apamama as cayman and the
apayaya as jaguar, that *unai*—beyond time—is dropped from the telling,
and *callari rucuguna*—Ancient Times—is invoked. In this particular
beginning, which continues the tale given above, a woman learns from
Nunghuí, as Chagra mama, how to keep the agouti out of the manioc.

> Nunghuí took a stick and on its end placed a peccary skull. The stick plus
> skull came to life and went *tuc tuc tuc*, hitting the agouti all around the chagra
> and driving them from the manioc. Nunghuí gave this to the ancient huarmi,
> who in turn buried it under the ground.
>
> The jaguar and cougar boys wanted to cut this stick, so that they could hunt
> agouti in the chagra, making it their domain, the domain of the jungle, again.
> They come to cut it, got to fighting among themselves because they didn't
> agree on who should try to cut which side, and fell into a river, where the
> caymans came and ate all but one. A pregnant jaguar escaped to have another
> son.

There are dozens of stories which establish, in various ways, that in Ancient
Times the domains discussed earlier in this chapter were established with
the clear division between women, related to soil and, less securely, to
water, and men, related to the forest. Linear times exist from the
beginnings to the present with fixed domains, which the ancient peoples
knew how to span or merge. Mythic time and structure, by contrast, exist
outside of domain structure, and hence require no domain spanning or
knowledge merging.

Ethnic Identity and Mythic Metaphor

Among the Canelos Quichua men who truly "belong" are metaphorically
addressed on ceremonial occasions as *huauqui puma*, jaguar brother. Such
men who are regarded as being *of* Canelos Quichua culture are said to be
descended from the ancients through a puma line; some are the black
jaguars, *yana puma*, some the phantom giant monkey jaguar, *chuba puma*,
others the cougar, *taruga puma*, deer puma. Apayaya, father's father's
soul or ancient male soul, is connected with a puma ayllu soul beyond time.
The first soul, aya, is simply inherited from the father, *yaya*, but the
grandfather soul must be acquired. Such acquisition involves a process of
status rise wherein the questing Runa moves upward in a hierarchy of
shamans, embedded in competition with his brothers over the acquisition
of ancient souls. As the quest for souls increases, so must knowledge of
mythic structure increase, for it is within this structure that the metaphor
necessary for the understanding of visionary experience occurs.

Ancient grandmother souls, collectively apamama, are the mythical female vehicles that men use to enter the water domain. Apamama, from the standpoint of any male Runa, refers specifically to the woman who gave birth to his inherited soul, his father's father's wife. And when he thinks of the future, he must think of transmission of apamama substance through his own wife. If he wants to transmit his inherited soul with the power and ancient life force which has come to him in the male line, then he can marry a woman from those descending from his father's father's wife's uterine relatives, all of whom he would class as apamama in the second ascending generation. A simple model that he may manipulate is represented in Diagram 2:1 below.

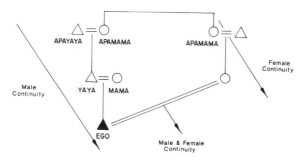

Diagram 2:1

Women, too, seek to transmit their inherited female soul, implanted by mother's mother's husband, to their offspring. They can do this by marrying a man who directly descends from the mother's mother's husband's agnatic relatives, whom she classes as apayaya in the second ascending generation. A simple model that she may manipulate is represented in Diagram 2:2 below.

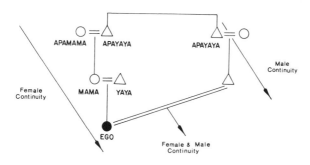

Diagram 2:2

Kinship statuses constitute an *idiom* of social transmission which, among other things, triggers metaphors which express a male-female parallelism *in* transmission, a mutual dependence *for* transmission, and a logic for cross-generational marriage. Metaphorically, according to this model, ego male takes as wife the daughter of a woman connected to a cayman ayllu, beyond time, and ego female takes as husband the son of a man connected to a jaguar ayllu, beyond time.

Apamama, as cayman, is one of the seats of Sungui, the water spirit master. Women in general get their knowledge from Nunghuí, the wife of Amasanga. Men get their knowledge about ancient souls from Amasanga. Intersubjective sharing of knowledge between man and woman takes place in the huasi, that tangible-material and social-symbolic enclosure of space and time where man and woman unite to transmit their collective, accumulating knowledge to their descendants.

VISIONARY EXPERIENCE

Mythic thought serves as a basis for the analysis of dreams. Such continuing analysis is crucial to the world view of the Sacha Runa. As night stars fade toward dawn, and before the eastern sky is lighted by the sun, dreams reach a vivid intensity and the Canelos Quichua awaken and talk softly to one another about these recent visions. This begins around 4:00 A.M. or earlier, and by the time of first light, at 5:00, knowledge and reflection about these night visions provide more symbolism for intersubjective analysis of the Runa inner selves. This transition period from night to day is one in which souls have left bodies and wandered, and domains have returned to their mythical merger. Amasanga and his wife, Nunghuí, have joined one another in the tree trunk and roots, the crops are filled with soul substance, and animals wander between jungle and chagra.

As the domains separate with the coming of pre-dawn light women visit Sungui's domain to get fresh sweet water to boil, cool, and mix with the fermented manioc mash. The designs on the mucahuas take on an intensity at times, in the eyes of the beholders, as insects, boas, turtles, grubs, stars in contrasting black, red, yellow, and white painted on the serving ware make visual representation to mythic structure. Such representations help the pre-dawn drinker to orient his dreams into the whole of a domain-structured isomorphic meaning system, allowing him to bring multiple metaphors to bear on the work-a-day world which he is about to confront beyond the huasi universe. Just before dawn male falsetto shrieks rend the air, and many men play special spirit songs on transverse flutes. The songs are regarded as being those of a small bird, *paspanchu*, which sings just before a storm breaks. The theme of such songs can be expressed by the words "evil is coming but I meet it calmly." Day begins.

Muscuna means to dream or to engage in visionary experience. All people dream, and all are therefore imbued with soul substance, since it is the soul, aya, which enters the realms introduced to the dreamer. To know, *ricsina*, to interpret the dreams, one must think, ponder, make observations, and talk to older people who know more. As one "learns"—the process called *yacha*—he must seek other visionary aids, the master one being an individual experience with Datura. This experience is partly discussed in the next chapter, under the heading "Yaya." Ayahuasca taking also provides a context for visionary acquisition of knowledge and power. Such a context is a small group affair involving a shaman and his clients. This is discussed in Chapter 5.

Visions, or at least thoughts going back in time, which people regard as visions, called *muscui* or *muscuyu*, occur during large ceremonies. Stimulated by lack of sleep, gallons and gallons of chicha and a wine-like drink made from fermented manioc and fungi, together with a repetitive drumming on snare drums, men and women collectively dream and sing to themselves for seventy-two hours or more. During this annual or semiannual ceremony, today known only as *jista*, the Canelos Quichua divide their central Runa territory into two halves, the *cari jista*, male ceremony, and the *huarmi jista*, female ceremony. These two basic divisions are also called *Quilla jista* and *Jilucu jista*, and reintegrate Runa people and Runa mythic structure by reenactment of crucial relationships. This ceremony enacts and portrays fundamental concepts of division between the inheritances of the two parts—male and female, Amasanga and Nunghuí, the puma and amarun—and their fundamental reintegration through common descent due to the union of ancestral brother and sister. The ceremony is presented and discussed in Chapter 6.

Visionary experience spans and integrates jungle, water, and soil domains, the sky and the underworld, and opens the entire sequence of linear time to enduring mythic structure. Men and women, through their collective participation in household perpetuity, also link these domains, through intersubjective interchange of their special knowledge, thought, and vision, and through a division of toil which allows for exploitation of the world of the Sacha Runa. The next chapter focuses directly on this male-female unit, the huasi.

NOTES

1. *Ricsina* is the root form, meaning "to know," "knowledge." The concept *Sacha Runa* always invokes discussion of knowledge, whether used in the sense of a person who can live in the forest, or the spirit of the forest which can bring knowledge to living Runas through dreams and visions.

2. The Canelos Quichua use the Spanish terms *norte* (north) and *sur* (south) when they need to refer to these cardinal points in a discussion with outsiders. But in their cosmology, as far as I can determine, the term *chimbajta*, from *chimba*, each side, is used for both north and south. Upriver and downriver, *janaj* and *urai*, can also be used on a north-south axis, the direction depending not only on the direction the river flows, but also the orientation of social groupings. For example, *from* Paca Yacu, Villano (in the north) is *janaj*, up, and the Yatapi River is *urai*, down. But *from* Villano, Paca Yacu (in the south) is regarded as *janaj*, and north into Auca territory as *urai*. What seems to be happening is that at both Paca Yacu and Villano the orientation of "up" is toward the far edge of the Runa territory, in distinction to non-Runa, who are "down." Achuara, then, are "downriver" in the south, and Huarani Auca are "downriver" in the north. *Janaj* and *urai*, in Quichua, seem to be used among the Puyo Runa exactly as the terms *tsumú* and *yakíia* in Jívaro proper, at least as it is spoken just south of the Pastaza River.

3. These fish, variously referred to by the common Spanish name *Bocachica*, are classed as *Prochilodus nigricans* by Eigenmann and Allen (1942:309). Although in Highland Quichua *challua* is the generic term for fish, among the Canelos Quichua it is the specific name for this species and *yacu aicha* is the generic term for fish.

4. Karsten (1935:386–392) presents comparable materials from Canelos differently, and some note must be taken of my specific disagreements and interpretations. A traveler can easily elicit material as Karsten does, getting bilingual Quichua-Spanish informants to offer "demon" as *supai*, particularly at Canelos, where the Catholic Church has had the greatest effect. Some spirits are indeed demoniacal, but the basic contrast, in all social and ritual contexts, is between aya, as soul, and supai, as spirit. Aya, for the Canelos Quichua does not, I will insist, mean "dead"; the dead represent a different dimension of the biosphere, as I discuss below. But *the dead do have souls, and the supais do, too.* I think that Karsten's list of "demons" is one of convenience for the Canelos informants. Many people told me that it is far easier to give lists of supais than to help the investigator understand the order existing in this universe.

From my work with some bilingual Quichua-Jívaro proper and Quichua-Achuara people, I also dispute the Karsten relationship (1935:386, 454) that asserts the equation of Quichua *aya* = Jívaro *wakani* and Quichua *supai* = Jívaro *iguánchi* (*iwanchi*). In Jívaro *wakani* simply means "soul," and *iwanchi* means "demons," "forms of the natural non-human world that can kill a man" (Harner 1972:144). In Quichua, bilingual, bicultural Jivaroan–Canelos Quichua informants make the equation Jívaro *iwanchi* = Quichua *aya*, and emphatically deny that the Quichua *supai* is the Jívaro *iwanchi*, but become more confused about a relationship with the concept of *wakani* as translated into Quichua. The closest I can come to *wakani* is in discussing the "ancient specter soul," called *arutam wakani* by the Jívaro proper (Harner 1972). Then, in Quichua, I can easily elicit in a variety of contexts *huandujta upisha muscuna*, Datura-induced vision, as the intercultural correspondence.

It should also be noted that the concept of *muisak*, "avenging soul . . . which comes into existence only when a person who has seen an *arutam* has been killed . . ." (Harner 1972:143), becomes *muiska* through common Jívaroan metathesis (Harner 1972:224), which is remarkably similar to the Canelos Quichua *muscuí*, soul dream, which comes during their ceremonies. The Achuara-Quichua bilingual, bicultural people with whom I worked cannot, or will not, discuss anything having to do with the arutam, which they regard as a Jívaro proper soul, spirit, or demon (they aren't sure which).

The crucial point is that, for some cultural transformational reasons, the Quichua soul concepts are closely equated with the Jívaro demon idea. Again, the Canelos Quichua can be pressed into making the translation of "aya equals soul," "wakani equals soul," therefore "aya equals wakani," but the people who know both cultures don't make their transformations in this way until forced through the mediation of Spanish, and beliefs in Christian "souls and demons," to make such relationships between the cultures. I return to this point in Chapter 6, note 7.

5. In Canelos Quichua, *allpa* refers to productive soil in which the forest and crops grow; it also refers to clay that can be worked to produce pottery. Terra firma is also included in the meaning of allpa. Allpa contrasts with *turu*, mud, and *chapaj*, mire. Both mud and mire span the domains of water and productive soil (yacu and allpa), but they are of no utility to humans, nor do the forest and crops grow from them. They are associated with the domain of water, in its dangerous forms associated with excess rain, floods, and earthquakes. *Chapaj* is a metathesis of *pacha*, which means "earth" in Andean Quichua. Jungle Quichua speakers know this, and invoke the Andean word only when referring to the "underearth." *Ucu* derives from *ucumu*, straight down (from a designated center); its opposite is *cusca*, straight up (from a designated center). The dividing point of straight up and straight down is the allpa of any designated space. An individual's own body and household are the usual loci for figuring up and down.

6. Some Canelos Quichua like to tell stories of the *Paccha supai*, waterfall spirit, which comes from the river to frighten them during hunting trips to areas rich in large game. The Paccha supai walks amidst thunder, rain, and darkness making a frightening, rhythmic noise, represented onomatopoeically as *tulús-durúng, tulús-durúng*. In such stories a core element is the ability to awaken quickly and confront the spirit as it comes to them. This spirit, however, is an Amasanga fear manifestation, not a Sungui manifestation. It is clearly analogous to the Jívaro proper arutam specter (Harner 1972), but is not sought out by the Canelos Quichua as it is by the Jívaro proper. There is one further supai, *Ulas huarmi*, which is a female Amasanga representation existing in rivers where the land rises to form dangerous, rocky rapids.

7. Symbolism of the otter, porpose, manatee, and other water mammals is unquestionably important in thoroughly working through this section on world view. For example, the giant river otter is called *yacu puma*, water jaguar, and the teeth of the fresh-water porpoise are thought to have very special properties which men can use to attract and sexually arouse women. Unfortunately most of our field work was carried out in the higher western territory of the Canelos Quichua, where the only water mammals are a small river otter and a kind of muskrat, neither of which takes on any special significance. My guess is that farther east, where large river mammals may loom large in cosmology, they will be found to occupy contrastive and complementary sections of a mythical transformation group, replacing other western elements which do not exist in the lower forest.

8. This term has sometimes been translated as "vine of the dead," presumably following Incaic usage (Harner 1972:153). The Canelos Quichua derivation most definitely excludes association with the dead, *huanushca: aya* = soul, *huasca* = vine, "soul vine." In Jungle Quichua to derive the English phrase "vine of the dead," or the Spanish phrase *bejuco de los muertos*, one would have to elicit, in some context, *huasca huanushca manda*, and whenever one suggests *huanushca manda* as a derivation or synonym for *ayahuasca* he is instantly corrected, and the distinction between *aya* and *huanushca* (who are believed to have ayas) made.

Ayahuasca is one of several *Banisteriopsis* species (Dobkin de Rios 1972, Schultes 1972:33–40, Reichel-Dolmatoff 1972, Harner 1972, 1973, for general discussions) known to the Canelos Quichua. Some people from Paca Yacu refer to the *ayahuasca huahua* as *quilla huasca*, moon vine.

9. I am told that there are still other names elsewhere. We grew two species of

Banisteriopsis (ayahuasca and mucu huasca) and a third (yaji) which was either another *Banisteriopsis* or *Psychotria* adjacent to our house during our field work. Some shamans take the male, mucu huasca, to have a somewhat different visual experience.

In general, snake symbolism pervades much of the shamanistic paraphernalia, although these ideas are usually submerged in other aspects of ceremony. A snake is regarded, at times, as a *supai huasca*, spirit vine, and the tips of the leaves in the bundle shaken by the shaman are, under the influence of ayahuasca, viewed as snakes' tongues.

10. The actual phrase is *apayayaguna ama mancha chuan nguichu, huaccha mani, huaccha mani: apayaya*—grandfather category/, *guna*—plural/, *ama*—negative/, *mancha* —frighten/, *chuan*—negative complement to *ama*, with emphasis/, *nguichu*—you, plural/, *huaccha*, orphan/, *mani*—I am.

11. In Canelos, and occasionally in Puyo, the aya rumi is called *tayaj rumi*. Furthermore, tayajs are regarded as ancient Runa ancestors in specific opposition to the Zaparoan Gayes. In telling the legend of a Gayes invasion of Canelos the tayajs are said to have come to life to defend the site, side by side with the inhabiting Runas. Some say that the tayajs used bows and arrows. People at Canelos proper also indicate that *tayaj rucuguna*, tayaj ancient times, existed "before the flood," which was "before creation." Since these concepts occur only at Canelos, or among people who have spent a great deal of time in Canelos, and since they do not fit well into the general temporal and mythic structures when these are induced in specific contexts of Canelos Quichua life (discussed below), I am drawn to the tentative conclusion that the idea of tayaj time as "before the flood" is one introduced by the church. Also, I think that *tayaj* is simply a Canelos proper idiomatic presentation of *aya*, soul.

12. The *idea* of Docero (who is sometimes called Locero or Luceru) and Cuillur occupying an east-west axis when they are in the sky is always expressed. But different speakers place one in the east, the other in the west, and also differ about which is morning and which is evening star. Some say it doesn't matter, they are both the same star, following the sun's course all around the heavens. The central idea is that they represent an east-west axis close to the earth domain when they are in the sky. When they descend to earth they become an older and a younger brother who are not predictable, always getting involved in squabbles. Which star Runa is younger and which is older does not matter, and different speakers differ about their relationships. For a book of myths featuring these stars, as told by various Jungle Quichua, see Orr and Hudleson 1971.

13. Many people around Puyo and Canelos, and elsewhere as well, add the Spanish *tiempo* (time) after the Quichua term for "now," "old," or "grandparent." One can elicit, for example, in sort of a "classroom" way, *cunan tiempo rucuguna*, or *callari tiempo rucuguna*, or *apamama tiempo rucuguna*. But in actual conversation I have never heard *tiempo* inserted, and the shortest possible phrase such as *apayayaguna* invokes time, even without the *rucu*, in this case. Some speakers give time characteristics in speaking of the past, such as "peaceful times," "times of war" or even "times of sadness."

14. The mythic dimension of Canelos Quichua life is sufficiently rich, varied, and complex to demand attention apart from this book. Indeed, a full analysis of Canelos Quichua concepts of creation of people, including the relationships between the sexes, and the people and all of the life forces of forest, sky, water, and underworld domains demands major research.

15. One important variant of this myth was elicited in which the wife of the moon was Quilla mama, with whom the moon had a daughter, Jilucu, and the incestual tale proceeds from Quilla-Jilucu incest as father-daughter incest. Jilucu is the common potoo bird (*Nyctibius griseus*; see Meyer de Schauensee 1964:121–122). It is true that on a beautifully moonlit night one can hear the bird calling *ji-lúuuuuuu-cuu, cuu, cuu*.

16. I enclosed "sisters" in quotation marks because in Canelos Quichua mythology achiote is *huarmipangui* (*huarmi*—woman/, *pa*—emphasis/, *ngui*—you), which means "man who acts

like a woman"—i.e., makes chicha, prefers men to women in sexual relationships, plants and prepares manioc.

17. The actual phrase is *aiai alajma ama tiushi huaichu huauqui: aiai*—ouch/, *ala*—mushroom, mythic brother/, *j*—possessive/, *ma*—emphasis/, *ama*—no/, *tiushi*—pinch/, *hua*—to me/, *i*—command/, *chu*—negative complement to *ama*/, *huauqui*—real brother. Sometimes, in telling this, the speaker elaborates and says, "Ouch, don't do that [pinch me], I'll lose part of my ear!" Also, sometimes in the telling people argue over whether the sort of mushroom found by the wandering Runa on the tree should be cooked or eaten as is; this sort of audience interplay gives a sense of impending humor, and allows the speaker time to think of some new twist by which to provoke cascades of laughter. One example is where the speaker addresses the mushroom and says, "I don't know whether you are good to eat or not, so I'll just sample a piece now and take you home to cook later," reaching out to pinch off a bit. . . .

3

Huasi

Two microcosms of the Canelos Quichua biosphere exist. They are embodied, respectively, in the household and in the individual. Both integrate the domains, dimensions, and symbolism of the universe. The union of an adult man and adult woman and their mutual establishment of a household—huasi—establishes a small universe from which each undertakes to exploit and maintain nature, to bring nature and culture together, and to integrate nature and culture with flesh, spirit, and soul. Such individual maneuvering generates continuous variety in the organization of symbolic relationships.

HOUSEHOLD

The traditional house of the Canelos Quichua ranges from round to oval. It is built on the ground and has a thatched roof. In the recent past the houses at Puyo were completely enclosed with chonta walls, while from Paca Yacu eastward there were no walls. Canelos itself had (and still has) both enclosed and open types. If the house axis is east-west then the woman's part is in the east end and the man's in the west. If the axis of the house is north-south, then it does not matter which side is the woman's and which side the man's, but the contrast between two houses is maintained. The man's side is called *jatun huasi*, big house, and the woman's *ichilla huasi*, small house. The center, *puñuna huasi*, sleeping house, combines male and female attributes and symbolizes continuity of that which both man and woman bring to bear on their future, from their individual and combined presence and from their individual pasts.[1]

Symbolism of the ichilla huasi revolves around the following equations: transformation of raw manioc to food by cooking, transformation of cooked manioc to drink by woman's "substance," transformation of earth (clay) to serving bowls and storage jars by woman's work, knowledge, and souls, and the merging of earth and water domains by the combining of fermented

An oval house near Puyo, 1973.

A round sacha huasi in purina territory on the upper Conambo River, 1972.

manioc and water. In the case of chicha making, the woman "eats," *mucuna*, the manioc and, after it has become part of her body, returns it to storage where it becomes a water food, or drink (some types of chicha are actually called *yacu*). Women see to the continuity of corporeal life by cooking food and making chicha, and to soul and spirit continuity by providing a pertinent array of pottery.

The jatun huasi is where other people are received. Such *runa pasiana*, people going by or passing through, sit on a long bench which is usually the remains of a broken canoe. This bancu symbolizes a boa. The man himself normally sits on a carved bancu in the form of a water turtle or a tree cayman, *ruya largartu* (the same as the apamama discussed in the previous chapter; the name derives from the fact that the mythic tree cut for a canoe turned into a cayman). He sits toward the center of the house on his individual bancu, as the runa pasiana sit toward the entrance point of the jatun huasi and face the male host. Symbolically, guests and host sit on the stools of Sungui, hewed by a man from Amasanga's forest, and are served chicha—the merger of soil, water, and feminine substance—by the man's wife, sister, or daughters.

The very center of the house symbolizes the center of the universe, for cusca and ucumu are reckoned from that point. The husband and wife sleep on either side of the center on a sleeping platform, *caitu*, the wife with a little baby, *llullucu*, on her left side, her husband on her right. Married or unmarried pubescent children sleep on platforms built on the opposite side of the house center, and prepubescent children sleep where they want to, on the floor or with parents or other children on their respective platforms. Both the man and the woman "hide" some special stones and other secret substances near their bed, and hence near one another. Conception, birth, funerary wake, curing, and shamanistic trips with Ayahuasca mama take place here, too. Souls are thought to leave the body and enter other domains during dreaming, and those domains are closest to the center of the house. Here husband and wife sleep and dream together; one frequently wakes during a dream to mention the soul's movement to the other. In this household center the couple travel nightly to other domains, and quietly share their visions and subsequent interpretations with one another as the night wears on. Awakening well before dawn, husband and wife move toward their respective houses. The woman performs necessary tasks of merging water, manioc, plantains, and meat into a food preparation, and the man plays a flute, gathers herbs for curing, or takes up one of many crafts for an hour or so.

By dawn, after all household members have eliminated in the surrounding house garden and washed in a nearby stream, the man joins his wife in the ichilla huasi, drinks chicha, and eats whatever the woman has prepared. Much discussion of the previous night's dreams, their meanings in terms of the Runa world and other worlds, and preparations for a day of toil from dawn to late afternoon or dusk are made.

The ichilla huasi itself may have an auxiliary house to store pottery, *asua churana huasi,* chicha-pottery house. If not, then all of the large jars for storing chicha, the serving bowls, cooking pots, and serving dishes are stored on racks in the ichilla huasi. Toward the eastern end of this house is the fire, which consists basically of three logs ingeniously placed spoke-like around a hot central fire made with chonta sticks and coals. The logs are simply pushed in together as they burn, providing a nice, stable warmth which can be stoked into a cook fire within minutes. Over the fire hangs a *ñajinchi* basket to smoke leftovers or foods to be taken on a hunt or trek. Dogs often cuddle up into the logs, gaining what warmth they can prior to a wet day of accompanying Runas in the forest or chagra, or a day of waiting for their masters' return while they guard the house. Lower jaws, *quiru,* of the *huangana,* white-lipped peccary, and *lumucuchi,* collared peccary, are stuck into walls in the ichilla huasi, as are monkey skulls.

Sufficient plantains for about a week's consumption are stored in the ichilla huasi, but manioc for only a day or two is kept there, as it spoils very rapidly when removed from the earth. When maize is harvested dozens of bushels are placed on racks above the ground. The chicha itself is a prominent feature of the woman's house. The large decorated jars range in number from two to a half-dozen or so, and are filled up to pot's shoulder with chicha mash, which is for the family's consumption and for household visitors as well. The mash is mixed with water just as it is served. Water is not stored in the huasi but brought fresh, as needed, from nearby clear, rocky streams or from underground brooks. It is boiled before dawn and used to mix with chicha; when the boiled water is gone fresh water is used for chicha mixing for the rest of the day.

Other paraphernalia in the ichilla huasi include a very large wooden bowl, *bátia* (from the Spanish *batea*), used for mashing cooked manioc to mix with masticated manioc, wooden pounders, some with carved heads, smaller bowls for shucking beans or panning gold, flat turtle-shaped planks, *taula,* for pressing dried tobacco leaves, and various sorts of baskets for carrying foodstuff or clothes. For grating plantain pulp into a bowl a file-like piece of spiny palm aerial root, *shiquita,* is used. Clay for making pottery is plastered to a pole, or to the outside of a chonta side, and other flat turtle-shaped planks, *tatanga,* for rolling clay coils, together with rocks and clays for coloring and a petate-like stone for mixing water and stone-dust dye, are either stored in the ichilla huasi or put in the special pottery shed.

Where houses exist in a settlement the *huasipungu,* household garden, extends outward from the kitchen, but the "front" of the house adjoining the jatun huasi is kept clean to the ground. Where the household is solitary or part of a linear riverine settlement, the huasipungu extends in all directions. Common plants of the huasipungu are four to five species of taro and yautia, sweet potatoes, occasional cucurbits, jicama, papaya, tropical forest sugarcane (two varieties used primarily as a remedy for accidental curare poisoning), some manioc, capsicum, various common remedies and plants to attract fish, develop breath power and control for blowgun use, and make dogs hunt. One of the latter is dog Datura, *allcu huanduj*. A small nightshade, *mutya*, grows wild and is left for the small seeds and pulp inside the Chinese lantern–type pods which are nibbled on by children.

The jatun huasi contains hunting paraphernalia, chief among which are the long, tapered, shiny black blowgun, *pucuna*, with white-lipped peccary or deer tibia "soul" mouthpiece, which comes from the Achuara of the Copotaza River or farther east, and the dart quiver, *matiri*, with the shaved bamboo darts, *biruti*, which all men make for themselves. *Jambi*, the dart poison, hangs in a small calabash shell, *jambi puru*. It is usually purchased from the Achuara in Peru or Ecuador and then added to poison, which some Canelos Quichua in all the Runa territories know how to make from a vine, *jambi huasca*, and other substances, including the spine of the tulumba toad.

Fishing equipment is quite elaborate, especially where gill netting is productive. The *Lica*, sometimes over sixty feet in length, is used. This rectangular net is spun from the leaf of the palm known as *chambira*. In the case of the lica the leaf is first cooked and the inner fibers removed. These are washed, dried, and grouped into a bundle, *huangu*, from which they are spun by a chonta stick, *piruru* or *piruruhuá*, with a turtleshell piece attached as a weight. Small rocks are dipped in shiny black cooked chicle, called *pungara*, and woven into the bottom of the lica while still tacky. Then a number of round plugs made of balsa or another comparable substance are affixed to the top, for floats. The round dip net, *huishina*, is usually obtained from the Quijos Quichua.

The net carrying bag, *shigra*, is ubiquitous. It is also woven from chambira palm-leaf fiber, but not from the inside as is the lica. Fibrous substance is pealed from the leaves, dried, stripped, and then rolled on one's leg to produce a good strong twine, which is then woven into the net bag or into a hammock. Birds (especially the toucan) stuffed with cotton or residue from dart scrapings, feathered headdresses, *llautu*, a drum, *caja*, a three-hole transverse flute, *juliahuatu*, and an over-the-shoulder ditty bag, *tslambu*, are also characteristic items in this masculine domain. Ubiquitous purchased objects in the jatun huasi include muzzle-loading shotguns and machetes.

Runa pasiana are always served chicha in the jatun huasi. A careful, stylized conversation accompanies the chicha drinking and sets guests apart from the intimate domain of the household center, and apart from the individualism of female production in the ichilla huasi. Shared inter-household emotional experience through the mediation of chicha drinking will be discussed in more detail in a later section on chicha.

Food is normally served and eaten in the ichilla huasi. Manioc, other tubers, and plantains are boiled in a yanuna manga and served on a banana leaf. Smoked meat, smoked fish, and fresh fish are also boiled and either placed on the same common leaf or served individually in the black eating bowls. Fish is sometimes boiled and served with manioc leaves. Corn and *chontaduro* fruit (from the *pejibaye*, peach palm) are boiled, piled on banana leaves, and served in large amounts. A single person may eat six or eight ears of corn at a sitting, as well as twenty or more chontaduros. Chicha is also drunk here, but the stylization characteristic of jatun huasi drinking is absent. To move to the kitchen is to drop the formality, and individuals act as their personality dictates, not according to a particular visitor's mood and feeling. There are no "visitors" in the kitchen; there are only individuals.

Special items owned by both men and women are kept in the center of the house. These include magical substances, special feathers for making headdresses, shrunken sloth or monkey heads, monkey and peccary skins for drumheads, soul and spirit stones, steel axe or adze heads, new or dress clothes, and other expensive paraphernalia purchased from trade centers.

Many people have more than one house, each adjacent to the other. In such cases the ichilla huasi has a male side, a female side, and a central sleeping place as discussed above. The jatun huasi maintains a man's side and woman's side also, but the entire house is used primarily for greeting and housing visitors. Shamans in particular are prone to have more than one adjacent house, and some of them have three.

To understand the full ramification of the concept of huasi we must now turn to sexual division of labor, discussed under the headings "Chagra" and "Hunting and Fishing."

CHAGRA

Two items of foreign manufacture are crucial to contemporary Canelos Quichua existence: the axe and the machete. Otherwise only a heavy chonta spear-shaped digging stick, *tula,* is used. Men generally work with axes and large, heavy machetes, while women work with somewhat smaller machetes, their digging sticks, and bare hands.

The first task in clearing any chagra for manioc planting is usually done by

On the way to a chagra.

a couple, together with whatever children they may have. Working parallel to one another with machetes the workers clear all vines, brush, and small bushes of up to about an inch in diameter. Everything is cut down into the surface roots, making the jungle mulch and humus covering the soil as clean as possible. All the residual, cut plant materials are pulled to the edge of the half- to two-hectare area, to dry and mulch there for about ten days.

Then the man, working with adult sons and sons-in-law, if he has any, cuts the trees down with axes. The men, sometimes on the advice of the women, are careful to leave a variety of palms for wood, fiber, fruit, and palmito foodstuff. In the lower elevations they leave rubber trees for their fruit and for the latex used in pottery manufacture. Caimito, chirimoya, and guama trees, many bushes from which vegetable dyes are extracted, and huayusa trees are also left.

Women and children immediately begin to clean the chagra. They do this in a bent-over position, swinging the machete so as to clean about half an inch under the mulch-loamy surface, clipping the tiny weeds and surface roots before they can establish a ground-level tangle that would usurp the immediate soil-surface nutrients which must go to the manioc. Logs felled by the men are also cleaned of their encompassing Araceae, Bromeliaceae, Orchidaceae, and many other plants, and these are thrown on the flanking compost pile. Logs and trunks remain in the chagra.

Men and women then lug the lightweight six-foot stems of manioc to the new site. These stems were previously cut; they store nicely for months when stuck intact into the ground with leaf stems removed, and they maintain their viability, putting out only the tiniest of new roots until cut into smaller segments. When ready to plant the women cut the stems into eight-inch sections and push them into the ground at an eighty-degree angle, arranging them in groups of three or four so that the penetration points turn away from each other. In this way the manioc clones grow outward from each other within a central group. Women also scatter beans around the chagra at this time, though such beans are not often used for food. Rather, they are used to fix nitrogen in the soil, prolonging the utility of this newly planted chagra space. From this point on women tend the manioc, keep weeds down, and maintain a watchful eye on encroaching agouti and paca. When evidence of such animal intrusion takes place the man is informed, and he usually sets a trap for the agouti and builds a tree platform near the chagra, in a place where palm nuts are falling, to shoot the paca.

The man places his mark on the new chagra by planting palm suckers (and sometimes seed sprouts), small huayusa transplants, genipa seeds, and achiote (Bixa orellana) seeds. The woman, in turn, plants rubber, chirimoya, and caimito seeds. The man often builds a small huasi on such a new chagra, and the woman with her children may stay there for two or three days at a time working from dawn to dusk; she sings songs to Nunghuí, and sometimes performs dances for her as well. The woman's children help her, and also explore, search, and play in chagra and adjoining forest, imitating bird calls, looking for animal and bird signs, and now and then finding a large (one-pound or more) land snail or land turtle,

Cutting the manioc stem prior to replanting.

Chagra near Puyo, 1971.

which they capture for food. They catch fish, crabs, shrimp, and snails in the streams, and carry water to the woman in the chagra. Games are played in which they call to their mother like birds from the forest; she responds by singing or cooing to them from the chagra, and the interplay between mother and children—chagra and forest—awakens memories of myths about forest and chagra interaction. Tales previously told by men or women in the huasi are re-enacted at night in the chagra huasi as the mother sings and recounts such tales to her children.

All varieties of manioc planted in the Puyo area are grouped into two categories, white, *ruyaj lumu*, and red, *puca lumu*. Their young, small tubers are both relatively tasty up to the time of the plant's flowering, which occurs in from three to five months, but quite bitter (and toxic from prussic acid) for a while after the flowering. Sitting in the ground for a month or more increases their size, restores their flavor, and lowers the level of toxicity. The manioc is ready for first harvesting in about five to six months after planting. It is the responsibility of the women to be sure that tubers with a bitter flavor—those which produce toxic reactions—are not brought to the huasi. As manioc is harvested work takes on a rotational pattern as the woman, with the help of her husband and children, harvests and plants at the same time. The woman simply pulls up a manioc stem, whacks off small and large tubers with a machete, and divides them into separate piles; then she snicks off about a dozen eight-inch sections and pushes them back into the ground. A few remaining large intact stems, with leaves removed, are placed together in a clump, to be used later when new ground is cleared.

As the manioc goes into this second planting men place suckers from a few of the dozen or more plantain and banana varieties in the ground. A sucker is simply cut off another plantain, carried to the chagra, and planted. More beans and several types of cucurbits are also planted at this time by women. After a complete planting and second harvest of manioc in this area (by the end of about a year to two and a half years), men plant more plantains and clear a new section of forest for new manioc chagra space. In this way the fifty-yard-wide chagra slowly rolls along through the jungle, with the manioc harvesting-planting cycle in the front, women in charge, and clearing down to the ground the technique. The tail end of the chagra, *chagra siqui*, controlled more and more by men through plantain planting, becomes increasingly tangled and brush-like until, after the plantains mature in about eighteen months to two years, the entire rear area is allowed to go back to jungle, or planted in maize or naranjilla for cash gain.[2] If no cash crop is planted, the beans are collected from this area to be replanted in the newly cleared area. When maize or naranjilla is planted, the beans are collected by women after the men finish their harvest. Plantains will continue to bear for at least eight more years in the second growth area. Depending on availability of land, land contour, and edaphic factors, the chagra is moved outward from three to five miles from the original site for a period of twelve to twenty years. Tall, mature pejibaye palms planted on the original chagra indicate "possession" of the beginning land, as that land returns to second-growth forest. The couple returns to their original site to begin the process again, although now they are harvesting from the far end of their personal territory, while beginning a new chagra on the other (original) end. Residence is established in the llacta system at the beginning of the chagra, and a second, temporary residence moved outward as the chagra is moved. Whether or not the increasingly distant huasi becomes regarded as primary depends on other social factors described in the next chapter.

Evil and danger exist on the chagra, for poisonous snakes, especially the bushmaster and a small green-chartreuse relative, the palm viper, are numerous. There is scarcely a person who has spent ten to twenty years working chagras who has not been bitten, some several times. Most people seem to survive, but many people do die from snakebite. The Canelos Quichua have several remedies against such danger, which is regarded as part of life—a never-ending potential threat which can strike suddenly, because of anger of the supai itself or by the direction of evil shamans. All poisonous snakes are killed with a stick, never with a machete; their heads are severed and buried with the stick plunged through, holding them down into the ground. Women study the patterns on the skin of the dead snake carefully, seeking to capture the *churana*, marking, of the vanquished supai on the rims of their mucahuas.

We noted above that some of the tail end of the long territory carved out by a man and woman and their children for the manioc-cycling chagra is used for such crops as plantains, bananas, maize, and naranjilla. Maize and naranjilla seeds are simply broadcast into the remaining bush; then the second-growth brush and vines are again cut and partially cleared. Snakebite in such brush clearing is much more frequent, since the palm viper and bushmaster fall or fling themselves from over the heads of the machete wielders. The meticulous ground-level cleaning associated with manioc is not undertaken. Instead, compost-mulch from the chagra edge is spread over the area, together with the brush cut down on top of the seeds. This slash-mulch cultivation is much the same as the one used in the wet Pacific Littoral (Whitten 1974). The naranjilla plants are frequently transplanted to get better spacing, but are weeded only to maintain pathways to the ripening fruits.

Nightshades (Solanaceae) abound in the Puyo area, with a half-dozen or more varieties of a vine-plant locally classed as potato, six species of naranjilla (only one of which has commercial value), semi-wild cherry tomatoes, capsicum, tobacco, and Datura. Except for certain kinds of Datura which are kept hidden, and the sporadically commercial naranjilla, these nightshades are randomly planted and also grow wild throughout all chagras. Jicama (Quichua *ihua*) beans are also planted randomly, and though the beans themselves are poisonous they produce a large, deliciously sweet white tuber which is eaten raw. Various lilies and anthuriums are left to grow, and the lily bulbs and new anthurium leaves are harvested for food and medicine.

A variety of Old and New World taros and sweet potatoes are grown, but are more often found on the smaller huasipungu, next to the house, than on the chagra. They are basically women's property and the product of women's labor. Many cucurbits, three of which are called *isha*, are grown. The isha produce long vines which go up the chonta or guama trees, flower, mature into three- to eight-pound elongated "squashes" in about eighteen months, and fall to the ground, where they are gathered. Nightshades and cucurbits are planted by both men and women, with women taking a leading role in the agriculture. They do most of the dirt-level clearing, planting, harvesting, and carrying to the house. The basic female crop is manioc, but women are identified as "owning" all root crops. By contrast, the basic male crops are maize, plantains, and naranjilla. Both men and women share in planting, care of, and harvesting the other crops, with woman's knowledge and work predominating.

Tobacco, *tahuacu*, is grown in fairly large amounts (50 to 100 or more plants) away from the chagra and often on the purina chagra. The techniques of preparing a manioc chagra are used. The planting and care of the tobacco is a woman's responsibility, though pressing and preparing it is the joint work of husband and wife. In the past cotton was also a special crop, grown and tended by men, but today naranjilla and maize have replaced it in market value. Peanuts and many other nuts are more important crops in areas east of Puyo.

Men accompany women to the manioc chagra day after day, and actually do many of the tasks which everyone agrees are supposed to be female sex-specific. In addition to helping the women out in their domain-defined drudgery, men also hunt in the territory surrounding the chagra, fish in nearby streams, and gather forest products such as copal and other medicinal saps and plants. Agoutis, squirrels, marmosets, coatimundis, and armadillos live on the fringes between forest and chagra, and small tropical forest deer, about the size of a pointer dog, are common. Wood to be used in household crafts is cut from logs felled on the chagra.

In addition to agricultural work women must carry firewood to the household. Identification of *sources* of firewood, however, is a male responsibility. In fact, men generally cut the wood and carry it to the chagra or near to the household, where the women complete the task of bringing it into the ichilla huasi.

Purina Chagra

The Canelos Quichua prefer to have a second chagra from six to twelve hours' hard walk outward from their huasi. *Purina* simply means to walk or trek in Quichua. This chagra is also called *miticushca*, hidden. The process of establishment of the purina chagra is much the same as that discussed above. The territory is determined by squatter's rights of an intermarried action set—a group of individuals who simply agree to share a distant territory and to defend it if necessary against other similar groups. Again, the husband-wife unit is the fundamental one; cleaning takes place for manioc as discussed, but the couple does not visit the chagra again after planting for about six months. Then they return to reclean the chagra, and they often remain at their remote outpost for several months before again moving inward toward their residential llacta in a Runa territory nearer the centers of trade. Some special crops, especially tobacco, and fish poisons are grown on the purina chagra. Great variety is not characteristic, unless the couple regard this as their more permanent settlement, in which case they may be thought as trekking inward rather than outward. Such people are always called *Sacha Runa*, signifying primary identity with a jungle area and no llacta tie to the trade center of a territory. Important activities undertaken near the purina chagra include hunting, fishing with barbasco, exploiting challua runs, catching and smoking large catfish, and turtle-egg gathering. The territoriality of the local llacta, part of the definable Runa territory, includes specific distant areas to which llacta segments trek to establish purina chagras. There they live for a time in a territory to which people in other territories have also trekked. Men always hunt, and the purina chagra zone is one territory in which game is sought. This zone, though, is partially determined by a man's social ties and responsibilities within intermarried ayllu groupings. There are also male hunting territories per se, which cut across such male-female purina chagra territories and depend primarily on continuity of knowledge transmitted through males, and on the activation by given males of the collective activity of a hunting group.

HUNTING AND FISHING

Forest and river quests for meat are strictly male concerns. A man is never so occupied that he is not at least thinking about game behavior and watching for actual signs of game and fish. His basic apparatus in hunting is blowgun and muzzle-loading shotgun. Darts are used for small birds, poisoned darts for larger birds and animals, especially monkeys, and a shotgun of about twenty guage with black powder, caps, and a large variety of rough shot for peccary, deer, giant anteater, jungle cats, and tapir. Men tend to kill off rapidly large game and monkeys near the chagra, and the chagra areas around the more populated llacta near the trade center of a Runa territory are often nearly (but never totally) devoid of large animals. Such game is mostly secured on treks to and from the purina chagra or in stipulated hunting territories.

Hunters enter a known territory for a period of about a week at a time to secure large quantities of meat, which they smoke and dry. Such hunts are undertaken by a group of five to seven armed adults with younger unarmed boys, *huambras*, ranging from twelve to sixteen years of age. The men walk rapidly for from six hours to a day until they are well into the territory they will hunt. They talk excitedly about the territory and its characteristics for the first part of the trek; but the last few hours of travel are quiet, as each man takes note of his surroundings, stops to comment on animal and bird signs, and carefully watches for other human signs. On arrival the hunters rapidly establish a rainproof *sacha huasi*, jungle hut, which is completed within half an hour. On the way to this central camp they cache chicha in the ground, wrapped in banana or heliconia leaves, at intervals of about four hours' walk. On their return trek the men talk little and move at a steady, ground-eating pace. They stop to rest only where the chicha is cached, and there drink it from fragile, decorated mucahuas, which they carry to and from their sacha huasi.

Men are able to imitate all of the sounds made by all of the animals and birds. They know their various calls, including sex calls, fear calls, eating calls, and the cries of young and old. Such ability is as crucial to hunting success as skill and accuracy with blowgun and shotgun. Thorough knowledge of animal and bird habits is also critical, for a number of types of deadfalls, ground and tree traps, and ambushes are used to secure game. Crucial in this is application of a man's specific knowledge of animal habits to specific knowledge of territory.

A whistle signal system is used when the Canelos Quichua travel in the forest, and they regard this system as their own human jungle call, *jujun pushca runata cayangahua sachaibi*. They say that Jívaro proper and Achuara recognize the whistle calls, but do not themselves employ them except in deference to Canelos Quichua. When a Runa hears a whistle from a stranger he returns it as a sign of peace and passes on, usually without either party actually seeing the other. Should either party want to approach the other he gives a falsetto hoot, *juuuuu*, and when answered quickly responds with the falsetto *juí* (like English *whee*), which both parties use as an alternating call as they move toward one another.

Before dawn on the first day in the sacha huasi each man smears red achiote paint on his face to "attract monkeys," or, as some put it, "to walk like a red howler monkey." They then move outward in different directions. Each man will kill what he encounters—usually large birds— but what is really crucial in this first day is the location of a troop of monkeys or herd of peccary. Having located such a group the entire camp moves its location, and the hunt then centers on killing enough monkeys or peccary, or both, to provide about 100 pounds of fresh meat per hunter.

Meat is singed and smoked at the central camp for at least two days, making it black and hairless. Prior to departure it is bundled in heliconia leaves and placed in a tightly lidded hexagonal-weave back pack. It is not looked at again until it is distributed on the hunters' return. Some fresh meat is eaten each night, but during the daytime hunt a man lives on some dried, smoked manioc, plantains, and his individual huangu of chicha, which he caches in the ground midway between base camp and what he expects to be his own outer limits of hunting for the day.

Fresh tripe is cooked in the hunting camp, or brought home to be eaten by the huasi members. But the "stomach" (the *shungu* includes throat, stomach, and heart) is never eaten. It is cut from the animal and the contents examined very closely. Hunters especially seek a *misha rumi* (a hard ball of hair) in the stomach of the tapir, which they take as a gift of a hunting stone from Amasanga. If one finds such a misha rumi in the stomach of a white-lipped peccary the hunter gives it to his wife, since it came as a gift from Nunghuí.

Soul acquisition takes place on the hunt as well as meat acquisition. The skin of the spider monkey, or sloth, is sometimes removed from the skull and shrunk by placing hot stones within it. The soul of the monkey or sloth accompanies the Runa back to camp and on to the huasi. Such a head is later given as a gift to someone to whom the head-taker is indebted. Monkey skins are also taken and worn as part of a headdress; they often signal, or suggest, acquisition of a human, non-Runa, soul, *machin aya*. Men also keep the entire plumage of some of the birds which they kill, especially the curassow, guan, trumpeter, parrot, toucan, macaw; they skin the bird and later dry it in the huasi. The souls of these birds also stay with the taker. Baby birds, especially those named above, and some baby animals—monkey, agouti, sloth, coatimundi, otter—are captured to be brought back into the household and raised as pets. They are "company" to the adult animal and bird souls brought to the huasi.

Invasion of a hunting territory for soul acquisition and meat, and especially the killing of monkeys, is a dangerous business, though, and the wrath of the Juri juri is easily provoked. When the Juri juri is heard at the sacha huasi the men flee to another area. Later, through consultation with shamans, at least some of them will learn how better to deal with the danger of the particular Juri juri zone, or else decide to hunt in another area.

An encounter with a jaguar or other jungle cat, or with a boa or anaconda, is regarded as a direct encounter with an ancient sacha supai or yacu supai hunting the Runa hunters. The cat or snake is immediately attacked and killed. In the case of the boa virtually every aspect of it is of value, and the Runa hunters prepare skin, oil, teeth, brain, and vertebrae for the special, secret yacu supai substances used to attract women, attract fish, and prevent conflict. Jaguar and ocelot teeth are kept, as are the teeth and jaw of the white-lipped and collared peccary. Snakes, large jungle cats, anteaters, and deer are never captured for household use, although some small boas and ocelots are brought back to be immediately sold in such frontier towns as Puyo and Tena.

Enchanted lagoons, huatsalalas, also exist. In fact, I was told the story of "The Cayu of the Huatsalala" (see p. 49) on the return from a hunt by a group of Puyo Runa. Immediately after telling me this story they went on to explain how they had nearly been trapped by the enchanted lagoon. They marched round and round it for hours before coming to their senses, and collectively blew tobacco smoke at the lagoon, thereby breaking the spell. Only after establishing their counter-power, which they derived long ago from ancient jaguar souls, did they explain that the area was "theirs." It was their territory not only because they knew it, but because people from nearby areas of San Ramón and Canelos could not break the enchantment of the lagoon and therefore could not hunt the abundant peccary of the area.

Fishing is also a male pursuit, though women gather fish when barbasco or some other fish poison is used in large quantities. Small fish (from a half-pound to ten) are netted, harpooned, trapped, or caught on hook and line. Large catfish are caught on hook and line or poisoned. Although the Canelos Quichua can weave their own fishline from fibers, purchased line is preferred. All hooks and harpoon points are purchased from trade centers. Otherwise, all paraphernalia for fishing is manufactured from native substances.

Use of a large net, long conical trap, or a little fish poison are the primary means of fishing, while smaller dip nets and harpoons are supplemental. Men and children fish in small streams any time they wish, and a steady if small supply of protein is nearly always available through such endeavor. One means of fishing a small stream is with the long rectangular lica, which is cast by one man in a circular pattern across the current. Fish which swim the center of the current are caught in this manner. Another way is to take a bit of fish poison, mash it, and seek out a sucker-mouth fish under rocks or in a hole; when the fish is discovered a bit of the poison is released near it, and the fish is harpooned, netted, or just grabbed as it rapidly but only partially succumbs to asphyxiation. Sometimes a man skillfully cuts the fish's tail off with a machete and then grabs it by the gills. When the water level is dropping, poisoning and netting methods are especially effective. On a rising water level a long conical trap, called a *yasa,* woven from pin-duj cane, is used in small estuaries and streams. Two or three of these traps are placed with their mouths facing upstream, and as small fish run downward during periods of high water they enter the yasas. Wiggling to get out they move farther inward, becoming permanently trapped by the spring action of the reeds. Yasas are often embedded in a dam-like pile of brush which prevents fish from moving conveniently downstream; the mouth of the yasa provides the entryway through the brush, and hence into the Runa pot. To appreciate the yasa's efficiency, though, one must acquire a taste for somewhat disintegrated flesh, for the fish die quickly and begin to decompose within the trap.

Sometimes, when waters are low and clear, groups of men and women combine to fish with barbasco or some other fish poison. If barbasco is to be used, both men and women prepare it by pounding, at the place where it will be put into the stream. As men wade into the water with net bags full of barbasco mash, other men, women, and children position themselves downstream to pick up the fish as they float to the surface or careen downriver in the throes of asphyxiation. A trap or screen "dam" may be built a mile or two downstream as well, and asphyxiated fish collected as they run into it.

The Canelos Quichua prefer to drop barbasco in a jungle river away from their own habitation site. Barbasco fishing is regarded as a great deal of fun, but certain tensions are also created in this activity. Barbasco causes the shimmering water domain to take on a deathly palor, and the fish which are normally "given" in small amounts by Sungui go "crazy" (*nuspa aicha*, crazy meat) as the Runa families invade the water domain using a chagra substance and hunting techniques. Women who are in deep sorrow have a special use for barbasco: they eat it to commit suicide. They say that when life in this world is unbearable they prefer to eat barbasco and go to live under the water, like a fish.

The stomachs of all fish are quickly torn out and thrown back into the water, otherwise every part of the fish is eaten and the bones sucked. Small fish caught by all means other than barbasco fishing are usually cooked and eaten fresh, or only slightly decomposed. Large catfish are smoked and dried in a sacha huasi and handled exactly like animal meat. Some families trek to specified fishing territories where they also have a purina chagra, and specialize in obtaining tradeable dried fish. I would say that of all "favorite" foods of the Canelos Quichua, smoked fish is at the top of the list.

Having now briefly sketched the fundamental subsistence activities engaged in by men and women in their united endeavor to maintain themselves and provide continuity for their offspring, let us review the primary statuses of intrahousehold life.

MAMA

Mama refers to a man's *huarmi*, his woman or wife, when the idea of continuity of household tradition is part of the referential context. It also refers to his own mother, the reference point being man's father's wife, the corporeal source from which a man received his father's substance by birth from his mother. Any woman associated specifically as wife of the household founder is both *asua mama*, chicha producer, and *asua churana mama*, producer of chicha pots. Both of these production processes deserve special attention.

Chicha

The household's lifeblood is chicha. No household is without this precious food for more than half a day, and it is rare that the household ever runs out. To make chicha a woman first removes the outer skin of the manioc, then washes and boils about eighty pounds of the smaller tubers. About twenty

Making chicha.

minutes is needed for the boiling, after which the still-steaming tubers are pounded in a large wooden bowl. Asua mama places a large handful of the pounded mash in her mouth and gently masticates it for an hour or so as she pounds away. Then she takes it out, puts it in the bowl, and puts another handful in her mouth. Ordinarily her daughters, or a very close niece or sister, help her. As the pounding is completed women continue to refreshen the manioc in their mouths, sometimes eating a handful or so but keeping their mouths full throughout the day, while they perform other household tasks. While making chicha they do not work outside the ichilla huasi and seldom leave it. By day's end there is enough "starter" manioc in the wooden bowl to assure mild fermentation; at this point the mash is placed in a decorated storage jar, where it begins to work into the life-sustaining, thickish, mildly tangy gruel widely known as chicha.

Women impart a seemingly endless source of variety to their chicha making. For example, sweet potatoes may be pounded in with the manioc, or other secret tuber substances added which subtly change the color, flavor, or alcoholic content. Berries, papaya, bananas, plantains, caimito, chirimoya, rubber-tree, and chontaduro fruit are also used; a special chicha is often made from the latter two when they come into season, and strong banana chicha is made for chagra-clearing mingas.

With the eighty pounds of raw manioc, which of course boils down to a lighter weight, three ordinary-size (eight- to twelve-gallon capacity) storage jars will be filled three-quarters full. They will then be partly set into the earth[3] to allow the chicha to ferment in a nice, even, coolish temperature. Banana, heliconia, and balsa leaves are placed on top for a cover and bound securely with a liana. The woman ideally makes new chicha while she still has a supply on hand for family, friends, and guests, so that she can allow it to sit for a day or two. But people may drink the fresh chicha immediately. The household begins to run short of chicha in eight to twelve days, at which time the process of resucitation of household life substance is repeated. During an average ten-day period of normal drinking the household serves between forty and sixty gallons of chicha, figuring that each mucahua-full is about two-thirds water, and some of the chicha is simply eaten by women and children without mixing with water. A strong man himself drinks two or more gallons a day. Obviously chicha consumption is fundamental to the Canelos Quichua diet. This is no mere supplemental beverage or "beer" to be enjoyed now and then. This is the primary food substance in quantity and in caloric intake. Men and women can go for days with no food other than chicha. And even when they have plenty of meat, fish, and manioc, they feel deprived without their combined ration of several gallons of chicha per day.

Chicha serving and conversation in the jatun huasi is highly stylized. The man's wife is always asua mama in a visiting context. She symbolizes the everlasting continuity of the Canelos Quichua's special food by a merger of water, manioc, and female substance. She quickly takes a handful of chicha mash from a storage jar, places it in a mucahua, pours about two cups of water in, mixes it with her hand, and moves rapidly to the jatun huasi. There she again mixes it with her right hand, kneading the various lumps and removing any fibers, and hands the full bowl to a visitor. The visitor accepts with outstretched hand, both server and served looking in opposite directions. The woman quickly turns to inspect the chicha for tiny bugs or specks, removing them with thumb and forefinger, the man then blows gently on the surface of the chicha and drinks.

The woman then hurries back to the kitchen, fills either a large or another small mucahua, and comes back to the drinker. If she has chosen to use the larger serving bowl, she continues to pour as he completes about half the bowl and holds it out for replenishing, still not looking at the asua mama. If she has elected to return with a smaller bowl, she sets that next to the man, or he takes it with his other hand. Three or four mucahuas may be so lined up next to the drinker. And when several women serve one man he often winds up with several mucahuas, each being replenished by the respective server.

The person drinking the chicha concentrates on his conversation with the woman's husband, who continues doing whatever he was doing when the guests arrived. As the conversation goes on the asua mama keeps careful watch on the chicha, coming quickly to take specks out or to refreshen the drink by mixing with the right hand. She also takes good-sized lumps from the serving bowl and eats them, sometimes handing them to children. A normal drinker, especially one who has not had more than a quart of chicha before entering the house, drinks at least two quarts before signaling that he has had enough. This is done by passing the mucahua outward as though asking for more, but moving it quickly away from the bowl and looking at the asua mama as she tries to serve more. Usually she insists persuasively until he has drunk about a quart more; then she desists, moving on to repeat the serving procedure with other guests, and finally with her husband and children.

When there are many men to be served they line up on the long bancu, and the woman begins at one end and moves along the line, often not releasing the mucahua but insistently "pushing" the chicha by making the man drink to her steady pressure.

Great intensity of intersubjective emotional flow accompanies such chicha drinking in the jatun huasi. If a man is happy, he endeavors to

Storing chicha.

Mixing chicha with water prior to serving.

Drinking chicha.

Allu asua (fungus chicha). Specks are parts of the charred manioc skin.

communicate happiness, friendship, and warmth to his hosts, and they reciprocate. But if he is angry or sad, he drinks and spits and curses and the man and woman of the house join him in deeply emotional ways—crying, becoming angry, or just looking shocked and miserable until the speaker vents his anger or sorrow. Then, slowly but surely, they reassure, agree to take action, and seek to envelop the visitor in a web of friendship and warmth. Interpersonal hostility between guests and hosts has no place in the jatun huasi. Indeed, it has no place in the huasi at all. The Canelos Quichua seek to regulate disorder in the small huasi universe, and the stylized chicha-drinking context is the one setting in which this is constantly done.

The Canelos Quichua know how to make a heady "wine" called *vinillu* (dimunitive of Spanish *vino*). Preparation of this involves both men and women. Manioc is roasted with the skin intact in the chagra. Either men or women may do this cooking. The outer skin is usually charred black when the manioc is considered done. Then the tubers are taken to the household, stacked, loosely covered with balsa leaves, and allowed to sit in the ichilla huasi for about a week. An orange powder-like fungus (probably neurospora) is sprinkled in with the tubers. Orange, white, black, and yellow fungi develop in the tubers, and within ten days everything inside the skin has succumbed to the bright orange growth. The entire tubers, skin and all, are then pounded in the wooden bowl and parts placed for a moment only in a woman's, child's, or sometimes a man's mouth. A storage jar is specially prepared with a round basket or wood-and-leaf filter, *panshi* (or *pansi*), halfway down, and the mash is placed on this. As the mash, called *allu asua*, mold (fungus) chicha, or *allu mucushca*, masticated mold (fungus), ferments, it drips into the bottom of the jar, and in about two days there are two to three quarts of these drippings, which are the vinillu.[4] The allu asua itself is removed to retrieve the vinillu and is replaced in the same jar for continued fermentation, re-dripping, and storage, for it will also be served. As the allu asua ferments, small orange worms, *allu curu,* and a few tiny scorpions, *allu iputindi,* hatch, and live in the fungus chicha until the rising alcoholic content kills them, or until they are consumed. The vinillu itself is delicious when fresh—much like a good cider. The effect of vinillu is comparable to that of a beverage with an alcoholic content of 12 to 16 percent, perhaps due to a cyanide psychotropic effect rather than alcoholic content. Vinillu may be added to regular or fungus chicha to produce a more intoxicating brew, or just drunk as is.

Vinillu and fungus chicha are normally served only on special ceremonial occasions, but sometimes they are made just because people in the household get the urge for vinillu.

Laying a coil on a tinaja.

Pottery

Women manufacture multicolored pottery for storing and serving chicha and black pottery for cooking. The former is decorated with stone-derived paints and coated with a tree resin called *shinquillu*. There are three basic types of chicha pottery: the storage jar, *tinaja* (Spanish), or *asua churana manga*, or *shinquillu manga* (Quichua), the serving bowl, *mucahua*, and the figurine called *jista puru*, fiesta vessel, or *sisa puruhuá*, flower vessel. The black cooking ware includes the *yanuna manga*, cooking pot, *yacunda*, huayusa cooking pot, and *uchu manga*, capsicum cooking pot. The basic process is the same in their manufacture.

Women find adequate clay deposits in river banks and brooks, or by penetrating an underground deposit in the forest. Men carry the clay for them to the ichilla huasi, where it is dried, pounded somewhat to get air bubbles and tiny stones out, and then wet to the exact consistency necessary for coiling. Coils are rolled out on the turtle-shaped tatanga by a woman who sits on the ground or on split bamboo. No temper is used. Coil by coil the pot, serving bowl, or figurine is built up. Then the woman kneads the piece into the exact form desired. Mucahuas are regarded as the finest art form available, so let us consider them first.

Having built up the sides and formed the mucahua, the woman then strives for thinness of sides and, for the experts, a large size. Sometimes she builds a pretty base, *chaqui* (foot), and occasionally even adds clay pellets in the base to serve as a rattle. A piece of calabash, *huihuishu pilchi*, is used to scrape the sides of the mucahua. The woman then nips around the rim, closing it with lips and teeth but leaving no markings. The mucahua is then set on a rack inside the ichilla huasi to dry for a few days. When dry a white slip called *allpa* or *ruyaj allpa* (white clay) is added. When this is dry, polishing with the female soul stone, aya rumi, is done, and a woman's special merger of the first of three souls imparted. This is the *Manga allpa aya mama*—soul of the clay giver, Nunghuí. Special designs which will be placed on the mucahua come from Nunghuí; it is to her that women ultimately owe their ability and through her that their eternal soul substance will live on.

Now comes the design itself, that subtle combination of general female knowledge and special secret technique which the maker has acquired from either her mother or her husband's mother. She begins with the other two basic stone color dies—black and red—which are mixed in separate stone mortars. We consider here the system which occurs when a black-and-red-on-white mucahua is made.[5]

In decorating the white mucahua with black and red, the woman imparts the second and third souls. The *ahuashca huarmi aya*, woman's soul built into the clay by labor and knowledge of technique and design, is one of these. The other is the *huarmi huasimanda ayatian*, household soul continuity. This soul or life substance includes the couple and their children. As the woman begins to impart these souls through design she "thinks" special songs taught to her by other women. The songs themselves "belong" to the being about which she thinks-sings, and so she often begins with the phrase _____ *huarmi runa mani*, "_____ woman is a person," filling the blank with whatever spirit or soul is the song possessor.

First she paints a strong red line using a thick brush made of her own hair. This is called the *mamataishasca*[6] or *mama churana*, which symbolizes female continuity either as "body" or "dress" of woman. Next she paints a finer black line parallel to the red, and calls it *cari pintashca*,[7] husband color, or *turi pintashca*, brother color. Immediately a woman making such a beginning picture, and discussing what she is doing, in context, points out that, from the cari pintashca line—i.e., using the male position as the reference point for discussing design meaning—the larger red line is *paiba mama churana huarmi*, his female mama churana. Pottery design, as it is created by women, contains a basic set of symbols that asserts male continuity only through the body of woman. "Brother line" and "husband line" are used interchangeably by women in discussing the black

pottery lines. Suggestive in this is that a brother has descended from the
same couple as the sister, hence the sister passes on the brother's substance
in her pottery tradition. Also suggestive in this is that brother and sister are
"married" (made together) on the pot, symbolizing the moon-bird union
discussed in the previous chapter.

Elaboration of the black lines takes place, usually by building more
parallel ones, and then adding more red lines into a particular pattern.
Then smaller black lines, or dots, are added. Such decoration is called
huahua churana, baby dress or body. Any tiny red line is mama churana,
but the tiny black ones are "baby bodies." It must be stressed that only
women and babies have *churana* in pottery metaphor. The male lines,
always symbolized by longer black lines, are *pintashca*, just as anything
with obvious decoration is "painted."

As the design unfolds a number of highly stylized figures are created.
Common among these are the boa, iguana, cayman, water turtle and land
turtle, bends in the river (called *quingu*, zigzag), various snakeskins,
petroglyphs from rocks seen in the forest, stinging insects, spiders,
spiderwebs, caterpillars, stars, flowers, grubs, eagle claws, and tree
trunks.

Each mucahua tells some secret story relating to the life situation of the
maker. Women strive for a degree of communication of individual,
household, and ayllu traditions and ideas on each bowl which is only
suggestive to the general member of Canelos Quichua culture. The closer
one is to the ayllu, household, or individual and the more one knows, the
more precise the interpretation that can be made. Ultimately, only the
woman herself knows all of the meanings of the design, including contrasts
and complementaries of inside-outside figures, or figure segments, the use
of special rock paints, and inner knowledge of secret integration of design,
myth, and acquired household souls from Ancient Times.

In making pottery figurines women range from portraying the tree
mushroom, moon, jilucu bird, and sun and stars from mythic time and
structure to anything they have seen that has captured their attention. For
example, I have seen jukeboxes, pith helmets, hard hats, and even full
pottery masks in the form of a Mexican movie wrestler's mask, along with
the more traditional fish, lizards, caymans, snakes, turtles, people, canoes,
calabash shells, bottle gourds, chirimoya fruits, jungle animals, snails, and
insects.

Mucahuas and figurines are fired in the same manner. After painting the
black-and-red designs on the white surface the mucahua is placed inverted
in an old broken pot which is, in turn, placed over a low fire made between
three logs. It stays there, heating up, for ten to fifteen minutes, and then is
covered with hot ashes from the fire and the fire stoked with chonta wood

Making mucahuas and figurines for serving chicha. Woman in foreground is applying dye, using a bit of her own hair as a brush.

Piling hot ashes over mucahua during firing.

and other firewood. The mucahua is fired with intense heat for about twenty minutes, as the initial fire burns down. It is lifted off with a machete and hand while glowing white-hot, and within thirty seconds is tested by touching it with the shinquillu resin. As soon as the resin stops sizzling or burning it is rubbed over the entire bowl. As this happens the colors change, taking on the intensity which will then be characteristic of the bowl or figurine. Most shinquillu is essentially clear, but there is a variety which gives a pink tinge to the white slip. Knowing the exact heat and timing for the firing is crucial, and such knowledge must take into account the clay and dyes being used. For example, if a certain white clay which is supposed to turn to black is used, the heat must be such as to effect the transformation. If the heat is inadequate it may come out a dull gray, or remain white and flake off when the shinquillu is applied. In such cases the woman making the bowl will say the soul of the rock is "dead." But she knows that another woman can make it "live" through secret knowledge. Also, when the shinquillu is rubbed on, some dyes smear or flake.

From Sara Yacu to Montalvo another process complements that described above. Here rubber sap, *lichi* or *lichihuái*, is used in addition to the shinquillu. In such cases shinquillu is not rubbed on certain portions of the bowl or figurine. The pottery piece sits for twenty-four hours after firing, and the uncooked milky sap is then gently placed over the surface lacking resin and allowed to sit without any disturbance for twelve more hours. A light, smooth, milky film then covers the design. This produces some fading of the design in a year or so.

The large storage jars are made in about the same way as the mucahuas, except that they are thicker and made to last for years rather than a few weeks to two years, as is the case with mucahuas and figurines. Boa or water turtle designs (symbols of the Yacu Supai Runa) frequently encircle the tinaja, but all of the designs mentioned above, and more, are also applied. The tinaja may be fired inverted or mouth up; the entire process takes about an hour. First the painted tinaja is placed on the three logs of an open fire, sometimes set into a broken tinaja and sometimes not. Then a mound of firewood and chonta is built up around it, completely covering it, and allowed to burn throughly. If the colors do not appear properly, the tinaja is refired. Then shinquillu is added to the outside. The inside of the tinaja is lined either with a black tree pitch mixed with copal, or with cooked rubber sap, or with a combination of the two. Regardless of what is used, the substance is placed in the hot tinaja and rubbed around with a stick as it sizzles and smokes until a thick black coating covers the interior.

Such coating is not usually applied to the smaller tinaja used for feather storage, *huillma churana manga,* or, today, as a "bank" in which to place money and other valuables. Such storage banks are capped with plantain or heliconia leaves and hung from the roof poles in the center of the house.

Black pottery is made in the same manner as is the multicolor, except that the eating bowl, *callana,* is thicker and figurines are not made. The main difference is in the firing. Presumably, carbon is given off in the smoke because of incomplete combustion in an oxygen-poor firing atmosphere, for the bowl, which is fired inverted, emerges with a brilliant shiny black interior. Canelos Quichua women state that the shiny blackness derives from wood resin transformed in the wood smoke to the pot's inner surface. Black cooking pots have flared rims, while the capsicum cooking pots do not. Pots for brewing huayusa are distinctive in design, since they have a bowl-shaped bottom, narrow middle, and a very wide, flaring shoulder and rim. Black pots for cooking ayahuasca are the same shape as those used to cook ordinary food. It should be noted here that huayusa, ayahuasca, and usually capsicum are cooked by men in the ichilla huasi.

YAYA

Yaya means "father," which the Canelos Quichua derive from *aya,* soul. From the standpoint of a woman, her husband is *cari,* or less frequently *cusa,* husband. She calls her father *and* her husband's father yaya. She will pass on to her children her husband's father's soul, as well as her own soul inherited from her mother. Her own father's soul goes to her brothers. A man assuming the father role within the household must be able to make all that is needed (except pottery), give expression to aya and supai needs through musical instruments, cure his household of ordinary disease, and provide meat and fish.

He is a woodworker as well as hunter and fisherman, for he makes house, canoe, paddles, stools, platform beds, bowls and pounders, hunting traps, and so forth. He weaves nets and fish traps but shares basket making, net bag making, and (though rarely today) cotton and thread weaving with women.

To musical instruments, especially the three-hole transverse flute and the drum, he imparts an ancient human soul, and sometimes a male forest supai soul as well. He captures animal and bird souls which he keeps near the center of the house in their skins and plumage. As animals and birds die, their souls gently leave their bodies through their mouths and remain in the close vicinity of the body, which the hunter brings home. These souls convey Amasanga power on their respectful capturers. On entering the house with his game and accompanying souls, the hunter goes to a hammock in the center of the house, puts the game down, sits, and quietly drinks his fill of chicha in the presence of the newly acquired souls, which can give him more forest spirit power. With such power greater skill with design and aesthetics can be acquired; as some men say, "While a man works on the material form, Amasanga works with him on the inner substance."

At night he dreams with the help of his souls, and considers his dreams

Repairing a blowgun.

and their significance before dawn. If he finds inconsistency between the newly acquired souls and substances in his stomach—other tiny supai souls—then he brews and drinks huayusa in sufficient amounts to vomit out the evil or incompatibility. Sometimes in such dreaming great strength comes to him from distant Runa souls, and he awakens to play the drum and let the one or two imparted souls resound and "sing." The singing of the distant human or forest spirit soul comes out through the drone of the snare itself stimulated by the monkey-skin resonator. During these pre-dawn hours he also makes feather crowns and other things from the plumage and skins with which to adorn himself when signaling soul acquisition. He also plays the transverse flute, just before the strong new sun rises, and night and day are restored to their respective Runa divisions.

Fixing kapok on a dart.

The headdresses which the man makes are especially significant in Canelos Quichua culture. The llautu encircling the head symbolizes the amarun (boa-anaconda-rainbow). Red, yellow, white, and black are the basic colors, and here white substitutes for yellow (i.e., serves the same classificatory purpose), blue for black, and orange for red. Red symbolizes blood and yellow the sun. Moreover, red symbolizes potential conflict as well as continuity, and yellow signals attraction or union. Men put the red part of a circular headdress in the front when they want to ease a conflict situation, and yellow in the front when they want to attract women. Red symbolizes continuity through birth—*consanguinity*—and yellow symbolizes the necessary attraction between men and women for sexual relations—*affinity*.

The toucan embodies the four Canelos Quichua basic colors noted above. Beyond time, when animals were human, the sicuanga was a powerful Runa warrior who killed other animal Runas without fear. He was *huanchij*, killer. He was like a sky boa flying through the air in lance form. Men try to kill adult toucans and capture young ones, keeping one or two around for their powerful ancient souls and weaving their feathers into boa headdresses.

Huasi Founder

To become a huasi founder, as distinct from simply a male member of a huasi established by father or father-in-law, a man must undergo special visionary experience with Datura. Men and woman both keep secret, hidden Datura plants, or simply know where other Runa have hidden plants and use theirs. The Datura is gathered by the taker sometime before the sun begins to lose its power around 3:00 in the afternoon. Normally it is cut well before noon. One or two parts of the limb of the Datura plant, between two knots, are cut. Then the man seeks a secret place in the forest, builds a sacha huasi shelter, and returns home. That night he may drink a small calabash of tobacco water, through his nose, to clarify dreams and make them become more vivid. The next day he boils the Datura stem into a tea, walks to the area in the woods with his wife, and drinks the brew. For a while he is very agitated, drunk, totally unaware of his surroundings, and wants to travel like a madman. During such a state he could walk or stumble into a fast-moving river or fall off a ledge. His wife restrains him until, struggling to escape, his soul leaves his body, the body "dies" (becomes unconscious), and the soul begins a trip through the forest, while the woman guards the body. The soul sings a special *taquina*, shaman's song, as it walks along, and flowers bloom all around it. The various kinds of bees and wasps as spirit helper souls (*bunga* or *putan*) come and buzz around his

and later a bancu in the form of a cayman, from the same tree.

Making a canoe . . .

feet. Stinging insects come, as spirit friends, for he is now *of* the huanduj supai, he is one of them. Snakes, all of them spirits, wind around his legs, and mediating birds as supais flutter around his legs too, and accompany him on his journey.

He finds a place to sit, and time and space become one so that he sees back to Ancient Times and forward into the future. He sees the souls of the spirits, and takes a crucial step toward understanding the world of the Sacha Runa; Amasanga appears. Now the man's soul as contemporary Sacha Runa and Amasanga as ancient Sacha Runa look deeply into the soul and soul's substance. The Runa must explain to the ancient one why he has entered the dimension of the huanduj. He must look into himself, his dreams, past life, and his desires for the future and explain these to Amasanga. This is a difficult time, for Amasanga forces Runa to undergo self-analysis and come to grips with an emerging self. Hidden evils in the shungu must be purged and the Runa must explain himself to the ancient Sacha Supai Runa as he becomes contemporary Sacha Runa.

After the Runa has cured himself of his own evils through insight the Amasanga examines him for spirit darts, which have entered his body through the projected envy of his wife's other suitors. The Amasanga helps the Runa soul to see these, too, and then Amasanga cures Runa by sucking out the darts. Such darts remain in the world of the Amasanga as spirit helpers and take the form of the various bees and other stinging insects which accompanied the Runa on his taquina walk.

Once the Amasanga is satisfied that the Runa soul is "cured" he mediates between the Runa and the underworld people, *ucupachama manda runahuá*, calling on the little underworld shaman to come and help the Runa in his quest for a continuing future and strength in the present. The underworld shaman helps the Runa to see the way to pacts with various supais and also indicates the dangers inherent in seeking power greater than that of safe huasi yaya, household founder. Then he departs. The Runa soul and Amasanga Supai Runa converse more and the ancient supai shows the Runa some secret plants with curing properties, and also where soul stones containing ancient Runa souls are hidden in the forest floor or in the bases of trees. Then the visions begin to dissolve, the soul returns to its body, and the body and soul substance merge as the man falls into a sleep. He awakens that night or the next dawn, feels no hangover or aftereffects, and returns home.[8]

In such Datura experiences, the first of which is undertaken when a man brings a wife home, or joins her in her father's home, the individual Runa becomes increasingly strong, knowledgeable, confident, and brave. Should the man have a bad trip and wish not to continue sporadic visits to the huanduj world, he "stops" in a process of household growth, and continuity of his ayllu and household substance becomes dependent on other factors. Men successfully coming out of a huanduj dream, *huandujta upisha muscuna*, believe that souls of ancient Runas accompany them, help them, and protect them from the ever-present spirit darts sent by envious and angry contemporaries.[9] Such men begin to talk louder and to expand the size of their houses, studying even more diligently techniques of making things, and looking more carefully into their own genealogy to identify the specific ancient soul helpers.

Knowledge itself does not come exclusively from the combination of visionary experience and individual study and reflection. A man must also acquire the information necessary for intrasocial interpretation from either his father or wife's father. Right after his experience with Amasanga a man converses with one of these two yayas, seeking more information about ancient souls, ayllu structure, and interpretation of visionary experiences themselves. Such questioning usually provides a stimulus to a yaya to continue his own means of power and knowledge acquisition, the yacha process. To some degree, ego's acquisition of yaya status stimulates his own or wife's father's acquisition of some degree of yachaj, which means "possessor of learning," the shaman's status.

CONTINUITY

This chapter began with intra-household symbolism stressing male-female dichotomy at the antipodes of a cardinal axis, and the resolution of the dichotomy in the center, where the straight up and straight down axis to other antipodal worlds (sky and underworld) exists, and where the souls of animals and ancient Runas stay. Dreams and hallucinogenic experience partially resolve these antipodes for respective yaya-mama founders, and such partial resolution sets up a movement toward increased knowledge and shared personal power between cari and huarmi which will be transmitted to their male and female offspring. We also discussed the different responsibilities and activities of the yaya-mama founders in maintaining the economics of the household and in providing access to past and future times through dichotomized tasks.

Children grow up in a milieu in which the yaya and mama founders represent real parents acting, discussing, and instructing in a biosphere that begins in the household and ramifies outward to huasipungu, river, chagra, purina chagra, and hunting territory, first by being carried in the mother's sling and later by foot. Boys and girls learn everything about both the mama and the yaya roles and activities, including their mutual secrets, dreams, hidden substances. Little boys and little girls help the mother perform necessary tasks of huasi and huasipungu and accompany her to the chagra. Little boys accompany the father in his short sojourns to hunt and fish in the llacta territory, and little girls begin to carry babies in slings and take on more and more female chores. By the time boys are eleven or twelve they hunt and fish alone, sometimes accompanied by girls of the same age. In this way knowledge of hunting and fishing, a male pursuit, is learned by women. One girl is normally kept closer to the mother by the age of eleven, to help her in the daily drudgery and to receive more intensive instruction in symbolism and secrets of continuity.

Freedom to delve into all aspects of adult behavior is permitted most children up to around thirteen years of age. But by then they are participating as their physique allows them in sex-specific male and female tasks. And by then they know that the full male-female culture which they have learned must continue in their future huasi not only within their own personalities, but by union with a mate capable of continuing the special traditions into which they have been socialized. For some girls and boys mate selections are made for them by age thirteen, but others search for a mate up to nineteen or twenty years of age, at which time the cari-huarmi union, which will eventually result in the yaya-mama statuses and roles, takes place.

The foundation of household is basic to economics and to cultural continuity of the Canelos Quichua. Each household is theoretically and actually able to sustain itself in total isolation from all other people should the couple decide to live as veritable Sacha Runas, away from contact, in a distant jungle house. Symbolically, too, a huasi is a whole in and of itself, connected to distant and ancient ayllu and forest spirit souls through male and female huanduj experiences and in the female pottery tradition. Male acquisition of animal and bird souls connects the huasi with mythic structure beyond time, and male and female songs which come from beyond time and from ancient and distant Runa and supai souls perform the mediation with time, distance, and domain structure to assure huasi continuity.

There is one thing the household cannot provide without violating a prohibition on marriage: it cannot, within itself, provide actual continuity by spouse selection. A spouse must not be a brother or sister, but brothers and sisters seek to find a spouse who is not only attractive, exciting, and economically valuable to them, but who also embodies the cultural and mystical substance capable of fulfilling the continuity drive of their own inherited and acquired ayllu culture. The continuity of apayaya and apamama brought into the household by yaya and mama embed a man or woman seeking a spouse not only in a real net of kinsmen and friends but in a broad structure expressed through the idiom of kinship and shamanism—the maximal ayllu, an everlasting system of transmission and alliance going back to Ancient Times and continuing into the future as long as Amasanga and Nunghuí survive.

NOTES

1. Round and oval houses are now nearly gone in the Puyo area, but they are abundant downriver, especially away from the river bank of the Bobonaza. Nevertheless, even among the Puyo Runa this fundamental symbolism endures, and the orientation described in this section exists, except in households of Quijos Quichua men living in settlements with their actual Quijos Quichua brothers. Puyo Runa now strive for variety and novelty in house style. As they do this they add layers of symbolic meaning based on the patterns described below. Some people, for example, build a rectangular jatun huasi with adjoining oval kitchen, and hold their intracultural affairs in the kitchen, away from the prying eyes of curious, deriding nationals. Some build two-story houses with ichilla huasi and jatun huasi below, reserving the private upstairs part as the central sleeping house.

2. Variations in this pattern also occur according to social and economic factors impinging on the population occupying the area. When the family working chagra A runs into chagra B, one of the two parties must "hop over" the alter chagra and continue on the other side. Such bumping and hopping procedure is the cause for endless disputes, and resolutions of such disputes come to cement conflicting parties into wide micro- and macro-territorial alliances which, while conflicting within, nonetheless evolve as an increasingly solid system opposed to adjacent territories.

3. The pattern of placing the tinaja in the earth midway to the maximum width is common from Paca Yacu eastward, and ubiquitous at Curaray and Montalvo. From Puyo eastward to Canelos and the headwaters of the Curaray and Villano rivers, however, there is much variety in how the tinaja is placed in the soil. In the westernmost area it is sometimes placed on a frame to keep it completely off the ground.

4. Karsten (1935:121) reports the name *shutushca yacu*, dripped water or drippings, for what must be vinillu.

5. In addition to the white slip there is also a more brilliant white clay which some women use to create a white-on-red pattern. Secrets involved in the white-on-red are well guarded, and I have the impression that there may be a special set of symbols involved in this patterning as well. All of the white-on-red that I have seen has been made by painting the entire outside of the mucahua or a band around a tinaja with the usual white slip. Then, when dry, red is added, allowed to dry for a few hours, and then decorated with broad white bands flanked by black ones. In some cases I know that two firings were necessary to get the white to come out, before the shinquillu could be applied, but I do not know whether this is always the case. Finally, in terms of variation, I saw one mucahua (in Canelos) which was all black lines on white with no red band or red spot. This is the only such specimen out of perhaps 5,000 mucahuas, and something that I have been told "never happens." The mucahua was collected and is today housed in the *Sacha Músiu* (Jungle Museum) in a small hamlet of Río Chico, about two hours from Puyo, where it will be viewed for years by those interested in the rich variety encompassed by the fundamental symbolism herein discussed.

6. *Mamataishasca* is the pronunciation of this line among the Puyo Runa and well illustrates the variety of ways by which labeling in this pottery-making symbolic domain occurs. For example, *mamata* or *mamatai* (/mama/-/ta/, *mama*-emphasis; /mama/-/ta/-/i/, *mama*-emphasis-imperative) leaves us with two possible stems for the *shasca* suffix. One is the *aisa* or *aisana*, body covering, since a change from *s* to *sh* is common among the Puyo Runa. Then the *asca* suffix would simply mean a completed action. But the Puyo Runa love word games, and a couple of men, not women, pointed out that *aicha* means meat, in this case fish meat, so the woman's "covering" was really her flesh (associating women with fish). Frequently, in pointing out something like this, men immediately remind me that the same lures used to catch fish serve to attract women. Another derivation of this term is /mama/-/ta/-/i/-/chasca/, *mama*-emphasis-imperative-united, wedded, or sowed, if we take

chasca from *chayashca*. Informants will accept either of these derivations, but invariably point out that *mama churana* is what the phrase means, if the elicitor cannot satisfactorily work out the *mamataishasca* derivation. Even more double meanings and word play can result if someone offers *mama churashca*—this signifies the completed action of the "placing" of the *mama* line, and, sexually, completion is not attained until the *cari pintashca* has been painted. Then, with the male black lines enclosing the red, the "mother" line is really "placed." A sociolinguist fluent in Jungle Quichua and aware of the Canelos Quichua love for word play (they even mix terms and constructions from Spanish and Jivaroan) could, I think, write a volume on word play and pottery symbolism.

7. Among the Puyo Runa *ñaño*, brother, is occasionally used by women when speaking to someone who knows Spanish, and this is one of those contexts in which it is commonly employed. In Jungle Quichua itself a woman addresses and refers to her brother as *turi* and her sister as *ñaña*. The man uses other terms (*huauqui* and *pani*, respectively). In rural Ecuadorian Spanish *ñaño* is frequently used by men and women to mean *hermano* (brother). For some reason it is rare to elicit the term *turi* when the woman making the black line refers to it in kin terms, and common to elicit *ñaño*.

8. For women the process is similar but I know less about it. They supposedly have their own huanduj, which they hide and guard from men, even their own husbands. When they take their Datura they are guarded by a woman companion, or several women, rather than by a husband. In their conversations with Nunghuí they seek knowledge of their own body soul, and of an integration of this soul with designs which will be imparted to pottery. They also seek answers to meanings of special designs they have seen, and special relationships in mythic structure which they will portray in clay paintings. During such experiences they learn special songs of the supai, and perceive special relationships in mythic structure which allow them to sing more beautifully. They also learn ways to send their songs outward to visit the person sung to, without danger of return of the song, and without danger of the song being intercepted by the wrong person or supai.

9. Comparison of this Canelos Quichua "soul strengthening" by a Datura trip to Amasanga and the supai world should be made with that described by Harner (1972:135–143). Fortunately, there are some Jívaro proper intermarried with the Puyo Runa, and they unhesitatingly translate the Jívaro term *arutam* or *arutam wakani*, "ancient specter soul" (Harner 1972:135), as the Quichua *huandujta upisha muscuna*. Considering Harner's excellent description with what we have already discussed, it seems to me that one major transformation from the Jívaro proper to Canelos Quichua soul-acquisition concepts is that the Runa-Amasanga visitation allows the Runa to see more clearly his relationships with ancient souls, his position in the everlasting ayllu system, and abilities to acquire power in the form of ancient apayaya souls. But he does not acquire a new soul in this way. Furthermore, although he seems to excude confidence and speak louder after such a trip, he does not seem to feel an overwhelming desire to kill. Rather, in the cases familiar to me, he seems to have an overwhelming feeling of his own invincibility. Once the Canelos Quichua man has visited Amasanga and emerged strong and invincible, he "knows how to dream" and understands the meanings of visions and sensory experience which were previously obscure, jumbled, or muddled. He may begin to take tobacco water before retiring, drinking it through the nose to have clearer dreams. In this sense I think that the relationship between the Canelos Quichua *muscuna*, dream or vision, experiences, together with their continuous acquisition of animal and bird souls, is also comparable to the Jívaro *muisak*, "avenging soul," notion also discussed by Harner (1972:143–149).

4

Ayllu, Marriage, and Llacta

The Canelos Quichua maintain a polysemic, extendable metaphor of identity based on concepts of descent from ancestors who acquired jaguar souls from the Ancient Times people. A system of genealogical classification which derives from apical ancestors in Times of the Grandparents links people in Present Times to one another. Shamanistic structure links contemporary people directly descended from Times of the Grandparents back to Ancient Times. Through the idiom of kinship and shamanism the Canelos Quichua cognitively span the hiatus in their ethnic charter through Times of Destruction and link Runa families in their contemporary huasis to ramifying kin ties of their current social networks. This chapter considers the *repetitive patterning* of consanguinity and affinity and their relationship to marriage, territoriality, and cultural continuity.

No information on social organization can be elicited from the Canelos Quichua in the Quichua language without constant reference to stipulated genealogical statuses. Terms such as *yaya, apayaya, masha, huauqui* are employed every day to refer to actual people in stipulated or demonstrated consanguineal or affinal relationships to one another. Extensions of these genealogical criteria are also employed to create a set of referential statuses which is put to multiple usages in all social contexts. The totality of usages of this set of referential terms constitutes an ayllu structure. This referential system of the Canelos Quichua provides each individual with a malleable set of reference points out of which structure and dynamics are constantly created. The referential system of kin classes can be set forth as a standard ego chart. Indeed, many of the Canelos Quichua found the groupings of kin types into kin classes convenient and efficient, and worked the following diagrams out for me with little difficulty and almost no dispute, except where Spanish language and concepts intruded.

Once the "easy" part had been worked out, however, friends and

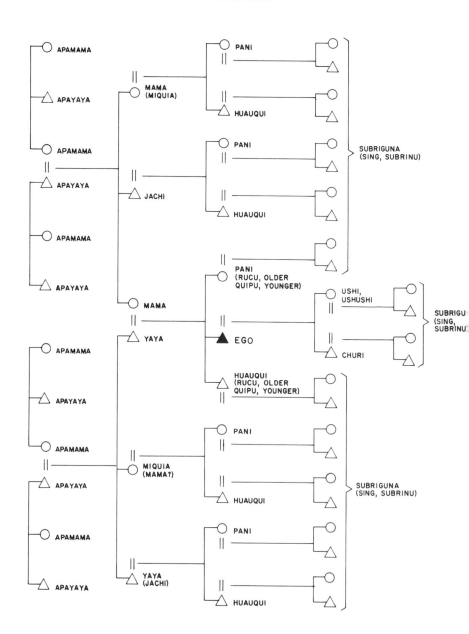

Consanguineal kin classes, male ego

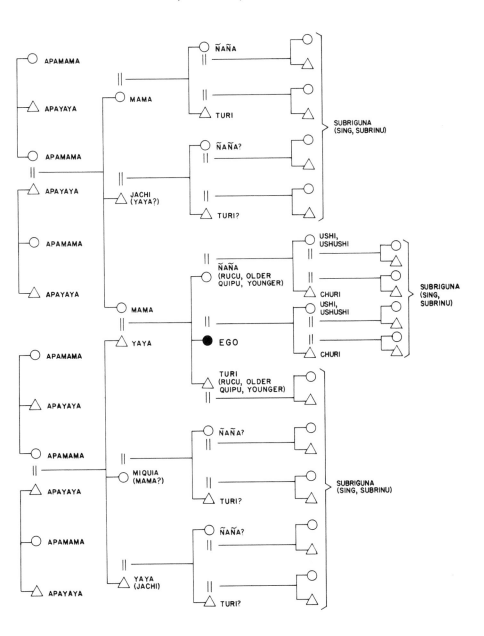

Consanguineal kin classes, female ego

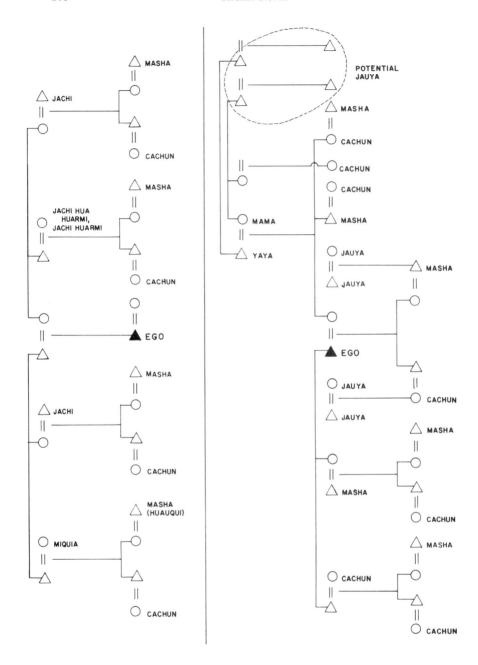

Affinal kin classes, male ego

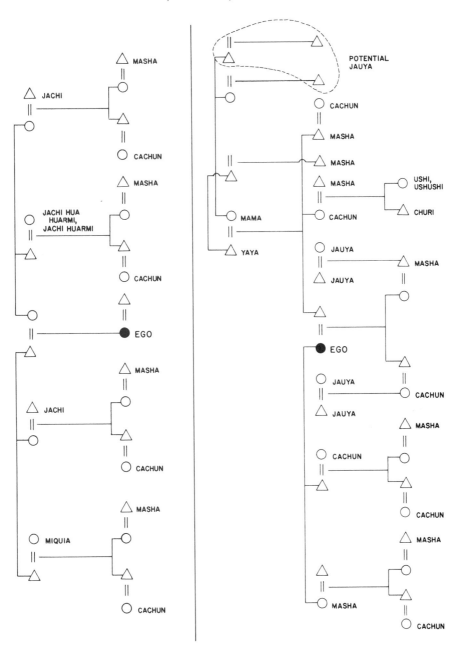

Affinal kin classes, female ego

companions set to the task of letting us understand how structure is developed out of the kin class framework, and showing the relationship of such obvious biological constraints as sexual relationships, birth, puberty, and death to kinship and ethnic perpetuity. The purpose of this chapter is to communicate the fundamentals of this system.

In brief, the referential kin class system provides the Canelos Quichua with an inherited and acquired network of "relatives" which itself constitutes a structure. But out of such form, which no individual or group can manage as a totality in most contexts of life, other structures are built. One of these is the maximal ayllu, a structure which links mythic structure, ancient time, and known history to the present and future. The reference points for this system are ultimately the stipulated *souls* of the apayaya-apamama ancestors who intermarried and acquired their substances from Ancient Times people. The maximal ayllu is a relative constant, or invariant structure, among the Canelos Quichua. All of Canelos Quichua social organization, including relationships with other peoples, is conceived of in terms of segments of maximal ayllus linked by affinity.

Another system is an ego-centered network of ritual or mystical co-parents called *gumba* (derived from the Spanish *compadre, comadre*), which lateralizes a series of strategic partners for a given ego. This ego-centered system solidifies some relationships in the maximal ayllu but attenuates others. The gumba network is fundamentally an address system out of which some kin class terminologies may be transformed. Polysemy, extension, connotation, and metaphor (Scheffler 1972:313–322) are crucial processes in such transformations.[1]

The two systems—ayllu and gumba—revolve around the processes of shamanistic power and authority quests, in which successful acquisition of mystical skill and social support generates a localized stem kindred, also called ayllu. The shamanistic processes involve both the metaphors inherent in the maximal ayllu (acquisition of souls, transformation into a jaguar—see Chapter 5) and the strategies played out in the gumba network. This dynamic system mediates between the referential and address systems, producing the polysemic and extension rules necessary to understand the fluctuations and shifts in kin class usage.

We begin with ayllu dynamics, which are expressed through terms used to designate stipulated and demonstrated genealogical statuses. The resulting terminological relationship system, in referential and address applications, provides a structure which serves as a basis for classifying individuals in genealogical space. The social categories of relationship which constitute this structure are based on the complementary concepts of *consanguinity*, blood relationships, and *affinity*, intersexual relationships through which blood relationships are potentially created.

KIN TYPES AND KIN CLASSES

The anthropologist Alfred L. Kroeber (1909:77–84) long ago established that there are six possible primary positions in a shallow consanguineal net radiating from any individual, *ego*. These positions are called *kin types*. The six consanguineal kin types are father, mother, brother, sister, son, and daughter of ego. Affinally, of course, we must have an *alter* to any ego. Ego and alter together make up two more kin types of the spouse relationship: husband and wife. With these kin types any position in a kinship system, no matter how distant or complex, can be easily identified. Here is a set of conventional symbols which we shall use to portray kin type:

Father	F	
Mother	M	
Brother	B	consanguineal
Sister	Z	
Son	S	
Daughter	D	
Husband	H	affinal
Wife	W	

Using this system of notation we can rapidly locate a position in genealogical space by combining various linkages. For example, FBD is father's brother's daughter and MMZHDD is mother's mother's sister's husband's daughter's daughter. This system of notation is a convenient one for beginning our understanding of ayllu structure. The Canelos Quichua easily employ such a system to locate the exact genealogical position of a given person. For example, MMZHDD is *mama mama ñaña cari ushi ushi*.

When the Canelos Quichua describe a real or potential social relationship they employ a few cultural rules to create an adaptable, self-perpetuating system by which they link people whom they have never seen before to a postulated continuous kin structure, ayllu. What we seek here are the recurrent rules applied by the Canelos Quichua in determining *linked social statuses*. These linked social statuses are called *kin classes*, as distinct from kin types. We have already introduced some classes, such as *yaya* and *mama*, and provided an ego chart of all such classes. Here are the Canelos Quichua primary kin classes, with their corresponding kin types.

Consanguineal Kin Class, Male Ego	*Kin Type*
Yaya	F, FB, WF, MH
Mama	M, MZ, FZ?, FW, WM
Huauqui (older: *rucu;* younger: *quipu*)	B, FBS, FZS, MZS, MBS, FBDH
Pani (older: *rucu;* younger: *quipu*)	Z, FBD, FZD, MZD, MBD

Churi (older: *rucu;* younger: *quipu*)   S
Ushi, Ushushi   D

Consanguineal Kin Class, Female Ego *Kin Type*
Yaya   F, FB, HF, MH
Mama   M, MZ, FZ?, FW, HM
Turi (older: *rucu;* younger: *quipu*)   B, MZS, MBS?, FBS?, FZS?
Ñaña (older: *rucu;* younger: *quipu*)   Z, MZD, MBD?, FBD?, FZD?
Churi (older: *rucu;* younger: *quipu*) S, ZS, HZS
Ushi, Ushushi   D, ZD, HZD

NOTE: WF, WM, HF, HM, MH, and FBDH are affinal kin types from our standpoint, but fall into the Canelos Quichua consanguineal kin classes.

Inspection of these referential kin classes makes certain factors obvious. First, a man and his wife use different terms for brother and sister, so we see the *criterion of sex* at work. Second, the affinal bond of husband and wife merges the statuses of father and mother for the two spouses, an example of the *criterion of affinity* in stipulating consanguinity. Third, a father's brother is often classed with ego's father and a mother's sister is often classed with ego's mother. This criterion is called *merging* since collateral and lineal relatives are classed together. Fourth, the merging of siblings and cousins into the same kin classes differentiated by ego's sex combines the criterion of merging with that of sex. Fifth, a man calls only his own sons and daughters by the kin class term, but a woman classes not only her own sons and daughters but also those of her sister and husband's sister, another illustration of both the criterion of sex and that of affinity. Understanding of such criteria necessitates closer inspection of the connotations attached to the terms, and extensions of the primary terms.

Extension Rules: Consanguinity, Sex, and Affinity

Huauqui and *pani* (male ego) and *turi* and *ñaña* (female ego) are definitely extensions from a household context to collateral men and women who are the children of siblings, and therefore collateral actors in socially homologous settings. Intra-household brothers and sisters and brothers and sisters who share a parent are prohibited by rigid incest taboos from marrying, but such a taboo does not extend to the collaterals. Indeed, cousin marriages are ubiquitous, but not between spouses classifying one another as huauqui and pani, turi and ñaña. Men use the huauqui extension in a metaphorical manner to invoke mythical collaterality through jaguar lines, and to allude to the commonality of origin through the ala transformation of a lost brother. It has already been noted that yaya and mama kin classes span consanguinity and affinity for a married couple. A man refers to, and addresses, his own and his wife's parents as yaya and mama, and a woman similarly extends the yaya and mama terms to her husband's parents. Although husband and wife *extend* consanguineal terms upward to their respective parents, these same parents reciprocate *affinal* referential and address terms:

> Ego calls S *churi* and DH *masha*
> Ego calls D *ushi* and SW *cachun*

The kin classes masha and cachun are purely affinal. Let us see all of the kin types which compose them:

Affinial Kin Class, *Male Ego*	Kin Type
Masha	<u>DH</u> (calls ego yaya)
	ZH, WB, WZH (all call ego masha)
	BDH, ZDH, FBDH (may call ego masha)
	MZDH, MBDH, FZDH (do not call ego masha)
Cachun	<u>SW</u> (calls ego yaya)
	BW, WZ, WBW, FBSW, WMZD (all call ego masha)
	ZSW, BSW (may call ego masha)
	MZSW, MBSW, FZSW (do not call ego masha)

Affinal Kin Class, *Female Ego*	Kin Type
Masha	<u>DH</u> (calls ego mama)
	ZH, HB, HZH, MZDH, HFBS (all call ego cachun)
	ZDH, BDH (may call ego cachun)
	FZDH, FBDH, MBDH (do not call ego cachun)
Cachun	<u>SW</u> (calls ego mama)
	BW, HZ, HBW, MZSW (all call ego cachun)
	BSW, ZSW (all call ego cachun)
	FZSW, FBSW, MBSW (do not call ego cachun)

The primary status of masha is an asymmetrical one between a couple and their daughters' spouses. These men owe allegiance and service to the couple who gives a daughter in marriage. The primary status of cachun is a less asymmetrical one between a couple and their sons' spouses. The first extension of this kin class is between male ego and his ZH and WB and female ego and her BW and HZ, as illustrated in Diagram 4:1 below.

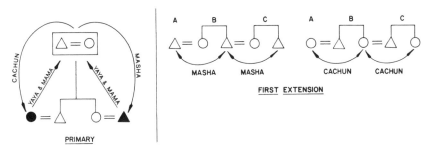

Diagram 4:1

Here male ego A is subordinate to B who is subordinate to C, but female egos A, B, C are nearly equal in status. Three resolutions of the subordinate-superordinate status for men are common in Canelos Quichua social organization. In one of these, two brothers marry two sisters, thereby joining forces vis-à-vis wives' parents, brothers, and sisters. In another, sister exchange is practiced. In the third, a series of subordinate-superordinate statuses effectively equalize the asymmetry. The first is illustrated on the left, the second in the center, and the third on the right, in Diagram 4:2 below.

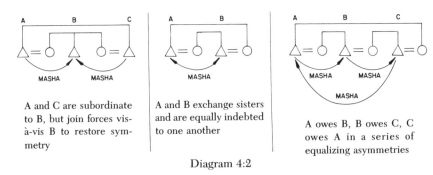

A and C are subordinate to B, but join forces vis-à-vis B to restore symmetry

A and B exchange sisters and are equally indebted to one another

A owes B, B owes C, C owes A in a series of equalizing asymmetries

Diagram 4:2

Further information is gained by combining this list of kin classes and kin types with that given on page 112. We immediately see that the cachun class designates the *female siblings* and *affines* of real or potential kin status huarmi (W, male ego), cari (H, female ego), huauqui (male ego), turi (female ego), and male children's spouses. Masha designates the male affines and siblings of real or potential kin status huarmi (W, male ego), cari (H, female ego), pani (male ego), ñaña (female ego), and female children's spouses. Ego male and ego female maximally extend their reciprocation of cachun-masha terms as represented in Diagram 4:3.

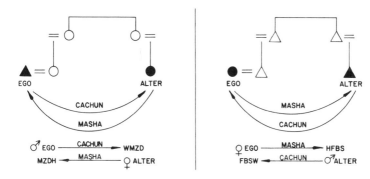

Diagram 4:3

When sex linkages are not the same, reciprocal extension of affinal terminology is not expected. I return to this below.

Men and women also extend the masha-cachun affinal class down one generation, not only to their children's spouses but to the spouses of children of brothers and sisters as well. This is done even though a male ego does not normally classify his brothers' and sisters' children as churi and ushi. Understanding these extensions, and the position of the four kin types belonging to the cachun-masha classes that do not reciprocate the same term to ego male, leads us to examine more closely ego's first ascending (parental) generation. Let us return to yaya and mama. Except for mother's brother, siblings of yaya and mama may be classed together with yaya and mama. In fact, in eliciting kin terms this is what is usually given to the field worker for FB and MZ unless the informant has been exposed to Quichua-speaking Spanish speakers, in which case the speaker may give all the siblings of yaya and mama as *jachi* (male) and *miquia* (female) in an attempt to translate Quichua into the Spanish equivalents for uncle and aunt.

Some consanguineal ambiguity always occurs in Canelos Quichua classification of parents' siblings. This is because affinal status of the parent's siblings, determined in previous generations, is also involved in his or her kin class, relative to any ego. Usually, FB is classed as yaya, MB as jachi, MZ as mama, and FZ as miquia. A connotation of shaman status enters with the concept jachi, and resolves apparent ambiguities in actual kin groupings (see Chapter 5).

Collateral Kin Class, First Ascending Generation (most usual)	*Kin Type*
Yaya	FB
Mama	MZ

Jachi	MB
Miquia	FZ

By introducing affinity and seeking an extension rule (Scheffler and Lounsbury 1971:106) a much more definite, unambiguous statement can be readily elicited that applies to kin class in ego's first ascending generation:

$$MB = FZH$$

The primary term for MB is extended to FZH. MB, jachi, and FZH, jachi, are *always in the same kin class*, whether or not FZ is classed as miquia, as she usually is. Furthermore, MBW is the *only* affinal position in this generation to have *no referential kin class designation* in the abstract. She is jachi huarmi, unless she is also miquia through a father's sibling or other relationship. (For example, FW, other than ego's M, is miquia, FWZ is miquia). This MB = FZH equation suggests a *sister exchange* equation in the parental generation—a symbol of affinal equivalence between MB and FZ. This sister exchange structure is presented in Diagram 4:4 below.

Diagram 4:4

Now we are ready to return to the kin types MZDH, MBDH, and MZSW, MBSW, whom male ego addresses as masha and cachun but who do not reciprocate the same term. Ego calls his MZ's children's spouses (MZDH, MZSW) masha and cachun because they are married to his classificatory brothers and sisters. This is because M and MZ are mama and both carry the female continuity of apamama, their mother. Such spouses have no reciprocal kin term for ego because the criterion of affinal extension of yaya and mama only connects a person to his spouse's actual parents (except where the sex linkage is the same, as illustrated in Diagram 4:3 above). From their position ego is beyond the masha-cachun class.

We noted earlier that Canelos Quichua social organization is conceived of as linkages between segments of maximal ayllus, and that these linkages were built up out of affinal ties. Understanding of further extensions of the masha-cachun kin classes involves us in the formal system of linking ayllu segments. When ego (male or female) marries, he/she extends the parental terminology upward to the spouse's parents, as we discussed above. But the parents maintain the affinal relationship signaled by the cachun-masha terminology. Ego and his wife terminologically signal a minimal intersecting of ayllu segments, while their parents invoke the alter ayllu, "in-law" terminology, which denies intersection and stresses segmentation.

The parents of spouses have a special relationship category for one another, *jauya*. Prior to the formalization of a jauya bond, parents of marrying children ask at least a couple of friends or relatives, frequently brothers and sisters, to join them in the spouse negotiations. Those who accompany the primary spouse-negotiating parents may address one another as gumba, and they in turn are addressed by the alter spouse-negotiating group as jauya, an extension of the reciprocal terminological status existing between parents of the marrying couple.

Spouse's parents' siblings and their offspring are also called jauya during actual spouse negotiations, and some of these people retain this affinal status if their actual participation in marriage procedures was active or pivotal. They reciprocate the terms masha and cachun. If ego male or female participates in the marriage procedures of his/her MZSW or MDZH (his/her cachun and masha), then he/she is called and referred to by them as jauya. When this occurs, ego extends the masha-cachun terms even further to include all spouses of those who call him/her jauya.

Ego also assigns MB's children's spouses (MBSW, MBDH) to the cachun-masha kin classes because the people tagged are regarded as married to his/her classificatory brothers and sisters. Rationale for inclusion stresses that the classificatory siblings are such because they descended from one of ego's apayaya statuses, a consanguineal extension of the position of FF for men and MMH for women. Since cousins married one another in Times of the Grandparents those classed as cachun and masha also call ego jauya, if ego participates in their marriage procedures. Such participation triggers wider extension of the masha-cachun classes in ego's address terminology.

The principle behind cachun and masha tagging is important, and well illustrates the MBSW and MBDH statuses. I have never found ambiguity in the cachun-masha tags in the referential system, and have often found ego to figure that MBS and MBD are his "brother" and "sister" because they are *married to* acknowledged masha or cachun. Maximal and segmental ayllu structure can be teased out of the linkages which develop through a network of masha and cachun classes.

Moving from the mother's to the father's side of ego's immediate set of consanguineal and affinal kinsmen, we find more evidence of equated affinal preference. The kin class for FZSW and FZDH is still cachun and masha, respectively, but people feel better about these tags if the person in the class has a known genealogical connection to the classificatory sibling's spouses as well. FBSW is clearly cachun, but FBDH is classed, in the abstract, as huauqui by male egos. We seem to have this extension rule:

$$B = FBDH \text{ (male ego)}$$

I am at a loss to explain this extension. I know of no one who applies this extension rule in any context for any purpose. Ego addresses FBDH as masha, but the person so addressed does not reciprocate any kin class term to ego.

Under some circumstances there is a preference on the part of a father to marry two of his sons or daughters to a pair of sisters or brothers. There is a definite preference among Achuara brothers to marry classificatory Canelos Quichua sisters, and many women also express a preference to marry a classificatory ZHB. If ego and his brother were to marry two sisters, themselves children of ego's FB, then perhaps the extension would have a genealogical basis, but I have no cases of such a parallel cousin marriage.

Let us now introduce the second ascending generation reckoning from ego.

Kin Class   *Kin Type*
Apayaya   *FF* (male ego), MF, FFB, FMB, MFB, MMB, *MMH*
                   (female ego)
Apamama   *MM* (female ego), FM, MMZ, MFZ, FMZ, FFZ, *FFW*
                   (male ego)
                   WFM, WMM (male ego)

It is immediately apparent that complete merging of kin types between collateral and lineal relatives occurs. For a male ego, *apayaya* refers specifically to FF and *apamama* to FFW. Other kin types designated by this kin class are thought of as extensions of this relationship. For a woman apamama refers to MM and apayaya to MMH, and other designated kin types are their extensions. Such extensions are readily explained by the Canelos Quichua as being the result of repetitive cousin marriage and sibling exchange in Times of the Grandparents.

Combining this information with the unambiguous extension rule equating MB with FZH, we could describe the Canelos Quichua kinship structure as one of bilateral cross-cousin marriage, a system of restricted exchange (Lévi-Straus 1963:121–122). The process is indicated in Diagram 4:5 below. For ego's wife, alter, see Diagram 4:6.

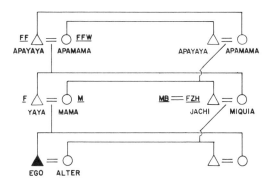

Diagram 4:5

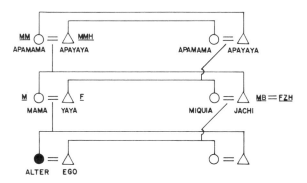

Diagram 4:6

Here ego inherits his soul from his father, in a direct transmission sequence from FF and FFW, and his wife inherits her soul from her mother
in direct transmission sequence from MM and MMH, who naturally turn
out to be the *same married apayaya-apamama couple*. In this model, ego's
and alter's parents are the brother-sister children of the original apayaya-
apamama couple. Such an elementary structure provides the mechanism
for brother-sister common substance to be reunited in marriage every
generation. But there is a problem with this model if we want to apply it to
Canelos Quichua kinship as an elementary structure: *ego and alter classify
one another as brother and sister when they are known double first cousins,
and incest rules prohibit such acknowledged brother-sister marriage.* Some
marriages of ego to a person who is both MBD and FZD do occur for one or

two generations, when distant groups such as Canelos Quichua and Quijos
Quichua combine through sibling exchange and marry their children to one
another to consolidate a llacta. But the incest prohibition nonetheless
prevents our analysis of this system as an elementary structure.

The model that often emerges from a discussion of kin structure with the
Canelos Quichua can be represented in one of the forms in Diagram 4:7
below.

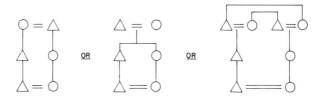

Diagram 4:7

If we take the FFW (male ego) married to MMH (female ego) or apayaya
married to apamama (primary statuses) replication every other generation
as the cognitive basis for figuring the ideal transmission and recombination
of male and female soul substances, expressing ayllu continuity, then
Diagram 4:8 can be applied.

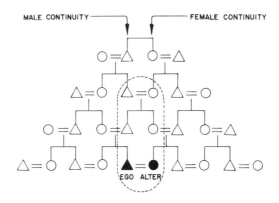

Diagram 4:8

This is a bilateral, cross-cousin (FZD = MMBDD) marriage system of
parallel transmission of kin class status, but, contrary to the analysis of

Scheffler and Lounsbury (1971:35) for such a system, there is no MBD-FZS–spouse equation rule. In this model MB and FZH serve as isomorphic linkages between ayllu segments. MB (jachi) becomes yaya to ego's Z, and WF (FZH,jachi) becomes yaya to ego. Both ego's W and Z link him to masha statuses WB and ZH. Further reciprocal extensions, we have noted, depend on actual marriage negotiations which forever alter the extant set of social statuses to which ego imparts structure.

These models are helpful but inadequate. The Canelos Quichua kinship system is open-ended and autotransformable according to vicissitudes from an outer world. But the rules and models do yield, or suggest, transformational relationship systems which provide a basis for cultural continuity. Kin class analysis of Canelos Quichua affinal and consanguineal terms quite clearly indicates an *ideology* of parental or grandparental cousin marriage and a kin equation suggesting sibling exchange.[2] Contemporary Runas practice sibling exchange under some circumstances. The concurrent rule, however, which prohibits marriage between double cross-cousins, results in a complex structure which is often handled by cross-generational marriage.

In Chapter 2 I introduced two simple models which a male and female ego could manipulate to build conveniently the linkages between apayaya and apamama continuity. The models were separately constructed to suggest a basic FM(FFW)ZD marriage for male ego and MF(MMH)BS marriage for female ego. Taking a brother-sister ego locus and combining these two models, we get the picture presented in Diagram 4:9 below.

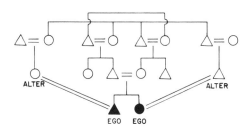

Diagram 4:9

This model demonstrates common marriages made by male and female egos among the Canelos Quichua. For their partners, alter male and alter female, marriage is, respectively, alter male = FBDD (FZSD), alter female = MZSS (MBDS), which are also common marriages. Marriages such as the one indicated in Diagram 4:10 are also common.

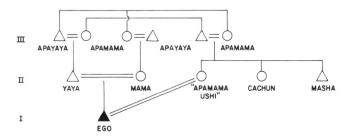

Diagram 4:10

In Generation III two men (ego's apayaya) exchanged sisters (ego's apamama). Another of ego's FFZ married another man, technically unrelated to the two men and two women from whom ego will inherit and acquire his soul substance. In Generation II ego's father took a wife who is technically his FZD but was not so classed because FZH's parents lived in another Runa territory and his father and mother had no kinship ties with his wife's immediate family. In ego's own generation ego also took a wife who is technically both his FFZD and his FFWBD, a perfectly acceptable marriage class, although one which *could* be reckoned as a double-cousin, unacceptable, class. In Canelos Quichua kinship, extension of any consanguineal bond into the apayaya-apamama generation by invoking a transmission rule negates lingering taboos which can be applied by extending sibling bonds through filiation procedures. This is done by figuring each kin type linkage. By invoking a matri-transmission rule ego simply uses an apical kin class designation, apamama ushi (grandmother's daughter), and he has an acceptable and desirable wife class by which to reckon his chosen huarmi. He also maintains his male continuity from the father line, and marries into the apamama line of his mother. By making a common cross-generation marriage he takes a spouse from a non-cousin sector of genealogical space. Furthermore, by his marriage he creates a cachun class of women for his classificatory siblings, and a potential masha class of men, should more marriages proceed into this group by ego's classificatory brothers, or his father's or sons' classificatory brothers. Finally, his new affinal mama (WM) is the sister of his father's affinal mama (FWM) and his new yaya (WF) is masha to his father's affinal yaya (FWF). By replicating some statuses in his father's gumba-jauya network his own segmental ayllu linkages become increasingly firm.

Linkage Classes

A fundamental principle of ayllu structure is the proposition that women in sister and wife kin classes, real and potential, link ayllu segments to one another. Sisters and wives invariably wind up in common kin classes. A woman is born into an ayllu reckoned from her mother to mother's mother and mother's mother's husband (MF). When she marries she links ego to her father and mother, and brings into the huasi the MM apamama continuity. Ego is linked as a son to WF because of the female huarmi linkage; but, because he is not *of* the wife's father's substance, transmitted through WM, this "father" uses the masha (affinal link) term for ego. The wife also links ego to her brothers and sisters in just the same way as ego's sisters link him to their spouses. All men so linked reciprocally share the kin term masha.

Ego is linked to his non-classificatory (kin type) brothers and sisters through the common consanguinity created by the FF = FFW affinity, transmitted directly to ego. Brothers and sisters also share the special form of continuity brought to their common birth by M through her MM. Brothers transmit some of the same yaya substance to their children, but transmission of the apayaya substance depends on factors of shamanistic acquisition (discussed in Chapter 5). Sisters transmit their common mama substance to their children, but may differ on the apamama substance according to whether they took special pottery direction from their own mother or their husband's mother.

Within ego's generation the linkage classes through male and female transmission from common grandparents are potentially attenuated because of the *acquisition aspect* of soul substance possession from Times of the Grandfathers, and from the *choice involved* in women's learning of pottery traditions and associated continuity symbolism from Times of the Grandmothers.

AYLLU STRUCTURE

In his own generation ego male incorporates brothers, sisters, parents' siblings' children (huauqui and pani classes), and female in-laws classed as cachun. Ego excludes the men whom he classes as masha from his maximal and segmental ayllu, for they belong to "another ayllu." Women, then, span male ayllu divisions for they are pani in one and cachun in others.

Ego male includes all people classed as yaya, mama, jachi, and miquia in his ayllu, as well as all classed as apamama and apayaya. Much merging takes place in such classification and the merging allows for choice in ayllu membership. For example, a man may reckon his descent from an apayaya who was, in effect, his FWFF. Remember, ego calls wife's father yaya, and even though the wife's father does not call ego churi in the living present, movement into Times of the Grandparents introduces other factors. For example, if through dreams and soul-acquisition Datura quests ego believes that he has acquired his FWFF soul, then he begins to figure his position in maximal genealogical space in terms of other acknowledged descendants from this apical ancestor. Such a quest involves his wife as well, for she often refigures her apamama status.

Ego male readily classes his daughters as part of his ayllu, for they provide potential linkages to other ayllus, as well as potential bonds to strengthen his gumba network. Ego's sons are also part of his ayllu. His SS, SD, together with the children of his brothers and cousins, all *subriguna* (from the Spanish *sobrino,-a*), are all *potential* ayllu members, but ego male does *not abstractly* reckon subriguna as part of the ayllu.

Ego female includes her own children and those of her sisters and husband's sisters as churi and ushi, son and daughter. For a female ego the female subriguna are *very important ayllu members* for they are the potential affines for future alliance and security.

Men divide ayllu structure along spatial lines as well as genealogical. *Ñuca ayllu*, my ayllu, refers to the people reckoned from Times of the Grandparents residing in ego's Runa territory. This is the *territorial clan*. *Caru ayllu*, distant ayllu, means ayllu members residing in another Runa territory, or even a non-Runa territory. Combination of territorial and pan-territorial ayllu members constitutes the *maximal clan* for male egos. Women reckon ñuca ayllu both in immediate and distant dimensions. They include their father's territorial and distant clan reckoning, together with the territorial and distant clan segments into which their sisters and mother's sisters have married.

Obviously the ayllu is both ancestor-oriented and ego-oriented. Convenient though it is to separate kin groups based on these contrastive orientations, the phenomenon of soul acquisition from Times of the Grandparents, which may merge affinal and consanguineal linkages for a given ego but not for others in his stipulated descent group, leads me to discuss ayllu structure from both ancestor and ego perspectives.[3]

LLACTA STRUCTURE

Members who share ayllu bonds spread through a Runa territory and sub-groupings lay particular claims to named subdivisions, llactas, which radiate out from the mission, trade, or administrative site of the territory to a distance of two to six hours' steady travel. Every territory contains from six to twelve generally acknowledged llactas and several more in the process of formation. Llacta formation coincides with llacta fission and realignment, the concept being a dynamic one which involves members in constant conflict and conflict resolution. Each llacta has an original founder, a powerful shaman able to control generalized mystical power or danger and directed spirit attack.

Llactas are consolidated around a stem kindred segment into which men and women representing one or more other ayllu segments are married. As the stem kindred reaches a population of seven to ten male huasi founders, together with their wives and growing families, a currently maximal population of about 70 to 100 people (including babes in arms) induces fission. Fission takes place through staggered purina, by the out-movement of some members to another llacta or another territory, or even out-movement to another culture such as Quijos Quichua or Achuara Jivaroan. By staggered purina I refer to a process by which a number of the families of a given llacta are on purina at one time, while other families are on purina at another time. Land scarcity and game scarcity are the voiced reasons leading to fission and dispersal of llacta members.

Llactas are also depleted by diseases which sweep epidemically through Runa territories, and probably by greatly increased parasite infestations which accompany moderate crowding when contiguous llactas near the administrative-trade site of the Runa territory increase their populations. Epidemics lead to immediate dispersal to purina chagras, and increased parasite infestation leads to complaints of generalized mystical danger (contagion) and directed spirit attack. The latter is imputed to shamanistic duels. Illness and ideas about spirit attack lead those who are ill to get out of the llacta territory for a time; purina chagras and alternative opportunities for residence in another area provide refuge. Search for cures for illness and reconsideration of ayllu bonds necessitated by shaman duels (see Chapter 5) also lead llacta members to move, realign, or elect a veritable Sacha Runa existence in a remote jungle area.

Ayllu members, we have noted, share their llactas with members of other ayllus, and this is where the fundamental female linkages of the ayllu structure become all-important. Ego male is linked to other men, with whom he cooperates in group hunting, group fishing, reciprocal labor exchange, trade expeditions, and territorial defense. But equally important is ego male's linkage to potential competitors for chagra, forest, and river resources through affinal bonds as well as through consanguineal bonds. In two or three generations children and grandchildren of the original linked segments become a single residential segmental and extended ayllu descended from apayaya-apamama intermarried apical ancestors. These descendants continue to reckon other Runas similarly descended from stipulated intermarrying ancestors in Times of the Grandparents, as part of their everlasting ayllu (maximal clan). Such ayllu consolidation (a stem kindred) is the core of a segment of an extended clan within a llacta. Constant recruitment of new members as children grow and marry gives to every llacta a symbolic duality of people "originally" *of* the llacta (those who reckon descent from founding apical ancestors) and those who have been recruited *to* the llacta. Even those who have been recruited to the llacta, however, often lay claim to membership on the basis of common ayllu bonds, reckoned through one or another linkage in Times of the Grandparents.

People who are stipulated descendants from ancestors reckoned as crucial in llacta formation have claim to subdivided chagra land within the llacta, each claimant's land bordering another's. In order to recruit in-laws a man offers a portion of the land which he claims to a son or son-in-law. By so doing the man loses part of his own llacta segment, but he gains a growing, strong ally. Furthermore, until such land has been subdivided two or three times the man may not really be -capable of exploiting or protecting it. He must recruit men who are in his debt and women who are in his wife's debt. If successful he not only gains land-based allies to consolidate his intra-llacta zone against encroachment by llacta mates, but also the work force necessary to exploit his own established land claims.

Llacta structure also embodies two native concepts dealing with the politics of llacta maintenance vis-à-vis adjacent llactas. These are the concepts which I translate and analyze as *embedding* and *outposting*. Embedding refers to the placement of some llacta members near the named, symbolic focus of the subdivision, where they are socially circumscribed (Carneiro 1970:737–738) by the larger numbers of members. This involves the embedded huasi unit in more chicha giving, more intensive interaction and maintenance of good will, and greater jeopardy from directed spirit attack and shamanistic duels. The Quichua concept of such embedding is simply *llactaimi causanchi*, living in the llacta.

Outposting refers to the placement of a huasi regarded by one llacta group as being *of* their llacta, *llacta manda*, adjacent to or even within the territory of another llacta. This is simply called *ñucanchi llacta manda _____ mayambi tian*, "one of our llacta visiting _____ llacta." Outposting removes the huasi members from intensive, frequent contact with their own other llacta members, and involves them more directly with alter llacta members. People who are outposted are capable of either going over to the adjacent llacta or forming their own.

Through time llacta centers and llacta boundaries shift and fluctuate as those outposted maneuver advantageously. Such maneuvering inevitably changes the nature of groupings in a Runa territory. For example, let us consider the case of three brothers, sons of a shaman, who marry three sisters in three different, adjacent llactas. Each of them has several residential alternatives within the llacta system. A man may live in his father's llacta near the llacta central locus, in which case he is clearly embedded and signals expansion of his father's ayllu in that llacta. Alternatively he may live on the outer fringe of his own llacta, outposted to that of his father-in-law. He may live with his father-in-law near the central locus of this alter llacta, in which case he is regarded as outposted by his own ayllu segment and llacta but embedded in his father-in-law's llacta by his father-in-law's ayllu segment and llacta mates. Or a man and his father or father-in-law may be found near the fringe of one or the other llacta, both outposted, so to speak, but such a residential maneuver signals potentially new llacta formation.

If each of the three sons mentioned above arranges residence in such a way as to claim some outposted allegiance to different llactas, while at the same time locating their *actual residences* near one another, and if their father comes to live with them, they become the central ayllu node of their own llacta, and anyone joining them from their previous llactas becomes a "newcomer."

KINDRED AND MARRIAGE

Within llactas, shallow, three-generation stem kindreds represent the core segments of territorial clans as nodal residential units. The stem kindred is ideologically predicated upon a shamanistic node; within each stem kindred adult male egos form their own personal kindreds. Both stem and personal kindred maintenance is dependent upon recruitment strategies and land allocation. Factors of llacta boundaries and membership, residence, and spouse selection vary, but certain structural aspects of the relationship between ayllu and huasi endure. Let us first turn to the common, repetitive variants and alternatives, through which ayllu and huasi structures are maintained and adapted.

Residence

There are three residential alternatives practiced by a huasi unit among the Canelos Quichua at any given time. First, the man and his wife may go off to live on their own in either a remote jungle area or in another territory where ayllu members reside. This alternative is not common, but its possibility often keeps the couples' parents and ayllu or llacta mates from becoming too possessive, domineering, or demanding.

The second alternative is to reside in the vicinity of one set of spouse's parents, leaving the other set with some sort of compensation. This is the most common option. Where two or more llactas border one another within a Runa territory, interesting organizational strategies are played out by a couple electing this option. If the boy comes from llacta A and the girl from llacta B and the couple elect to live in llacta A, the girl's brothers may well make special offers of land space, and allegiance, to the boy to make sure that he regards himself as *of* llacta B (where his wife's parents reside), and potentially *outposted to* llacta A (where his own parents reside), even though he is regarded by his own llacta mates as *embedded* there. Through time, residential changes of the couple may alternate between llacta A and llacta B, *especially if they can establish a chagra within a couple of hours' walking distance from both llactas.*

The third alternative occurs when two men who have married each other's sisters, or two (classificatory) brothers who have married two (classificatory) sisters, arrange the marriage and residence of their children so as to fortify intra-llacta, inter-ayllu dominance. This normally occurs at the foundation of a llacta, and, after the second generation, powerful sanctions of incest accusation are applied if married double cousins attempt to reenact this pattern by arranging intermarriage of their offspring. The pattern is most common when inter-ethnic marriage takes place in the first generation. In fact, I know of no such arrangements between acknowledged Canelos Quichua intermarrying ayllu groupings. The ones I am familiar with involve Quijos Quichua marrying Canelos Quichua or bicultural Canelos Quichua–Achuara in one generation and perpetuating double-cousin marriage in the second.

Spouse Selection

Marriage choices and plans revolve around four alternatives. The first occurs when a man captures a baby boy from another people outside Canelos Quichua territory and rears him to marry one of his daughters. These arrangements are not common but they have occurred in the past. Revenge stealing has also taken place, and the placation of aggrieved parties one or two generations later by gifts, or even by the sending of a marriagable spouse to a related member from the other culture, leads to some very strong alliances between some of the Canelos Quichua and members of other cultures (Achuara Jivaroan, Jívaro proper, Zaparoan, and Cocama, that I know of).

The second alternative is either the outgrowth of the first or the result of diminution of hostilities resulting from a killing between members of different cultures. In this alternative a male child is sent to an aggrieved father who has lost a son or to a man who has lost a brother. The child is

reared to marry the man's daughter, and further reciprocities again cement
relationships between members of kindred segments of two different,
normally antagonistic, cultures. A variant of this alternative occurs when a
man with children escaping a killing in his cultural territory seeks asylum in
the vicinity of a well-established Canelos Quichua man, or a man
endeavoring to consolidate his llacta territory. Such an escapee offers his
young sons in marriage to the man's daughters in return for asylum.

Children reared to marry under such circumstances are instructed in the
origin of their apamama and apayaya substance, and encouraged to return
to their natal territory to learn language and custom, taking their Canelos
Quichua wife and several male and female unmarried youths from their
wife's father's family with them.

The third alternative occurs when two sets of parents negotiate the
marriage for a son and daughter before the daughter reaches puberty.
These marriages, in particular, cement relationships between strong men
in different ayllus, and contribute to both llacta alliance (between members
of often distant llactas) and ayllu continuity when the affinal bond endures.
But if a man abandons the woman a lifetime feud is initiated.

The fourth alternative involves the direct mutual choice of a young man
and woman for one another as spouse. In this case, the most common one,
the man asks his father to negotiate with his chosen mate's father for their
marriage. Such negotiations can be interminable if not triggered by other
factors, one of which is simply "capture" of the bride by the groom and
flight to his father's household (and sometimes bride's father's brother's
household in a different llacta), forcing negotiation to take place.

Canelos Quichua marriage stresses mutual, reciprocal possession of two
individuals, cari and huarmi. The terms of affinity, or marriage, used by the
cari-huarmi pair for each other, and applied to them by other llacta
members, are *huarmiyuj,* possession of a woman, and *cariyuj,* possession of
a man. The interactions of marriageable man and woman generate
interdependent systems of obligation and responsibility, each of which is
grounded in a primary dyadic relationship. For the man these are (A) the
cari-huarmi relationship, which will become a yaya-mama huasi unit;
(B) the yaya-churi relationship between ego's father and himself; and
(C) the yaya-masha relationship between ego's wife's father and himself.
For the woman there is (A) the same huarmi-cari dyad; (B) the mama-ushi
relationship between ego's mother and herself; and (C) the mama-cachun
relationship between husband's mother and herself.

Residential choice skews the relationship of one dyad or another. To
satisfy the transactions involved in the maintenance of one dyadic system,
cari or huarmi often create tension in another. Multiple, complex sets of
transactions within each dyad cumulate and ramify, invariably modifying

the quality of interactions in another. As the cari-huarmi union solidifies and maintains the impetus behind other dyadic and network transactions, the spouse-negotiating category, jauya, forms, its central focus being on the parents of the marrying pair.

A couple undertaking the task of reorganizing their lives and continuing to maintain their close ties with natal families while developing new ties with new families face a set of social expectations which place severe strains on the affinal bond. Attenuated or weak affinal relationships simply don't stand up under such pressure. Affinity between man and woman signals a whole system of linkages whose ramifications are forcefully brought home to the young couple. The strains in their immediate kinship networks force the couple to symbolic activity attendant on creation of the huasi as a micro-cultural, micro-social universe embedded in Canelos Quichua symbolism and the maximal ayllu. Datura trials for man and woman and subsequent instruction in spirit helpers and soul acquisition (man) and pottery tradition (woman) bring the couple into increased awareness of their role in cultural perpetuity as well as in socioeconomic affairs. A couple whose affinal bonds and huasi universe do not strengthen and persevere toward local llacta and inter-llacta interpersonal maintenance, or worse, a couple who find one another incompatible, simply break apart, each beginning anew the search for a viable partner.

A man is expected to take an active role in searching for a wife. All opportunities afforded by traveling are utilized to learn of spirit substances useful in attracting women, and in trying one's luck at attracting women as well. Ordinarily a man finds a compatible lover by the time he reaches twenty years of age. Sometimes, in his quest for knowledge, a man decides it is not so hard to love many different sorts of women, and makes his decision about a spouse on the basis of advantages offered by the girl's father. Women also actively seek husbands. They learn of secret magical substances making them beautiful, perfect the female household tasks of chicha making, and learn the underlying meanings and techniques of pottery manufacture. Many girls also travel with senior male relatives to distant territories or towns, and are not infrequently "stolen" by handsome beaus while there.

Regardless of how the selection is made—and the range is from thunderstruck love at first sight to courtship over a period of years—a man eventually tells his father that he intends to marry a particular girl. Whether he does this by simply bringing her home or by asking his father to negotiate their marriage, at any movement indicating pending affinity between a boy and a girl, the respective jauya category between the couple's parents is signaled.

The jauya category starts to form on the boy's side, as his father begins the task of trying to structure the series of events making up the marriage episodes, which take about three years to complete. At the same time, however, the girl's father and mother also begin to lay out strategies for the same episode series. In essence this is what occurs.

The man's father arranges a visit to the girl's father. In such arrangements he asks one or two brothers or residential in-laws (ZH but never WB, as far as I know) to accompany him, and to share the burden of providing necessary gifts of food and drink. Today many gallons of raw cane alcohol are a crucial, indeed central, gift. Drinking goes on for a couple of days or more. Those accompanying the father of the groom are jauya vis-à-vis everyone who comes to drink in the girl's father's household, and (at least in Canelos and Puyo) they are *tentatively* or *potentially* gumba to the groom's father. Only later, when the bride's father has also selected one or two gumbas to continue to negotiate marriage arrangements, will the jauya term be reciprocally applied between individual members of the spouse-negotiating categories. When this occurs, ego's father strengthens his personal gumba network by close incorporation of some brothers and sisters' husbands, differentiating this net from his WB masha statuses. Conversation about what a good hunter-provider the boy is, and what a good chagra-working chicha maker the girl is goes on as people drink, eat, and dance, and when the couple dance together "marriage"—cariyuj-huarmiyuj—in its preliminary form is signaled. Thereafter, the couple begin to sleep together within the house of the bride's parents.

Most emphasis is in giving enough to the bride's father to compensate him for the loss of his daughter. At the end of a two- to three-day period (sometimes longer) the groom's negotiating set leaves. The married couple may stay on with the girl's father, in which case the groom is seen as paying off a debt of labor in compensation for his marriage to the girl. More often the couple accompany the groom's parents, but it is understood that the groom still owes the girl's father his labor for from six months to a year. Two or three such visits by the groom's negotiating group may be necessary during the first year of marriage.

Many kin relationships are remembered during this period. Maximal ayllu members are recalled and discussed, and advice sought from knowledgeable elders about grandparental origin nodes, from which it is hoped that the man will acquire a soul and, on the female side, continuity will be transmitted through pottery tradition. Both spouses work for the parents in the house where they are residing. Although they would like to set up their own chagra and household this is extremely difficult, for they are constantly involved in work within the chagra and residential unit of the parents.

Both sets of parents normally want their son or daughter to stay home, or at least to remain in the vicinity of the parental household. Each parental pair usually tries to make an attractive offer to the young couple to accept co-residence. Division of the man's or woman's father's chagra land is the basic offer made. But this in itself produces conflict among other llacta members, many of whom may object to a new youth holding land in their territory, when a father-in-law makes the offer. The youth may fare no better in his own father's territory, however, for those in his yaya and jachi categories may object to division of land of their brother (the youth's father).

Objections are usually based on the fact that there is, in practice, much overlapping in land claims. Given the system of swidden agriculture, such overlapping is not a critical point of contention until more and more of the land is worked. When a father or father-in-law offers a son or son-in-law a segment of his land, it is clear that more of the chagra territory will be worked, with possible loss to holders of other llacta chagra territory.

Within the newly married man's father's llacta actual fights may break out between him, or his brothers, and other residents. Although he is important as a new adult to his father's expanding kindred, he also comes to understand that he may not be able to live comfortably in an arena of conflict. To remove himself from such conflict, and also to fulfill the obligation to his father-in-law, he frequently goes to his wife's family's house and begins a period of service to in-laws. Here he is obliged not only to help clear land for his father-in-law's chagra, but he must also provide firewood to his father-in-law's household, normally a woman's task.

A father-in-law often offers land to his new son-in-law as an inducement for him to remain. Such an offer also produces conflict for those in the youth's masha category, i.e. his wife's brothers, who see such land as potentially theirs. Again, fights may break out, and accusations of sorcery may also be reciprocally made between those in ego male's and ego female's ayllus.

Instruction in pottery technique is a very important signal as to where, and under what conditions, a girl will eventually reside. A mother who took pains to train a girl in this difficult skill may insist that such a continuity of apamama symbolism must remain in the vicinity of the girl's natal huasi, convincingly maintaining that the continuity of Nunghuí and the ancients is tied to the girl's skill. The move of such a girl to the husband's parents' huasi is seen as a transposition of ayllu continuity to another territory. This is not necessarily negatively valued by the women involved, but a relationship between the women in the jauya category must be established where agreement as to the continuity of apamama substance from Ancient Times to the present is reached. Should women find conflict or discontinuity in their mythic structure or histories, they may object to the girl's movement and do everything possible to dissuade her from joining her husband. Or, if they don't like the man's mother, or his family, they may invoke mythic or ancient discontinuity to instill doubt in the girl's mind.

A woman who has not been so trained, however, may be taught techniques and symbolism by her husband's mother, learning to maintain ayllu continuity from the apamama times through her affinal female relatives. This, in turn, often involves her in other work and service to her mother-in-law as she becomes more and more obligated to her, and to her husband's mother's sisters.

Sometime in the second year, occasionally earlier, the wife's family may visit the husband's family. If it is expected that the husband will reside with the wife's father for an indeterminable period, then the wife's spouse negotiators bring meat and alcohol. If not, then it is expected that the husband's spouse negotiators will provide chicha, food, and some cane alcohol. People party and recount ayllu history and legend, the hope being that accord in all aspects of spouse negotiating will occur.

If accord is reached, all well and good; but even fission may resolve some problems should the families not get along, for if one or the other spouse-negotiating group is displeased it may leave, the couple then making a choice as to which side to take. Once again, a weak affinal bond simply cannot endure in such a conflict situation, and there is always the possibility of affinal fission within the second year.

By the end of three years more reciprocal visits, or even gifts sent by traveling Runas, cement whatever relationships have finally been somewhat tortuously worked out. By this time the husband has normally worked for his father-in-law for from six months to a year, and he and his wife have established a chagra in some area. As soon as their chagra is planted, though, the couple is cut off from the parental food supply and forced to forage as best they can. Again, surviving this strain seems to strengthen the huasi unit. Furthermore, people who feel sorry for a struggling young couple may help them out, thereby cementing friendship bonds among a dispersed and localized network of people within consanguineal and affinal categories in a Runa territory. Any time during this three-year period the couple may register their marriage with national officials, receive a church marriage at one of the ayllu ceremonies (discussed in Chapter 6), or even be married in the Catholic church of Puyo or Canelos by special arrangement.

The concept of one ceremony to cement the affinal bond, however, is not a Canelos Quichua one. The idea of at least three years of spouse negotiation and arrangement of the various peoples involved in a referential kin class system, constructed kinship network, and territorial-land claiming unit constitutes the reciprocal sense of huarmi and cari acquisition—cariyuj-huarmiyuj—which can be called "marriage." The end result is a structural unit—huasi.

The birth of the couple's first child, at least among the Puyo Runa and the Canelos Runa, is accompanied by the immediate establishment of a gumba bond between the couple and another married pair. The man is usually F, B, ZH, or WZH to male ego, and the woman is HBW, HZ, or Z to his wife. I know of no cases of WB serving as gumba. Of course, WB *becomes* gumba *to* ZH because the gumba co-parent class is reciprocally applied. But the bond is *formed* by ego asking ZH, not by a request to WB, as far as I know.

This gumba bond supersedes all other dyadic, classificatory, or categorical terminological designations, and is expected to establish a close, life-long, reciprocal, symmetrical relationship between the couples. The child becomes the gumba's *llullucu marcashca,* marked child, and the gumba is *marca yaya* (male) and *marca mama* (female). These bonds are also expected to endure throughout a lifetime. The ritual co-parent chooses the child's first name, and the child's parent its second name. Men name boys, women name girls. Some of the secret spirit substance of the gumba is also conferred on the child, and if both father and co-father are shamans and there is reason to believe that the child has some special power, the child will be thought to have the potential for becoming a powerful shaman.

Extension of the gumba terminological designation is often made by co-parents' brothers, sisters, and children, though reciprocal maintenance of this term, and the implied symmetrical ties superseding kinship and affinity, is by mutual choice. Formation of such a gumba network within and beyond llacta boundaries signals the end, or nearly the end, of spouse negotiations. There is considerable variety, of course, much depending on when a woman has her first baby, where she has it, and whether or not it lives.

Canelos Quichua symbolize the enduring ayllu structure and its replication with each marriage by figuring ways in which a man can take a spouse from the same category from which his father's father took a spouse. Such acquisition assures the couple continuity of inherited soul substance, and, equally important, a set of relatives who see themselves as replicating inter-ayllu exchange patterns taking place in Times of the Grandparents. An ideology of structural replication seems to gloss over individual tendencies toward bellicosity during spouse negotiation, thereby reducing some potential strains on the cari-huarmi union.

There is also a tendency for distant llacta spouse acquisition, perhaps due to the difficulty of satisfying demands and expectations of both sets of parents. The repetitive linking of ayllu segments in relatively distant llactas, together with the consequent establishment of more cachun classes and an ideology of replication of structure from Times of the Grandparents, extends an awareness of ayllu and ethnic unity through llacta and territorial divisions. Furthermore, serial marriage and polygyny in the past, clearly evident in my genealogies, together with great fertility and fecundity of the acknowledged apical ancestors, create a large marriageable class for any ego. All such potential spouses *can* be reckoned as "cousin," and cousin marriage is ubiquitous. But individual choice of a desirable, compatible mate, as well as a need to bolster the affinal bond constantly in the face of strains produced by the spouse negotiators, leads to decisions far more complex than a cousin-marriage model can explain.

KINSHIP AND CULTURE

The structure of huasi and the structure of ayllu are relative constants around which maneuvers involving llacta, ayllu segments, land, and social status revolve. Each ayllu segment maintains its special culture and special, sometimes secret, ethnic awareness. For example, every ayllu segment contains members who reckon descent from Jivaroan, Zaparoan, or Quijos origins and retain and perpetuate certain facets of these cultures through myth, design, medicinal secrets, or shamanistic procedure. Such culture, including secrets, is transmitted to residential in-laws. In this transmission process sub-territorial, though *inter*-llacta, concentrations of knowledge exist. People in such intertwined ayllu segments trek together to the same general purina territory, and the male members trade with men of other cultures, particularly when they speak the requisite languages. Out-marriage from each intermarried center within a territory serves to concatenate knowledge within the maximal territory, producing the territorial Runa. Further out-marriage, as well as movement of entire kindred groupings outward from one territory to another, disperses such knowledge among groupings in other territories, who themselves transmit to one another.

The size of Canelos Quichua territory itself provides many large refuge zones for independent huasi units seeking to escape the pressures imposed by territorial clans. Moving into distant jungle territory and engaging in individual and household acquisition of soul power through Amasanga and Nunghui is a viable alternative to either embedding or outposting within the llacta system. In time, the members of such a sacha huasi become particularly valuable to llacta members near an administrative center because of their greater knowledge of a jungle territory. Reincorporation of such Sacha Runa into certain llactas insures the territorial Runa of a diversity of knowledge which can be applied to purina chagras, hunting territories, and the search for valued jungle products.

DEATH AND REORGANIZATION

Death conjoins a world of souls of the dead, *huanushca aya*, with the living Runa. The living soul—that substance which maintained the life of the person—leaves the dying person through his mouth and remains in the vicinity of the body. A corpse is brought to its own house and laid out in the center along a cardinal axis. Its soul then travels freely within the house. Both men and women resident in the house and the brothers and sisters begin immediately to chant a heart-rending wail. The women let their wail resound, and the men bottle theirs up in their throats, covering their mouths with their hands. The wail invokes memories of all the good things done by the deceased and also brings memories of the deaths of other loved ones. The grief that is projected and shared around the dead person is indescribably deep and moving.

Interspersed in such crying is a discussion of *why* the person died when he did. Illness, accident, and snakebite are usually dismissed as secondary causes, and the real reason for the death is explored as everyone tries to place blame. Frequently neglect or a mistake by people resident in the huasi is named, and quite violent arguments may result. These are usually resolved by projection outward with an assumption of an evil "somewhere" that struck out at the beloved deceased. More and more people in the territory come bearing small gifts of tobacco, copal (for lighting), and chicha. Near the centers of trade they bring packs of cigarettes, candles, and cane alcohol. The general grief enactment goes on, interspersed with arguments over causality of death, until two or more hours after dark.

By this time most sisters of the deceased, together with their close female relatives, move to the ichilla huasi, where they continue to wail and visit with one another. Men, except the actual brothers or sons of the deceased, begin to enact grief's opposition—uproarious humor. Such "play," *pugllana*, takes place near the corpse. The first game is always the same. It is described as *huairu* by the Salasaca of highland Ecuador, and known by this name in Nordenskiöld (1930:211–213) and Karsten (1935:467ff.). Karsten (1935:480), Cooper (1949:517), and Hartmann and Oberem (1968) give a picture of a highland analogue of the gaming piece, which has also been found archaeologically on the coast of Ecuador (Meggers 1966:88). The Canelos Quichua do *not* use the word *huairu*, which they relate to the *aya tullu*, soul bone. They carve a small canoe, *cánua*, out of a piece of plantain or manioc, putting three holes on one side and five on the other.[4]

The first game, called *sincu, sincu* (from the Spanish *cinco*, five), is played with this object. Two teams of five men each face one another; each team has twenty beans. Playing counterclockwise, each man tosses the canoe on the floor saying *sincu, sincu, sincu,* while members of the opposing side say *tuhuama, tuhuama, tuhuama,* "tip over, tip over, tip over," and all shout when the canoe comes to rest. If it lands upright or if the side with five holes lands up, the thrower's team gains a point and puts a bean aside; if the canoe lands upside down or with the three-hole side up, the player loses. When one side gets twenty points it rises and each man in turn gives a resounding finger snap to the forehead of each opponent, who in turn shouts *aiai* to screams of hilarity by all present.

Canelos Quichua exegesis[5] of this game is that the soul of the deceased has become hungry and has sampled the chicha but cannot be satisfied. The game is played to entertain it, to allow it to flow in and out of the players, testing the relationship between the world of huanushca souls and living souls. Everyone must stay awake during the night of the wake, so that their souls do not travel as vision makers to conjoin directly with the fresh substance of the unsophisticated dead soul. Those who do try to sleep are rudely and loudly awakened, and I have been frequently told that in the past a fire was lit under such people. Throughout the night, and sometimes through a second and even third night as well, ayllu members of the deceased, together with the in-married relatives, play within the contained universe of the huasi while women serve chicha, visit, and wail. Death conjoins huasi and ayllu and touches each with the enduring soul substance of its own inevitability.

After midnight, or toward dawn, as people become tired and sleepy, several other games are played, among them a sort of blindman's bluff. Someone who has drunk a good deal of chicha or is a bit drunk from alcohol is selected, blindfolded, and spun in the vicinity of the corpse. The soul of the deceased immediately enters the blindfolded man, who tries to grab someone in the room and frighten him by enacting the visitation of a wandering soul of the dead. People shriek, run, and if grabbed shout *huaccha mani, huaccha mani,* "I am orphan, I am orphan" (I have not acquired a soul of the deceased).

Another game is the "monkey foot" or "foreign people's foot" game, *machin chaquichisca pugllashunchi.* A man is trussed up with his feet tied behind him and his arms tied to his feet, immobilizing him. Then he is pushed by someone so that he crashes down near the corpse, sometimes even whamming into it. Again, the huanuschca aya enters the person and he thrashes around on the ground, trying to kick out at someone just as the mythic man described in Chapter 2 kicked out at the giant anteater.

Between such games virtually anything can be played, and games recently learned from outsiders are often tried, improvised upon, adapted, and incorporated into the death ceremony. Throughout the night the idea is expressed that a newly liberated living soul of the deceased is walking as an invisible person, entering anyone it wishes, and throughly familiarizing itself with the collected souls within the huasi universe. It also shows itself to the inner substances of the collected Runa, but the living themselves, even the shamans, cannot see the huanushca aya.

The appearance of the sun ends the intra-huasi ceremony and game playing, for the penetration of the yellow rays within the huasi destroy the closure of the household universe and open the entire universe to the huanushca aya. Although the soul may be called back for two or three nights, especially when people have traveled for some distance to attend the wake, the coming of the sun is a signal for burial. By the second or third signal—within two or three days—the corpse is interred.

Burial preferences and concepts vary greatly, and an anthropologist working among the Canelos Quichua may today elicit all sorts of customs characteristic of many people of the tropical forests of South America, except tree burial. A corpse may be buried in the center of his house and the house abandoned, or in a cemetery near the center of the Runa territory, or adjacent to a llacta, or in a secret place in the forest. People discuss what they will do with the corpse for a day or two, between the nightly wakes. Whatever is decided, however, the following *concepts* are expressed.

The deceased must be buried along a cardinal axis, in a container, *cánua*, symbolizing a canoe, together with some food, chicha, cooking, drinking, and eating pottery, clothes and adornments such as necklaces and headdresses, and exchangeable tokens such as gold, silver, or money. The corpse must also have a huanushca huasi, and one plantain stem must be planted near the head of the deceased outside the shelter. The liberated soul of the deceased leaves the area around the corpse before its interment. It begins a trip straight up into the sky world and straight down into the underworld. During such a trip the soul may be captured by a spirit. If it is not captured it eventually enters some living thing or else becomes a star. Stars fall to earth now and then and positioning in the sky world is not final. At the same time, a soul remains within the actual corpse, which also becomes a huanushca aya, and in time presumably is liberated by the blossoming of the plantain, though this, for me, is hedged in obscurity.

Other mucahuas, callanas, some chicha and a bit of cooked food, and sometimes toys fashioned from wood or pottery are left for the huanushca aya. It is thought that the traveling soul returns to the grave of its corpse, and animals or insects seen there may be taken as a visitation. As nearly as I can determine, however, the movements of souls, the duality of souls of the dead, and other aspects of death are conceptualized as fundamental mysteries by the Canelos Quichua. They are not rigidified into dogmatic codes, and no simple exegesis can be easily elicited. People's own experiences through dreams and induced visionary experiences leave much of the relationship between the living and the dead idiosyncratic. The greatest reorganization occurring after the interment of a corpse takes place over the consolidated accusations of sorcery. People just don't normally believe that it is time for the deceased to go, and they search for, and reflect on, sources of killing power. To understand this process, and its relationship to kinship, it is necessary to examine shamanism and shaman hierarchies.

NOTES

1. Although the term *gumba* seems to derive from *compadre-comadre* (in trade Quichua it is often rendered *compa*), I see no particular reason to suppose that this dimension of social organization is taken from the *compadrazgo* system of Hispanic culture. "Ceremonial friendship" (*hikü-hiko*) as described by Irving Goldman (1963:130–133) for Cubeo culture in the Northwest Amazon is a clear illustration of the same indigenous institution among a tropical forest people.

2. This analysis, combined with the "bifurcate-merging" (Murdock 1949:142) nature of avuncular terminology, when presented in the most usual form given on pages 115–116, raises the question of whether or not there is evidence for prior terminological separation of parallel and cross-cousins. We have been able to find none at all in east Ecuadorian Quichua. There is no question but that the current system has been subjected to all sorts of pressures to change over the past few centuries. Unfortunately, in Quichua we have no clues as to what it transformed out of. In the Achuara Jivaroan language the Achuara men of the Copotaza-Capahuari rivers (who intermarry with the Canelos Quichua) class FZD or MBD as a potential marriage partner, provided the girl's father and the man's father have no classificatory sibling relationship. Parallel cousins, by contrast, are classed with sisters, and marriage prohibitions obtain between them. Following more field work with the Achuara and completion of Theodore Macdonald's work with the Quijos, a reconstruction of Canelos Quichua kinship and marriage is planned, setting this system in a context of intercultural exchanges involving Jívaro proper, Achuara, Zaparoan, Quijos Quichua, and Canelos Quichua.

3. The work of many anthropologists influenced my mode of analysis in this abbreviated discussion of the properties of Canelos Quichua kinship structure. It is entirely possible that none of these scholars will welcome such indebtedness, however, since each has gone his own way, sometimes in opposition to the others. In no way is this presentation intended to be deliberately eclectic. I see commonalities in approach made through certain distinctions in recent literature (itself based on earlier work), even though the overall approaches of those cited often proceed in quite different directions. Specifically, I am indebted to Meyer Fortes (e.g. 1969) for his extensive discussion of issues involved in employing the concepts of "descent" and "complementary filiation," and to Claude Lévi-Strauss (e.g. 1969) for the equally extensive treatment of elementary and complex structures, exchange, and reciprocity. Morton Fried (1957) most clearly set out concepts of stipulated and demonstrated descent. Ward Goodenough (1970) clarified the distinction between ego and ancestor orientation so well in his discussion of anthropological etics and emics that I hesitated at first to merge it here and there in my discussion. But *ancestor soul acquisition by ego and transfer of orientation point from ancestor to ego* necessitated my approach. I think that the Canelos Quichua system can be analyzed as a "parallel transmission of kin-class system," recently

explored and clarified by Harold Scheffler and Floyd Lounsbury (1971), from whose work I have learned a great deal. But again, insistence on *male transmission system–female transmission system mutual dependency, resuscitation, and recombination in each huasi context as the couple brings apayaya and apamama substance to their future continuity* demands sufficient attention in its own right and leads me for now to eschew elaboration of data relevant to their classification. Lowland and Andean kinship structures unquestionably share a commonality of form which crosses vastly different ecological systems, and presents anthropology with a system which still requires considerable work to portray adequately. It is hoped that this description of Canelos Quichua kinship and the next chapter on shamanism and kinship will clarify some issues in the literature, even though the data were collected in a time of rapid change.

4. Hartmann and Oberem (1968) give a full review of the distribution of the huairu in highland and lowland South America. I am especially indebted to Rudi Masaquisa, whose interest in this ethnography and in the distribution of Quichua culture throughout South America eventually provided the material necessary to clarify some issues with regard to the huairu (or huayru) of the Andes and Amazonia. He saw a couple of the canoes carved out of manioc which I had collected at a wake near Puyo, asked me about them, and listened to my tapes. He asked if there were comparative data and I showed him the material in Karsten (1935) and in the *Handbook of South American Indians* (vol. 5). Sometime later he gave me an old huairu bone supposedly made from the aya tullu of an ancient person. I took this back to my field site and was somewhat surprised to find that virtually everyone knew what it was and where it came from ("Salasaca pampa"), and began to explain much more about the nature of souls and why the Canelos Quichua do not use this kind of huairu. Among the Puyo Runa and among the Canelos and Sara Yacu Runa it was decided that this was the soul bone of a powerful shaman from Canelos killed a long time ago in Salasaca pampa.

5. Exegesis comes only in context—that is, in an actual wake setting, at night, while the wailing and gaming are going on. The wake itself is known by a combination of the Spanish word for wake, *velorio*, and the Quichua *pugllana*, a common phrase in Quichua being *viluribi pugllangahua raichi canuata, llambu, llambu: viluribi*—wake/, *pugllangahua*—let us play/, *raichi*—hunger/, *canuata*—canoe/, *llambu, llambu*—everyone, everyone. People will not discuss these events unless a death has occurred, their reason being that the huanushca aya will return.

5

Shamanism and Ayllu Regulation

Ayllu structure, as we have seen, is conceived of by the Canelos Quichua as a postulated network of linked souls extending back before Times of Destruction to Ancient Times. Through oral history and world view the Canelos Quichua impart demographic aspects to the different time periods, and relate them to ayllu structure and shamanism. In short, there were more ancient Runas than there are contemporary Runas and all of the ancient people had some knowledge which was lost during Times of Destruction. The totality of lost knowledge was considerable, but is not completely irretrievable. Those apayaya-apamama ancestors emerging from Times of Destruction were few in number. They intermarried among themselves to produce the living, and recently deceased, ancestors of the contemporary Runa, who have once again begun to expand their population.

The contemporary Runa ayllus (segmental, territorial, and maximal clans) exist as expanding, outward-ramifying consanguineal-affinal chains of linkage reckoned from contemporary shamans and from the shaman parents of contemporary old people. The shamans provide crucial linkages to the Ancient Times people through their acquisition of the ancients' souls. To become yachaj involves a developmental sequence of soul acquisition which reunites apayaya-apamama substance with the ancients' substances and at least partially regains knowledge lost in Times of Destruction. The process of shamanistic power quest also conjoins a Runa ayllu structure of partially controlled soul linkage with the world of the spirits.

In Ancient Times, unlike the present, people knew how to direct the movement of the huanushca aya so that it could be reborn. When the ancient people died their souls entered rocks and enduring logs, from which sources contemporary shamans acquire the living, encapsulated soul of the dead Runa ancestor. Souls of the ancients are also captured by such spirits as Amasanga and Sungui, and powerful shamans acquire these ancient souls directly from these spirits. When a contemporary Runa considers his own soul substance he must reflect on the ancient souls acquired by people in yaya, jachi, and apayaya kin classes, for souls of the same ancient substance form linkages to one another.

Many contemporary adult Canelos Quichua lack a yaya shaman; but none are without an apayaya shaman ancestor, and none are without one or more jachi soul possessors in the immediate ascending generation. In fact, recognition of shaman status for a man is signaled in the descending generation by an increasing number of men designating him as jachi. Even a man other than actual father (FB) previously classed as yaya by referential kin criteria becomes addressed as jachi when it is believed that his soul acquisition and mystical knowledge to cure and to kill is sufficient to regard him as a powerful shaman, *sinchi yachaj*. Because of postulated cousin marriage in Times of the Grandparents, every ego knows that many yachajs are related to him in the MB = FZH (jachi) kin class. Those whom ego calls jachi reciprocate the term *alaj*, my mythic brother. An asymmetrical system is established whereby a powerful shaman is regarded in both a consanguineal and affinal kin class of the first ascending generation; he, in turn, lateralizes his terminology to that of the ethnic "brother" for those who *call him* jachi. Use of the term alaj by a shaman for younger, less powerful men symbolizes a present reawakening of lost souls in ego's generation; and an expanding number of jachis, for any ego, in the ascending generation symbolizes the acquisition of past power acquired for contemporary ayllu and ethnic continuity.

A person is born with an inherited human soul, aya tullu, in his right shinbone. Since his father acquired some spirit helpers in the establishment of the huasi, and since there are always animal souls in the huasi, children also involuntarily acquire some spirit helpers at birth. These enter through the child's mouth and exist in the shungu area. The baby is *llullucu Runa*, an "unripe" jungle person. As he eventually toddles out toward the wider environment beyond the huasi and has firsthand encounters with the forest and river, he becomes *huahua*, child. To progress beyond the child stage, however, he must demonstrate some control over his own involuntarily acquired spirit helpers, and voluntarily acquire some additional spirit aid. As this is accomplished the child becomes *huambra*, youth.

Huambras seek to utilize mystical substance to complement their developing personality and knowledge, to help them embed themselves more fully in ayllu and ethnic structure, and to maintain flexibility and alternatives with regard to llacta responsibilities. They seek to avoid conflict with members of their own sex, and to make themselves attractive to members of the opposite sex. To do this they acquire various mystical substances, called *cuyachina yuyu* or *simayuca*, which they place in a chambira or similar pod, *misha puru*. The substances are well known to all men, women, and children. They include the brilliant blue wings and body of the *cantarica* beetle, a "secret" female substance called *yutu papa* (literally "quail potato," possibly a small, wild sweet potato), balls of hair from the stomach of the tapir, a cooked red achiote mixture, bark from the red *mindal* tree, and a leaf also yielding a red dye, *carahuira* (bark or husk of the wind), boa brain, fer-de-lance rattle, scrapings of porpoise tooth, dried and pulverized bat, brains and bones of several small birds, and fungus, *supai allpa*, which grows in a misha puru or mucahua buried in the ground with animal or plant substances inside.

misha puru (50% reduction)

Preparation of his special small pod of magical substances involves the huambra in discussions with older people about meaning and metaphor in substance preparation and power acquisition. He often must travel to distant areas, trade with people he does not know, and also learn more of the jungle environment. Substances and some articles from other peoples are readily incorporated into his mixture as the huambra tries to learn transcultural as well as intracultural secrets.

A small universe compatible with the youth's personality and conceptualized biosphere is alluded to as "growing" within the pod: tiny flowers open and bees buzz around as the whole thing "ferments" like chicha to produce a living spirit-helping universe close to the youth's own soul substances. As the huambra now begins to have special experiences which he relates to the created, voluntarily acquired, encapsulated spirit universe, he pays more attention to his dreams and discusses them with members of his household. Continuous dream interpretation draws data from daily life and mythic metaphor enriching both local culture and the unfolding Runa personality.

Small amounts of these substances are often used as invisible paint which the huambra puts on his face, arms, and torso, working with attractive

designs which he "feels" and which feeling is thought to be projected to
others. Spirit danger exists, though, for the youth could easily prove
himself too attractive to a supai, which might then lure him off into jungle,
soil, or river domain to live forever away from the Runa world. Youths also
collect bird and animal souls and make feather crowns and animal-skin
headdresses to maintain close contact with captured soul substances.
Beyond huambra status lie degrees of ability at self-protection from
generalized mystical danger, *paju* (illness not caused by a spirit dart), and
direct spirit attack, *shitashca* ("blown"—illness sent in the form of a spirit
dart). Powers to cure and project sickness separate the status of huambra
and yachaj.

The paju-shitashca contrast requires some further clarification at this
point. Generalized mystical danger is everywhere. Separation of the Runa
from the spirit world takes place through cognitive classification of the
known, but Runas are perfectly aware that illness has invisible, unfathom-
able causes. Sometimes medicines work, sometimes entreaties to spirits to
leave the body work, sometimes such remedies are useless. Direct spirit
attack is something else, for evil intent is imputed to a human or spirit
source. Anybody can, in anger and with little forethought, send forth pain
or illness in the form of a spirit dart. Such "blown" spirit helpers can often
be removed or returned to the sender with little difficulty. By contrast,
some spirit darts are very difficult to dislodge and do severe injury or cause
death; they are sent by powerful shamans, or spirits working through
powerful shamans. The developmental sequence of power acquisition
defines a categorical hierarchy of shamans which is directly related to ayllu
structure.

Huambras *must* reckon ayllu structure from father on back to FF and
FFW (FM). A yachaj reckons not only in this way but also outward from
himself. Ayllu bonds constitute a structure of protection in mystical space
from generalized mystical danger and from direct spirit attack. The latter
peril comes in the form of spirit darts or animal demons which zero in on a
shamanistic power source and follow intra-ayllu lines of increasing
vulnerability from shaman to huambra to huahua to llullucu.

Ordinary shamans protect themselves by reciprocating knowledge
across affinal linkages. For example, shaman A's sister is married to shaman
B and shaman A's wife's brother also becomes a shaman, C (see Diagram
5:1 below).

Diagram 5:1

By sharing knowledge and helping one another in shamanistic technique, ayllu (kindred) nodes A, B, and C will have overlapping protection against spirit penetration. The shamans are in a kin class of masha to one another, but *they change this class to huauqui to signal their combined shamanistic power-presence.* Ideally, each shaman will be gumba to the other as a transition from masha to huauqui. In two or three generations their descendants will regard one another as belonging to the same maximal ayllu, reckoned from any of the three shamanistic nodes. But such descendants also become more vulnerable to spirit attack because they share common stipulated descent from intermarried apayaya shamans. To understand such ayllu vulnerability as a complement to ayllu protection more information is needed on mystical danger and direct spirit attack. I turn first to the spirits themselves and ways by which Runa seek to control them, working upward in degrees of power from ordinary spirit helpers and ordinary Runa to spirit helpers with acquired human souls to the powerful shamans.

SPIRIT HELPERS AND THE SHAMAN

Small bees, *putan* or *bunga,* are the basic Amasanga spirit helpers. They are everywhere and their drone sound is a dream bringer. All Runa have some putan supais in their stomachs. These spirit helpers bring dreams, even to babies, and in a rudimentary way help a growing Runa to interpret his experiences in the visionary dream world. They also link male and female Runas to Amasanga and Nunghuí. Envy by one Runa of another may lead a person to mobilize his spirit helpers to do harm. In the very simplest form of this procedure a man merely places his hand over his mouth in the same way as he covers the blowgun mouthpiece when he blows a dart, takes aim at the person he wishes to harm, and blows.

A spirit helper leaves his throat and speeds toward the victim. It may hit him and lodge in his skin. But more likely it is seen by shamans, caught, and returned in the form of a chonta spirit dart, a *supai biruti.* The returned dart lodges in the caster and must then be removed by a shaman. Such a cure is accompanied by a lesson as the shaman chastizes the thrower for his envy and indicates the supai helper duality in envy maintenance—the dart which may harm another can equally hurt the sender. Sent supais do harm, but their targets are often not the desired one.

Once a Runa has undergone a Datura experience with Amasanga he understands more thoroughly the nature of the spirit helper world. He knows that envy is an inevitability of human life, and that he must protect himself and his huasi members. He sets about gaining more information about general mystical danger which exists as a result of the spirit world's interpenetration of Runa bodies, and specific spirit attack coming from directed spirit darts.

A common exposure to mystical danger is called *huaira*, wind, which is today related to the Spanish *mal aire* (evil air) by the Puyo Runa and Canelos Runa. Children with the common ailments of vomiting, diarrhea, and mild fevers can be cured without the aid of hallucinogens, provided the illness is caused by mild skin penetration of spirit substances intending no ill will. The specifics of such curing vary considerably, but the fundamental principle involves a tobacco-smoke cleansing of the back of the child from head to foot. Smoke is blown on the child's back, and moved down the child's body with a leaf or leaf bundle. Then the front of the child is cleansed with warm ashes from a fresh fire stoked up to light the tobacco cigar. When the child's front has been all rubbed downward with ash the curer fills his/her mouth with water dipped with a calabash shell and blows it on the fire to extinguish it. The child is then symbolically cleansed with the remaining water.

When the parents are unable to cure their child in this way they seek more medicines in the forest and try them. Should such herbal preparations fail, direct spirit attack is immediately suspected, and they must either try to counteract the attack, or visit a yachaj or sinchi yachaj. Such visitations are costly in goods and often time, so most adult men, and some women, set about increasing their own system of spirit counterattack.

The first line of protection from direct spirit attack is the acquisition of more spirit helpers. These are *yachaj sami tsintsaca*, shaman's magical darts.[1] Such darts are purchased for 100 sucres (U.S. $4.00) each, or for a material item worth this amount of money. Purchase is from one's father or grandfather, if he is a shaman, but preferably from a classificatory (MB-FZH) jachi. Such purchased spirit darts include living chonta splinter, small frog, living hair, small snake, stinging caterpillar, spider, *machaca* moth, blood-sucking insects, bees, stinging ants, chonta soul stone, and also sentient scissors and Gillette razor blades.

The buyer—a hausi founder—studies a bit with the shaman, gaining instruction in the nature of mystical substance, human envy, and motivation for harm. Then both drink ayahuasca; the shaman calls Amasanga in the form of two black jaguars and Sungui (or Yacu mama) in the form of two anacondas, and, with their help and knowledge, a shaman's spirit helper dart is coughed up by the shaman from his own stomach. The spirit moves around in the shaman's hand, proving its viability, and then the buyer takes it and swallows it. Spirit helpers are accumulated in this way for several years, while the huasi founder continues to receive instruction from the shaman. The buyer must refrain from bringing these spirit helpers up out of his stomach. His spirit helpers become increasingly accustomed to the Runa's personality and soul substance, and help him understand the nature of illness and curing. A person may keep these spirit helpers for a lifetime. They protect him from generalized mystical danger and often from direct spirit attack. But eventually most collectors move into a novice yachaj class.

To do this a Runa spirit-buyer studies more intensively with a shaman in either yaya-apayaya kin class or jachi kin class. Then the aspirant shaman spends an interval fasting. He eats only plantains and drinks a brew of mashed fresh small bananas and tobacco water called *yapishca palanda*. He must eat no salt, capsicum, manioc, drink no chicha, and refrain from sexual intercourse. There are also secret prohibitions imposed by the selling shaman if he really wants the Runa to become yachaj. If he wishes his client to fail, he may omit a prohibition and the man's shaman spirit helpers will return to the shaman when they are invoked by the buyer. At the end of the fast period, which may last weeks or months, the aspiring Runa takes a good big dose of yapishca palanda, sleeps, and the supais inside him all come up and out, not only in bee form but now as tsintsacas ready to be blown as chonta spirit darts against enemies. If the Runa can, at this point, refrain from the almost overwhelming temptation to blow these darts out against enemies and can simply re-swallow them, he becomes a curing shaman, well imbued with proper knowledge gained through instruction from the selling shaman. He is now *cusca yachaj*. Should he begin blowing darts around, as many do, he is *yanga yachaj*, meaning basically that he is untrained, uncontrolled.

A cusca yachaj cannot be injured by the approaching spirit darts of a yanga yachaj, for his spirit helpers see the incoming dart and rush to the site of penetration to form a hard, impenetrable callus. The incoming dart glances off and wings along the man's ayllu structure until it penetrates a huasi, and there it goes into a more vulnerable body of baby or youth. With the aid of spirit helpers and information gained from Amasanga, most huasi founders, whether or not they are cusca yachaj, can remove or deflect such unwanted spirit darts sent by envious, untrained yanga yachajs. The supais go back to the shaman who sold them to the blower, and in this way the shaman knows that one of his clients has not only forgotten or ignored his lessons but has also lost his spirit helpers.

The relationship between sickness, envy, and ayllu structure now begins to emerge. Illness which cannot be cured by body cleansing, herbal remedies, or simple entreaties to the spirits is regarded as the result of direct spirit attack. Normally such spirit attack is the result of malign intent on the part of a yanga yachaj who sent spirit darts toward an enemy. The darts often cannot penetrate the enemy and so lodge in a more vulnerable person in the targeted person's ayllu. Sent darts follow ayllu lines to the victim's huasi, and if they don't find a vulnerable person in that huasi, or if the resident supais drive them out, they move back into the ayllu structure and zoom toward another huasi until a vulnerable person is hit. Obviously, given such a spirit propensity for attack within the ayllu of the victim, people refrain from blowing darts at their own ayllu members. A spirit gone wild within one's own ayllu, having glanced off the intended victim, is a terrible thing. No one in his right mind would want a caroming supai biruti loose in his ayllu, heading toward nearby huasis with vulnerable members. The most obvious targets would be the sender's own children.

ANCIENT SOULS, SPIRIT HELPERS, AND POWERFUL SHAMANS

To understand ayllu foci and the larger range of shamanistic power it is necessary first to understand the means by which ancient shamans saw to their own perpetuation. These shamans had two abilities. One was the art of *sumi*[2]—the ability to change one's own body into that of an animal. Ancient shamans could change themselves into a jaguar at will and travel as a cousin of the supai puma, which is the flesh representation of Amasanga. The other art was that of soul projection into an everlasting stone, large rock, or indestructible tree trunk (sometimes into a stone itself embedded in a tree trunk). Such a stone with a bottled-up living human shaman soul inside usually occurs in the shape of a polished axe head. Other ancient shamans could acquire the soul power and soul substance of deceased shamans by drinking a preparation from a secret substance called *puma yuyu* or *puma tucuna*, jaguar succession. The acquisition of the second shaman soul allowed the taker to practice sumi, and when he died to project his own soul into a soul stone, where he could later accompany yet another shaman who had gained the knowledge to awaken the soul in the stone.

On the death of a shaman with an acquired second shaman's soul, the deceased places his own soul in a stone, and the ancient acquired soul is released. Such a released soul, still a powerful ancient shaman, enters the body of an owl or harpy eagle, *apapa*. All owls and eagles are ancient souls.[3] On the death of the apapa the ancient shaman's soul is transformed into a special polished shaman's stone, shaped like the drawing below. Those fortunate enough to acquire such a yachaj rumi place it on top of an aya rumi, using the soul stone as bancu for the shaman's stone. One bottled-up ancient soul then transmits its power through another bottled-up soul at the bidding of a contemporary shaman.

At a time of expanding populations and large ayllus there were enough shamans to assure continuity of all of the dead shamans' souls, and the ayllus were bound by multiple linkages through the dead souls to Ancient Times. But during Times of Destruction, when population declined, the

Runas were moved all over Upper Amazonia, stones became lost, and many of them changed their form and location. This occurred when the shaman transformed his enclosure of rock, called *tutu*, bud, into a tulumba toad and hopped off seeking living shamans. Such movement and loss of living souls of dead shamans created an enormous power pool in Canelos Quichua territory and beyond, due to the surplus shaman power which came about as the souls of the deceased outnumbered the living.

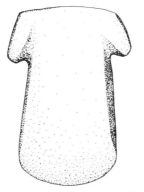

yachaj rumi
(50% reduction)

aya rumi (50% reduction)

In Times of the Grandparents shamans collected various soul and shaman stones, drank huanduj, consulted Amasanga, and in many cases successfully learned how to build compatability between themselves and their many ancient shaman soul helpers. Among other things, they learned that at death souls of ordinary people go first into the underworld or sky world, and then return as directed by spirits to enter animals and birds. Many animals and birds, themselves spirits, *have an acquired human soul*. The increasingly wise grandparental shamans drank ayahuasca, smoked and drank tobacco, and learned to acquire, command, and control the spirits with acquired human souls; they became sinchi yachajs.

In this learning period the grandparental shamans had to leave their territory and seek out foreign shamans in the high Andes and in deeper Amazonia, where remnants of information necessary to work within the Canelos Quichua power source still existed. That shaman who successfully maneuvered in the spirit world with the help of ancient shaman souls, and with the support of territorial and foreign spirits, studied even more, underwent various trials and ordeals, and rose to a position where he himself could become a living stool for certain spirits. Such a bancu, with the mediation of Ayahuasca mama, could allow Amasanga or other spirit masters to speak directly through the shaman's mouth.

The bancu often sought to perpetuate his special abilities by projecting

Sinchi yachaj.

an ancient shaman's soul from his own ayllu into a son or grandson of his ayllu. He also asked a shaman colleague in a gumba relationship, and of the kin class WB, MB, FZH, or FFWBS, to impart a complementary ancient soul. Because of this procedure some children, youths, and adults have a pair of imparted ancient souls and an involuntarily acquired proclivity to become a powerful shaman or bancu.

Contemporary powerful shamans do not ordinarily send mere spirit darts at adversaries. They send spirits with living souls of dead humans winging at victims. Whenever a powerful shaman dies it is due to the projection of such supais by another powerful shaman. A common powerful shaman spirit dart is the *cuchapitiuri biruti*, lagoon toucan dart, which comes out of the female water domain at the command of the shaman, flies overhead making a high-pitched *quich huiaj* sound, and zeroes in on the enemy shaman like a powerful chonta projectile fired at close range by a silent gun. Another such projectile is a lightning dart. But the recipient shaman is usually able to muster his resident souls and spirits to create an iron shield at the point of entry, and the toucan or lightning spirit dart glances off and continues to follow ayllu lines into a vulnerable person (anyone not a powerful shaman) in the same or a nearby huasi. When people within the ayllu of a powerful shaman begin to suffer great pain, and to die, it is due to an evil dart or a directed spirit possession sent by a powerful shaman. Even though being a member of an ayllu with powerful shaman ancestors and contemporaries is dangerous, it is necessary because inter-shaman feuds begun generations ago continue, due to the desire for revenge not only among the contemporary members of depleted ayllus but among the living souls of the dead, who (as spirit helpers) may eventually rejoin powerful shamans who are at war with the descendants of their enemies.

A powerful shaman who has drunk puma yuyu and learned the art of sumi studies for years with other shamans, communicates with powerful spirits through Datura quests, and collects an array of soul stones of various colors. Eventually he establishes a pact, *pactashca*, with the supai of a particular llacta. He first blows a spirit dart into a large rock or tree, creating a depression or bowl. The dart may even be a lightning bolt. Then he mixes Datura in the depression, drinks it, and visits Amasanga to receive permission for the power to make pacts with other supais. Amasanga again calls the underworld shaman, and he in turn examines the aspirant's motivation. Now the successful powerful shaman sees his way to incorporation of great power through the female water domain spirit master, Sungui huarmi or Yacu mama, and the foreign soul master, Juri juri, in both male and female manifestations. He perceives Amasanga and Juri juri as the *same* huanduj supai, dispenses with the Juri juri's territoriality, and merges him with Amasanga as forest soul master spirit helper. He becomes not only sinchi yachaj but llacta founder. The stone or tree site where such llacta foundation takes place is sacred to the Canelos Quichua. From the time of the shamanistic founding of such an area ayllu members defend their rights to the llacta against all adversaries, and come to stand in a position of higher rank (in their own eyes) than their in-married affines who are members of other ayllus.

Frequently more than one powerful shaman lays claim to the same llacta near the trade locus of a Runa territory. The children of such powerful shamans are often intermarried, and the shamans often cooperate. Sometimes, however, power acquisition results in enemy shamans occupying the same or adjacent territories, and the spirit darts wing back and forth in shamanistic death duels. Such duels tend to bring considerable destruction of life, and the ayllu segments move off to hidden purina chagras for a time, to allow the central territory to "cool off."

Shamans themselves, if sufficiently powerful, continue their vendettas and attempts to kill adversaries over long distances. For example, one may project his own soul into that of a harpy eagle, transform its appearance, take over its ancient shaman soul, and fly toward the enemy shaman. Here is an actual account of such an attack witnessed by a dozen people.

APAPA ATTACK

One night powerful shaman Orlando, possessor of a jaguar soul and founder of a llacta among the Puyo Runa, was sleeping with his wife in a well-fortified house. There were chonta stakes all around the oval house, but a small window-like space only a foot wide and a foot and a half deep existed at the far end. In through that space came a great owl. The apapa had to turn sideways and fold its wings to get through the space. It came right at Orlando, who immediately awakened, having seen the apapa coming in his dream. He grabbed a chonta stick, one of many which he kept lying around for this purpose, and swung at the apapa. *Whack!* he hit it. Still it came on. *Whack, wham!* He swung and swung and broke its wing. Then the apapa grew larger and tried to envelop him with the other wing. By now not only Orlando's household members but also those of adjacent houses had arrived to watch the duel. It took Orlando an hour to kill the apapa, which was, in fact, a bancu shaman from Sara Yacu. While Orlando fought the apapa containing the shaman's soul, his former wife's brother living in Sara Yacu sent toucan and lightning projectiles directly at the shaman's body. Together they killed the bancu, and Orlando kept his soul captive as an apapa spirit helper.

The next day he signaled acquisition of the bancu's soul. To do this Orlando skinned and mounted the apapa on a cross, put it upright in a balsa raft, and floated it down the Pinduj River.

After telling me this story the sons, daughters, and in-laws of the shaman explained that attack of one shaman by another when in sumi transformation was the ultimate deciding factor in a long-standing feud. One or the other shaman must die, and the victor acquires the loser's soul, which itself is an acquired soul from Ancient Times shamans.

Awareness of the relationships described above becomes most clearly presented through group shamanistic sessions where participants drink ayahuasca.

AYAHUASCA VISIONARY EXPERIENCE

Ayahuasca mama, the serpentine vine spirit, and the "orphan female" spirit Yaji allow shamans and powerful shamans to maneuver in the domain of spirits. Where Datura allows any Runa to collapse space and time and see *all* the spirits, Ayahuasca mama, herself a spirit *of* the huanduj, provides the necessary linkage to spirits which have acquired human souls. Through the mediation of the souls acquired by spirits, the shaman, through his acquired souls, is able to converse with selected spirits. The more familiar he becomes with the spirits through their souls, the more proficient he becomes in using their powers without harm to himself. Powerful shamans must learn to control spirits well beyond Amasanga'a domain.

Ayahuasca Preparation

The soul vine is cut and yaji leaves gathered before dawn, either by the man who will take it or by one designated by the shaman. About eighteen nine-inch vine segments and twelve to twenty yaji leaves are placed in the kitchen, and the cutter rests, dreaming and thinking, in the center of his house. Sometime around 9:00 A.M. a girl messenger comes from the shaman, confirming that a drinking session will be held in the evening, and the man drowsily remains in his bed or hammock for another hour or so. Then he cuts wood and prepares the base for the fire at the east end of the house. He rasps the outside of each vine strip to get rid of bark that is "too strong," splits and twists six or seven strips, and places them in a four-gallon cooking pot. He repeats the process until all eighteen strips of ayahuasca are in the pot. He arranges the firewood logs, places chonta sticks in the center, and starts the fire. Then, with the advice of any youths or children in the room, usually including his own son and the shaman's daughter, he puts in about nine yaji leaves, evenly distributing them around the split ayahuasca vine strips. Next he blows tobacco smoke all around the pot to clean off any unwanted spirit substances that might have entered with the ayahuasca spirit. He whistles a secret song which has come to him from Amasanga, then fills the pot three-quarters full with cool, fresh water. He places the pot over the fire and sits down to watch it cook.

The shaman's daughter or cooker's daughter brings the man a bite or two of plantain, which is all he can eat until the ayahuasca is ready for use.

In two and a half hours the cooker removes the pot, takes the stems and leaves out, and gently arranges them into a wreath on the north or south side of the room. Then he puts the pot back on, adds more chonta sticks, and begins to simmer off the rest of the water. In a little over three hours from the time when cooking began there is only a cup of dark brown fluid left, and everyone in the room—cooker and children—watch closely, commenting every ten seconds, until within a minute or two all agree that the ayahuasca is ready. The cooker takes the pot off the fire and places it within the wreath of cooked vine segments and leaves.

The ayahuasca is now ready to drink. The cooker's wife enters the kitchen to prepare food, and the cooker eats a normal meal and goes about other work until around 5:00 P.M., at which time he prepares himself for ayahuasca visionary experience. He rests, sleeps a bit, dreams and reflects on himself, his household, his life, and his ties to other times and other places. He puts himself in a peaceful frame of mind; friendship and love for his fellow Runas engulf him.

Ayahuasca Curing[4]

An ayahuasca-curing session with a powerful shaman is conducted when a person suspects that spirit darts have entered his body. The symptoms are normally the sudden onset of sharp stomach pains and the inability of the person to cure himself through herbal remedies, but any illness may be attributed to penetration of unwanted spirit substances.

People who will accompany a shaman on his ayahuasca experience with various spirits gather in the jatun huasi before or just after dark, together with others who will not participate. Conversation among all reflects a mood of friendship and warmth; political, economic, or social problems may be discussed, but everyone avoids raising the talk to a level reflecting anger, envy, or hostility. The shaman has been sleeping. He awakens, talks to the various people, drinks some chicha, has his daughter receive and "guard" the ayahuasca brought by the cooker, and often returns to sleep a bit more. At 8:00 he returns and indicates that it is time to drink ayahuasca.

All women who do not have a specific role in the curing session leave, but men are free to stay and take ayahuasca if they want to, or simply to observe. The session is held either in the center of the shaman's house or in the center of his ichilla huasi if he has more than one structure. Two women assist the shaman. They are either the shaman's wife and daughter, or the shaman's wife and the wife or mother of the principal person to be cured. The women prepare eight-inch cigars and tobacco water from *runa tahuacu,* human tobacco (also called *sacha tahuacu,* jungle tobacco). Tobacco prepared by women is necessary for cleansing objects and people of surface supai substance, and for clarification of the shaman's vision in searching for magical darts and in understanding their true spirit form and origin.

Women sit just behind the centrally placed shaman, around a very low-burning fire; men gather around the other side of the shaman, leaving a long boa bancu between them and in front of the shaman as a seat or bed for the person to be cured. The shaman sits on his turtle or cayman stool. Crucial to such a curing session is cooperation of the spirits of the water domain, the yacu supais.

The shaman's principal female helper pours two ounces of ayahuasca from the delivery pot into a small calabash shell, *ayahuasca puru,* and hands it to the shaman. He checks its volume and may ask for more or pour some back into the pot. He blows tobacco smoke into the drinking bowl, whistles his special shaman's tune while thinking the words, and drinks it all. The woman hands him a calabash of tea-like huayusa in another calabash shell, *huayusa puru,* with which he gargles. The woman then gives him another dose of ayahuasca, which he cleanses, whistling his song, and then he passes it on to the person to be cured, if the person is a man. He offers ayahuasca to all men present, and the strong preference of all drinkers is that all men in the session drink. Such drinking is not a requirement, however, and even patients sometimes decline the soul brew.

While the shaman is passing ayahuasca around, the two women helpers drink runa tahuacu water through their noses, to clarify their own visions prior to the entry of the yacu supai. As the ayahuasca begins to take effect the men continue talking about various things, maintaining the exact level of conversation established earlier before the session began. They do this as the earth trembles and as a great waterfall, *jatun paccha,* comes down around the house.

If there are evil substances in the shungus of the takers, or if they are harboring envy and the desire to blow out their resident supais, illness will overwhelm them and they will leave the room to vomit. But the Canelos Quichua generally search themselves during pre-session dreams and so feel only a bit of nausea, interpreted as latent evil, which, revealed to the shaman, is coaxed out of them. In fact, although I have attended many ayahuasca sessions, I have yet to see a Canelos Quichua become physically ill during this early period of adjustment to the effects of the drug.

By the end of about twenty minutes all the drinkers hear the waterfall and know that it is "ancient," *rucu paccha.* They know that supais are entering, and that the water, soil, and jungle domains are merging within the shaman's huasi. They continue to talk about mundane aspects of their own lives in the presence of the supais, themselves with acquired Runa souls. As the spirits begin to appear as visions, each drinking Runa identifies what he sees; the shaman and the women confirm or correct his vision, and the shaman keeps the Runa from fearing it. First come two boas which the shaman sees as jatun amarun, giant boas, and the women tell him are Yacu mama. The women softly assert, *Yana amarun runa mani,* "black anaconda is a person." Then the shaman sees two giant black jaguars which he identifies as sinchi yachaj.

The men become more and more drowsy, yawn extensively, laugh gently, as the women continue to make cigars. At the end of about half an hour most of the men have urinated once or twice outside the house and have settled down with the giant boas and jaguars in a domain-merged shaman huasi universe to view inner substances and to travel to far places. The shaman's job now is to concentrate on what is wrong with the victim, but other men are free to travel in the spirit world to the limits of their capabilities. They must take care that they do not get themselves so far under a river or under a hill that the resident supai will keep them there.

The shaman takes his first cigar from his wife, blows smoke around the room, whistles his taquina song, and calls his spirit helpers, who come in the form of bees, butterflies, fireflies, and sparks. Sometimes he plays a musical bow, or violin, to call them. Unlike a huanduj experience, only those called by the shaman come, and he knows each of them. They are all huanduj ayas, the same ones that come to the flowering of the Datura blossom. While whistling he thinks the words, "Datura is flowering and wants its bees." As the spirit helpers come the shaman tells his daughter to bring him the curing leaf bundle, *shingui shingu panga.* This low-growing palm leaf gets its name from the ancient spirit shaman, *shingu shingu puma*—a medium-sized black jungle cat. The shaman cleanses the bundle by blowing tobacco smoke over and through it. He then begins to shake it, whistles another song to himself, *huanduj supai runa mani,* and begins to "see" as Amasanga sees, through the help of the Datura spirits. Then he sings a third song to himself, again with his own special tune. As he shakes the bundle the tips of the leaves become flickering snake tongues, each with three tips. The snake tongues signal the existence of hidden *jambi,* medicine-poison, within the bundle. He calls on Ayahuasca mama to bring Yacu mama to him as amarun runa, boa person. The boa (or anaconda) comes, examines his shungu, and decides that it and its contents are good, *alli.* Should the boa find evil, *manalli,* he would immediately make the shaman vomit; then the evil would have to be examined and disposed of by the river spirits before curing could take place.

Once the shaman has "opened" like a huanduj flower and gained the perception of Amasanga and the curative power of Yacu mama, he is ready to deal directly with the supai world and to cure the victim of supai penetration.

The patient removes his clothes, is covered with a sheet or blanket, and the shaman shakes the leaf bundle all over the patient's body, from head to feet. He never uncovers, views, or cleanses the genitals. He then blows tobacco over the entire body to cleanse it of accidentally accumulated supai substance. He begins to chant a song, keeping the words bottled up in his throat, so only he and the supais can hear it. After a verse or two he opens his sounds, so that all know what he is singing. With the power of the amarun runa behind him he sings to the Juri juri and to distant powerful shamans to call back their supai helpers. He tells the Juri juri and foreign shamans that their spirit helpers have inadvertently lodged in the body of a "poor, defenseless, baby" Runa. He says that the Runa has done no harm and has been struck by darts not meant for him or for his ayllu, and he sends pleas to all the powerful shamans, including spirit shamans, to call back their helpers. After about half an hour of such sung entreaties to distant shamans, the curer stops singing and shaking the leaf bundle, and then blows tobacco steadily on the body, first the front and then the back. He picks up some substances which only he can see, puts them in the leaves, goes to the wall of his house, pushes aside the chonta poles, and shakes them out into the air. He has picked up spirit helpers being called by their masters, and he flings them back into the air beyond the huasi so that they can return from whence they came.

He has cured the victim from exposure to generalized mystical danger (paju)—from harm caused by spirits accidentally lodged in his body. Now the shaman must concentrate on the results of direct spirit attack—supai birutis or tsintsacas which are lodged in the victim's body as a result of directed (shitashca) spirit helpers sent by a hostile shaman.

The shaman's wife hands him a bowl of runa tahuacu water which the shaman drinks through his nose. He then takes a fresh cigar from his daughter, lights it, and blows smoke on the victim. The embedded darts appear in their real form—poisonous snake, lizard, spider, water toucan, machaca moth, ball of hair, black stone, or any of dozens of other supai manifestations. He may also drink another dose of ayahuasca at this time, after which he waits about half an hour more for the visions to come, and repeats the songs to the bee-like spirit helpers, Amasanga, and the boa people.

He indicates the position and form of the lodged supais to members of the session, and with his help those taking ayahuasca see them as glowing a brilliant blue under the skin, in the stomach, or in a vein or artery. Those who perceive suck in their breaths, *ahhh*, and wonder who would send such evil toward such a good Runa.

The shaman drinks tobacco water again, blows smoke on the area, and leans over an enlodged supai. He places his mouth completely over the area, and his own spirit helpers come up into his mouth to help him. He sucks noisily and the supai is removed from the victim and taken down into his own stomach for identification by his spirit helpers. Then the shaman places both hands on his head and vomits the foreign spirit up into his own mouth; he *retains its own acquired human soul*. He then moves to the side of the house, pushes the chonta stakes aside, and blows the spirit dart with a *shuuuj* sound outward toward its ayllu of origin. He repeats this process for half an hour to an hour until all supai birutis are removed. Sometimes he blows the removed spirit dart into a tree outside his house, rather than sending it back as a warning to the originating shaman.

This process of sucking, swallowing, regurgitating, and blowing away the spirit while retaining its soul may end the curing session. After the victim is cleansed with tobacco smoke the shaman cleanses all of his attendant sons, and then his wife and daughter, any other female helpers, and any participating or observing members of the victim's family. In such a session winging the darts back to the sender's ayllu is considered to be a fair warning to beware of careless spirit dart blowing. But occasionally, when the shaman thinks he himself is under direct attack, the attack source must be identified and a counterattack launched.

On such occasions he drinks more tobacco water and sings a different song, called *pasuca*,[5] in which he calls the Juri juri from various territories in three feminine forms: Urcu supai huarmi, Juri juri huarmi, and Amasanga huarmi; they come to him separately but merge again as a single powerful, evil spirit. The ground under the house trembles, and as the shaman sings the pasuca, these huanduj huarmis take possession of him. He stops singing and speaks the spirit's animal cough—the very Juri juri sound which so terrifies hunters when they are in a distant hunting territory. Under possession of the powerful spirit an ancient human soul possessed by the spirit is blown with a loud *shuuuj* toward the ayllu of the enemy shaman. Death will result in the targeted ayllu, and the targeted shaman, together with acquired ancient souls of his ayllu, will rapidly learn the source of such redirected spirit attack. In these killing vendettas, which go on for generations, ayllu structure both merges and splits apart. No person can claim ayllu membership with both sides of a pair of warring shamans or with their stipulated ancestors, for to do so would be to become vulnerable to the directed supais of both sides.

The shaman performing a pasuca spirit-killing may call on any powerful spirit master of a particular domain with whom he has made a pact. The spirit always comes as one of two or three manifestations in female form. The most powerful shamans call distant lagoon, whirlpool, river, and even ocean shaman spirits—each the possessor of many human soul helpers. Eventually, as the shaman acquires more and more ability through pacts with powerful supais, he becomes the dreaded bancu—stool of the spirit shamans. Such shamans are frequently, if not always, possessed by spirits, or by the enduring souls of dead humans living in the spirits themselves. These shamans come to embody the inexhaustible power source of the ancient shamans, for they are always able to replenish their supply of spirit helpers and ancient shaman soul helpers through direct power acquisition from the spirits themselves. But bancu status is so dangerous to the rest of the Canelos Quichua that powerful shamans set about killing members of the bancu's immediate family by sending spirit darts and malign supais and by the commissioning of the Jívaro proper and Achuara "powerful assassin," the huanchij.[6] Alliance with non–Canelos Quichua becomes crucial in the maintenance of life for those descended from bancu shamans.

After the pasuca the shaman continues to shake his leaf bundle, examines all members of his family for unwanted spirit substances, sucks out spirit darts that may have entered during the rather hair-raising pasuca ritual, when Runa shaman and supai huarmi power merge, and then cleanses the entire room of unwanted spirits. People leave and go to sleep, seeing the pair of great boas coiling this way and that and the pair of black jaguars rubbing against them as they dream away the night.

In the morning the domain-structured natural world exists for the viewer together with a movie-like replay from time to time of the jaguars, boas, and other scenes from the night before. Bathing in a cool river helps restore the Runa body to its normal state, though twenty-four or more hours must pass before the heavy hangover effect disappears.

AYLLU STRUCTURE AND SHAMANISM

Several points emerge from this discussion which underscore the role of shamanism in the continuity of ayllu structure. First, powerful shamans acquire souls from grandparental shamans who themselves had acquired souls from the ancient people. Only they know, for sure, what souls they acquire, and their outward flow of information to acknowledged ayllu and alter ayllu members varies. Second, shamans directly acquire ancient shaman souls, thereby providing symbolic continuity through Times of Destruction—through stipulated descent and demonstrated filiation.

Third, powerful shamans provide mechanisms for unifying and separating, expanding and contracting ayllu space according to criteria of soul power acquisition, defense from mystical danger and directed spirit attack, and the ability to counterattack.

Shamans also signal cooperation by transforming affinal to consanguineal status within a set of mystical cooperators. They commonly span ZH and WB masha statuses with the shaman kin class huauqui, as shown in Diagram 5:2 below.

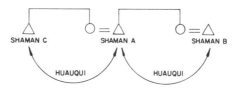

Diagram 5:2

Shamans A, B, and C, each of whom is in the kin class masha with relation to one another, call each other huauqui to cement their mutual protection pact. Then, recall another phenomenon introduced at the beginning of this chapter, illustrated by Diagram 5:3 below.

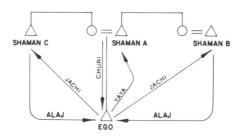

Diagram 5:3

Ego places shamans B and C in kin class jachi, distinguishing the MB = FZH class as ayllu nodes distinct from yaya, his own ayllu node. Shamans B and C reciprocate alaj to ego, classifying him as "mythic brother." In the next generation, as ego 1 transmits information on shaman nodes and ayllu structure to his offspring (ego 2), we find the situation illustrated in Diagram 5:4 below.

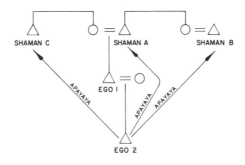

Diagram 5:4

The shamans are all apayaya from Times of the Grandparents, and regarded as power extensions of primary (male ego FF) apayaya shaman
power. From the shamans' perspective such male grandchildren are only
potential ayllu members. Incorporation into shaman ayllus will depend on
factors of soul acquisition by the shamans' children and the children's
children. By employing the MB = FZH kin class equation from the reference point of his own father (ego 1), ego 2 may combine grandparental
nodes B and C as an apayaya node parallel to FF, necessitating a classificatory apamama affinal connection (FFWB or FFZH). The resulting structure can then be portrayed as in Diagram 5:5 below.

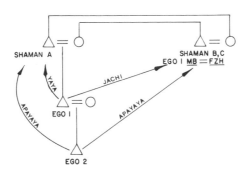

Diagram 5:5

Shaman status B, C, now one referential position in ayllu space, becomes
part of a dual apical structure from which ego 2 reckons descent. Recalling
our discussion at the end of Chapter 2 and in Chapter 4, we know that ego

also seeks a wife classifiable as transmitting apamama substance from Times
of the Grandparents. Considering shaman status in the domain of kinship
offers multiple possibilities for the consideration of primary apayaya and
apamama statuses. Let us again consider Diagram 4:10, but with shaman
nodes added, in Diagram 5:6.

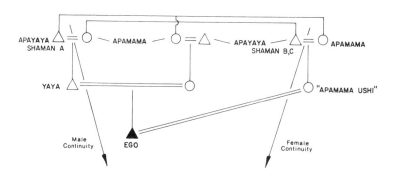

Diagram 5:6

In this illustration ego figures a patri-transmission node as shaman A and
a matri-transmission node as shaman B, C, an apamama affine. He marries
so as to include in his own offspring the continuity of his own patri- and
matri-inherited substances. What is crucial is the idiom of parallel
transmission of shaman status and the role of marriage in uniting or
recombining stipulated ancestral nodes of ayllu structure with imputed
acquired power. When ego actually acquires power from the deceased
shamans in the apayaya-apamama generations (if he moves into shaman
status), he may change his name and further manipulate his ayllu
membership so as to shift his descent position. This becomes necessary at
times due to the inter-ayllu vendettas discussed above. For example, in
Diagram 5:6, should stipulated powerful shaman descendants of shaman
A's ayllu begin a killing feud with shaman B, C's ayllu, then fission of all
people between the A and B, C lines would take place, with people
acknowledging membership to one or the other but not both. Or, should
categorized B, C statuses come to be composed of actual shamans dueling
with one another, either B or C would remain as apayaya, but the other
would be denied such apayaya position. With some resolution of such a
duel, however, merger may again take place. Resolution is particularly
likely with the Canelos Quichua when the people as a whole, or a major
segment of a Runa territory, is faced with severe external pressures.

NOTES

1. The term *tsintsaca* derives from the Jivaroan word *tsentsak* (Harner 1972:118–125, 154–166). The Canelos Quichua and Jívaro proper concepts, so many of which are similar (those of spirit darts, Sungui [Tsungi], the bancu, etc.) should be compared, I think, as variations in a belief-system transformation set, and also as ethnic complementarities across actual geo-ethnic territorial markers. Completion of such a comparison demands information from Achuara, Zaparoan, and Quijos Quichua concepts, which also seem to form comparable cognitive structures and geo-ethnic, socio-mystical systems.

2. *Sumi* is not a Quichua word. It should not be confused with the Quichua term *suma*, pretty. *Sumi* as the Canelos Quichua use it may derive from the Tupian term and concept *sumé* (e.g. Métraux 1948:702–703).

3. I think that *apa*, as in *apayaya*, derives from *apapa*, the *pa* being a bound morph expressing emphasis. Should this be the case, the grandparental prefix *apa* would represent the ancient soul, just as *yaya* derives from *aya*. But Achuara, Zaparoan, and Jívaro proper also use the prefix *apa*, and I don't want to go beyond the possibilities of mutual existence of a morph within a broad inter-language transformation group and attempt to derive it from only one language of the group, especially when two of the three languages are as yet linguistically unclassified.

4. In this section I am considering the case of a powerful shaman conducting an ayahuasca session. Lesser shamans can proceed only to identification of the darts, and can loosen them to bring relief to the victim.

5. *Pasuca* derives from the Jivaroan *pasuk*. Comparable data for the Jívaro proper are given by Harner (1972:158–159, 163–164).

6. *Huanchij* in Quichua is the same as *kakaram* (*kakarma*) in Jívaro proper. For a full discussion of these Jívaro proper "powerful ones" see Harner (1972). The same term is employed by the Achuara, but the complex varies somewhat from that of the Jívaro proper. The status of huanchij itself does not now, to my knowledge, exist among the Canelos Quichua, and those occupying such a position some twenty years ago were all, as far as I know, bicultural Achuara–Canelos Quichua people.

CHAPTER

6
Ritual Structure

A ritual context—a setting in which stylized behavior takes place—is often established by a man within his own huasi. In its simplest form this basic huasi ritual brings power to the individual and household. While resting during a return from a hunt a man weaves a basket-like headpiece from split vine or reed. On entering his household he walks to the center, gives the game to his wife, and, after drinking chicha for ten minutes or so, begins to weave feathers and animal skin into the headpiece. Particularly favored are a combination of monkey skin and the entire plumage of the giant toucan, curassow, cock of the rock, or guan. Should the hunter be fortunate enough to have killed all of these, he may make a really elaborate headdress of monkey skin with the toucan on top, beak sticking out over the man's face, two or three large black birds arranged down behind, and the cock of the rock on the bottom on a frame, so that when the man moves rapidly the bird seems to fly.

When the headpiece is ready the man plays a private soul song on his transverse flute, dons the rig, takes up his drum, and begins to move counterclockwise around the house, beating the peccary-skin side and allowing the monkey-skin side, with attached chambira-fiber snare, to resound inward toward the center of the room. The beat is always the same, 1-2-3-4/1-2-3-4, with the fourth beat either absent or distinctly diminished to allow the snare to "sing" out its buzzing *muscuyu*, soul-dream, sound. This ritual walking, where the man takes about one step every four beats, is called *yachajui*. The sound of the drum beat represents Amasanga-controlled thunder, and the snare buzzes the spirit helpers' dream song. Thoughts of distant living and dead relatives come to the man and to other household members as he continues to circle. The souls of other animals awaken and also sing their own songs, which the man and woman think-hear. The women may, individually, sing one or another of the songs, beginning with the phrase ———— [e.g., *paushi huarmi*, curassow woman] *runa mani*, "the curassow woman is a person."

165

As he walks round and round, the women residing in the house rush to bring him strong chicha and begin to force it on him, pouring pint after pint down his throat. When particularly strong thoughts strike him and he feels his power increasing, the man shouts to the women: *asua, asuata apamui mama*, "chicha, bring me chicha, chicha giver." And they do, more rapidly than before, pouring more and more down the man's throat. The man may stop the circling pattern to move toward a woman, signaling that he wants to dance. The woman immediately complies, placing both of her feet together, lifting her skirt slightly, and then with near-hopping motion swinging her body from side to side and throwing her long hair back and forth. After three to four minutes the man resumes his circling pattern, and the women serve chicha to one another and to everyone else in the household.

A man hearing the familiar huasi ritual of male power and soul liberation through snare and song may go to the house, accompanied by his wife. As he nears the jatun huasi he gives a loud, falsetto *juíiii*, and all within answer *juí, juí*. He enters, women rush to him as his own wife moves toward the kitchen to help, and they jostle one another in an effort to pour two or three bowls of chicha down the incoming man's throat. The chicha sloshes and flies around to the delighted cries of the women, *jí jí jí jíiiiiii*, the first four sounds going upward in a falsetto scale and the *iiii* falling back off in a decrescendo. Sloshing chicha represents the rain which accompanies thunder. The entering person may play a flute, or pick up a drum and follow the man already playing, in which case everyone shouts *parihú, parihú*, meaning "equality" or "togetherness" and including, in this context, not only the men and women participating, but also the souls of spirits and animal souls liberated by such behavior. Now the circling men pivot and come back clockwise, allowing the mixed resounding heads and snares with their ancient and distant ayllu and spirit souls to resound outward from the house, into the forest, and over the river domains, where Amasanga, Nunghuí, Sungui, and all the Yacu Supai Runa can hear them. Now people shout *uyariungui, uyariungui*, "sound bringers, sound bringers," referring to both the drum snares and the drummers.

When the circling man, perhaps accompanied by another, has drunk two or more gallons of chicha he usually wants to take his power elsewhere, so he lurches from the house, his wife following, and continues his beating as he walks on toward the house of a friend. Should his companion in his own house seek to join him, the resident women of the original huasi will mass near the door and douse him with chicha as he leaves. In some areas he may have to walk twenty minutes to half an hour through the jungle at night, but he enters the designated house still beating and, with the loud delighted *juí* yells of its members, continues the circling pattern. As he circles in the new household, women force more chicha on him, and when he leaves they give him a chicha shampoo. "One who walks like thunder must experience rain," they sometimes shout.

The sort of huasi power ritual described here is limited by its spontaneity. There is simply not enough chicha, let alone special "strong chicha," to allow a man to maintain this pattern, particularly if he seeks to involve others, for more than twelve hours. Nonetheless there is often enough drink to carry the man until near dawn. Today, where aguardiente—raw cane rum—is used to speed up intoxication, people tend to begin passing out within two to five hours' time.

The pattern just described is common when a man returns from a hunt, and may also be used as a "warm-up" for a minga work party. One also encounters it when visiting, particularly when game is brought by a visitor as prestation to a distant host. Fundamentally, the ritual signals the personal, acquired, power of the man initiating the behavior, an assertion of intra-household power through chicha flow and male capacity to absorb its life substance in large amounts, the connection of the men and women in the household to distant and ancient ayllu souls and to acquired animal souls, and the merger of Runa and supai souls.

AYLLU CEREMONY

Once or twice a year a large-scale ceremony is held in and near the administrative locus of each Runa territory. Although this ceremony has no name other than *jista*, from the Spanish *fiesta*, and although the Catholic Church has formally and conscientiously contributed to some aspects of the public ceremony, it is nonetheless a central characteristic of Canelos Quichua culture. [1] As we will see in the next chapter, it is also a pivotal point of articulation between the stipulated antiquity of Canelos Quichua culture, the vicissitudes of contemporary penetration of outside forces, and the adjustments necessary to insure a future through social adaptability.

In this ceremony distant and local ayllu members from separate llactas group together to create a mutual mystical power field devoid of spirit darts. The men are visited by Amasanga, the women by Nunghuí, and both are visited by the souls of dead, distant ayllu members, and eventually by the Yacu Supai Runa. Men conjoin their souls with those of animals. Women sing or think-sing flower songs, especially of the *lumu sisa*, manioc flower, and open their minds like the opening of flowers of food-giving plants to the female-power spirit bees. Such mind opening allows for integration with mythic time and enactment of mythic structure. While enacting such structure women pour huge quantities of chicha, fungus chicha, and vinillu into (and onto) the participants. Both men and women cross domain boundaries and play with animal souls and with spirit souls and mystical presence.

The structure of this ayllu ceremony is partitioned into two parts, a female *huarmi jista* and a male *cari jista* (see Diagram 6:1 below). These are also known, respectively, as *jilucu jista* and *quilla jista*. The two parts are symbolically joined by both consanguineal and affinal ties, reflecting the mythic union of the male moon and his sister, the female jilucu bird.

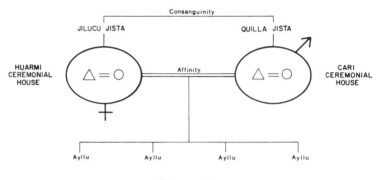

Diagram 6:1

Other participants in their various houses are arranged around the two parts, as descendants from an ancient brother-sister union, each related to others by stipulated common descent, from Mythic Time, from Ancient Times, and from Times of the Grandparents. All participants in this unified, partitioned ceremony are known as *jisteros.* In structural opposition to the jisteros are the *lanceros,* four dancing warrior men representing affinal attack power, which both complements and opposes the mystical power symbolized by the jisteros.

Preparations of the Jisteros

At least two male *priostes* (organizers) are chosen at the end of an ayllu ceremony and charged with the responsibility of carrying out the basic obligations of the next ceremony. (In Quichua such a person is called *amu chayuj,* ceremonial head, but the Spanish term is now usually used.) Everyone present at the cermony must agree to the priostes for the coming year. The chosen must be sure that there is ample manioc for chicha, meat for a feast, and an appropriately large setting for the respective partitions of the ceremony—huarmi or jilucu jista and cari or quilla jista.

Except for the planting of an extension of the prioste's chagra in manioc for chicha, which occurs any time from six months to ten months prior to the ceremony, the priostes and their wives do little until a month before that date, which is ordinarily set by a visiting priest when he announces a Sunday for formal mass and a feast. Once the date is known the priostes choose from five to ten *ayudantes* (helpers; also called *chayuj manda*, of the ceremony) from men classed as masha from the standpoint of ego, or ego's father. Brothers are ayudantes only if their father is also chosen, or, in the case of a prioste with adult sons, he will ask his sons to help him. But the basic unit is a group of people reciprocally classing one another as masha. A brother-father unit goes along only when the father-son tie knits it together; such a unit uses the father as locus for reckoning relationships. The ayudantes are known as *cajoneros uyariungui*, sound-making (and dream-bringing) drummers. All the ayudantes will hunt, but not necessarily in the same group with their respective prioste. Furthermore, other men in a masha class will also be asked to go on the hunt.

The wife of a prioste is known as a *jista huarmi*, ceremonial woman, and *asua mama*, chicha giver. Assistants of the jista huarmis are the ayudantes' wives, who are also called asua mamas. They make pottery for the fiesta, gather manioc, make chicha and fungus chicha, grate plantains for soup, chop and cook the meat brought by the hunters, and generally oversee everything having to do with ceremonial preparation.

The first real sign of preparation is the arrangement of the administrative site of the Runa territory into two or more parts. The priostes wait for pressure from strong huasi heads resident in this area. Ordinarily such men are the sons of shamans or powerful shamans, themselves studying to achieve shaman status and known as powerful individuals. (They are not the designated annual "officials,"[2] who have little to do with ceremonial preparation and ritual performance.) The priostes, finally succumbing to the pressure, reluctantly agree to initiate the somewhat tension-filled reorganization of llacta and ayllu residential units.

The priostes agree to a site for the cari jista house in the west, north, or south and a huarmi jista house in the east, north, or south. They and their ayudantes then either build large new oval houses in these areas or borrow existing houses that are well situated for the ceremony. The ayudantes, a few of whom come from distant territories, also move their actual residences so as to be on the side of their respective ceremonial partition. People from whom the house borrowing is done also move around, either to get themselves in one or the other partition or to get more or less out of the partitioned structure itself. From the time of the establishment of the Runa territory center into a structure of two parts, which itself may be subdivided into one or two more parts if there is more than one cari jista, a ceremonial mix of people occurs which varies considerably from that which is characteristic of the intermarried ayllu segments resident in the area

Genipa face painting.

where the ceremony takes place. Much informal visiting, face painting with genipa, and chicha drinking goes on. Men hunt individually or in small groups, and the ritual pattern described at the beginning of this chapter takes place. Men and women strive for knowledge about, and visions or dreams of, their distant and dead ayllu members, and share such knowledge with other ayllu members now resident in the ceremonial structure. Much overlapping of apayaya, apamama, and ancient people statuses occurs, and people remember other alliances between ayllus. The idea of common descent of all participants is intensified and related to the present union-in-polarity represented by the quilla-jilucu, male-female, brother-sister, affinity-consanguinity integration. Integration through cousin marriages in Times of the Grandparents and the acquisition of souls from Ancient Times by all of the immediate ancestors of the contemporary participants are also discussed. Men call each other *huauqui puma*, jaguar brother, and *ala*, mythic brother. Animated discussion about dreams takes place before dawn each morning, and repeated affirmations as to the life strength of forest soul master Amasanga and clay giver and chagra master Nunghuí are given.

  Women make some new mucahuas, tinajas, and figurines, and men make headdresses, animal-skin and bird-skin cloaks, drums, and shoulder slings, *jalingas*, with seeds, peccary teeth, animal paws, boa ribs, and whole stuffed birds. Both men and women paint their faces and sometimes arms and torsos with genipa as children of the tears of the stars, common descendants and siblings of the Quilla-Jilucu union.

This jistero preparation swings into a sequential routine two or three weeks prior to the final Sunday feast day. This usually occurs near the end of December and in March or April, but it may also occur in mid-October. Since the final day is given in terms of a Western calendar, it is convenient to present the various activities in this manner, even though the Canelos Quichua do not reckon their sequence in this way. Here is a two-week sequence.

FIRST WEEK

Sunday. Men dividing into hunting parties signals the "countdown" toward the ayllu ceremonial performance. The hunters divide themselves into three or more groups which cut across the ceremonial division. Each group is led by a strong, acknowledged hunter, familiar with a particular hunting territory within two days' forced walk from the ceremonial site. Each leader invites a couple of very good hunters and also some huambras in his masha categories to accompany him, including in his group men who do not know the hunting territory. In this way not only ceremonial divisions but also hunting territory divisions are crosscut by the hunting group membership. Having made this division, haggling takes place over which prioste will pay for the powder, shot, dart poison, and provide the chicha for the groups which he himself will not accompany. The haggling stops quickly, though, with agreement that the prioste must foot the bill for the group in which the majority of men belonging to his jista partition will hunt. Should either prioste feel that his helpers are disproportionately distributed, the hunting groups will change membership, the overall attempt being to send off three or more hunting groups into different territories with the equal probability that the net result in wild peccary, tapir, monkeys, and fish will be the same when the helpers return their catch to the respective prioste's ceremonial house.

Monday. The decisions about hunting groups made, the partitions regroup before dawn; the men go off to collect firewood in large amounts, and the women go to their respective jista chagras to roast manioc, lug it to the house, and store it under damp leaves to develop its fungus for the making of fungus chicha and vinillu. These two tasks are often initiated early in the morning, before dawn, and continue until about 9:00 A.M., along with the ritual behavior described earlier in this chapter.

Tuesday-Thursday. Helpers themselves initiate small morning rituals to get help from other people to bring in more firewood or finish parts of their houses, while women continue roasting manioc in the chagra and bring manioc, plantains, and sometimes corn to the house. Men see to their hunting and fishing paraphernalia and plan their hunts, sharing information with those ignorant of the territory to which they will trek. Thursday night the hunters sleep together in their respective hunting groups; they drink chicha, talk, and then attend to their own dream patterns to seek good feelings for the coming trek.

Friday. An asua mama ceremony launches the hunters toward their respective territories. Before dawn the hunters line up in their hunting groups, each with gun slung over left shoulder, tslambu ditty bag with soul stones, powder, shot, and caps over chest and on right hip, shigra net bag with fishing net, wrapped chicha, and plantains secured on the back with head tumpline, machete across right arm, and blowgun in right hand. The women, decorated with black face paint, force chicha on them; they drink and drink and then the women smear red achiote paint on their faces. The hunters shout *juíiii,* and as they do this the women switch the backs of their legs with stinging nettles and the men go roaring off, shouting; they usually run the first mile or so before settling into a trot for about five hours.

The men are off to invade Sungui's domain for fish, and to take foreign people's souls from the monkey troops. They also seek peccary or tapir to provide large amounts of meat for the guests who come on the final day of the ceremony, and to acquire the misha hair balls of Amasanga or Nunghuí. Birds will be collected by each hunter for his household's use and to provide plumage for his own ceremonial costume. The *tsantsa,* shrunken head, also called *cushcamanda* or *cuscamanda uma,*[3] is taken from the monkey. It may be sown into a skin vest or jacket made from monkey skin, or worn on the man's back, with the jalinga, during the fiesta.

After the hunters' departure, the women dig clay and lug it to the house. There they plaster it on the walls to dry, and set up the entire center of the house as a pottery- and chicha-manufacturing area. The asua mamas work in the prioste's house, or, if it is too crowded, in other ayudantes' houses. Other hunters' wives also set about preparing extra chicha and pottery, but they do this in their ichilla huasis; only the asua mamas establish the entire puñuna huasi as a female unit during the hunters' sojourn.

Saturday. Women settle down soon after dawn to make mucahuas and ceremonial figurines. In addition to the large array described in Chapter III, each woman also makes one or two pottery trumpets, which, with three imparted souls, will be presented on the final ceremonial day to someone of high rank. Each woman works sitting on the floor on a split-bamboo or other sort of seat, bent over more than double for at least eight hours at a time. Brief respites are taken to nibble a bite or two of food, and perhaps to serve chicha to a visitor. But more often than not women don't have time for chicha serving during this pottery-forming period. A woman may make a dozen or more mucahuas and an equal number of animals on this first day. While working away in her uncomfortable, tiring, ache-producing position, a woman thinks Nunghuí and other spirit songs, and frequently sings one of them. Her attention is given over to the spirits she is imparting to the vessels, and to the creativity through form development which she is undertaking.

During this time women tell one another myths, choosing segments and themes related to the shapes they are making and the designs they are considering. Innuendo is sought, for the shapes are just emerging, and no painting has yet been done. Each woman suggests to others a segment of mythic structure, but the real iconographic representation of this structure will not emerge for a few days. Each woman is molding a special created mythic universe segment, to combine into a ceremonial whole with the other female-produced segments.

SECOND WEEK

Sunday. The women bring manioc and plantains from the chagras for food and to make chicha. Saturday's headaches and backaches are followed by Sunday's drudgery as the women trudge to and fro carrying up to 100 pounds of manioc per trip on their backs in tumpline-affixed hexagonal-weave baskets. Sunday night finds all women asleep soon after sunset.

Monday. All asua mamas, together with their mothers, sisters, nieces, and other female friends, spend the day cooking and pounding manioc, masticating it and the fungus manioc, and placing each in about eighteen storage jars, to produce at least 350 to 400 gallons of chicha for each prioste house. All will be consumed during the ayllu ceremony. The ratio of chicha to fungus chicha is about six to one, and, of course, gallons of vinillu are drawn from the fungus chicha.

During this day women think-sing Nunghuí and other chagra songs, especially a manioc flower song to Nunghuí, a Quilla-Jilucu song, a song about the sun going into the river and turning it red, songs about the great flood, death in the sky and under the water, and songs which belong to deceased women. In normal symbolism the sun is yellow, male, and symbolizes affinity, while the color red symbolizes consanguinity, blood, and conflict, and is also connected to the water domain as Sungui's central color of the rainbow-boa manifestation of the Yacu Supai Runa. Sun yellow is the opposite of rainbow red; the former dries water, the latter is associated with rain. By merging these affinity-consanguinity colors and the attendant male-female, sky-river domains, women begin to establish

Pottery figurines for an ayllu ceremony ready for decorating and firing.

the essential quality of the ceremonial universe: *a reversal of everyday opposition, segmentation, and alliance.*

As women mix male attraction of women (symbolized by the sun) with death in the water domain and female continuity (symbolized by the sun turning red under the water), they also think about the possibility of the hunters being enchanted by Sungui or Juri juri, or even killed by other people guarding the hunting territories. As they provide more and more of the life-giving chicha, they consider origin myths and their collective descent from a common union. Monday, in this sequence, is a special, sad day for reflection on female centrality and the myriad of symbols, metaphors, and structures which converge upon the women in the center of the ceremonial huasi, as they continue to provide continuity and represent unseen reality of Runa time and space.

But it is not the huarmi way to bemoan life's unknown complexity or potential tragedy, and the women find humor in everything; as they end the day and remove the last of the chicha mash from their mouths, they sing out songs to the sky, jungle, soil, and water domains, and ask for high sky rivers and birds to carry their songs to hunters, to other far reaches of Canelos Quichua territory, and beyond. That night they dream of the results of their song flights, and share with dreaming hunters a sense that once again all will go well with the coming ceremony. Vision is sharpened by the chicha making and song sending and receiving, and the next day the women return to pottery preparation.

Tuesday. This is the final day of unified female action. Women once again work on pottery all day, making some black and some red callanas,[4] and especially painting and firing their mucahuas and figurines. As the male and

Two sides of the same   Alli Runa.   Sacha Runa.
drinking mug.

A new machin runa, a boss for one of the   Pregnant jilucu bird.
oil companies.

Cichlid.

Poisonous snake ready to strike.

Sucker-mouth catfish.

Representation of a jukebox.

female lines are placed and formed into patterns related in a variety of ways, representations from many time periods form into a striking array of decorated pottery figurines. Portrayals from mythic structure such as the tree mushroom, jilucu bird, moon, sun, jaguar, giant anteater, and cayman emerge. Other representations from Ancient Times such as Amasanga, and images from the world of shaman power including various attack supais such as stinging ants and caterpillars, are produced together with the newest things around, such as model jukeboxes, baseball-cap-wearing *guiringus*, gringos, and life-size hard hats. Designs emerge on mucahuas and on the figurines with a predominance of boa, turtle, and sky motifs. Many of the figurines are two-sided. For example, there are tree mushrooms with a star or sun face on the reverse side, and an *alli runa*, good person, with a *sacha runa*, jungle spirit person, on the reverse, and a jilucu bird (moon sister–sexual partner) with apapa (eagle-owl shaman soul bird) headdress. Equations which merge time periods and structural oppositions and which have layers of double, mirror-like, images are sought.

Through graphic art each woman enacts some personal integration of design, life, spirit, and soul substance. The mutual, collective endeavor of graphic portrayal generates an intra-ceremony female universe symbolizing, among other things, temporal and spatial reintegration and ayllu continuity. Women excitedly watch and listen to one another as they work along on their own projects. Individuals sing songs, and older women sometimes help out younger girls, even imparting small secrets to them.

Wednesday and Thursday. Women continue making pottery, making chicha, and in a few cases even take the vinillu out, replacing the fungus chicha to obtain more drippings. Other work is done as needed and a variety of tasks may be undertaken according to whether one is ahead or behind in preparation. Some new allu asua is started, to insure a fresh supply of vinillu on Sunday morning. Some hunters arrive, especially the groups in which the priostes participated. The women put them to work gathering anything needed, including more firewood, and they also hunt around the llacta for more birds, squirrels, or marmosets to complete the plumage and skin needed for their ceremonial costumes. Thoroughly blackened smoked meat and fish are hung around the center area of the house, while a reserve supply of peccary and deer meat is hung or stored near the fire in the ichilla huasi. This day is sometimes designated as firewood-gathering day, though most such gathering was done before the hunters' departure.

Friday. This is the official day of the hunters' return, and indeed, the larger one or two groups of hunters may not return until the afternoon of this final preparation day and first ceremonial night. As the day wears on,

people in the ceremonial area become quieter and quieter. Task after task
is completed, the pottery finished and stored in the ichilla huasi, the chicha
fermenting in all the big storage jars. The vinillu has been put away or is still
dripping in jars. For the first time the houses serving as factories have been
swept clean, and fresh sand or gravel has been placed on the ground floor.
Songs cease by midday, and conversation ceases by afternoon. People
reflect on the possibility that the worst has happened, that the men have
died.

   A half-hour or more before the first distant falsetto *juíiiiiíii* shouts rend the
air, worry and fear dissolve in cari or huarmi jista, for the women are
informed by friendly runners that the hunters are coming. By dark both
cari and huarmi jista hunters return to their respective ceremonial partitions. The majority of the animal meat and fish goes to the ceremonial
houses, but hunters give fowl to their own wives. Women in the ceremonial houses store peccary and tapir meat in the kitchen and hang smoked
chunks of fowl, peccary, deer, and tapir from the ceiling of the house center. Men drink, laugh loudly, beat drums or play flutes, and tell fragments
of tales from the hunt. Emphases in such tales are on the high hills they
climbed and the rushing waters they crossed and fished. Crucial here is the
verbal portrayal of near-disastrous encounters with Paccha supai, Juri juri,
and Sungui and the successful acquisition of peccaries, monkeys, and fish.

   As they tell these tales the most successful hunters hang blackened
monkeys from the center pole and make fun of them, abusing the acquired
souls believed to remain in the area of the charred, smoked bodies. Other
men join in, making crowns for the monkeys, placing cigarettes in their
mouths, and otherwise treating meat and souls of the killed machin runa
with the opposite of normal respect. This is not meat given by Amasanga,
but the bodies and souls of foreign people taken from the Juri juri. With the
storage of meat and the taunting of the hung machin runa the annual ayllu
ceremony is launched.[5]

Preparations of the Lanceros

There are four lanceros in each Runa territory except Puyo.[6] Unlike the
priostes, they serve for more than a year, and they are not chosen at the end
of an ayllu ceremony. When a man moves from one Runa territory to
another to reside with his wife in the llacta of his wife's father and brothers,
he is a candidate for the lancero position. A man's wife's father and her
brothers control the prestation of a wooden macana when they have in their
local residential ayllu a person in the masha category already designated as
a lancero. These wooden knives are scarce; they are supposed to have come
down from Times of the Grandfathers, and they are made from a very hard

wood (not chonta) which grows in the low, damp forests from Montalvo eastward. Invitation to an incoming in-law is a mighty prestation, for it obligates the newcomer to give a household chicha party at each annual ayllu ceremony. In this ceremony chicha, fungus chicha, and vinillu must be served in large quantities, and the women must have a large, ceremonial array of pottery mucahuas and figurines. But the man is not expected to hunt, collect foreign or animal souls, or walk in the power circle beating his drum. Rather, he will learn a dance (described below) involving quadrangular movements that form various sorts of squares, wear a special headpiece, and symbolize opposition to the unity-polarity of the ceremony. When a lancero has been named and has accepted the invitation, he becomes a continuing figure in the territorial ayllu ceremony, as opposed to the priostes, who serve for only one year. This continuity is conveyed to priests or nuns, either resident or in charge of a parish central to the territory, and they provide the lancero with silver or copper bells to wear around his calves a few weeks prior to the annual ceremony.

Preparation of the lanceros involves them in extra clearing of chagra land each year, and their wives must undertake the work described above for the asua mamas of the jisteros each year. Otherwise, the four lanceros must practice their dance, make the special headdresses with four tall macaw-tail points, and learn from powerful shamans more about their special role in enacting segments of mythic structure. Such learning involves them more deeply with persons in the jachi kin-shaman categories, and draws them closer to ancient soul and spirit power sources through knowledge acquisition. Such a centripetal force toward the wellsprings of ayllu power makes the mashas more and more a part of the transmission of their wives' ayllu knowledge within their residential Runa territory.

The lanceros are members of a mythical *taruga*, deer, ayllu. All deer carry the souls of ancient deceased people. Beyond time, when animals were human, the deer was a dancing warrior, and the dance of the lanceros in the ceremony represents the pre-attack pawing behavior of a snorting deer about to lower his small, sharp horns and protect his family and territory. In older Present Times, within the lifetime of contemporary old people, it is said that the lanceros, together with other male companions, went off to attack the Jívaro proper and take heads for a ceremony to be held later, after the priest had departed. This was the *runa huanchisha jista*, dead human ceremony. In such attack the lanceros were led by "powerful ones," huanchij, the killer, and sicuanga, the toucan-lance-warrior. When the lanceros symbolize attack of another people, especially the Jívaro proper, their mythic taruga ayllu is transformed into a *taruga puma ayllu*, and their dance pattern is that of *apamama puma*, a mythical female cougar ayllu node of the cougar line of cats.[7] In the ceremonial structure the lanceros symbolize both the enduring, territorial-protecting, deer-with-human-soul and the attack-killer cougar.

On the night of the hunters' return each of the four lanceros drinks chicha in his own house and performs the ceremony described in the beginning of this chapter. Lancero men talk of killing and complain about the work they have to put into the ceremony. They do not come together as a dancing ensemble until the next day. While drinking chicha, however, they move from one lancero house to another. Individually, but not as a group, one or another of the lanceros may visit one of the jisteros' houses, in which case he and those accompanying him are received in the same way as a visiting alter prioste (described below).

CEREMONIAL ENACTMENT

The enactment of the annual or semiannual ayllu ceremony is easily conceived of in terms of its basic three day–three night pattern, beginning when the last hunters arrive late Friday afternoon.

Friday: Ceremonial Beginning

Just as soon as all hunters have returned, and it is known that the meat has reached both of the ceremonial houses, one of the ayudantes—who must have demonstrated his hunting skill by a large kill—picks up his drum and begins to circle counterclockwise, beating the standard rhythm. Immediately other men shout the falsetto *juí juí*, and cry out *parihú, parihú, jistata ranuuuuuu*, "togetherness, togetherness, the ceremony be-ginnnnnnnnns" (literally, "is constructed"). Hardly does the circling drummer get started on his vision and thought-bringing shaman-power circling pattern than the women appear before him with large (quart capacity or more) mucahuas brimming with chicha. He drinks and drinks, first from one and then from another—taking in probably a half-gallon of chicha with large gulps. If he can't swallow it all he may blow out a cupful or more, in order to gulp more offered from another asua mama's bowl. Usually he can't drink it all down fast enough, thereupon getting the remainder of a mucahua-full on his headdress as a chicha shampoo. *Jí jí jí jíii*, cry the women and rush back to the chicha storage jars for more.

The prioste takes a seat at the far end of the jatun huasi as this behavior proceeds, and his wife gives him a two-quart mucahua of vinillu from which he drinks as he wishes, and into which all the asua mamas continue to pour more vinillu until none remains. He sometimes hands this bowl to other men or women, and they drink and return it. Normally the prioste does not play the drum; he simply drinks and gives others his vinillu in his own ceremonial house, while the ayudantes and the asua mamas drive the ceremonial behavior along.

A brief meal break takes place before the ceremony really gets under way. Women hastily place fowl, manioc, and plantains on banana leaves on the floor near the center of the house, and all grab, slurp, and gobble. Immediately afterward an ayudante or two begin their drumming-circling pattern, the prioste resumes his seat, and other ayudantes of the prioste arrive bedecked in skins and plumage, drumming as they come. All ayudantes now circle round and round, as their wives urge chicha on everyone else. Other members of the priostes' and ayudantes' families and visiting friends and relatives take seats on the long bancus around the house. Women go from one to another actively pouring chicha, fungus chicha, and vinillu down their throats. Sometimes four or five women converge on one person, each continuing her pouring as the selected receiver gulps, blows out liquid, and even stands on the bench in an effort to avoid the inevitable chicha shampoo.

By dark, identical behavior is taking place in both ceremonial houses. The central ayudante, who demonstrated great prowess in hunting, maintains his drumming and a calm demeanor in spite of the enormous amounts of chicha he is expected to drink. As visitors to the house begin to outnumber the asua mamas and their daughters, other male ayudantes begin to serve chicha too. Their adult married and unmarried sons also help do this, undertaking the woman's primary role as chicha giver. Now the drummers turn outward, letting the distant and ancient souls of the drum and house sing out. From this point on the circling pattern shifts from clockwise to counterclockwise every ten minutes or so.

In about an hour one or two drummers each invites an asua mama to dance. They do this by simply breaking the circling pattern, walking toward the women with a more rapid step—two steps rather than one every four beats—and invited women quickly respond, handing their mucahuas to other women, lifting their skirts slightly, and with both knees slightly bent begin a skip-hopping dance, throwing their bodies back and forth and their heads in opposition, so that their long hair flies to and fro. The drummers lift their knees higher and move forward and backward as the women approach them, moving from side to side, keeping their entire bodies in motion. A woman may sometimes playfully throw her hips or torso in such a way as to knock her male dancing partner off balance, to the delight of everyone.

As the drummers invite other women to dance, other men, both guests and ayudantes, do the same, and some produce transverse flutes to play while dancing. Each dancer plays an instrument—drum or transverse flute—and each song played while dancing comes from an ancient soul,

Drummers circling counterclockwise.

Drummer dancing with an asua mama.

Asua mama giving vinillu to a cajonero uyariungui.

distant soul, or special spirit soul. As the songs are played thoughts and visions come to other men and women and are said to mingle within the domain-loosened ceremonial house. The women are dancing to Nunghuí and think-singing songs to her as well. The men are playing out Amasanga power in the face of the meat taken from the domains of Juri juri and Sungui. Dressed as animals and birds of the forest and accompanied by the souls of those very beings, men play at assuming other identities, of other peoples, of other places, and in other cultures. A dance with a woman lasts

Chicha shampoo.

only two to three minutes, after which the man moves to another woman, or else resumes his circling drumming. After the flute players tire of dancing they, too, join the group of circling men.

All drumming and flute-playing men are yachaj in this context, representing the accumulated soul power of merged domains. They all have the power to bring visions, just as the huanduj supais—Amasanga and Nunghuí, Ayahuasca mama and Yaji—bring visions in non-cermonial life. Sinchi yachajs, founders of various llactas in the Runa territory and beyond, may also join the ceremonial pattern, which they do by playing a six-hole flute called a *pingullu*. The pingullu in Quichua is the shinbone, where the soul born to animal, bird, or human resides. Synonyms in Canelos Quichua for pingullu are *rima tullu*, talking bone, and *aya tullu*, soul bone. The powerful shamans either place a soul in a bamboo pingullu, or actually play the still-living soul of a bird in the apapa class, the dominant figure being the owl or harpy eagle.

The noise of perhaps fifty people talking loudly, three to five drums beating in unison or near unison, snares resounding with multiple humming overtones, and two or three separate flute songs intricately weaving in and out of one anothers' patterns drowns out all other sounds in the area. Some women and men sing in falsetto, too, letting their usually "thought" songs emerge to synergize with the other powers and forces now clearly thought to be within the ceremonial universe in the ceremonial house. Flutes and falsetto voices intricately weave in and out of the individual melodies to create a musical tapestry of counterpoint and reflection juxtaposed to the steady, tedious drum beat—snare drone.

About half an hour after dark the huarmi jista group makes its first visit to the cari jista group. With drummers in the lead beating away, flute players following, and then others who were in the house—men, women, and children—the ceremonial jilucu people walk slowly, noisily, to the ceremonial quilla people's resounding household. The sound from within the quilla jista house as the jilucu people approach is first that of increased snare buzzing and drum beats, for the incoming group endeavors to match a unison beat with that of the house. Drummers enter and immediately begin to follow those circling within, matching the beats and steps. They circle counterclockwise once or twice, and then there are many shouts of *parihú, parihú, jistata ranu* as the ayudantes are given more chicha than they can possibly hold, and the visiting prioste quietly sits next to the host prioste, each with his quart of vinillu.

Women and men in the host house rush back and forth pouring chicha, fungus chicha, and vinillu down the throats of male and female visitors. As the drummers go round and round and then turn to allow the merged cari-huarmi, quilla-jilucu vision-producing snares to resound outwards, more and more shouts and falsetto shrieks are voiced, for now the visiting drummers are leading the host drummers in sending the visions outward. Behavior described just above takes place: dancing, singing, chicha shampooing, circling. In about three-quarters of an hour the huarmi jista group prepares to leave, drummers moving toward the door. At this time there is a veritable deluge of chicha rushed their way, and most, if not all, get a thorough soaking in the life-giving fluid as they finally get out and begin to move back toward their ceremonial house. On the way they may move through an ayudante's house, drumming, dancing, drinking chicha, and collecting household members as they go. They eventually arrive back in their ceremonial house, begin circling, and await the reciprocal visit of the quilla group. In about ten minutes the visit takes place, and the scene is acted out as above with roles reversed.

These reciprocal visits go on until 10:00 P.M. or midnight, when many go to their respective households to snooze a bit and receive vivid dreams. But person after person talks, yells, and some jisteros continue to beat drums and come and go from the ceremonial houses until 1:00 A.M. No one can sleep for more than ten or fifteen minutes at a time because of the noise—and no one wants to. Domains are merged, souls are everywhere, spirits are present, and one could easily lose control of his own or acquired souls. So dreams are received and then commented upon, jokes are made, drums are beaten, and songs sung. By 3:00 even those rendered unconscious by alcohol and fatigue are up again, and the noise level rises all over the central Runa territory. Drums are beaten, flutes played, and animated conversations take place until 4:30. Around 5:00 a hearty meal and plenty of good warm chicha is served in each house. Ayudantes go to their respective ceremonial houses, and the second day of the ceremony is under way.

Saturday: The Bringing of Flowers

The ceremonial ritual described for Friday begins again in full swing about 5:30 A.M. Chicha, fungus chicha, and vinillu are again pushed in huge quantities. Some women bring out special mucahuas and figurines not shown the night before for fear of early breakage. Everyone is soaked in the sticky chicha and all heads buzz and reel from ingested vinillu. The stronger the hunter and the more vivacious the dream-bringing drummer the more the women pour chicha down his throat and dump it on the carefully prepared headdress. The meek and the shy aren't exempt, however, for they too are periodically singled out to be filled and soaked with chicha.

The lanceros may make their first appearance sometime Saturday morning. They arrive together, bedecked in the special headdresses, bells around their calves, carrying their wooden knives, accompanied by their own male aids and asua mamas. As their ayudantes circle with the other drummers the four lanceros move into the circle of drumming men and, with a sort of skipping step which makes the bells tinkle, dance back and forth in quadrangular patterns, moving their knives in slow flourishes. As they do this three or four of their women also move into the middle of the circling oblong of drummers and, as a group, dance next to the lanceros. Within a minute or two a few other men may begin to play their flutes, and within ten minutes other dancers so impede the lanceros that they either sit down to drink chicha or leave. When they do leave they go to the other ceremonial house, repeat the pattern, and then return to their own houses, where smaller-scale ritual drumming and drinking is going on.

The selected cabildo members of a year before may also pay a visit to the ceremonial house, carrying their canes of authority.[8] They simply enter, sit down, accept a few quarts or more of chicha and vinillu, submit to having chicha dumped on them to a moderate extent, and, having paid a visit to the other house, depart until the next day.

People from all over the Runa territory begin to arrive by midday. As they enter they drop a small bundle of yellow flowers, symbolizing affinity, in a large hexogonal-weave basket placed next to the prioste. The flowers are for the new Christian God. Women immediately converge on the male flower giver, trying to make him drink several quarts of chicha and soaking him with a shampoo, symbolizing the ancient, enduring water system of the rainforest. Women and girls move to the kitchen to see if they can help,

Reentering the house during the "bringing of flowers."

or hide from the shampooing, but they are usually pushed back out into the central house, where someone or other douses them with chicha. As the houses fill up with seventy-five people or so, the drummers get some respite from the gallons of forced guzzling, for everyone is too busy pushing chicha on the newcomers to worry about the actual jisteros. Similar behavior spreads to other houses, where newcomers will stay the night; jisteros leaving one ceremonial house may spend as much as two or three hours weaving through four to six other buildings en route to the other ceremonial house.

Late in the afternoon, between 3:00 and 5:00 P.M., the male jisteros go into the jungle to cut tarapoto palm, which will be used to make arches around the central plaza of the Runa territory, and to gather their own yellow flowers to contribute to the brimming baskets. On their return the men with flowers pretend to force their way back into their respective ceremonial houses. Some even raise machetes and bare teeth. As they do this their own asua mamas, now massed at their entry point, pour chicha down their throats and douse them thoroughly. The flowers are placed in the baskets and each ceremonial house enjoys its own dance with drums and flutes until it is nearly dark. During this period, when reciprocal visits are not made, people actually dream on their feet while dancing and playing. Powerful memories, thoughts, and visions of deceased ayllu members all come into the ceremonial huasi, mingle with the ancient souls in present time and structure, and cement those within the house into a very special vision-producing and vision-sharing unit.

With an hour or less remaining before nightfall the quilla people go to visit the jilucu people, and all together quickly set up the arches around the square and bedeck them somewhat with yellow flowers and red leaves (which, as far as I know, are just added for decoration). One can easily elicit a dominant symbolism at this point in the ceremony. The affinity suggested by the predominance of yellow and the division of the ceremony into cari-huarmi parts are representative of the incestual affinity of the beginning, which placed all Runas in the same ayllu.

The arches having been set up, the reciprocal visiting, drumming, and dancing continue at least until midnight and sometimes beyond. After the ceremony stops people continue to talk and shout until around 3:30 A.M., when brief naps are taken. People arise again at 4:00.

Sunday: Feast Day

In every household women are moving rapidly by 4:00 A.M. to carry water and to prepare a good substantial meal, which is eaten before 4:45. At about 5:00, the day of the feast is inaugurated in front of the Catholic church, designated *mushuj huasi,* new house, in the central square of the Runa territory.[9] At this time the four lanceros, led by a man playing a three-hole flute with his left hand while beating a special beat with his right on a small drum, dance for about fifteen minutes. Jisteros from cari and huarmi partitions join them and circle round and round as the lanceros perform a dozen or more quadrangular patterns. Then, led by the jisteros, all head for one of the ceremonial houses to perform, and then go on to the other ceremonial house to do the same. The near-riotous cacophony of collective individual playing and dancing goes on for about half an hour. Around 6:30 all the dream-bringing drummers, followed by the lanceros and anyone else who may have joined the party with drum or flute, go off to visit all the ayudantes' homes. Although the group leaves together, it splits into segments which cut across the ceremonial partitions. Three to five separate drumming sets, some with and some without one or more lanceros, weave here and there to within about a half-hour's walk from the ceremonial locus, visiting many houses and spreading the ceremony outward. Many men collect more palm branches on the way, and women and men collect more yellow flowers. On their return they drop some flowers in each of the baskets of the respective priostes' houses, and lean the palms up just outside. Then they are treated to more chicha and more dousing.

While the jisteros and lanceros are on their ceremonial sojourn, women in the ceremonial houses begin to prepare for a later feast, *camari*. They grate gallons of boiled plantain using a shiquita stick, hack up almost all of the meat, place it and grated plantains into separate cooking pots with boiling water, and cook for about twenty minutes. Around 10:30 or 11:00 the church bell tolls and all participants in the ceremony, plus most visitors, head toward it for a special mass. Here they are chastized and castigated by the priest for their drunkenness and admonished to carry out the rest of the ceremonial day with sobriety and reverence.

The strong hunters, those who have spent the most of the past two days drumming and drinking with scant rest, are supposed to agree throughly with the priest and tell him that they personally will see to "order" for the rest of the day. They seek to convince him by responses, in the church and as he leaves, that they are among the most sober of participants and should have his trust.

Right after the mass the lanceros lead the jisteros in a procession twice around the square, in and out of the yellow, split-palm-frond arches. Then, reassembling in the church, the first note of intra-ceremonial group hostility sounds. The priest must now receive a consensus of those assembled as to who will assume the prioste role for the next ceremony. Would-be priostes either volunteer to strong elders or are asked to volunteer. Invariably there are six to eight names, only two or three of which can serve. All have enemies who do not want them to be prioste, and such negative sentiments are openly voiced. In fact, the vehemence may reach the point of a near fight in the church, except that the priest then intervenes and reminds the people that there will be no ceremony unless agreement is reached. Eventually, within ten minutes or so, people stop shouting against two or three names, and the priest confers on each of those chosen the obligation to carry out next year's ceremony.

At around noon the annual ceremony enters the feast stage, as the priest and cabildo members go first to the cari ceremonial house and then to the huarmi one. The events and setting are the same in each.

Camari. A table is set for high-ranking guests, or outsiders, in one part of the ceremonial house, while one or two long benches with plantain-leaf covering are set in another part. Boiled plantains are placed on each. Outsiders such as priest, nuns, schoolteacher, or trader are served first, and nothing happens until they finish eating. Then the real camari begins. Ayudantes of the prioste place themselves at either end of each bench, and a clamor arises from all non-jisteros, those in the guest role as separate from those of the alter ceremonial partition, for food. People jostle one another to get a seat, throw a sucre or more on the bench, and yell to be served. Others just sit there, scowl, and look miserable. Servers and served enact a hostile relationship toward one another. Servers claim that a person hasn't paid his *jucha* (literally "blame" or "sin"), the one-sucre-per-callana food fee. Those served in turn claim that there is not enough meat in with the plantain soup, or that it is shungu, the one part of an animal or fish which no Runa will eat. Others claim they are being served snake meat, something else never eaten, or that they are being poisoned. Many simply dump the food into a bucket to eat later, but some try to offend their hosts by drinking as many as five bowls of soup and still demand more, while others are trying to sit down to eat.

As the camari goes on the drummers circle round and round, and powerful shamans and aspiring trained shamans play special camari soul songs on their pingullus. Eventually those who have eaten go on to the other ceremonial house, to again insult their hosts and receive demands for payment. The prioste and his wife do most of the serving, with the asua mamas and the ayudantes helping. Some asua mamas send ayudantes out of the house to collect a few sucres from someone who has not paid the jucha, and genuine acrimony is generated in such clashes. Some people try to settle debts based on loans, and again real insults and warnings are reciprocated.

By the time the eating is well under way or nearly finished in both houses, native people of high rank—cabildo members, some visitors from a distant territory, a powerful shaman—are seated at a table and served without jucha and without insults. But there is tension even here, for the person often does not want to eat more, and he is literally dragged in some cases to the table and soup poured into his throat, much of it falling on him. As this happens younger women, helpers of the asua mamas, may walk casually over to the person of high rank and pour chicha on his head.

As the eating abates and chicha is again served to all those sitting, dancing, or drumming, special pottery trumpets are given to people of high rank, particularly to the cabildo members. Such trumpets may have the face of a moon on the bell, or a mounted Amasanga on the center, at times they are even curved to give two tones, and some have two bells. The asua mama who made the trumpet fills it up and gives it to her husband, with thumb over the mouthpiece. He in turn carries it to the gift receiver, who drinks all the chicha in it, from the bell, and then begins to blow it. The three souls imparted by the asua mama—her own body soul coming from Times of the Grandmothers, the household soul, and the soul of Nunghuí—sing out through the blowing of a high-rank man, who in this context is said to be singing the song of *yami*, the trumpeter swan. This song is said to "torture" or "make everyone suffer" (*llambu turmindai*, from *turmindarina*).

As the pottery trumpets begin to honk away in a non-musical male-female merged soul noise and as other gifts of special pottery figurines are given away, the racket and activity within the ceremonial house crescendo even more. Lanceros again enter, are quickly fed and given more chicha, and begin again to dance in the center of a circling group of as many as twenty drummers. Powerful shamans play their pingullus, others play transverse flutes, and people begin to wonder if, during this ceremony, too much enactment of mythic structure will occur and the great flood of antiquity will return. As hard rain comes people comment on the possible need to build a great raft with soil and manioc on which to travel eastward. Men and women assume the roles of Docero, Cuillur, Indi, Quilla, Jilucu. Young girls begin to serve guests in very special figurines representing the core aspects of mythology, including a special tree mushroom made by the prioste's wife. Some women bring forth special pottery fish—symbol of the Yacu Supai Runa—at this point. Many of these fish figurines are made with an extra hole near the drinking lip. As a woman holds the figurine for the man to drink she keeps her index finger over the hole, but releases it as he drinks so that much of the chicha runs down his front. Some women even put round pottery snakes, representing deadly fer-de-lance, bushmaster, or palm viper, on their heads, dancing until they fall off and break.

Men, too, have a game they play, especially unmarried men with sweethearts, but also husbands with wives or sometimes sisters. The man picks up two blackened monkey or sloth heads with ancient souls within and gently touches the woman with one of them. The woman shudders, winces, cringes, and, after having been touched, reluctantly accepts the head as a gift. The man is touching the girl with the power of the Amasanga supai, male soul master of the forest domain, just as she is drenching him in the life substance of Nunghuí and Yacu mama. The woman in turn, having accepted a blackened supai head, proceeds to touch her brothers with it, as the first man goes on to touch other sisters with a second head, which he does not give away.

Chicha dousing and black-head touching crescendo and many younger men and women begin heaving grease, mud, or whole tinajas of remaining chicha at one another, leaving the house and running to and fro, carrying a free-for-all slop fight throughout the central area.

About 3:00 P.M. a more staid, formal camari is held near the front of the church, where the four lanceros and their families are fed, and where outside guests may also be invited to participate. The priest also marries several couples at this time, and, at least in Paca Yacu, a slow dance takes place for a few minutes, before the married couples return to their respective houses to give their own parties. Gifts of firewood, plantains, and a bit of black smoked meat are brought to the priest's house, and all drummers go round and round in the central square, women dancing within the circle.

Playing with chicha after the camari.

The lanceros insult the meal and act as bravely as they possibly can, talking loudly and rudely to cabildo members and other jisteros. They literally act like officials. (Indeed, in showing the headdress and explaining the lancero demeanor to bicultural Jívaro proper–Canelos Quichua from the Pastaza River near Puyo, the lanceros were immediately classed as warrior chiefs from Canelos, and it was said that these were the very people who used to lead attacks from Canelos into the Jívaro territory of Sharupe, on the right bank of the Pastaza.) The lanceros may talk loudly against Achuara and Jívaro proper during this last ceremonial day, even within easy earshot of Jivaroan, as well as Canelos Quichua, individuals.

While the lanceros busy themselves being as unpleasant as possible, other men and women join in the activities described above, playing havoc with the remains of the Nunghuí- and Sungui-derived soul power of the pottery and chicha. Tinajas are dragged to the central plaza still half full of chicha, which is flung around in a general free-for-all. The jisteros continue their drumming round and round in a circle near the camari table, and many women dance as a unit, throwing their hair to and fro. Then the lanceros leave this scene and go to the house of one of their members, where they drink chicha until a little before 5:00.

Dominario. At 5:00 the lanceros go to the priest and tell him that they wish a "benediction" for their *dominario*, a ritual to terminate the ayllu ceremony. This term presumably derives from the Spanish *dominar* (to dominate). A powerful shaman imbued with ancient knowledge comes quietly to the church. Sometimes a man of such power and knowledge cannot be found by the lanceros in their own Runa territory and has to be called from elsewhere. He moves to the front of the church, faces the square, and begins to play a melody on his three-hole flute while softly beating a rhythm on his drum. Inside the church several men prepare a ten-foot-long bamboo pole with four notches, into which they place copal to form the basis for four torches. The pole represents the great anaconda from Ancient Times. It is the corporeal representation of Sungui or Yacu mama, master of water and spirit master of the Yacu Supai Runa. The copal fire burning in the ancient amarun represents the powerful central red color of the rainbow, sky-earth symbol of the ancient water spirit.

The four lanceros assemble in front of the powerful shaman, and on his signal begin the last of their dances until the next ceremony. First they dance shoulder to shoulder, back and forth, swinging their wooden knives in a set pattern to the rhythm of their bells and the drum. Then the jistero drummers come back into the picture and circle the dancing lanceros, moving clockwise. Women break into the circle and dance as a group, tossing their hair.

Next the lanceros break into two groups and dance toward each other, moving back and forth, as the women continue their dance and the soul-bringing drummers continue their beat. On another signal from the flute- and drum-playing powerful shaman the lanceros put their backs to one another and work through a different quadrangular pattern. Then, on another shaman signal, they begin to dance back and forth, weaving in and out in a square dance–like pattern. About nine patterns are worked through by the lanceros, each more complicated than the previous one, as the women dance and the drummers play.

Inside the church the four copal torches in the bamboo log are lit; some jisteros, themselves descendants of the ancient jaguar ayllus, pick it up and assume the "dress," churana, of the ancient anaconda spirit on their shoulders. Then, with the dream-bringing drumming jisteros, they begin to circle the entire plaza. The ancient yacu supai is ritually freed from the water domain and for a moment "dominates" the land, flooding it with ancient water power. The shaman leader, imbued with ancient knowledge, maintains his melodies and rhythm, the lanceros (as taruga pumas) keep up their quadrangular dancing patterns, and the women continue their dancing adjacent to them. The women's dance is to Nunghuí, ancient garden and pottery-clay giver. The jisteros, led by the jaguar-borne anaconda, then begin to run around the plaza, and then back and forth around the square and through the church, knocking aside the flimsy partitions and crashing around in a jaguar-determined serpentine course, before running off, still carrying the burning amarun pole, first to one ceremonial house and then to the other, and finally breaking up into respective cari and huarmi units. The lanceros remain in the plaza, dancing for a while, and then ask the priest for a special benediction for them alone. First the shaman gives the benediction to each one, and then the priest does the same. Then the lanceros go on to whichever of the two ceremonial houses contains the remains of the jistero ceremony, dance some more, and then accompany the group to the other ceremonial house, repeat the same pattern, and return again to the house where they began. The ceremony is then technically over.

READJUSTMENT

I stated at the beginning of the section on the ayllu ceremony that the people in both jilucu and quilla ceremonial partitions, plus those arranged around these houses, regard themselves as related through common, stipulated descent from Ancient Times and Times of the Grandparents. Enactment of this unity in the central Runa territory, we noted, involved a ceremonial reorganization of household and llacta. After the dominario ritual people continue to party, but now they are enacting intra-huasi and individual rituals, as described at the beginning of this chapter. The enactment, however, takes place in a readjusting context where actors are coupled with people other than the normal huasi members, but without the ceremonial supports which have been employed for the past few weeks.

Insults which were received during the camari are now taken personally, and ayudantes and the past year's prioste may solidify their (usually affinal—masha) bonds to one another, in opposition to guests who abused them. Furthermore, people in each ceremonial house may feel that the other group did not perform equally—they may either have tried to outdo the complainers, or they may not have done enough. In either event actual complaints by the huarmi group against the cari group take place. Remember, the male hunting and ayudante groups themselves are mainly composed of people in masha classes, mature brothers being separated into their respective houses.

Lanceros usually come to visit one or the other of the ceremonial houses, as individuals, not as a group, and they too voice complaints at having to perform year after year rather than only once in a while. To stop the incessant complaining and to restore a party atmosphere, older participants, and sometimes the younger, produce raw, potent cane alcohol, which they earlier purchased from traders or lugged on their backs from Puyo to Canelos and then brought on downriver. Drinking leads to merriment; a prominent individual begins playing the drum, some people dance, and everyone decides to visit the other ceremonial house. There the alcohol is passed around and laughter ensues, but complaints may also be voiced. These are now very serious for there are no ceremonial restraints; brother may be insulting brother, and insulters may even reside in the same llacta. Furthermore, a person may show lack of gratitude for the house he has borrowed during the ceremony. The past year's priostes are no longer in charge nor held responsible, though they will be blamed for anything wrong; the new priostes who have done nothing may be abused for pushing themselves to the forefront.

Cabildo members absent themselves from such discussions, for it is inevitable that they will be abused for being middlemen between outside nationals and the Runa territory, but their relatives may be present to hear the complaints, and they may take offense. It is unnecessary to list all possible complaints to understand how easily such tired, psyched-up, drinking people can be offended, and how easily a verbal spark can touch off a fight.

Fighting

Invariably one young man offends another and blows are struck. This isn't regarded as very serious, until someone tries to break the fight up. Should one of the youths hit the intermediary, he may strike the youth, which may anger the youth's brother, who may strike him. The striking chain (or, in Canelos, the hair-pulling one) can touch off an exchange of blows between previously cooperating brothers or closely cooperating in-laws. These exchanges are very serious, for they may lead to permanent fission, setting up a chain of readjustment which ramifies to most llacta members.

Fights between spouses are also triggered as women try to intervene and are slugged by their husbands. This is also serious, especially when a man has an adult son who tries to intervene in his father's chastisement of his mother. Fights between spouses and between brothers are eventually mediated by outside intervention—by priest, or by political official if one exists. But fights between in-laws are resolved by a group of brothers ganging up on the in-law and driving him out. When one group of brothers attempts to expel an in-law who is accompanied by an equally strong group of brothers, a real battle may take place which will require years to resolve and may even lead, through time, to a feud extending through generations and involving people through many territories.

Considering the tensions which can break out, and the readjustments which will then be necessary in the immediate and distant future, it is remarkable how well the Canelos Quichua contain the post-ceremonial hostilities. Frequently, prominent people in a given ceremony are those who, a decade before, left after a fight and a series of mutual hostilities to found a new llacta. By stressing *alliance* with such now more distant relatives, and by playing down internal hostilities, some harmony in the immediate scene is achieved, and integration of the territorial and inter-territorial Runa is furthered. Also, young men who see the way of things with increasing hostility around them, and who have difficulties in maintaining a reasonable life in the immediate surroundings of growing negative debts (accumulated reciprocal insults through a period of time), may seek to ally with those coming from a more distant llacta or Runa territory. Affirmation of common descent at the ayllu ceremony gives ideological support to such new alliances.

In short, the tensions and hostilities manifest at the post-ceremonial drink and fight fests occur in a context where realignment and spatial mobility can take place. Drinking may go on for several days, with a great many breaches resolved by collective discussion and projection of the breach onto forces outside the Runa world but within their sphere of adaptation. For example, grievances against the local priest or local political officials may be enumerated, and two parties to a fight be shown to have the same grievance. Such grievances must then be presented to members of the cabildo, who in turn present them to the officials. Such grievances can prevent escalation of conflict between two men, thereby saving their kinsmen from potential conflict necessitating ramifying

Drinking aguardiente after ceremonial enactment.

alliances with relevant parties. At the same time outward-oriented grievance presentation strengthens, for a time, the role as mediator of one member or another of the cabildo.

Fighting itself among the Canelos Quichua has several specific degrees. I have been discussing the one least liked by the people, the one they call *ñucanchi pura llata (llatan)*, fighting among ourselves (literally, "our nakedness between two"). Another type is the *jacu macanacushu*, brawl (literally, "let's go fight with the macana"). This sort of fight takes place when one unit squares off against another, using hands, fists, feet, and teeth—*not* the macana—as sole weapons. When one llacta group fights with another and the visitors leave as a result, all may end reasonably well and grievances can be patched up by stronger territorial boundary creation and maintenance. The macanacushu fight, however, may also precipitate a schism which is not easy to resolve. For example, during a general brawl two cooperating men of the same llacta may square off in the pura llata, and this is the most serious breach to handle. In fact, it may lead one or the other to begin intensively cooperating with members of a heretofore rival llacta, again strengthening such boundaries within a Runa territory.

Two forms of fighting stress killing. One is the *jacu huañuna cushun,* a war with another group for the purpose of killing as many people as possible. The other is the *jacu huanshigrishu,* which is a specific, planned killing of another person. I am told that the former used to be carried out after an annual ceremony and were invariably aimed at the Jívaro proper, the Untsuri Shuara, of the right bank of the Pastaza River.

Illness, Vendettas, and Motivations to Kill

No one feels very well after the ayllu ceremony. Food poisoning from overripe smoked meat and fish combines with the extreme gas pains and bloat caused by the copiously consumed chicha, and possible cyanide poisoning from the fungus chicha and vinillu. There are sorcery accusations and heightened curiosity and wonder at the world of spirits, which also participated in the ceremony.

Shamans and powerful shamans are visited, and in some cases strong accusations are lodged by important members of one ayllu segment against another. Such accusations usually revolve around existing long-term shamanistic feuds and ayllu vendettas. After the ayllu ceremony, however, some new genealogical connections of participants may be remembered, and more people reshuffled a bit to fit one or another side of an existing vendetta.

One solution to ramifying schismatic factionalism involving more and more Runas on one side or the other of powerful shamans locked in killing duels is the direct elimination of one of the shamans. Since the Canelos Quichua believe that they cannot directly kill a powerful shaman, they seek to make pacts with distant Achuara Jivaroans or with Jívaro proper to do the job for them.

To approach Achuara powerful killers, Canelos Quichua shamans prefer to use sons or sons-in-law who know their language and customs; this serves to maintain alliances extending between Canelos Quichua, Achuara Jivaroan, and Jívaro proper and guarantees a multi-ethnic core of strong

Canelos Quichua men able to move between the power fields of the
Canelos Quichua shamans and the direct attack prowess of the Jivaroans.
Many bilingual Achuara–Canelos Quichua men serve as ayudantes or
priostes in each ayllu ceremony. Such participation signals their willingness to be incorporated into Canelos Quichua life, often as sons-in-law of
powerful shamans.

Incorporation of such Achuara, and also Zaparoan, though I know almost
nothing about the latter,[10] brings yet another concept of *Sacha Runa* to our
discussion. Native people who know a language other than Quichua, and
who can travel with impunity to other groups—isolated, skirt-wearing
Jívaro proper, Achuara Jivaroans on the Copotaza or Conambo rivers,
forest-dwelling Zaparoans—are known as Sacha Runa. The designation in
this context implies knowledge of peoples of the tropical forest transcending the culture boundaries of the Canelos Quichua, and removed from the
centers of national invasion. Dream-bringing drumming by such Sacha
Runa, as ayudantes, opens the Canelos Quichua power force not only to
forest soul master and clay- and garden-giver spirits, but also to whatever
souls and spirits, yet unknown in their entirety, may exist eastward,
southward, and northward in the vast damp forests from which the Canelos
Quichua emerged and to which they owe their everlasting ayllu and ethnic
continuity.

The ayllu ceremony begins with a peaceful if tension-filled merging of
spirit and Runa domains, crescendoes to a near dominance of domain spirit
masters, and ends not only with a symbolic reestablishment of these
domains, but some inevitable readjustment in kinship and territorial
alliance as well. Readjustment and continuity through the annual or
biannual ayllu ceremony expand the ethnic charter to other jungle peoples,
particularly as a last resort in thwarting possible pervasive ayllu factionalism through shamanistic vendettas.[11]

NOTES

1. The relationship between church policy and administration and ayllu ceremony is
discussed in the next chapter. Among the Puyo Runa, with whom I did most of my field work,
the ceremony is now held away from the central Puyo area, in the larger, and/or oldest of the
dispersed llactas with established hamelts, *caseríos.*

The data in this chapter are presented so as to describe the basic aspects of the ceremony as
it exists today in Canelos, Paca Yacu, Sara Yacu, and Montalvo, as it existed in Puyo prior to
the large-scale colonization by non-native nationals, and as it presumably exists in Curaray. I
have seen everything presented here, except where explicitly noted, at the annual ceremony
at Paca Yacu. Among the Puyo Runa I have participated in five annual or biannual ceremonies
based on the described model, and served as *cajonero uyariungui* in one. Also, in many
smaller-scale ceremonies, ranging from spontaneous ones to the founding of the museum in

the caserío of Río Chico, aspects of the larger ceremony were played out, and instruction was given to me as to the symbols and metaphors involved. During all such participation people from the Runa territories mentioned above were present. In addition, people working on the Lowland Quichua Project have visited the annual ceremony at San Ramón and still another caserío on the Pastaza River. These data, together with those taken from priests and from the archives at Canelos, give considerable weight to the material presented here. Finally, it must be noted that full participation is called for to get data on this ceremony. Only after an anthropologist has (literally) immersed himself in chicha, fungus chicha, and vinillu in one or more ceremonies can data pertaining to symbolism, metaphor, and elaboration of ceremonial structure be presented; this requirement perhaps accounts for the sparcity of data on the ceremony in the work of Karsten (1935), and that of various authors writing in the *Oriente Dominicano*.

The weakest aspect of this portrayal concerns the symbolism, metaphor, social position of the *lanceros*. *The Puyo Runa do not include a lancero group, dance, or attendant symbolism in their annual ceremony*, nor, as far as I know, do the Curaray Runa.

I have not called the divisions of the *jisteros* "moieties," even though the term means "division in half." This is because I am reluctant to give weight to speculation on a prior division in half of each territory or unit. The concept of opposition of allied groups, indeed of opposition and resolution in all aspects of social and symbolic life, is crucial to Canelos Quichua ways. I have deliberately submerged Catholic observation based on imposed dogma of a moiety system among the Canelos Quichua (described in the Dominican literature in terms of *partidos*) because such a division seems based partly on the ceremonial opposition, partly on the territorial division into llactas, and partly on concepts of "upriver" and "downriver" groupings, each of which operates at a different level of culture. A technical paper is planned on this subject.

My impression of this ceremonial pattern near the centers of intensive trade and colonization is that the symbolism and activity patterns are becoming more condensed, but expanding in numbers of locations and in frequency of performance. An example of condensation is the incorporation of *cari jista* and *lanceros* in the same house at Paca Yacu on one occasion; an example of expansion is the giving of five different ceremonies on more or less "traditional" lines in different llactas of the Puyo Runa near Christmas, 1972, at about the same time. In one of these there were three ceremonial houses ranged along a road on which the jisteros walked in total disdain for colonists trying to move traffic.

Discussion of this ceremony in the metaphoric correspondences manner described by Fernandez (1973:1366) will be undertaken in a separate article. I agree thoroughly with his statement that "the ritual system is, in essence, a system of enacted correspondences" (see also Fernandez 1974). However, completion of such an analysis prior to discussion of the entire ceremonial structure in this book would, I think, greatly delay publication and thereby prevent others from also working on aspects of this subject from comparative points of view.

2. The Catholic Church imposes a varayo or cabildo system, briefly described in the Introduction to this book and analyzed to some extent in the next two chapters. The cabildo members are selected or elected, according to Runa territorial style, disposition of clergy, and gathered native people. Four or six officers are chosen to serve essentially as brokers between clergy and people for one year; then a new group is selected at the insistence of the people. The Dominican plan of control of natives in Canelos Quichua territory, which includes church dogma regarding native ceremony, service of natives, and social oppression of all Indians in the area, is given in their documentary guide, *Reglamento o norma directiva que observarán los misioneros en las reuniones de los pueblos*, which I read at Canelos in the spring of 1973. Among the Puyo Runa the cabildo system has been replaced by a five-man board made up of president, vice-president, secretary, treasurer, and lawyer, who communicate directly to the

Ministry of Social Security rather than to the Dominican order. Nonetheless, the church has tried to fragment the comuna of the Puyo Runa in recent months by again imposing the varayo system on one or two llactas and labeling the llactas as new church territories.

3. *Cushcamanda* or *cuscamanda uma* means "head from cusca," a head which comes from a position "straight up." Monkeys and sloths are killed by a blowgun aimed straight up toward the tops of the trees, which border on the domain of siluí, the sky. This is the exegesis of the Puyo Runa when they wish to use Quichua rather than the Jivaroan *tsantsa* for the head brought back with a captured foreign person's soul.

4. The fundamental color of the callana today is black, *yana*. But some people make red callanas, though they do not like to use the term *puca*, red, for the bowl. Where *yana manga* may be accepted as synonymous with *callana*, the term *puca manga* makes people wince. Some women at Canelos still conscientiously make a white callana, *ruyaj manga*, one of which I collected in 1973 but the significance of which I am ignorant. Black is the Canelos Quichua color for Nunghuí and Amasanga, and meat (animal and fish) is served in black ware, in all *discussions* of ceremonies. It is clear that Jívaro proper women use red for the Nunghuí color and serve food in red, or black-and-red, ware. It is probable that the three colors—black, red, and white—had some ceremonial significance in past times, and among some of the old women today in Canelos, Paca Yacu, or perhaps Sara Yacu such significance may still be brought to light.

5. To make a three-week ceremony, just extend activities described under "Wednesday and Thursday" for another week. In such cases of longer preparation work is less intense, and an even larger array of pottery and chicha is produced, which makes the ceremony itself more intense.

6. In some areas of Quijos Quichua territory lancero dances also take place, at the annual town fiesta at Tena and Archidona, and at local chonta ceremonies just east of Archidona. Many aspects of the Quijos lancero dance are the same as the one I witnessed at Paca Yacu in November, 1972, which is the only Canelos Quichua lancero involvement in the annual ceremony I have seen. I speculate that the lancero dance is of Zaparoan origin, and that, among other things, it perhaps represents Zaparoan attack power (see also note 7 below).

7. The play on words and languages between Quichua and Achuara Jivaroan is well illustrated by the concept *taruga puma*, cougar. In "proper" Canelos Quichua a cougar is *puca puma*, red cat. In Achuara Jivaroan jaguar and dog are classed together as *yawáa*, hunting animal. The cougar is *japa yawáa*, deer cat, and the Canelos Quichua simply translate the Achuara to Quichua as *taruga puma*, particularly in the absence of Quijos Quichua speakers. That there is more to the concept of "deer" and "cougar" than this, however, allows us to understand how Karsten could have derived the equation Quichua *aya* = Jívaro *wakani* and Quichua *supai* = Jívaro *iwanchi*. In Chapter 2, note 4, I noted that bicultural Jivaroan–Canelos Quichua informants make the equation Jívaro *iwanchi* = Quichua *aya*, and emphatically deny that the Quichua *supai* is the Jívaro *iwanchi*. The Canelos Quichua, as we saw in the last chapter, believe that all birds of the apapa class (eagles and owls) are embodiments of ancient shamans' souls. They also believe that all deer are embodiments of ancient Runa, non-shaman, souls. They state simply, in certain contexts, that *taruga* = *aya*, deer = soul. Writing about the Jívaro proper, Harner (1972:150) states, "The Jívaro interpret the presence of such creatures [owls and deer] at these old living places [garden sites] as evidence that the animals are temporarily visible embodiments of true souls. The true souls, when they are in these visible forms, are referred to as 'human demons' (*šuar iwanči*)." Through the concept of "deer," then, we understand more completely the correct transformation of concepts from Jívaro to Canelos Quichua, the former adding the corporeal representation (deer) to the concept of soul to create a "demon" *representation* which equates with the Quichua soul representation, the latter of which lacks a demon component to corporeal substance. The

equation Quichua soul = deer = Jívaro demon is easily established, and further suggests that the Alli Runa–Sacha Runa duality (discussed in the next chapter) is joined in ritual enactment through the mediation of the taruga puma ayllu of the lanceros.

I think, but data are inadequate to be sure, that the combination of taruga with puma is also made to suggest a parallel ayllu of deceased souls, represented in the annual ayllu ceremony by the lanceros. Whether or not ethnic (Zaparoan) relationships can be made to combine with concepts of living and deceased I am not sure, but I recommend more attention to this area.

8. This is not done among the Puyo Runa because there are normally no canes of authority. Among the Puyo Runa, members of the governing board do attend, and are treated as described in the text. Lately the Catholic Church has attempted to take advantage of the prioste system and the caserío governing system to designate either prioste or local representative as varayo, and has even bestowed two canes of authority on nonresident, non-participant individuals in one llacta system.

9. This ceremony is called *albano* (and I have heard *albazo*, which is the name of a highland Ecuadorian folk dance) by Canelos Quichua who know any name for it, *and* by the Dominican *Reglamento* mentioned in note 2. It presumably derives from the Spanish *alabar* (to offer praise). A Zaparoan group on the Tigre River was also known as the *Alabano* (see Steward & Métraux 1948:638). In Quichua the only name I have been able to learn for this translates as "let us go to the new house to drink at dawn," *mushuj huasii upi ringahua tutamanda: mushuj*—new/, *huasi*—house/, *i*—in/, *upi*—drink/, *ri*—reflexive?/, *ngahua*—let us/, *tutamanda*—dawn.

10. Among the people with whom I worked, especially bicultural Achuara–Canelos Quichua, or children of Achuara parentage, there was a great reluctance to discuss Záparos. There are many bilingual, bicultural Zaparoans living on the Bobonaza and to the north, but it is very difficult to elicit acknowledgment of familiarity with the language; unlike the case with Jivaroan languages, there seems to be some stigma among the Canelos Quichua in admitting Zaparoan parentage. The last person to admit being a Zaparoan speaker among the Puyo Runa, the wife of a powerful shaman, was murdered in 1970. Jívaro proper are blamed for the killing. It is possible that another field worker embedded in a set of people with more Zaparoan and less Achuaran influence would learn much more of the former and less of the latter. I think that there is strong Achuara-Záparo hostility but that the Canelos Quichua power sources, and their concepts of generalized spirit-human Sacha Runa, mediate such hostility, provided that both Achuara and Záparo are within the confines of Canelos Quichua territory and stipulated descent systems.

11. Within a month after the annual ceremony distant Achuara and Zaparoans arrive to trade with the Canelos Quichua at Montalvo, Sara Yacu, and Paca Yacu. Goods from the southeast and northeast such as dart poison, porpoise teeth, feathered headdresses, and blowguns are brought to be exchanged for kerosene, black powder, shot, caps, and clothes.

Puyo Runa Adaptation and Change

CHAPTER

7

Puyo Runa Baseline

Near the base of the precipitous eastern slopes of the central Ecuadorian Andes small, clear, pebble- and alluvium-laden rivers rise and fall as the rainfall changes in intensity and duration. Rising rivers rush into the Pastaza, causing downriver swelling in the lower Pastaza and Marañón. There, somewhere in Upper and Central Amazonia, hundreds of thousands of sucker-mouth challua[1] begin an upriver run, seeking out the food-filled tributaries of the larger rivers. On the largest Pastaza tributary, the Bobonaza, the end of the challua run is Canelos. But thousands upon thousands of challua miss the mouth of the Bobonaza and continue on up the Pastaza, eventually turning into another affluent, the Puyo, where they continue the upstream movement over cataracts and rapids during high-water periods. As they run they literally clean and polish millions of pebbles and rocky ledges of a particular kind of fast-growing algae, moving on and on in search of this food. Finally they encounter their ultimate barrier—an impassable small waterfall near the Puyo River headwaters.

At the end of the nineteenth century, before the coming of Andean and coastal colonists, this waterfall on the upper Puyo marked the northwest residential boundary of the Puyo Runa. The people ranged through a markedly differentiated territory from the upper Puyo River to the Pastaza, trading, raiding, and intermarrying with Quijos to the north and northwest, Canelos to the east, and Jívaro proper and Achuara Jivaroans to the southeast, south, and west.[2] Within their central Runa territory challua runs provided periodic large catches with nets, harpoons, and weirs. When water was especially low, fish poisoning provided somewhat lesser catches of characinids, cichlids, and other varieties. Between the river highs and lows, harpooning, trapping, and small-scale poisoning of the innumerable small streams, lagoons, and low swampy areas provided all people with ample eels, ñachi, a minnow-like fish with powerful jaws, chuti and pashin or huanchichi,[3] pike-like one- to three-pound fish, knife fish, sucker-mouth catfish, other small catfish, and the ubiquitous characinids and cichlids. Crabs, shrimp, water and land snails, turtles, and tortoises were abundant.

The forest of the Puyo Runa ranges from 3,000 to 1,000 feet. It spans montaña and hylean ecologies in a very diversified rainforest system, which includes soils enriched from Andean sediment and ash from the active volcanoes to the nearby west which abut a *ceja* cloud forest zone. Just to the east lies the Siguin Cordillera, a worn, third cordillera cut through by the Bobonaza River, the major connecting link of the Puyo Runa with other Canelos Quichua territories to the east.

Monkey troops, especially squirrel, woolly, howler, and spider, were once variously distributed in Puyo Runa territory, or within a distance of a half-day trek. Deer, agouti, paca, and armadillo were numerous, and herds of collared and white-lipped peccary were not uncommon. Wildfowl were relatively abundant. But the Puyo Runa did much of their hunting in designated territories which were also favored hunting areas of people from Canelos, Paca Yacu, and also the Jívaro proper, Achuara Jivaroans, Huarani Auca or Zaparoans,[4] and the Quijos. In turn, many Jívaro proper and Achuara Jivaroans chose to hunt in the territory of the Puyo Runa, as did some peoples known as Caninche, who occupied the rugged El Siguin Cordillera zone between Canelos and the Tashapi River.

Hunting, territorial defense, the making of alliances through intermarriage, and raiding to kill men and steal women and children all synergized into a dynamic system. The subsistence economic basis for this system was root crop and plantain cultivation, supplemented by abundant tarapoto and other palm hearts, chontaduro palm hearts and fruits, various nuts, fruits, cucurbits, and maize. While men fished, hunted, raided, and traded, women took care of much of the subsistence agricultural base.

The oval houses, fortified all around with strong chonta staffs, were built on hilltops within a one- to three-minute walk from clear, cold water supplies, and within a three- to four-minute walk from the Puyo-Pindo rivers or one of their many small tributaries, which spread outward like fingers into nearby Andean foothills. Each household was headed by a man who was either yachaj or huanchij, or both, together with at least one married son and one or two married daughters with their husbands. Each huasi unit made up a minimal social grouping joined to other such units by ayllu bonds, by bonds of mutual, open reciprocity developed through marriage alliances, and by the need to defend the common central Runa territory radiating out from the contemporary site of Puyo.

A continuous water supply,[5] access to fish in rivers and swampy marsh, a hilltop residence for defense and comfort from lower-level insect molestation combined with rich land for cyclical slash-mulch swidden root crop agriculture (called "permanent settlement swidden cultivation" by Harris 1972:249) and several nearby hunting territories. By the time an adequate Baños-Mera (Barrancas) mule trail was established in the late 1920s, the Puyo Runa had become central actors in trade with the Napo peoples, with Canelos, and through Baños with the sierra. Bilingualism (Jivaroan and Quichua) characterized the Puyo Runa, and reconstruction over the past sixty years indicates that every huasi unit contained within it, or within the immediate residential ayllu segment of its founder, some male members identifiable as either Achuara or Jívaro proper, and many households contained Quijos and Zaparoan men and women as well.

EARLY DEPOPULATION

Early maps (Morales y Eloy 1942:tab. 34–44) drawn in the seventeenth and eighteenth centuries indicate European and colonial exploration of the area from Baños through Puyo to the Pastaza, Copotaza, and Bobonaza rivers. There is no question but that the auriferous gravels of the area stimulated considerable contact between Andean traders and people living in the Puyo and Canelos area (Villavicencio 1858:411, Oberem 1974). Basically, in these centuries the Spanish crown's insatiable mercantile thirst for gold articulated well with the church's insatiable desire for bureaucratic expansion. Territorial expansion of the latter provided rationale for the former's extraction policy. Native people provided the labor for gold panning and the human capital for soul saving in the two spheres of Spanish colonial activity in the frontier forests east of the Andes and west of Central Amazonia.

Stirling's (1938:24) brief synopsis of the known early history provides an excellent, succinct description:

> The Dominican convent of Quito sent out four priests in the year 1581 into the territory of the Jívaro and the Canelos. . . . Diego de Ochoa and Sebastian Rosero penetrated into the mountains of Penday and Poya [Puyo] near the source of the Pindo River. During the year 1581 the town of Canelos was founded at the mouth of the Pindo and missionary work was started at this point. However, the Spaniards were continually harassed by the attacks of the Jívaros and it became necessary to change the location of Canelos twice. It was finally established on the left bank of the Bobonaza on the spot where it exists at the present day. This mission was officially turned over to the Dominicans by Charles II in 1683 but it did not progress, and by 1788 it contained only 22 converts.
>
> About this time Father Santiago Riofrío arrived, and under his administration the mission began to make headway. He succeeded in adding three small villages to the territory of the mission in 1789. These were Nuestra Señora del

Rosario, San Jacinto, and San Carlos de los Achuales. In 1803 the Dominicans
relinquished control of the mission and it was placed under the Bishop of
Mainas.[6]

In 1803, then, the central zone for dispersing priestly services and for the
collection of gold and other desired forest products became centralized
farther from the Ecuadorian Andes, at Borja, below the Pongo de
Manseriche in what is now Peru. Here the Portuguese penetration
westward petered out and the Spanish movement eastward from the Andes
waned. According to Phelan (1967:42): "In this story of penetration into
the Amazon on one of the 'rims of Christendom,' the key role lay with the
Church, in this particular case, the sons of St. Ignatius Loyola. That the upper Amazon basin is today Spanish and not Portuguese is primarily the
result of a few dozen Jesuits."

The 200 years of Andean-Amazonian Spanish thrusting took its toll. The
most significant aspect of such contact was tremendous contagion from
foreign diseases, especially smallpox, chicken pox, measles. Total depopulation may have occurred in the area of the Puyo Runa as people either died
or fled to distant sacha huasis in the face of the clear, if invisible, blanket of
death.

All of the available data on depopulation comes from documentation east
of Canelos,[7] where Jesuits carefully recorded the effects of disease
decimation, enslavement to the *encomienda* system, and Portuguese slave
raiding. For example, the historian Phelan (1967:47) tells us, "Once
the epidemics began in the Province of Mainas, their impact was
overwhelming. About 44,000 of the 100,000 partially Christianized natives
died during the first epidemic of 1660. Another wave of smallpox occurred
in 1669, killing 20,000 Indians. No more epidemics took place until 1749,
when measles spread through the land, taking a massive toll
in lives. Smallpox recurred in 1756 and in 1762, delivering the *coup de
grâce* to the once-promising missions of the Jesuits in Mainas. Along with
Indian revolts and Portuguese slave-raiding expeditions, the epidemics
reduced the missions to a scant 18,000 neophytes by 1762." David G.
Sweet (1969) has reconstructed the depopulation between the seventeenth
and nineteenth centuries in Upper Amazonia. A glance at a few of the
figures for native peoples just to the east of the Puyo-Canelos zone is
telling: Mayna (Zaparoan), 90%, Roamayna/Zapa (Zaparoan), 100%,
Pinche, 70%, Gae/Semigae (Zaparoan), 50%, Andoa (Zaparoan), 70%,
Avijira, 60%, Coronado/Oa, 80%. Sweet (1969:103) considers these all to
be Zaparoan, and derives a total depopulation figure of 80 percent for them.

The vague period sometime prior to the early nineteenth century is
accurately conceptualized as Times of Destruction. Dispersion of the

surviving Puyo Runa undoubtedly occurred, so the Puyo legend of attenuated ayllu links before Times of the Grandparents is apt. Also, stipulated transmission systems accurately portray descendants as inevitably attached to many scattered llacta groupings in various territories. Old people of the contemporary Puyo Runa, and people from all other Runa territories, insist that a mantle of contagion and death hung over the area between the Puyo and Pastaza rivers, and that for a long time no one could live there. Those who traveled into the region to hunt or develop a purina chagra not only risked death but often brought contagion back to Canelos, to the Curaray-Villano headwaters, to Copotaza, or to other Runa territories.

RE-POPULATION

By the first quarter of the twentieth century Karsten (1935:27) could write about the Bobonaza, Copotaza, Llushín, and upper Pastaza River areas that "although these rivers are situated only a few leagues from the eastern cordilleras, they were not properly explored until a few years ago." This statement is an erroneous oversimplification, for nineteenth-century travelers such as Simson (1886) seemed to find no problem in hiring competent guides at Baños and Canelos to take them hither and yon across east central Ecuador, from the Bobonaza River to the Curaray and Napo. Nonetheless, it does seem that the Puyo Runa enjoyed a period of population buildup and a brief respite from intensive, continuing contact, from around the beginning of the nineteenth century to the onset of the twentieth. We know that in the mid-nineteenth century there were some bilingual Jivaroan-Quichua people in the Puyo area (Simpson 1886:84–100, Spruce 1908:127–141, Valladares 1912:24–26), allied with Canelos and Sara Yacu peoples against Jívaros of the right bank of the Pastaza (Simson 1886:90). But the sharp rise in population began around the turn of the present century. Events described in published sources at that time (Valladares 1912) can be related to the oral history obtained in field work. For this reason our discussion of the Puyo Runa will begin with the period from a little before 1900.

The period begins with rubber demand–sponsored cataclysms in the east, and upriver movement by mauraders on the Napo. These stimulated an increase in the native population around Puyo, which in a short time was matched by a non-native national increase there. The sustained contact between Puyo Runa and non-Indian Ecuadorian nationals and foreigners characterizes the era between the 1930s and the present, and is the subject of the next two chapters.

The Amazonian Rubber Boom

Technological invention seems sometimes to spawn terrible social malig-
nancies which spread through an ecosystem in such a way as to permanently alter, cripple, and kill it. European mercantilism and its gold
extraction based on refined shipping and communication was one such
system; the African slave trade feeding insatiable demands for new cash
crops was another; and the rubber boom in Amazonia clearly belongs in this
class of malignant social forms.

Forces which conjoined the Canelos Quichua biosphere with processes
of burgeoning Western technology were the direct result of world demand
for raw materials. In the late nineteenth century rubber became the
product which stimulated re-exploration and re-destruction of Upper
Amazonia and a new subjugation of many peoples. Women of the lower
Bobonaza never dreamed that their expert, secret knowledge of coating
carefully painted mucahuas and chicha storage jars with latex could be of
interest to the new giants of industry in England, Germany, France, and
the United States. But that special Sacha Huarmi knowledge was on the
verge of worldwide demand.

> Despite its intriguing potential, rubber's progress... was marked by
> meteoric ups and downs.... though manufacturers esteemed rubber for
> purposes as diverse as beer-engine pumps, fire hoses, catheters and fishing
> boots, its uses were still but a drop in the bucket. Not until the winter's day in
> 1839 when Charles Goodyear... accidentally touched a gum-and-sulfur
> mixture to a hot stove lid in a Massachusetts village store to find it charred like
> leather was the riddle of rubber finally solved.... Goodyear... evolved
> vulcanized or weather-proof rubber—and from this historic moment the
> Amazon rush was on [Collier 1968:42–43].

Amazonia was the land of rubber trees; people native to the vast territories
knew how to gather the latex. They were cajoled, tricked, and eventually
enslaved into service. By the late 1800s the boom was at its peak. Although
rubber seeds had been exported from Brazil and were growing in
greenhouses in England to be transplanted far from their disease vectors on
plantations in Asia and Africa (Collier 1968), the elaborate system of
collection, centralization, and shipment of the latex outward from inner
Amazonia to the United States and Europe was expanding exponentially.

In 1888 the central headquarters of Julio César Arana, baron of the trade,
was located on the upper Huallaga River, eastern Peru, near the
conjunction of Andean foothills at Lamas and the Upper Amazonian
territory at Yurimaguas. His "trading post" was at Tarapoto, "a forgotten
6,000-strong community" (Collier 1968:43). A deadly, west-moving arc of
rubber searchers, slave seekers, and money-hungry desperados was

established just beyond the eastern, southern, and northern parameters of Canelos Quichua territory, well within the old Maynas mission territory. Havoc reigned in this land of Panoans, Jivaroans, Zaparoans, and other peoples, and many groups sought refuge in the Canelos Quichua forest.

The *caucheros* (from the east Ecuadorian Omagua term *cahuchu*—Collier 1968:42), as the rubber searchers were called, developed a system of reciprocal raiding and terrorism as they attempted to control a jungle zone and maintain a captive labor force to exploit wild latex. "Constant thefts of Indians by one 'cauchero' from another led to reprisals more bloody and murderous than anything the Indian had ever wrought upon his fellow-Indian. The primary aim of rubber-getting, which could only be obtained from the labor of the Indian, was often lost sight of in these desperate conflicts" (Campbell 1912:10). Rubber was the product to be sold on the world markets. But on the tributaries of the Upper Amazon the native peoples were the immediate prize and the target of the rubber-boom social malignancy: "The object of the 'civilized' intruders, in the first instance, was not to annihilate the Indians, but to 'conquistar,' i.e., to subjugate them, and put them to what was termed civilized, or at any rate profitable, occupation to their subduers" (Campbell 1912:10).

As the arc moved westward into Canelos Quichua territory, with bases at Montalvo on the Bobonaza and at the junction of the Villano and Curaray,[8] many things occurred. Various eastern and northeastern Indians intruded into the territory as cauchero allies, other Indians intruded as refugees from cauchero slaving, and the Canelos Quichua lost their direct trade relationship with the Huallaga River area. This later situation apparently gave rise to a diversity of trade alliances and strategies to maintain a supply of salt, dart poison, black powder, shot, caps, and muzzle-loading shotguns, steel machetes, axe heads, and beads (Oberem 1974:354). For the Canelos Quichua all of these goods, except steel tools, had previously come from the southeast.

Working with archival sources, Oberem (1974:354) writes about "the Canelo": ". . . the Dominican missionaries made great efforts to channel to their Canelos mission part of the salt produced, by means of salt water evaporation, by the Jíbaro northeast of Macas. The missionaries were so successful in their efforts that, to the present day, not only the town of Macas, but also the Canelo territory is supplied from this source. This trade between the Canelo and Jíbaro could not, however, meet the demand. Therefore, around 1914, both the Canelo and the Quijo again began to make successful salt trading journeys [to the Huallaga River]." Many of the old Puyo Runa remember the salt trips to the Huallaga River, but some affirm another route, where other trade was carried on. Bilingual Canelos Quichua–Achuara Jivaroan from the Puyo area would walk from Indillama to the headwaters of the Copotaza, secure canoes from relatives, and go down the Copotaza to the Pastaza River. There they would walk inland to the headwaters of the Huasaga River, and go down it to a site known as Huambishu, where they would rendezvous with other, related, Achuara from farther east and trade steel tools for salt, feathered headdresses, and dart poison. These Achuara also traded with the Cocama and Candoshi farther east; sometimes Peruvian Cocama would also come up the Huasaga to trade at the Achuara site of Huambishu.

National Penetration

International activity within the borders of a sovereign state inevitably sets up national processes of consolidation of international boundaries. The expansion of the rubber boom not only wreaked havoc upon native peoples of Upper Amazonia, it also stimulated the young, Andean-based governments of Ecuador and Peru to renew waning interest in their tropical lowlands. The Ecuadorian Oriente is so placed as to require enormous energy to extract and transport products to sources of demand. Goods must either flow upward over montaña and Andes (and then downward again to the coast), or downward over waterfalls, rapids, and cataracts to the navigable rivers of the Amazon basin. The rubber boom consolidated the network of river transportation east of the current boundaries of the Ecuadorian nation, and a little later the Panama Canal provided the necessary connecting link for Andean countries through their western Pacific ports.

Ecuador's national strategy of infrastructural territorial and resource consolidation during the late nineteenth and early twentieth centuries was to create linkages to *both* eastern and western waterways, and to provide access from coast and Oriente to Andean cities and towns (Linke 1960:112–117, Hegen 1966:60–62, Garces 1942, Whitten 1965:29). Convinced by foreign experts familiar with the conquest of the Appalachian and Rocky mountains in the United States that narrow-guage railroads were the answer to the total lack of infrastructural support for national exploitation of extant tropical territory, Ecuador began explorations aimed at delineation of the routes of a projected Andean-Amazonian system. One such venture was the proposed Ambato-Curaray railroad, which was to move from Ambato through Baños-Puyo-Villano to Curaray (Anonymous 1935, Jurado 1970:9). The critical socio-geographical linkages between Andean developers and lowland residents took place in the territory of the Puyo Runa.

Situated as they were, at the headwaters of the Pindo-Puyo rivers and just up a high ridge from the Bobonaza headwaters, beyond access of river penetration from the east, the Puyo Runa ecology provided not only an adequate setting for their subsistence life, but also refuge from the rubber-boom holocaust to the east. People penetrating from the Andes around the turn of the century were absolutely dependent on the Puyo Runa. Not only did the local inhabitants control access to trade goods coming from the south, east, and north, but they also were easily able to provide subsistence game, maize, and plantains while retaining their own necessary fish, taro-yautia, potatoes, sweet potatoes, manioc, and other root crops.

But it was exploration and Andean expansion which was in the minds of the Puyo penetrators of the late nineteenth and early twentieth centuries, not subsistence, and Puyo Runa culture—especially its core relational system revolving around the concept of Sacha Runa—became crucial to national exploration and eventual infrastructural expansion aimed at exploitation. The Puyo Runa offered expert knowledge of the forest of *montaña, hylea, eté,* and *várzea.*[9] They not only guided the explorers through the complex ecosystem of soils, trees, shrubs, fauna, and flora, but also led them to safe contact with other Sacha Runa speaking other languages. These natives—Jivaroan and Zaparoan, among others— apparently conceptualized their territories according to various transformational symbolic and metaphoric relationships, and enforced usufructory rights within geographic zones. The zones themselves were made up of various intercultural alliances with shifting ethnic markers.

National penetration revalidated the Canelos Quichua relational system by offering a new challenge. The challenge presented by national-sponsored intrusion was accepted by huasi founders and ayllu nodes, themselves connected by alliance, consanguinity, and a meta-system of dynamic symbolic relationships spanning Achuara, Zaparoan, and Quijos cosmogony north of the Pastaza River. Individuals from Puyo walked, with "explorers," into all parts of eastern Ecuador and on into lowland Peru, re-expanding and reconsolidating attenuated ayllu and alliance relationships, seeking a firmer grip on the purchase possibilities of their own ecotype, within general Canelos Quichua society and culture.

The scant but adequate literature on the Puyo area during the period of national expansion leaves little doubt that the native people were part of what Helms (1969:329) has termed a "purchase society":

Members of purchase societies appear as rural participants within a wider *economic* network formed either by industrializing nations searching for raw materials for their growing industries, or by trade with agrarian states. Geographically, purchase societies can be found on economic frontiers of states, in territory that is beyond de facto state political control (although often falling within the official de jure boundaries claimed by the state), but lying within economic reach of state activities. From the point of view of the local

society, the overriding factor, the channel that directs and influences all other
activities, is the need, small at first but constantly growing, for items of foreign
manufacture.

This period of late nineteenth-century–early twentieth-century national
exploration initiates the period of Puyo Runa Times of the Grandparents.
The period launches a native people on a reoccupation of an ancient
territory. Consolidation of the territory necessitated extraterritorial alliances which helped to build up local population and provided a
multi-lingual, multi-cultural basis for continued Puyo Runa expansion. At
the same time, the period initiated more extensive mutual trade as Puyo
became a locus for the inflow of marketable jungle products such as pelts,
gold, spices, drugs, dyes, and dispersal of items of foreign manufacture
such as axe heads, knives, machetes, cotton shirts, skirts, and trousers.

Left to their own devices of trade, alliance, and civil guerrilla strife to
protect rights of usufruct in their forest domain, the Canelos Quichua,
spearheaded by the Puyo Runa at the turn of the twentieth century, might
well have evolved a state within a state (on the unsubjugated frontier of a
nation) analogous to that of the sixteenth-century Zambo republic in
northwestern Ecuador (Phelan 1967:7–8, Whitten 1974:40–41), or to other
possibly comparable states in Southeast Asia (Leach 1954:197–226,
Lehman 1963, 1967). But another factor of national-international intervention also penetrated in the form of the soul-saving Catholics.

Dominican Dominion

By 1877 the mission of Canelos was reestablished as the locus of the
territorial archdiocese, and the Dominicans laid claim to the territory of the
contemporary Canelos Quichua, now including the mission of Gayes
(González Suárez 1970:201). In 1899 a Dominican friar, Alvaro Valladares
(1912), moved from Canelos proper to Puyo, bringing with him a group
of bilingual Jivaroan and Quichua men. Each of them is today thought
of by his children and grandchildren as a powerful shaman or raiding
warrior. Each, it is said, was already familiar with the Puyo Runa territory, and each was the acknowledged descendant of other known
powerful ancestors ranging from what is now Mera to the left bank of the
Pastaza, the Tashapi River, the Arajuno River headwaters, and the
Villano-Curaray headwaters. These men had diverse ties through ayllu and
marriage alliances, and they previously had spent part of each year in
Canelos proper and part of it on purina in respective territories. Valladares
(1912:24–25) states that the population of Puyo had been decimated around
1870 by a "Chirapa" Jivaroan attack, and that at the time of his arrival there
were fourteen native families, two families from Baños, and one from

Macas living there. The same number of "white families" was noted in 1927 (Yepez 1927:6).

With the reestablishment of the Dominican outpost in Puyo, probably near the site of the original Canelos mission, attempts were initiated to curtail native peoples' direct access to strategic resources and to impose juridical authority stemming from non-native concepts of usufruct and punishment. Three crucial aspects of the Dominican perspective on Indian subjugation emerge from the order's working plan.[10] First, the concept of the inherent inferiority of native peoples; second, the exclusion of native peoples from full participation in trade or other commercial negotiations; and third, the imposition of hierarchical control with the priest as the pinnacle of authority.

The Canelos Quichua seemed to accept such intrusion into their social order under certain conditions, notably when the refuge function of a zone became crucial due to exterior destruction, and when services were provided to buffer territorial encroachment by non-natives. The church provided a refuge for many peoples fleeing slavery to the east and north, and fleeing intensified internal fighting between Canelos, Jívaro proper, and some Achuara Jivaroans. It also proclaimed sovereignty of valued territory as mission-controlled, at first preventing colonists and fortune seekers from filing land claims on native hunting, fishing, chagra, and purina territories.

In return for such service it demanded weekly collective labor of young men for construction, cleaning, and maintenance of church buildings and grounds. To insure such labor it designated a group of varayos, which included a *curaca* (chief), *capitán* (captain), *alcalde* (mayor), *aguacil* (constable), and *fiscal* (treasurer). Reconstruction indicates that these officeholders were intermarried children of yachajs and perhaps former huanchijs. They provided a convenient communication linkage between the ayllu nodes of the Puyo Runa and the church authority.

The pivotal concept of Sacha Runa as "knowledgeable person" endured, for those serving as varayo quickly learned more of the Spanish language, the church-borne lingua franca Quichua spanning highland and lowland dialects, and more of the customs of the obvious authority holders in the frontier areas—the clergy. Also, as the priests visited other peoples, speaking various languages, in the immediate and more distant hinterland, they took with them recommended guides, together with some goods, specifically knives, thread, mirrors, hooks, and handkerchiefs, to trade for fish and eggs. As the already expanding trade networks were reintegrated in the westernmost area of Canelos Quichua culture, renewed priestly interest in the Sacha Runa souls contributed to localization of a trade nexus in the Puyo area.

The church's strategy for native subjugation under its own dominion established some parameters for a "native adaptation" to the frontier purchase society, as distinct from a "pioneer adaptation" which incoming colonists soon made. First, in return for the refuge zone function of a mission, native peoples—those defined as *indio* by the church—had to give the priest and his helpers manioc, plantains, and other subsistence crops. Second, although meat, fish, and eggs were purchased by the clergy, they were allowed to pay no more than half the cash value when cash was used, and a similar half-value or less in trinkets when cash was not used. Finally, the Indians were encouraged to maintain a fiesta structure with their own indigenous elements, but modeled on a general framework of folk Catholicism and Highland Quichua practices. However, the native peoples were prohibited from church activity during important Catholic Christian ceremonies such as Easter because of the imputed inability of Indians to grasp the sacred mystery of the sacraments. In this latter construct of native inferiority as regards Catholic dogma, there is no question but that the church set its native dominion aside from other proselytizing functions, establishing the basis for pernicious pluralism by separation of the native ceremonial calendar and juridical institutions from those of non-natives.

In short, repopulation of the Puyo Runa occurred in a zone offering refuge from eastern and northern destructive penetration, with a developing purchase society frontier cultural ecology mediated by church dominion over aspects of native economy and polity. By the turn of the twentieth century about a dozen large native houses were scattered around the area of contemporary Puyo; others existed from the last challua-run waterfall on the Puyo River down to the conjunction of the Puyo-Pindo rivers and on the Pindo. The activities of these Puyo Runa were somewhat conditioned by Dominican policies when there were clergy actually present, and when the Puyo Runa themselves were present in Puyo and its close hinterland.

ADAPTATION

Because of the importance of trade through this small nucleated and dispersed settlement of the Puyo Runa, other native peoples—many of them enemies of one another—began to settle within a six- to eight-hour walking distance from Puyo, especially on the Tashapi River, the lower Puyo River, and north of the Puyo River near the Arajuno River headwaters. Each of these areas of settlement was a purina area for some of the Puyo Runa, and the conjunction of people in out-moving (subsistence purina) and in-moving (trade purina) relationships was solidified by intermarriage and the creation of dispersed llactas by shaman founders of ayllu segments.

To the east and north things got worse and worse, so by the early twentieth century new alliances between some Achuara and Jívaro proper of the left and right banks of the Pastaza occurred, presumably to repel encroaching Candoshi, Huambisa Jivaroans, and eastern Achuara. The Puyo Runa grew stronger, and their territory became more and more a bilingual Jivaroan-Quichua refuge zone where enemies could live in tenuous peace within the confines of expanding trade opportunities and some church-defined refuge sanctuaries. As the cauchero thrust up the Napo itensified, Quijos Quichua and Zaparoans were caught between the well-established system of serfdom (Oberem 1971) and slavery. Many of these people moved into the Puyo area, or just north of it into what is now Fátima, near the headwaters of the Arajuno River, and interchanged sisters with some of the Puyo Runa ayllu nodes.

The trade advantages of Puyo, together with its refuge function and expanding indigenous-controlled territory beyond the reach of caucheros, led some western Achuara Jivaroans to send young boys to powerful Puyo Runa men known to be harboring revenge motives for killings in previous generations. Such boys were reared as sons-in-law and eventually married daughters of the Puyo Runa. They were carefully instructed in Canelos Quichua culture, but encouraged to travel back to their homeland on the Capahuari or Copotaza River from time to time, in order to maintain connections with their own Achuara culture and language and to solidify ties with Achuara shamans, killers, and manufacturers of medicines, curare dart poison, blowguns, feathered headdresses, and other trade goods sought by both Quijos and Jívaro proper to the north and the south. The parents and close relatives of such children made occasional visits to their Puyo Runa hosts, traveling through hostile territory and meeting, for safety, on a purina chagra of the host located somewhere north of the Pastaza River, west of the Puyo River, and south of Puyo proper.

Apparently ambushes and kidnapping in this important area of trade were fairly common, and the territory became known as a veritable *Auca Llacta*, land of Jivaroan insolence. In fact, dangerous though it may have been, it was the crucial hunting, fishing, and trading territory of the Puyo Runa. Llacta founders in Puyo with purina chagras in this territory moved with impunity, eventually establishing territorial segments with overlapping membership, and thereby reconsolidated, around 1900, the westernmost Runa territory of the Canelos Quichua culture area.

As exploration and trade over narrow and often corduroy but well-demarcated trails increased between Baños and Puyo, and the rubber boom–sponsored destruction to the east and north continued, still more people moved into the area, forming a geo-ethnic structure on which the contemporary Puyo Runa expanded. An intermarried group from the upper Copotaza-Tashapi (Caninche) and Capahuari–lower Copotaza (Achuara) settled in the area between contemporary Shell Mera–Puyo Pungo–Tashapi River, ranging along the Pastaza River no man's land and making alliances with some of the Jívaro proper from Arapicos and its vicinity. The ethnic contrast between the Jívaro proper and Puyo Runa in this area established the southern geo-ethnic boundary of the Runa territory. Another mixed Achuara–Canelos Quichua intermarried group from the Villano-Curaray headwaters, upper Conambo, and Canelos settled in the area from Puyo to the Pindo River, and fanned out to the Chingosimi River. They married Quijos Quichuas from the Ansuj River, relatives of whom moved into the area around contemporary Fátima. A few powerful Zaparoans, bilingual in Quichua, also intermarried with the Achuara-Canelos group and settled near the mouth of the Pindo River.

The contrast between Quijos and Canelos Quichua as residents in the respective Puyo-Fátima zones defined the northern border in ethnic terms, while the river headwaters of the Puyo and Arajuno rivers provided the geographic markers. More Achuara from the Capahuari and Copotaza rivers, related to other Puyo Runa, intermarried with Napo Quijos-Quichua. These northern Quichua speakers were fleeing oppression and enslavement attempts, and they encountered the Achuara in Canelos proper. The intermarried group moved westward and ranged along the Puyo River and a branch of the Pastaza River, forming an east-west axis crossing the north-south one.

Members in each of these groups were culturally part of contrastive ethnic-linguistic groups to the south (Jívaro proper), east (Záparo), southeast (Achuara), and north (Quijos), and their genealogical and marriage alliances also extended into these other cultures. Nonetheless, the cultural contrasts between territorially defined Runa llactas and territories considered to be of other ethnic groups became quite sharply defined. Reciprocal raiding occurred between the Jívaro proper and the Puyo Runa, between the Quijos of the Napo and the Puyo Runa, and sometimes between the Canelos Runa and the Puyo Runa. Reconstruction by informant work and literary sources indicates a general alliance between people in the Runa territories of Sara Yacu, Canelos, and Puyo against northern and southern ethnic units (see also Simson 1886:90).[11] Furthermore, reconstruction also indicates western Achuara (from the Copotaza and Capahuari rivers) alliance with the Canelos Quichua (especially at Sara Yacu and Puyo) against the same southern Jívaro, northern Quijos, and eastern Zaparoans. (Valladares [1912:34–36] dates Achuara alliance with some groups at Canelos from 1775.)

Diverse though the specific linguistic-cultural origins of the Puyo Runa were (and are), certain adaptive modes maintained continuity of a dynamic core ethnicity in this westernmost Canelos-Quichua territory.

Dualism and Ethnic Identity

Old people today like to tell stories of their parents during Times of the Grandparents which emphasize and dramatize the basic intra-Runa territory duality of *Alli Runa–Sacha Runa*. Alli Runa is the "good Christian Indian," a stereotypic association of traits projected onto a model of Catholic brokerage between external chaos and native adjustment. Alli Runa—cari and huarmi—accept less than fair share in trade from the church; the men work for no recompense for the Padre and their wives give the finest piece of ceramics and ample manioc to the same Padre. Their sons may even be sent to work for a few cents a month cleaning his house and garden plot, while daughters cook, sweep, and keep house for him and for the "Madrecitas." Sacha Runa, in this context, is the real person embodying a continuum from human knowledge and competence to spirit power. Sacha Runa walks without fear through Amasanga's forest domain with spirit helpers to ward off spirit darts, knowledge to help him get whatever he needs, from medicines to food, and strength to confront any human, animal, or spirit adversary. Sacha Huarmi maintains the subsistence base with the aid of Nunghuí, and mediates between the Amasanga-Nunghuí union and the Sungui water power.

Between the Pastaza and the Pindo rivers powerful shamans built huge, palisaded oval houses on high hillsides. *Tundulis* (Jívaro *tundúi*)—large hollow signal drums representing the power of amarun, the great anaconda—were placed by the powerful and knowing Sacha Runa on high hills. There they were used to acquire enemy souls and to signal other powerful Sacha Runa whenever there was danger of Jivaroan attack or encroachment by non-natives into the jungle domain. When the Sacha Runa warriors—the sicuangas, toucan men—sounded an alarm through the power of Sungui, in the form of a captured anaconda spirit, a force of Canelos Quichua power transcending kinship and cultural antagonisms is said to have developed. An important integrating mechanism for Puyo Runa expansion was their combined opposition to the encroaching Jívaro proper and non-natives. Dominican dominion outside of the forest area provided the articulation to a national system which in turn provided some benefits to those of Alli Runa demeanor.

Integration of the Alli Runa–Sacha Runa opposition in this intracultural dialectic with intercultural functions established a crucial ethnic marker for Canelos Quichua society and culture, a marker that by 1900 came to signify the Puyo Runa extenders of Canelos Quichua culture. *Alli Runa and Sacha Runa are one and the same;* one faces the refuge zone providing a trade locus in an expanding purchase society, the other maintains the relational system, itself a dynamic microcosmogony providing the impetus for continuing adaptation in the face of chaos. This duality allows us to understand more thoroughly Canelos Quichua resistance in accepting either Jívaro proper or Quijos Quichua culture as an ethnic structure, even though many Puyo Runa learned the relational system constituting these contrastive systems. Neither Jívaro nor Quijos provides the core duality of ethnic patterning as a fundamental cultural adaptation to the purchase society in a frontier ecology, but both contribute to the knowledge necessary for the maintenance of such duality.

Word and symbol play on the relationship between Alli Runa and Sacha Runa are nearly endless. For example, the Spanish term *alma* (soul) belongs to the Alli Runa as part of the salvation of the church's ministrations. Its transformation into Quichua is made by inserting the *a* vowel between *l* and *m* to produce *alama*, the national non-Indian pejorative term for the reputed Quichua "tribe" of the Bobonaza River area. The Dominican concept of alamas is that they represent Christianized heathen souls, converted "Jívaros," who may partake in aspects of the sacraments including baptism, marriage, and death rites. The alama concept is sometimes useful to the Puyo Runa when the church provides necessary functions, but it has no etymological relationship to the Sacha Runa concept of *alaj* or (for emphasis) *alajma*, my mythic brother.

Conceptual polarity suggested by this dualism is resolved when the church concept alama and the indigenous concept alaj are separated in their referential and address contexts. Only the clergy use alama referentially to include women and men participating in Canelos Quichua culture. Furthermore, they use it only in reference to people concentrated around the mission. The Canelos Quichua themselves use alaj in man-to-man conversation, and employ it most frequently when addressing distant non-relatives in Canelos Quichua territory. Women sometimes use alama in the church-localized context to refer to specific men, though by so doing they again invoke the duality between Sacha Runa and Alli Runa.

The same duality operated in the varayo system, and continued as this became a system of the cabildo. Basically, each officeholder had to maintain the Alli Runa–Sacha Runa duality. He and his wife and children had to maintain a position of respect vis-à-vis church officials and locate a huasi and nearby chagra in the central Runa territory while at the same time manifesting superior Sacha Runa qualities in personal power, hunting, purina chagra maintenance, and in connections with other potential and real allies and enemies. Successful varayos were powerful shamans married to sisters of other powerful shamans. The church attempted to filter folk Catholicism through such shaman varayos, stressing the dichotomy of God and the Devil, good and evil, saint and sinner while at the same time creating an obvious rank-class system: all whites considered superior, all natives considered inferior. The shamans, in turn, protected the native peoples from overwhelming Christian magic (e.g., changing wine into blood) by strong alliances with Amasanga, increasing their knowledge of church-controlled spirits (Jesus, Mary) to be incorporated into shamanistic performance. Amasanga, who became the Christian Devil for the clergy, was probably strengthened as the indigenous forest spirit, particularly as the church contrasted clearing with forest, God with the Devil, whites with Indians.

Microcosmogony

Whether or not my reconstruction is correct in all particulars, available evidence strongly supports the position that an important aspect of adaptation in each of the Runa territories, including the Puyo Runa territory at the turn of the twentieth century, was the adoption of a dualistic system of ethnic identity with the Catholic Church's reinterpreted system of folk cosmology playing an important environing role in the continuing elaboration of dynamic, adapting Canelos Quichua cosmogony. Folk Catholicism promulgated in the Canelos Quichua culture area in the Quichua language perhaps provided a pivotal revitalization mechanism validating a new articulation to frontier society. The church's attempts at subjugation were accepted by the Puyo Runa as the critical, manageable, non-native contrast for indigenous cultural maintenance and expansion. In such a contrastive position, Dominican dominion provided the necessary catalyst for a transformation in Canelos Quichua microcosmogony. Such a microcosmogony itself is both a form of protest and cultural validation, and presumably allows for increased articulation to imposed constraints and new forms of exploitation. James W. Fernandez[12] (1969:5) provides the rationale for this discussion. "*Protest* . . . can also mean a solemn declaration or affirmation of something. Most of the religious movements [which he has studied in Africa] have been preoccupied with reaffirming themselves, not in protesting against the larger situation. To understand them as they exist for their members, they cannot be studied exclusively as the institutional creatures of a much larger context. They are interested primarily in microcosmogony—constructing a universe of their own in which to dwell—and not in changing the universe to which they may be reacting."

Chapters 2 through 6 of this book were concerned with specific, culturally assertive aspects of a well-integrated relationship system set out according to my own observations and native exegesis. I am now arguing that the relationship system—Canelos Quichua culture—took a particular adaptive turn through its dialectic relationship with the Catholic Church. In one Runa territory or another, over several centuries, networks of trade of foreign-made goods articulated with a Catholic mission system governed by systematic rules for native subjugation and control. This articulation provided part of the material base upon which the Canelos Quichua mythical-ritual elements were transformed into a dynamic ethnic revitalization of diverse cultures. Around 1900 this Canelos Quichua system witnessed its greatest population expansion in the Puyo area.

Nowhere in Canelos Quichua culture is the core transformational duality of adaptive microcosmogony more apparent than in the ayllu ceremony, the particulars of which were described in the previous chapter. First, the selection of priostes is dependent on agreement by all. If the ceremony is to be held every year (or even more frequently), and if there is to be rotation of the priostes, then participants in the territorial-social dynamics of a Runa territory must at least temporarily suppress their animosities toward one another. Furthermore, shaman nomination of new priostes, individual motivation (volunteering as prioste), and use of the cabildo to present the priostes to the outside date-setter (the priest) create a viable relationship between established Canelos Quichua ayllu nodes (shamans), strong individuals (selected or volunteering priostes), the selected brokers (cabildo), and the church.

Second, men and women living beyond the confines of the fairly restricted central Runa territory—Sacha Runa—are drawn into residence near the church by their prioste and asua mama roles. They build a large house near the central area, in symbolic opposition to their alter prioste, and by so doing intrude into llacta structure and boundaries. They are also encouraged to stay there at least part of the year thereafter, thereby establishing a need to constantly reorganize the llacta system abutting the church-dominated plaza. Kinship and alliance bonds are ritually intensified during the annual ceremony, and the vision-provoking activities described in Chapter 6 affirm the widest and deepest possible commitment to relatives with Canelos Quichua culture and beyond, regardless of the particular bonds being built up in the area of mission and trade.

On the final day of the ceremony the church is designated as mushuj huasi, new house, and Alli Runa demeanor prevails as a blessing is sought from the priest by the jisteros (and, in the other Runa territories, by the lanceros). As the day's activities crescendo toward the dominario, the symbols of all the ancient sources of power are brought together until, just at dusk, the power of the giant spirit anaconda is borne by the jaguar men while the female mediators between soil and water dance (usually in the mud) to the root crop and clay-giving Nunghuí. All of the power of Sacha Runa and Sacha Huarmi is brought into the plaza, together with the power of the Yacu Supai Runa as the great anaconda metaphorically coils through the church. The church is new and the Runa ceremony ancient. Canelos

Quichua enactment signals the endurance of antiquity and indigenous continuity in the face of externally imposed constraints. Sungui power is a metaphor for flood, in this context, and the invocation of ancient water power could destroy the church; but to do so would mean a flooding of the territory and a consequent destruction of land and people. The ancient Sacha Runa is inextricably tied to the new, with the basic Alli Runa duality expressing this tie. Alli Runa articulates to the "new" through the climactic metaphor of destruction while maintaining the Sacha Runa ability to span Times of Destruction back to Ancient Times.

Fighting after the ceremony realigns and redistributes some members within the territory, sometimes cementing bonds which were previously attenuated. Uneasy post-ceremonial alliance in the Runa territorial locus demands some reliance on church settlement in disputes. Realignment and crosscutting ties in the hinterland necessitate multiple ayllu ties and marriage alliances. Concepts of alliance and renewed consanguinity are reinforced at ceremony after ceremony, and intensification of the Runa spirit and soul concepts and substances are enacted under the very shadow of the church. Indeed, the shadow itself provides the only Sacha correspondence in the otherwise sun-baked or rain-soaked plaza.

Finally, the periodic opening of the Runa biosphere—at the principal site of outside intrusion—to spirit and foreign soul penetration during the annual ceremony symbolizes continued transformation and cultural adaptation. By crescendoing ritual activity toward a collapsed domain-structured biosphere the Canelos Quichua "play"—their own exegesis, from *pugllana*—with the force fields which clearly penetrate their existence. Inevitable restructuring after the Sunday feast day signals not only return to a biosphere of the known, but introduces the aspect of continuous change and social readjustment in actual personnel and alliances, and individual enrichment in knowledge and metaphorical shifts gained through participation in a common ceremony with diverse Sacha Runa.

Territorial Consolidation

Actual population expands in a particular pattern near the center of a Runa territory when ceremonies are regularly held. Distant Sacha Runa are often brought in as priostes, and encouraged to stay for at least part of every year near the residences of original founders. In the Puyo area, westernmost of the culture zone, the founders are all upriver people, *janaj runa*, and incomers, whether from east, south, or north, are downriver people, *urai runa*. Specific alliances between upriver and downriver men crosscut one another, and divisive ayllu factionalism such as that created by shamanistic duels crosscuts claims that upriver founders are ultimately opposed to downriver in-migrants. Out-migration of any alliance group maintains upriver and downriver categorical oppositions in a new zone. Such redistribution establishes a basis for ayllu extensions between those in the central area and those farther out in the Runa territory or in another territory.

In Puyo, mediation of disputes by priest and cabildo placed authority patterns in an arena of negotiation between collective sentiment expressed by resident Alli Runa and the church's emissary. No cabildo member could stay in a position of authority without the consensus of the resident populace. A changing group of cabildo officers selected by consensus of resident natives, working with church authorities and curtailing shamanistic power among themselves, provided the authoritative basis for population buildup and nucleation in the church's domain. Ramifying affinal alliance ties, stipulated consanguineal links, and joined gumba chains grew and expanded with the categorical contrasts of "upriver-downriver" people and through the maintenance of bilingualism and intercultural diversity within the ethnic unit. Expansion and differentiation strategies endowed the Puyo Runa with a particularly valuable human resource pool for nationally sponsored "exploration."

Canelos Quichua cabildo members from Puyo and Canelos helped expand national knowledge of other native jungle domains in three ways. First, they guided explorations into their forests. Second, they carried national mail and military messages from Puyo eastward and northward. Some of the Puyo Runa were also commissioned as permanent *tamberos*, ferrymen, to take travelers across treacherous stretches of river. Third, they walked to Quito, sometimes carrying priests on their backs, to meet directly with the president of the republic and to discuss the eastern forests and their mysteries with Andean-oriented bureaucrats. Again, the Sacha Runa definition of "knowledgeable person" articulated well with the Alli Runa demeanor of "good Christianized Indian." Those who were the strongest, who knew the most, were selected to work most closely with those who could command an audience with the highest state officials—the Catholic missionary clergy.

Puyo Runa adaptation, then, was by 1900 and continuing into the 1920s characterized by participation in a purchase society within a frontier cultural ecology. A territory ranging from the Puyo River to the Pastaza and from Shell Mera to Cabecera de Bobonaza was consolidated by ethnically unified or allied people as part of Canelos Quichua culture, in distinction to Jívaro proper, Zaparoan, and Quijos Quichua culture. An aspect of this adaptation was the core duality in cultural patterning which attempted to use Dominican dominion as a useful artifice for articulation with certain aspects of the purchase society. The Dominican dominion itself was furthered by localization and expansion of the ceremonial system, because the more Indians it could report to be celebrating folk Christianity, the stronger its mission structure within the revitalized archdiocese of Canelos.

Commerce and Ethnicity

The church apparently took no public part in the major commercial trans-actions involving furs and gold, the crucial products for a capitalistic econ-omy developing out of mercantilism and feudalism in early twentieth-century Ecuador. Significantly, the Puyo Runa had access to both. They panned gold in various parts of their Runa territory and sold it directly to Andean traders. They traded trinkets, machetes, knives, and axe heads for furs with peoples to the east, and traded furs and gold for steel tools, guns, powder, shot, and other goods with the Andean traders. Such direct access to nationally valued products allowed the Puyo Runa to bypass the clergy, when they wished to do so, and deal directly with traders from the Andes, who either penetrated to specific sites along the Baños-Puyo trail or purchased goods brought to Baños by the Puyo Runa themselves.

This trade introduced the Puyo Runa to another sort of outsider—the apparently poor, itinerant, bilingual (Spanish-Quichua) trader who walked his way from Andes to jungle, subsisting on a peculiar gray flour, *máchica* or *mashca*, made from barley. These mashca-chewing men from *Ahua Llacta*—high territory, referring to people classed as non-Indian nationals by Canelos Quichua—developed dyadic ties with particular powerful Runas. It seems that each Runa-national dyadic exchange tie was discrete. Commercial transactions took place in Puyo proper, domain of the Alli Runa, where the individual, dyadic commercial ties to non-Runa evoked no question as to Ahua Llacta penetration into the large, Sacha Runa, domain.

Profits from the purchase and resale of gold and furs inevitably led to infrastructural expansion and to non-Indian settlement in Puyo, near the Dominican mission. Karsten's (1935:30) descriptions of two walks from Baños to Canelos, the first in 1916 and the second in 1928, give us an excellent contrast suggesting the dynamics of white intrusion.

1916:
From Abitagua [a high jungle ridge a few miles west of the contemporary site of Shell] one arrives in one day at Puyo, a small village inhabited by half-civilized Quichua-speaking Indians, whence one has to walk two days more through dense forest to reach Canelos.

1928:

A new road, suitable for big carts and travelling on horseback, has been made along the left bank of the Pastaza rounding the Abitagua to a place called Mera, from where it is only one day's march to Puyo. Mera, which some ten years ago only consisted of one house in a marshy and disagreeable tract, is now a big village with several hundred inhabitants.

With this settlement two radical shifts in the environing parameters of Puyo Runa adaptation occurred. An expanding colonist penetration took place, aimed at subsistence and profit. Violation of native usufruct characterized the former, and stronger articulation to national sources of monetary support, the latter.

But the relationship between Canelos Quichua and Ecuadorian nationals was to be subject to many forces of international political economy before the final establishment of pernicious secular pluralism aimed at Oriente natives. Significant in the immediate history of the Oriente was petroleum exploration initiated by Royal Shell Oil Corporation, the buildup and explosion of World War II, Peru's invasion of Ecuador, the rise of foreign plantation interests in eastern Ecuador, and finally the reentry of petroleum exploration to create at last a structure in which the Ecuadorian military could endeavor once and for all to obliterate the Sacha Runa biosphere and, inter alia, Canelos Quichua culture.

NOTES

1. See Chapter 2, note 3.

2. I refer specifically to Quijos-Quichua settlements on the Ansuj River to the northwest, and am guessing that the bilingual Jívaro-Quichua grouping reported by Simson (1886:88) as living at Río Topo is Achuara in dialect. My guess is based on the assertion by Jívaro proper from around Arapicos that other "Shuara" speaking a dialect similar to those of the contemporary Copotaza River lived between Río Topo and Baños, and on other assertions by people from the Copotaza who refer to their own dialect as "Achuara" that this same dialect, distinct from the right-bank Pastaza dialect, was spoken in this area. There is no evidence of Highland Quichua in the Puyo area during this period, but such contact between Canelos and the sierra had undoubtedly occurred during the colonial era (Naranjo 1974, Oberem 1974). Local history, including data from mission travelers, is given in Valladares (1912) and Jurado (1970, 1971).

3. The chuti—pike cichlid—is a day feeder and the huanchichi (Ecuadorian) or pashin (Quichua)—tiger fish—a night feeder. The former is *Crenicichla saxatilis (Tropical Fish Hobbyist* 1971:60) or *C. lepidota* (Sterba 1966:580–581, 705–708), and the latter a *Hoplias* species (Sterba 1966:87, 95). I have been unable to identify the ñachi. Many other inch-long fish, all used for food, exist in this area.

4. I refer to the territory encompassing the headwaters of the Lipuno, Curaray, Callana, and Oglán rivers. It is simply not clear from any reconstruction or from ethnohistoric sources what the relationship is, or may have been, between the contemporary Huarani Auca, famous

for their missionary spearing in 1956 (Eliot 1961), and people tagged as "Záparo" in many published sources (e.g., Steward and Métraux 1948:631).

5. I wish to emphasize the fact that Puyo Runa do not, by choice, get any drinking water from the major rivers, low swampy areas, or even small streams in which they fish, wash manioc, and bathe. They seek out clear, cold, underground streams from which to take their drinking water. House locations, then, are chosen not only with a stream for ablution and fishing, but also with a separate supply of clean drinking water.

6. Archival and published sources all vary a bit in regard to specifics of founding, re-founding, discovering, and rediscovering "Canelos" (including territories such as the mouth of the Puyo River, the current site of Unión Base and Puyo, Cabecera de Bobonaza, and the present site of Canelos). Pivotal publications on the Canelos mission, from which most other material seems to be drawn, are Jimenez de la Espada (1897), Villavicencio (1858), Vacas Galindo (1905), Rumazo González (1950), González Suárez (1970), Tobar Donoso (1960), Magalli de Pred (1890), and Valladares (1912). See also *El Oriente Dominicano 1929–1940* and Jurado (1970, 1971). For comparable material on the Maynas mission see Chantre y Herrera (1901), Juanen (1941–43), Figueroa (1904), and Uriarte (1952). A discussion of the significance of Canelos-Puyo missionizing, commerce, refuge area, and ethnic relations over several centuries is set forth in Naranjo (1974).

7. The crucial history of the Maynas mission under the Jesuits is in Chantre y Herrera (1901).

8. For discussion of Canelos Quichua customs written by a cauchero on the Villano-Curaray rivers in 1890 see Porras Garces (1973). Although he insists on using the term "Quijos" for the people described, there would seem no cultural basis for this. Compare the data, for example, with those presented in this work, and with the ethnography-ethnohistory of the Quijos by Oberem (1971).

9. Hegen (1966:19) gives the definitions of these rainforest zones as clearly as anyone, and I follow his usage.

The *Montaña*, the continuous forest of elevations between 2,500 and 1,000 m.; tree ferns and palms are characteristic. . . .

The *Hylea*, the forest below 1,000 m., covering the foothills and the piedmont in the Andean amphitheater, the peneplains in the north and in the south, and the lowland within the fall line as well as the floodplains. It is not uniform; a complex of physiognomic changes due to variations in soil, relief, and rainfall characterize it. Within the Hylea two distinct divisions are recognizable.

The *Eté*, the forest of the Tierra Firme within the Amazon Plain; it is always above flood waters and it stands on land with low ground-water level. It forms the core of the Hylea.

The *Várzea*, the periodically inundated formation of the Hylea on the floodplains of the valleys of the Amazonas and its major tributaries, forming relatively narrow ribbons within the Eté.

For additional technical material on parts of eastern Ecuador see Grubb, Lloyd, and Pennington (1963) and Grubb and Whitmore (1966).

10. See Chapter 6, note 2. All materials in this section are taken from the *Reglamento* which I read in Canelos, and from reconstruction with older Puyo Runa men and women, some of whom held varayo office.

11. Paca Yacu, though today a Runa territory of Canelos Quicha culture, represented a Bobonaza River trade site, but its members were often estranged from the inhabitants of Sara Yacu, Canelos, and Puyo. Paca Yacu was the territorial marker for Gayes Zaparoans who attacked Canelos from time to time, and also waged reciprocal raids with other Canelos

Quichua groups. Today the Gayes surname predominates in Paca Yacu, though Zaparoan is reputedly no longer spoken there. There are a few Gayes at Sara Yacu and Canelos, some of whom are said to still speak Zaparoan when the need arises.

12. This analysis owes a great deal to the work of Fernandez (e.g. 1969; see also 1974), whose analysis of African rituals triggered my own thinking about the significance of native ceremony and external chaos.

CHAPTER

8

Puyo Runa Ethnicity
and Adaptation

The land base of the Puyo Runa is constantly enriched by Andean soil and ash. As the challua of deeper Amazonia run upward to the Puyo, Pindo, and tributary streams in the swelling waters, so too do soil and rock flow downward, creating new deposits throughout the low areas during the inevitable receding of the ubiquitous floods. Land from Baños to Mera tumbles off the eastern Andean escarpment in huge masses, carrying its vegetation crashing downward off the precipitous slopes into the turgid, cascading waters which flow into the Pastaza. The Pastaza receives the rich soil and plant masses all the way down its thunderous course; its occasional rise of twenty feet or more and its frequent change in color from muddy white to opaque chocolate brown bear awful testimony to the periodic land movements on either side of its banks.

Such movements come about during the earthquakes of the Andean faults, and also during earth rumbles stimulated by the active volcano, Sangay, which today puffs out smoke and sends red lava down its beautiful snow-cone peak. Heavy, insistent rains between Baños and Puyo sometimes last for two weeks or more, causing massive slides; tons of earth fall, and slices of mountains from two to six miles across and a mile high come down. Smaller slides ranging from mere thousand-pound land masses to tons of half-mile-wide combinations of mud, rock, tree, and undergrowth occur at any time, seemingly without the aid of earthquake or deluge. Even on the bright sunny days ground water percolates through the young mountains, creating its own treacherous system of motion which combines with the more spectacular waterfalls to provide a perpetuation of water and land movement.

Through this route of land slides came mule trains, colonists, and more and more explorers. Among the latter were geologists for Royal Dutch Shell Oil Corporation, and perhaps others of a major rival, Standard Oil of

New Jersey (Galarza Zavala 1972:79). They began their mappings sometime around 1920 (Hegen 1966:72), during a period when rubber searching
and territorial consolidation on the Napo, Curaray, and lower Bobonaza
were still in a stage of sustained violence vis-à-vis native peoples. Fanning
out from the areas just east of the Abitagua range, explorers, hacendados,
and poor, dependent peones and homesteaders moved as best they could
outside the confines of national control and onto the edges of both
Dominican dominion and native jungle.

COLONIZATION AND NATIVE ADJUSTMENT

Settlement at Mera and consolidation of Baños-Mera trade by non-natives
forced Jivaroans from Río Topo and the Mera area back eastward toward the
Pastaza and Puyo-Pindo, as even more peoples—Quijos Quichua—were
displaced from parts of the north-flowing Napo tributaries. Most of the
former fanned out between the present town of Shell, up the Llushín
River, and to the present caserío of Chinimbimi while most of the latter
settled around the present town of Fátima. Some, however, intermarried
with people from each of the four points defining the north-south and
east-west axis of Puyo Runa territory. Such intermarriage plus consolidation of more "condensed" territories bordering those of the Puyo Runa
expanded the ethnic charter of the Puyo Runa from the Canelos Quichua
perspective, but confused the ethnic perspective from the colonists'
viewpoint. The convenient dichotomy for the outsiders became "Quichua"
and "Jívaro," the former tagged "half-civilized," "semi-Christian,"
"exploitable" for menial tasks, the latter identified with danger, the forest,
the unknown. The Alli Runa–Sacha Runa duality of the Puyo Runa fitted
perfectly into this conceptualization.

   With the eastward expansion of a national trade route, Ecuador began to
colonize and consolidate its Oriente. A contract was signed in 1928 with
Royal Dutch Shell for the construction of an Ambato-Mera motor road, and
speculation, exploration, and colonization increased. In its process of
national expansion Ecuador was clearly dependent on foreign capital which
came from two sources: petroleum exploration (Galarza Zavala 1972:79–86)
and plantation expansion. A Brazilian concern with unknown capital
backing began to establish extensive sugar plantations sometime in the
1930s, between the areas of Shell and the contemporary site of Tarqui.
Cane juice was distilled and the aguardiente sent by mule pack to Río
Verde and then trucked on to the sierra (Bemelmans 1964:117). Life on this
hacienda prior to the coming of a road is so strikingly contrastive with
mission, homesteader, and frontier town life that a statement from a

traveler-explorer (Flornoy 1935:36) who made a sojourn on the Bobonaza
sometime during the 1930s is worth quoting.

> A few miles away [from Puyo] is the *hacienda* of Zulay, an oasis of civilization
> which exists for the sugar cane plantations owned by a Brazilian and managed
> by four young colonials. Here, for a few days, we forgot our ordeals in tasting
> the sheer joy of civilized life: the delicious pleasure of sitting together on the
> veranda chatting and drinking *café au lait*, riding along the solitary path that
> runs downhill to the Puyo Mission, bathing in the ice-cold Pindo which flows
> clear and tranquil through the plantations, walking through the fields of sugar
> cane, idling deliciously during siesta hours listening to old French
> gramophone records. The four colonials who welcomed us with such charming
> forthrightness might easily have been airmen, sailors, diplomats or bank
> managers. Instead they had chosen to live on the fringe of the Amazon as we
> had chosen to explore it.

Flornoy's techniques of exploration make a telling point about native life in
the Puyo area: "At Puyo we said goodbye to Ayala, his men and the mules;
for the next stage, until we reached Canelos, our pack-horses were Indian
porters."

The porters were Canelos Quichua, fifty-six of them in this instance, who
were to lug 900 tins of food together with other necessities of an exploratory
expedition. The total weighed 4,500 pounds, and was packed into "fifty
cases and six parcels, plus three bags of waterproof canvas for personal
belongings" (Flornoy 1953:20–21). Carrying approximately eighty pounds
each, this group of Canelos and Puyo Runa trekked from Puyo to Unión
Base to Indillama, each the site of a native llacta founded by a powerful
shaman, up over the Siguin Cordillera, and down to the site of Canelos. On
the return trip the porters brought furs, gold, cinnamon, fibers for brooms
for sale in Puyo, and curare poison, blowguns, fishnets, and chicle for their
own use, trade, and distribution among other Puyo Runa. By definition,
porters were always "Quichua," the language connoting "beast of burden"
in the earlier periods of "exploration," as it does today in many parts of
Ecuador.

Another plantation was maintained by a North American writer, Richard
C. Gill, who is famous in ethnobotanical literature for identifying a single
vine as the source of curare (see e.g., Kreig 1964:161–162). His lifestyle, on
a site which must be near the hacienda Zulay, also exemplifies the striking
contrast of foreign residents' resources on this Ecuadorian frontier.
Writing about family life in 1931 somewhere near the present site of Shell,
Gill (1940:41) says, "Our evenings are calm, peaceful, away from the world
but keeping up with it. We change for dinner, have cocktails, and eat by
candlelight from a hand-rubbed *canelo*-wood table. Afterward, in the living

room, there are coffee, reading, games, appreciated radio. . . ." From such
an existence Gill was able to gather his information on curare (which came
to be used in open-heart surgery) and many other aspects of Canelos
Quichua life. In his search he drew together many aspects of the world of
the Sacha Runa, always careful to identify this world as "Jívaro," though
again, he worked within Canelos Quichua culture. Some of the Puyo Runa
and Canelos Runa still remember this early *guiringu* (gringo) who came to
ask questions about jungle life and send samples of their craft and
knowledge to another country.

The Puyo Runa men provided selected information about their forest
domain to explorers and information seekers. They carried cargo between
Canelos and Puyo, profiting from an expanding trade through which
purchase of desired goods—axe heads, machetes, knives—could be made
from Andean traders. They panned gold in their Runa territory and traded
steel tools for furs with other native peoples to the east, south, and north.
Up through the 1950s they carried national mail and served as mission and
military couriers throughout the culture area. They also undertook specific
jobs attendant on pioneer agriculture as they cut out segments of jungle
beyond, or on the edges of, their own territory, allowing the rapidly
expanding plantations to alter the ecosystem fundamentally. But they did
not move into a system of peonage on the haciendas. They chose, rationally
and with care, to exploit many facets of the incoming trade and work
opportunities without losing their own huasi, chagra, purina chagra, or
knowledge of hunting territories. Puyo Runa women continued to maintain
a subsistence base, as described in Chapters 2 and 7. Some Puyo Runa men
reestablished contacts through many hostile territories, and traveled
eastward and back as expedition guides. Some went as far as Iquitos and
Yurimaguas, Peru.

The hacendados' increasing requirement of an exploitable labor force led
to more and more in-migration of poor highland and coastal Ecuadorians,
many of whom endeavored to found a homestead while maintaining
hand-to-mouth existence as hacienda peones. The Puyo Runa avoided, for
a while, the "dynamics of underdevelopment" (Beckford 1972:183–214) by
focusing on trade, short-run labor necessitating their endurance and
knowledge of the jungle and its people, and maintenance of a subsistence
base.

Powerful shamans, almost all bilingual in Quichua-Jivaroan or
Quichua-Zaparoan, consolidated their llacta territories, and some began to
cure the poor peones of various national folk illnesses such as "evil air." The
funds received in such curing allowed the shamans and selected members
of their families to purchase land near Puyo, and beyond the guarded
jungle domain between the Pastaza and Puyo rivers. As they did this they

continued to maintain a house in or within an hour's walk from Puyo, while placing other sons and in-laws in the large oval houses built in the more distant llacta.

As the plantations grew and flourished beyond Mera, world demand for raw materials together with an imminent world war again entered to affect critically the course of east Ecuadorian history, and particularly the adaptation of native peoples. Royal Dutch Shell Oil began to construct a truck and car road sometime in the 1930s and it was opened to the new town of Shell (then Shell Mera), on the western edge of "plantation country," in 1937. At that time Shell Oil began its official exploration for petroleum in the Ecuadorian Oriente.

Puyo, about eight miles east of Shell, remained an essentially native area with only a "few houses" (Blomberg 1956:119) and continued Dominican dominion as swelling colonization blanketed the areas on either side of the treacherous, winding, slippery, sliding dirt- or mud-and-rock motor road.

Shell itself was located at the approximate site of a geo-ethnic no man's land, the southwestern corner, so to speak, of Puyo Runa territory, on the edge of the Pastaza River, not far from the mouth of the Llushín. Loosely allied Jivaroans from the Palora, Chiguaza, and Llushín rivers, together with some from the lower Copotaza, are currently identified as having laid claim to this territory prior to the expansion of plantations and the coming of Shell Oil. Whether these peoples were mixed Achuara-Jívaro proper or a clustered set of Achuara pushed from their neighborhoods by Jívaro proper expansion around 1900 (Harner 1972:36) is unclear. It is entirely possible, I think, that the dichotomy between Achuara-Jívaro proper breaks down in this area, but this must await further research. It is clear that alliances with various llacta groupings, and with some groupings of Jívaro proper, were made at the time of Shell intrusion.

The late 1930s are characterized by a large intrusion of well-to-do non-Ecuadorians and a flood of poor nationals. Germans (Jewish and Gentile), French, English, Dutch, and Danish nationals all entered Puyo via Baños and fanned out in various directions seeking asylum, fortune, trade benefits, and marketable information. During this period the Puyo Runa vigorously defended their Sacha Runa zone, while maximizing individual and group benefits deriving from the capital and goods of the *apachi* (non-Ecuadorian outsider) entering the now-growing trade site of Puyo.

Shell Oil built an airstrip at Shell,[1] and its engineers moved outward from it to staging bases in such areas as Arajuno on the Arajuno River, Ayuy on the Pastaza, and Taisha on the Pangüi. With these engineers went some of the most powerful men of the Puyo Runa as guides, hunters, and bodyguards. As camps were established here and there in distant jungle areas these powerful ones sent to them young sons twelve to fourteen years of age as camp boys, instructing them to learn the ways of the apachi and what they could of the local area and its own jungle inhabitants. This mixing of power and knowledge, and the use of such power to gain more knowledge, characterized the Puyo Runa in the epoch of Shell Oil exploration, just as it does today.

As the oil exploration went on, World War II erupted, and in July, 1941, Peru invaded Ecuador. Following the routes of the caucheros, the Peruvian army thrust up the various Oriente rivers, using some Jivaroan and Cocama troops.

Old people tell me that the *Canduishuar* (Murato and Shapra Candoshi) began to raid both Jívaro proper and Achuara at this time, and alliances formed between many Jívaro proper and Achuara groups to repulse and counterattack these eastern peoples. Subsequently, these alliances signaled hostility to interior Jívaro proper east of the Sierra de Cutucú and also to more eastern Achuara. Some of the allied fighters in-migrated to the various Runa territories, marrying Canelos Quichua and placing themselves in a downriver (inferior) position vis-à-vis the wife givers, in exchange for refuge. For example, a Cocama soldier married a woman from Curaray and both sought refuge in a llacta of his wife's extended ayllu among the Puyo Runa. His sons married daughters of the powerful shaman llacta founder. Other similar events occurred. Although formal hostilities soon ceased as Peru won half of eastern Ecuador at the Protocol of Río de Janeiro in January, 1942 (Galarza Zavala 1972:86–102), the struggle for the eastern border continued for some time.[2]

Up and down the Bobonaza River treachery and intrigue prevailed. The Peruvian army established garrisons across its new border, sealing off the more navigable reaches of Ecuadorian rivers and thus preventing national Ecuadorian access to the Amazon. One of these was at Andoas Nuevo, just below the confluence of the Bobonaza and Pastaza rivers. Throughout Canelos Quichua territory Peruvian and Ecuadorian military personnel sought out "spies" from among the personnel of many nationalities, and sometimes among native peoples. To be "Jívaro" (apparently including monolingual speakers of all non-Quichua languages and all natives in non-Western attire) at this time was especially dangerous, for such people were subject to accusation of Peruvian complicity. According to Harner (1972:33): "Around 1941, Jívaro-white relations became extremely tense due to the war between Peru and Ecuador. Ecuadorian troops attacked a Jívaro neighborhood near the Río Santiago reportedly because they believed that the Indians were from Peru and led by Peruvian army officers." The Puyo Runa insist that even the Puyo-Canelos trail was unsafe during the war years, as ambush by foreign nationals was always a possibility. They moved to and fro by other routes, one of which has now become the official trail to Canelos.

During World War II and immediately after, Puyo itself became the locus for most brokerage functions between eastern jungles and expanding nationalistic controls. It existed, still, just a few miles beyond the road terminus, in the heart of an expanding sugar plantation economy aimed at massive aguardiente production, and on the edge of a very rugged jungle territory, the home of aggressive native peoples controlling several languages and dialects of the eastern forests. The Puyo Runa adapted their lifeways to the increased encroachment of outsiders through maneuver in three broad arenas: local political economy; national bureaucracy; and territoriality beyond the town context.

Local Political Economy

Puyo responded to pressures of nonresident hacendados in its formal policies, and to vicissitudes of international trade in its local dynamics. Llacta groupings of the Puyo Runa formed specific alliances with one or another hacendado and also with one or two local traders. They supplied the hacendados with some free labor, particularly to clear forest areas, in exchange for occasional political help in maintaining their own forest region against encroachment by the poor in-migrants. As long as there was plenty of land the hacendados gladly kept the poor from flooding onto native territory, for they needed a dependent, permanent labor force of non-jungle people just as much as they needed a sporadic labor force of natives skilled in jungle ways.

In their alliances with certain traders, now settling to form actual shops in Puyo, the Puyo Runa contributed directly to the growth of a localized bourgeoisie. They brought pelts, gold, cinnamon, broom fiber in to the stores, and took out salt, candles, gunpowder, shot, caps, dynamite, fishhooks, pots and pans. Quichua was the local lingua franca of such commerce. Individual Puyo Runa formed ties of ritual co-parenthood with the petite bourgeoisie, by inviting them to be compadre and comadre for a newborn child (along with a native gumba), and padrino and madrina during their weddings. By so doing they endeavored to extend certain strands of their set of social relations to the newcomers. Through gumba linkages townsmen gained selected access to some marketable jungle goods—medicines, peccary skin (for leather), ayahuasca, feathers and headdresses—all of which had a market in Pelileo and Ambato. Usually the town resident extracted a servant from the Runa—a girl of ten to twelve years of age—who served for five years or more without pay. The Runas, in turn, extracted the necessary patronage vis-à-vis political officials, thereby assuring them, for example, witnesses in case of arrest or threat from new in-migrants. Credit was also extended through compadre-gumba links, and these credit extensions bound llacta groupings to particular families of Puyo merchants.

Formal recognition of these compadrazgo bonds, for the Puyo Runa, occurred at the special ayllu ceremony. The compadres of the Puyo Runa were always invited to the ayllu ceremony where Sacha Runa cosmogony was enacted. Most, if not all, marriages occurred during this ceremony, as well as many baptisms. Native symbolism of a changing biosphere was so employed as to impose the symbolic power of Amasanga, Nunghuí, and Sungui over the chaotic domain of town politics and commerce. Continuous readjustment of Puyo Runa strategies was based on the system of crosscutting national townsmen-native ties which provided both bourgeoisie and Sacha Runa with an open-ended system leading to potentially adaptive advantages in a rapidly changing frontier setting.

Some llacta founders married one of their daughters to a colonist, and a few native men adopted colonist existence, shedding both Alli Runa and Sacha Runa ways but maintaining special contact with powerful llacta founders in one or more of the Runa territories. Powerful shamans continued their careful economic strategy of purchasing and selling land, always taking care to maintain all transactions north and east of the Puyo and Pindo rivers. To the west and south the Sacha Runa biosphere was maintained by internal dynamics although linked to an expanding money economy on its edges.

Llacta founders placed one or two sons, and sometimes a daughter, in the local Dominican school in Puyo, where, with colonists' children, many learned to read, at least minimally. Other children of these founders were kept in the llacta zone, not only to work the chagra with their mothers but also to undertake the sort of study necessary for a Sacha Runa existence within a frontier ecology.

National Bureaucracy

It became increasingly clear to the Puyo Runa after World War II that their biosphere was in jeopardy, that expansion of the national infrastructure would serve foreign interests and would extend bureaucratic controls into the domain of the Sacha Runa. Self-appointed representatives, shamans or shamans' sons, used every possible intermediary—priests, engineers, foreign physicians, explorers—to make plea after plea for preservation of their land between Puyo and the Pastaza River. In their forthright quest for knowledge of the new political economy, and for the power to govern themselves, they sought out central figures in the national capital to gain bureaucratic sanction to maintain their territory, their lives. Several times Puyo Runa went to the national palace and met with President Dr. José María Velasco Ibarra and with representatives of the Department of Public Lands and Colonization of the Ministry of Public Works (*Departamento de Tierras Baldías y Colonización, Ministerio de Obras Públicas*). Their request was simply that their territory not be placed on the lists of "unclaimed lands" (*tierras baldías*) but set aside as their own.

Several factors apparently influenced the president's decision to grant the Puyo Runa request, including his own personal ties with a powerful shaman guide of the Puyo Runa (see Whitten 1975). But even such great caudillos as Velasco Ibarra (Blankston 1951) do not give away 16,000 to 17,000 hectares of native territory merely because of native pleas and a few personal ties. It must have been as evident to the president as it was to the Puyo Runa that the area around Puyo would soon be gobbled up by foreign interests. Zulay was expanding eastward and southward, German and Danish plantations were expanding northward, southward, and eastward, and serious talk of conversion to tea and cattle ranching had begun. Royal Dutch Shell Oil was still exploring, and other foreign plantations were strung out along a route from Puyo to the Napo River where there would eventually be a road. The national resources were inadequate to colonize and develop this extremely rugged area. By granting a large tract of land as indigenous territory, Velasco established a native "holding" action through which national officials could block foreign intrusions for a while. This also forced foreign interests farther from the Puyo area and increased the foreign expenditures on necessary access roads.

Velasco Ibarra eventually established a comuna, later named Comuna San Jacinto del Pindo, to extend from the Pindo River to the Pastaza, with the eastern boundary the Puyo River and the western boundary established later by various maneuvers in town, national, and native territorial arenas. Powerful Puyo Runa individuals were able to reach the pinnacle of national power at a time when nationalization of the Oriente lacked resources to consolidate its area in the face of foreign expansion. They used national power and bureaucracy to preserve their Sacha Runa biosphere, and by so doing tied themselves to the fate of national expansion.

Territoriality

By the mid-1940s llacta structure of the Puyo Runa territory had pretty much evolved to its present system. This region was not like other Runa territories of the Canelos Quichua, where many llactas abut one another near the mission-trade-administrative locus and radiate outward through chagra areas. The Puyo Runa, in response to constant pressure from colonization and plantation encroachment, spread their llacta loci around the rim of their territory, building on intermarried ties between the various groups mentioned in the previous chapter. Eight distinct llactas existed around 1945; one on the Pindo, just upstream from its conjunction with the Puyo, four on the Puyo itself before its conjunction with the Pastaza, one at the conjunction of the Pastaza and Pindo, one on the Brazo Chinimbimi, an arm of the Pastaza, and one radiating out from the headwaters of the Putuimi and Chingosimi. Each of these llactas was established by a powerful shaman, himself also a resident of Puyo or its immediate hinterland (e.g., to Unión Base). Each of these shamans had "marked" some spot of the outer rim of the llacta territory in his rise to power, and each had made pacts with resident Juri juri and with the various spirits of the hills, caves, and underground rivers. In each llacta a sacred quality existed, expressing the continuance of the Amasanga-Nunghuí union and their pact with the Yacu Supai Runa.

Members of these llactas intermarried, and descent reckoning followed lines of shamanistic soul acquisition which linked the evolving Puyo Runa back through Times of Destruction to Ancient Times people. Because all of the shamans were related through the intermarriage of their parents in Times of the Grandparents, the Puyo Runa developed a concept of a common territorial power pool which was acknowledged in the Andes by many indigenous peoples, across the Pastaza River among the Jívaro proper, and among the Copotaza-Capahuari Achuara.

The territorial markers on the outer rim of the Runa territory—hills, streams, stones, and even some special trees—became the spots of aggressive attack and frightening displays of solidarity of llacta members and their ayllu mates vis-à-vis outsiders. The Puyo Runa confronted, with arms, any and all members of the outside world who encroached upon the llactas. This was one aspect of Puyo Runa territoriality.

The other aspect involved individual and group acquisition of land beyond the sacred rim of a llacta, and its manipulation to gain the outside alliances necessary to maintain the basic Runa territory. Shamans purchased land declared part of the *tierras baldías* and resold it to strong, outside hacendados. Also, land was claimed as indigenous territory well beyond the llacta markers, and this land, too, was manipulated as exchangeable forest surplus for the increasingly necessary capital attendant on an expanding plantation and wage-labor economy.

NATIONALIZATION OF PUYO

In 1947 the Republic of Ecuador completed the Shell-Puyo section of the Ambato-Shell road. Puyo lost its Dominican-dominated trading-town atmosphere and became a national site for expansion in the Oriente. At this time Velasco Ibarra formally established the Comuna San Jacinto by executive decree, and the Dominican priest reclaimed the varayo staffs of cabildo authority. One year later Royal Dutch Shell Oil, now part of a consortium with ESSO, withdrew from Shell, laying off 900 workers within a few days, and the new president, Galo Plaza Lasso, rushed to Shell to declare, "The Oriente is a myth" (see Galarza Zavala 1972:104–106). Back came the oil-working Puyo Runa to the newly created comuna, along with many nationals who established residence in Puyo. Puyo itself became the seat of the canton of Pastaza.

The vacated buildings of Shell Oil were occupied by various Protestant missionaries and Summer Institute of Linguistics (formerly Wycliffe) evangelical Bible translators and researchers. A military garrison moved to the new canton seat to help the rural police keep order in the growing town. The Dominican mission began to extend its dominion to the newly formed comuna. Slowly, painfully, but inexorably, the Puyo Runa were pushed from the town, as their dependence on some aspects of town economy increased. Perhaps a dozen native families maintained a residence in Puyo through about 1955, though all of them had larger homes on the comuna. Today only one Puyo Runa woman remains with a permanent residence in Puyo.

Galo Plaza's announcement of the eastern "myth" may have slowed wage-labor–oriented colonists for a time, but shrewd businessmen and clever politicians began to enter Puyo, basing their strategies of capital acquisition on highland interests speculating on the future of a soon-to-boom Oriente. In the early 1960s Velasco Ibarra reversed Galo Plaza's public pessimism about the Oriente and gave new voice to an old slogan which continues to ring out into the present: "Ecuador has been, is, and will be the Amazonian Country."

Bit by bit the trappings of nationalization descended. As the canton seat grew toward becoming the site of the capital of new Pastaza Province in 1959, a great expansion of rules, laws, and offices occurred, together with an even greater swell of officials, police, lawyers, politicians, manipulators, sinecure builders, shop and saloon owners and managers, and a bevy of national planners and engineers. As Puyo grew in importance and swelled in population (to nearly 4,000 in 1962) other towns sprang up—Madre Tierra as a plantation town between Shell and the Chinimbimi, Tarqui as another plantation town between the Pindo and Chinimbimi, and Veracruz as yet a third plantation town on the new Canelos trail. By the 1950s a road swung north toward Napo and towns emerged just beyond its terminus. Other roads were hastily built to service the plantation towns, and from them improved road services developed to the plantation sites.

The Puyo Runa, settling permanently in their llacta territories, directly responded to nationalization of the zone. They began to form small, square or quadrangular caseríos on the llacta side adjacent to the comuna boundary, and made formal and informal requests that roads be built to them. It was extremely important to the Puyo Runa that access be provided to Puyo via truck, for although the closest caseríos, Unión Base (which was established just off the comuna) and San Jacinto, were only about an hour's fast walk from the growing market center, others such as Rosario Yacu were about two and a half hours away, and Chinimbimi and Puyo Pungo more than a day's hard trek from Puyo. Nationalization of Puyo created a weekly market through which many tropical products, particularly naranjilla, increased rapidly in demand.

Because naranjilla is particularly susceptible to many diseases and blights, it does well as part of a mixed crop in a horticultural swidden. The Puyo Runa men took a great deal of time from other tasks to join women in their swidden cultivation and put in large chagras of naranjilla, using the slash-mulch cultivation system. Returns on this labor were dependent upon access to a predictable water course for transportation by canoe and access to roadside sales or road transportation into Puyo. Some men did manage to haul a ton or so of eighty-pound baskets of naranjilla into Puyo from distant chagras, making about ten to fifteen trips for a three-man crew. But on the whole the naranjilla trade did little more than take a great amount of time from subsistence pursuits and greatly increase comunero conflict and tension over land access in areas nearest the developing roads.

As the formal aspect of Puyo bureaucracy expanded, verbal deals, understandings, and words of honor between Puyo Runa and Puyo nationals declined in favor of contracts, notes, deeds, and claims filed in Puyo, Tarqui, Madre Tierra, Mera, and in the agency for colonization in Quito. Land ownership around the comuna rim was rapidly gobbled up by non-natives, and although some of the Puyo Runa realized a monetary profit, they were unable to convert it into any sort of desirable territorial expansion. Moreover, much land was purchased on a promissory basis, and few natives ever saw full payment.

The result was a large-scale loss of individually held land off the comuna at a time when dependence on such land for cash gain was increasing exponentially. More and more the Puyo Runa had to cope *with* Puyo nationalization *through* a comuna structure. For this reason it is convenient to turn to the structure and development of the Comuna San Jacinto del Pindo, as it represents a special aspect of national expansion and, increasingly, a basis for indigenous survival.

COMUNA SAN JACINTO DEL PINDO

In 1937 the government of Ecuador established a *ley de comunas* (law of communes), which has as its first article this charter: "Every population

Colonists selling naranjilla near Puyo, 1960 (courtesy of Joseph B. Casagrande).

The Pastaza River overflows near Madre Tierra, 1960 (courtesy of Joseph B. Casagrande).

center not in the category of [civil] parish which exists in actuality or will be established in the future, and which is known by the name of hamlet, annex, suburb, district, community, *parcialidad,* or any other designation, will carry the name *comuna,* in addition to the proper name with which it exists or was founded."³ Note that comunas were not restricted to natives, or designated for large territories, in this original concept.

In 1947 President Velasco Ibarra decreed the establishment of a comuna to be called San Jacinto del Pindo between the headwaters of the Pindo and Pastaza rivers, with its eastern border formed by the Puyo River. The western boundary was to have been an imaginary straight line dropping from the Pindo River (on the map, Pindo Grande) headwaters to the Pastaza River, at the point where the Llushín River enters. But the western sector was an area of active colonization and land transactions between natives and individual colonists, themselves seeking homesteads on the edge of the Zulay plantation. Homesteading rapidly led to the opening of the road to Madre Tierra, its rapid growth, and the forcing of native peoples back across the Brazo Chinimbimi and to the edge of Cacalurcu. Similar expansion just outside of Puyo led to a colonist thrust down the Pindo River nearly to its junction with the Puyo, and then a southward one through an area of winding streams that coalesce to become the Chingo-simi River, within present comuna borders.

The Puyo Runa made their stands at Cacalurcu, Paz Yacu, on a point near the present site of Río Chico, where a powerful shaman once made a pact with the Juri juri, and at the present site of San Jacinto, where an old burial ground existed. Severe conflict between colonists and comuneros ensued for several years, and eventually the contemporary boundaries of the comuna were established by eingineers working for the Department of Public Lands and Colonization.⁴ At this establishment the comuna was formally called the *Comuna Indígena de Puyo* (Indigenous Commune of Puyo), and thirty-five separate, non-native, lots were surveyed and the rights to them granted to colonists from the Pindo headwaters to the edge of Cacalurcu. The original site of San Jacinto, near the Pindo headwaters (earlier known as *Mauca Llacta*), was given to the Dominicans for a convent. Within a few years almost all of these homestead lots had been purchased by plantation interests, and sugar cane rapidly replaced jungle-chagra swiddens.

The combination of this governmental move to associate *comuna* with *indígena* and to give immediate service to the establishment of colonists' lots at the time of establishment of comuna boundaries signaled a nationalization of Indian status in the Oriente. All comuneros were to be regarded as a "tribe" linked to a trade center (see, e.g., Anonymous 1951), regardless of ethnic origin. Individual indígenas were to be without national services in land claims within the comuna, for all comuna land was to be held "in common." As far as the government was concerned, interest in indigenous affairs extended only to the comuna boundary. Territory within those boundaries was ripe for mission expansion. These plural, racist, tendencies were soon to coalesce into national policy, applied through an expanding bureaucracy with separate offices for indigenous and colonist affairs.

Dominican Diminution

The Dominican order endeavored to create a replica of its earlyPuyo site on the new comuna. It apparently designated San Jacinto as the name of the comuna, encouraged establishment of the present site of San Jacinto (after its indigenous founding), and the comuneros were all urged either to live around the site, going on purina outward into the comuna, or at least to claim allegiance to this site as the locus of the territory still controlled by Dominican dominion. It appears, however, that Puyo Pungo and Chinimbimi developed their quadrangular caserío structure at the same time, representing, with San Jacinto, three points of the dispersed llacta system. Unión Base and Rosario Yacu also soon formed into caseríos, the former moving just north of the formal comuna boundary.

Shortly after 1950 the Dominicans established a small bamboo-and-tin-roof mission, and later a school, at San Jacinto. At this time San Jacinto took on the character of a site such as Paca Yacu on the Bobonaza—a place occasionally visited by a padre to find new souls to baptize, to attend an ayllu ceremony near Christmas, and, perhaps most important of all, to record in the order's archives the names of "baptized Indians." Such recording was still central to the charter of the Dominicans in the Oriente, and the expansion of their lists was their primary claim to increased aid from their archdiocese. Canelos remained the archdiocese center and the new comuna was claimed by the church as "the perpetual property of the indigenous communities of Canelos and Puyo" (Anonymous 1951:108).

The church reestablished a cabildo system, about the same as the old varayo one but without actual staffs. The cabildo was located at San Jacinto, and although charged with administering all indigenous affairs of the comuna, it actually functioned only as a mediation group between church officials and comuneros seeking Dominican aid in some endeavor. Ayllu ceremonies developed immediately in each of the new caseríos, and the priests were invited to them, together with national compadres from Puyo and the plantation- and colonist-dominated hinterland. But in spite of the church's nominal role, and some political help with the establishment of comuna boundaries after conflict with colonists, the governance of the

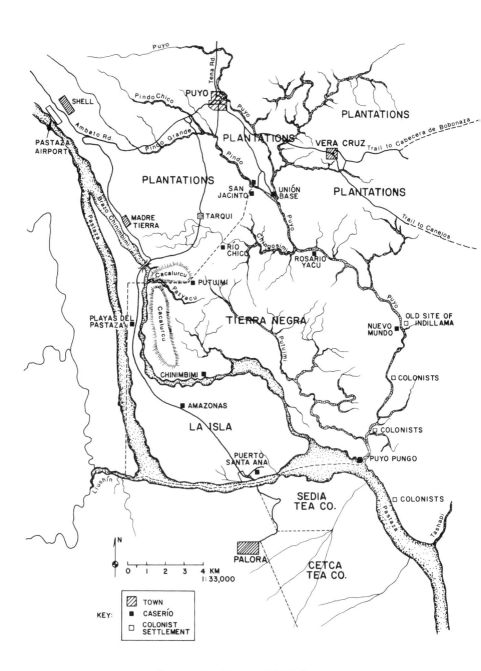

Comuna San Jacinto del Pindo, 1973

comuna was still fundamentally egalitarian, consensus being reached between powerful figures radiating from shamanistic ayllu nodes in each of the llactas.

Puyo Pungo was apparently too far from the Puyo mission for priests to make any sort of predictable visits, or to provide much assistance in secular affairs. The powerful shaman founder of this llacta and later caserío went to the new evangelical Protestant missionaries at Shell and invited them to come and establish a school there and evangelize them. Accepting the invitation, the missionaries soon built a small airstrip by which they could transport resources to build a school, dispense medicines, and establish a base from which to carry on their work. Summer Institute of Linguistics personnel, for their part, recorded the "Bobonaza dialect" of Quichua in this caserío.

Secular Adaptation

Through the 1950s the expanding native population on and near the comuna was beset by persistent encroachment onto the northern territory. The Puyo Runa stepped up their activity within the local political economy by insistent demands on church officials to aid them in the maintenance of their dwindling territory. They increased their land and commercial deals with compadres in town in exchange for informal support with the expanding number of local offices and sinecures. Protests were lodged every year in various governmental offices in Quito by many strong individuals acting in both formal and informal capacities.

In the early 1960s annual elections of the cabildo began, thus enhancing their representation of comuna interests. This official, elected body included a president, vice-president, secretary, treasurer, and *síndico*, a lawyer-type position originally held by a church officer but later by a comunero. The early cabildo devised a system of minimizing the land losses stemming from encroachment by individual colonists while maximizing short-run gains in an expanding money economy. The cabildo established a system of temporary usufruct transfer on a large area of the comuna known as *La Isla* (The Island) because of its isolation between the Pastaza and the Brazo Chinimbimi. They transformed this area into capital assets by informally dividing it into sections belonging to the llactas and allowing the members of each llacta to rent its land illegally to colonists while collectively continuing to condemn colonization of comuna land.

Comuna territory also served as a bulwark to foreign exploitation during the 1950s, when the Zulay plantation endeavored to purchase the Isla as did the British-managed, U.S.-financed Mitchell Cotts Tea Company. Their offers were rejected by the government. In 1963 a four-man military junta seized control of the government and immediately established a policy of land reform and colonization. One consequence of this was to place all comuna affairs in the hands of the Ministry of Social Security (*Ministerio de Previsión Social*), while all colonist and land reform activities were assigned to a newly created agency, the Ecuadorian Institute for Agrarian Reform and Colonization, commonly known by its acronym, IERAC (*Instituto Ecuatoriano para Reforma Agraria y Colonización*). The next year, Mitchell Cotts Tea bought 4,000 hectares of land on the south side of the Pastaza, across from the sought-after Isla, and moved its interests, called CETCA, to this new site. CETCA in turn sold land ranging to the Pastaza River to another company, SEDIA, and Zulay plantation began to convert from sugar cane to tea. Again, the government held firm in not allowing the foreign-based tea companies to get de jure control of comuna territory, but ensuing de facto relationships provided the structure within which comunero (Puyo Runa) usufruct strategies operated.

The new tea plantations needed an access road from the Pastaza River to the main route to the sierra, and the only feasible course was through the Isla. This need coincided with that of the comuneros, who for a decade had been demanding a road to the Pastaza so that they might exploit timber and naranjilla trade by use of truck service. Also, roadways made land more attractive to colonists and hence increased values sharply; the llacta members could thus make more profit from their land rentals if a road were built through the Isla.

Following the adaptive strategy of forming multiple alliances, the first cabildo directly confronted the set of national and international developments and brought the comuna's increased need for money into play. The cabildo itself needed a treasury to free the comuna from Dominican and local secular patronage and to pay for necessary trips to the Ministry of Social Security, which was based in Quito and had no local representative. The cabildo first granted the right to build a road through the Isla to CETCA, in exchange for CETCA's agreement to build a bridge over the Brazo Chinimbimi; this would effectively connect the Isla to a viable truck route. The cabildo then made a deal with a colonist-trucker by renting (illegally) a huge area of the Isla to him for a sum instrumental in establishing the needed treasury. Backed by the promise of a road and bridge, and with land on which to build warehouses, the colonist then gained from CETCA sole right to cross the bridge *without fee.*

The trucker soon made high, steady profits, expanded his number of trucks, and made the most of his monopoly on trucking naranjilla and wood. He illegally invested in other comuna land which he returned to colonists, with the agreement that they would produce charcoal. He purchased their charcoal at a low price and sold as high as possible to Puyo residents. He began to point out particularly lucrative land rental deals to helpful members of the cabildo.

Obviously the cabildo officeholders rapidly moved to a position in the local political economy far different from that of brokers between native peoples and Dominican officials. Election to the cabildo was limited to the five officers mentioned above, and elected officials had access to information and resources different from those of the ordinary comunero. A clear rank order of comuneros developed, with those of high rank in the national system (comuna formal structure) gaining differential access to the money economy. Differential access to strategic resources—land and money—came about within the comuna not through individual power and knowledge, but through maneuver within an established office vis-à-vis specific actors in an expanding national infrastructure partially controlled by foreign interests.

Other comuneros, too, opted to rent land, and some illegally sold plots, taking the money and leaving the comuna. Some of the renters converted their cash into cattle and some chagra area into grazing land by planting on it a hardy imported grass. This cattle complex[5] was rapidly developing in the Puyo area, and within a few years most of the forest around the town of Puyo had been completely replaced by coarse, high grass and grazing Brahman (and mixed) cattle. Firewood and charcoal became scarce items; the colonist *carboneros* of the Isla provided increasing amounts through the trucking monopoly.

Llacta founders continued to consolidate their populations on the edge of comuna holdings and llacta residents repulsed all endeavors at encroachment onto *Tierra Negra,* which was the entire comuna beyond the Isla. They also filed complaints against the resident colonists on the Isla, while making new deals to bring yet others in. Puerto Santa Ana formed a visible dispersed settlement of Jívaro proper, though with old ties to Canelos Quichua and Achuara of the Copotaza-Llushín groupings discussed earlier. Amazonas formed right on the new road, and Putuimi and Río Chico formed to the west, along a line, the *lindero* (boundary), which all comuneros began to maintain as a five- to ten-foot-wide cleared path between comunero and colonist holdings. A bit later Playas del Pastaza also located a caserío at its present site.

Expanding national consolidation manifest in provincial, canton, parish, and subparish structure gave colonists multiple avenues for pressing land claims with IERAC, but the comuneros were legally bound to the Ministry of Social Security. While IERAC had offices in Puyo, as did various governmental officials, the comuneros were expected to deal with one office in Quito. A surge of colonists entered the Isla in the mid-1960s, each individual making some deal with an individual comunero or subletting from a colonist, increasingly with de jure though technically illegal approval of the *teniente político* (political official) of Madre Tierra, the *jefe político* (political head) of Mera Canton, the governor of Pastaza Province, or even a provincial senator of Pastaza. During the period from the mid-1960s to near the present, the comuneros added the newly arriving Peace Corps Volunteers to their roster of outside helpers. The PCVs helped colonists and comuneros settle land claims, endeavored to help the comuneros understand the law and concept of a commune, and responded to caserío requests to formalize both the llacta holdings on the Isla and the boundaries between llactas themselves. In many ways, during this period, llacta and caserío formation endeavored to replicate the national system of rigid territorial boundaries of which they had seen so much since 1941. Schools came to Amazonas, Puerto Santa Ana, and Unión Base with the completing of narrow mud roads, and a school was also established in Rosario Yacu in a joint project involving the caserío members, some Peace Corps Volunteers, and the Mera Canton officials.

PUYO URBANIZATION AND URBANISM

To understand the dynamics of Puyo Runa adaptation through comuna structure, a bit more information about the growth of Puyo is needed. Casagrande, Thompson, and Young (1964:293) studied the colonization process in and near Puyo in 1962, and offer this lucid portrayal:

> ... if Baños reminds one of Leadville in the Twentieth Century, Puyo, while still smaller than Baños in total population, is more reminiscent of Virginia City in the heyday of the Comstock Lode. Seventy kilometers distant from Baños, Puyo was founded in 1899, but was isolated until completion of the road linking it with Baños, and hence with Ambato, in 1947. Since then its growth has been rapid, so much so, in fact, that considerable change was evident even during the brief three-month period that we used it as our field headquarters during the summer of 1962. It is the capital of Pastaza province, itself a recent creation, and seat of a *municipio,* or county government, which extends far down the road toward Tena. It is the site of a large church, the local headquarters of the Dominican order, two primary schools, two *colegios,* or high schools, as well as numerous places of business, including three hotels, a number of *pensiones,* a bank, four or five general stores, a sewing machine agency, two motion picture theaters, and many barber shops, grocery stores, *cantinas,* and other small enterprises. The Red Cross dispensary and one doctor provide professional medical care over a large part of the Oriente, and in addition there are a dentist and a government veterinarian in the town. Two gas stations provide fuel for the trucks and buses which constitute Puyo's lifeline to the outside world, and two garages help maintain the vehicles.
>
> Sunday is market day in Puyo. Extra buses run on the Puyo-Tena road all

day Saturday, and colonists pour into the town by bus, truck, horse, mule, and on foot. It is probable that Puyo's bars and theaters take in more money on Saturday night then during all the nights of the rest of the week combined.

Puyo had a population of 3,723 according to the 1962 national census; by 1969 it had nearly doubled (Gillette 1970:54); it was estimated at 10,000 or more by 1972. The main road was constantly being hacked through jungle and clay; it was extended from the edge of Fátima to beyond Archidona between 1962 and 1968. As it moved, plantations and homesteads replaced dense stands of jungle, and access roads were opened. Subsistence and barter economy changed into a money-market system. Development brought prosperity to the wealthy hacendados and many of the national colonists as new hamlets, small towns with schools and churches, appeared along the road from Puyo to Napo. The native peoples living near Fátima were forced eastward into their purina territory between Jatun Paccha and San Ramón, there to found another comuna. Concrete bridges replaced log and plank ones, and in 1972 a modern suspension bridge across the Napo River replaced the old barge-ferry and the hand-pulled cable car, providing a continuous road to Cotundo, beyond Archidona, on a route which will eventually connect with the Quito-Baeza road.

From a mud-street boomtown with ubiquitous false fronts and a flood of aguardiente and hell-raising marketers on weekends, Puyo had by the early 1970s become an organized, bustling, young bureaucratic seat of commerce, administration, and expansion. Main streets were cobblestoned, resonating under the steadily increasing numbers of buses and heavy trucks as Puyo grew more dependent on national distribution centers for goods and services and became a regional center for newly forming satellite towns. Thriving on the opportunities for local services, taxis and small-scale trucking businesses had their impact on the pace of life—more traffic, more traffic regulations, more reliance on modern transportation.

"Urbanization" refers to demographic growth patterns due to increased opportunities in the money economy, development of economic stratification with attendant hierarchical arrangements of social prestige to reflect monetary gain, and an increased importance of education and mass communication for political-economic functions. Puyo's growing importance as a regional center in the national-to-frontier relationships clearly reflects the urbanization process attendant upon nationalization.

National police joined the rural police, some of whom were sent to the outlying towns, even as far as Canelos. Telephone service, both local and long distance, complemented the older telegraph system. Electricity and a public water system were introduced in the early 1960s. Regularly scheduled flights from Shell airport aided the flow of people and goods, but the mail was dependent on road transportation. The most powerful vehicle of mass communication was the local radio station, Radio Pastaza, which opened in 1968. In addition to regular programs and paid announcements, it provided free service to all people wishing to send a message for public or private reasons. The station transmitted over a large area, eastward at least as far as the lower Copotaza River and Sara Yacu, sending out individual announcements, national speeches, and music programs ranging from classical through North and South American popular tunes to Quichua and Jivaroan songs.

The growing demand for goods and services was met by expansion and specialized development: a second bank, a colosseum and stadium, more saloons, a soft-drink bottling plant, beauty shops, more barber shops, increased hotel facilities. Along with the small but steady trickle of national and international tourists now came occasional groups of orchid collectors. Class-conscious town residents, building large modern houses, stimulated work for carpenters, masons, day laborers; branches of national cement, tin, and iron works located in Puyo. Pressure from wealthy home owners, hotel managers, and store owners for better services led to construction of an improved electric plant, a larger water reservoir, regularly imported bottled gas for cooking. Three Protestant sects (Jehovah's Witnesses, Seventh-Day Adventists, and a Baptist sect) set up storefront operations and later moved into more permanent quarters.

General stores had long been filled with the necessities of frontier and plantation life; to the machetes, shotguns, aluminum cooking ware, and plain fabrics for clothes and bedding were added Japanese-made plastic goods, dress materials and ready-made clothes, enameled pots and pans, cosmetics. Imported cigarettes, national brands of soft and hard drinks, and tinned luxury foods became available, for a price. Several brands of sewing machines were sold in six out of the more than thirty shops; imported silks and fancy trims indicated the lifestyle of some. Miles of barbed wire and barrels of staples reflected a staked-out hinterland; modern plumbing, pipes, wiring, and elaborate locks were requisite to a sanitary, enclosed home inside its locked-up property. Waste from these homes, and from hotels, poured into drainage ditches and streams, eventually emptying into the Pindo and Puyo rivers; garbage from the town was collected daily by several trucks and taken to convenient dumps in outlying areas. The developing national appliance industry shipped in refrigerators and stoves now that electrical service was improved and bottled gas available. Even the less affluent could manage to afford one of the many brands of battery-operated portable phonographs and a few of the newest discs from the record shop. Perhaps a bicycle could be bought when a car was out of the question. Unions, local and national, proliferated as an interlocking set of hacendados, store owners, and people with commercial interests increasingly manipulated the political economy for personal gain.

A branch of the national Public Health Service joined the previously established Red Cross and Dominican missionary health dispensary in Puyo in the late 1960s. The malaria station located its regional headquarters there, and national campaigns for preventive vaccination against epidemic disease focused on the new campesino (i.e. the new colonist). IERAC, too, located its large offices in Puyo, maintaining legal and technical aid to the colonists, but excluding comuna, i.e. indigenous, affairs from its normal services. A lone office with a sign on the door saying *Ministerio de Previsión Social* existed in the governmental edifice; it was almost always unoccupied.

Urbanization processes as sketched above are accompanied by an expansion of urban*ism*, the culture of cities. Crucial to the emergent culture in eastern Ecuador is the self-definition of participants as urban people. The charter of urbanity is defined by the ethnic designation *blanco* (white) in contrast to all people of the forest, the zone's native populace. Tropical rainforest ecology is rejected as part of the relevant urban environment; knowledge of and adaptation to the forest environment are debased, relegated to "savagery." Development of a code of urban ethnic egalitarianism not only masks differential access to basic resources among white town residents, it simply negates the native from all processes of urbanism.

The sierra and coast of Ecuador have long known a landed, wealthy elite, the blancos, beneath whom are many classes of people variously categorized. They generally aspire to blanco values, but are reminded in multiple contexts of poverty cast in the idiom of racial mixture that their status in life is beneath that of the elite. The nation, below the elite, is often characterized as *mestizo*, an imputation of mixture from Indian and European stock. *Mestizaje*, the ideology of mixture, coalesced in the Oriente, and in national ideology under military rule, to assert a oneness of a people. By negating elite-values, and in the absence of actual elite families in the eastern forests, the new colonists simply assumed membership in the blanco category themselves. To be "national" was to be blanco, and to be other than blanco (now synonymous with national mestizo) could only mean to be *indio*. The equation of town or cleared forest with blanco and forest with indio was repeatedly made. Under the ideology of racial mixture a powerful mechanism for exclusion of the non-mixed was generated.

Awareness of Indianness was enacted throughout the late 1960s and early 1970s in Puyo during the Founding of Puyo Day celebration on May 12. A *few* natives were invited to dance for the blancos, dressed in grass skirts and body paint—the national stereotype of the tropical forest Indian. Also, comuneros were asked to join the parade and carry lances, symbol of a now nonexistent native populace. Signs announcing the undeveloped Puyo of the past—always with drawings of *atrasado* (backward) Indians—were carried by other parade groups, along with drawings of colonists which portrayed *desarrollo* (development) and the future.

Foreign Exploitation

Foreign-based extraction and exploitation entered this system in the late 1960s. The Texaco-Gulf consortium had struck oil in the northern Oriente in 1963, and by 1968 exploration of the central Oriente had once again begun out of the Shell airport. Anglo-Ecuadorian Oil, Amoco, and Standard of California (among others), their subsidiaries, and contracted exploration companies provided a bizarre infrastructural validation to the processes of urbanism. With a deluge of airplanes, helicopters, and the system of base camps with their outlying bivouacs and supply lines, all provided with tinned goods and procedural plans from Shell—and out of Shell from Quito, London, Houston, Amsterdam, New York, and Toronto—the search for subsurface oil and the attendant explosion of capital for ancillary services created a veneer of security in an area still basically supplied by only one almost unbelievably treacherous stretch of road and an airstrip located in an area of nearly constant rainfall and fog.

Native response to the oil boom was immediate. From virtually every family of the Puyo Runa young men signed on to work with the exploration companies. Unless recalled by their families many spent one to two years in a forest zone. They did the major part of the initial camp clearing, built helicopter pads, and cleared the ten-foot-wide jungle paths where dynamite was exploded every half-mile by helicopter-borne foreign and national engineers. They also taught the other workers from the highlands and coast the basic aspects of the forest domain. In many areas foreign boss–native worker ties became close, but everywhere the national union system, often insisting on the inferiority of native workers, intruded; the very skills needed in exploration were denigrated and relegated to native labor wherever possible. The Puyo Runa, along with all the other Canelos Quichua, took advantage of the oil boom not only to gain cash but also to study again other ways, other customs. Some men visited Achuara and Jívaro proper groups long estranged from them, returning to their parents and in-laws with new information about the enduring diversity of the Sacha Runa.

Although some native oil workers amassed enough cash to purchase land, cattle, sewing machines, new clothes, a watch, and a radio—all necessary accouterments of the urbanized life to which they would return—most were thoroughly fleeced by one or another mechanism attendant on the boom. In many cases recruitment was by the labor organizer, who provided workers to the exploration company for a set fee

Amoco base exploration camp, Montalvo, 1970.

A camp in the forest with helicopter pad.

and agreed to pay the laborers and provide food, clothing, machete, axe, and shelter for them. Such recruiters actually managed to charge workers for such necessities, claiming extensions of loans against workers' earnings so that the workers had little or nothing when they signed off. The ways in which native and national labor were separated from their U.S. wage of 75¢ to $1.20 per day are far too numerous to list.

Many other Puyo Runa opted for a three-month term and signed off with about 2,000 sucres (U.S. $80) just before they would have had to join a union and commit themselves for a year or two of labor. By staggering the flow of such men for three-month periods, people in ayllu segments endeavored to maintain the necessary local manpower, with a trickle of incoming cash and knowledge. Even those who went for a few months were careful to study the ways of the gringo controllers, national bosses, national poor workers, and if possible meet, study with, and understand the lifeways of other indigenous peoples.

In Puyo itself bureaucracy swelled with sinecures, and commerce boomed with new goods and inflated prices. A deluge of workers from the highlands and coast left for the camps, and more colonists flooded into Puyo and its hinterland only to find their prospects to be stark and dismal. They had to find a way of life in a maze of legal and commercial paternalism near a road or town, or blaze a homestead in a jungle area with no skills, knowledge, or tools.

Many of the colonists who remained in this urbanized setting opted to settle on native territory. This occurred at the urging of an hacendado or trucker, and for a brief period by contract with a comunero in need of ready cash in an inflated economy. This strategy of squeezing the natives now found support within Puyo itself, for the need to maintain a native labor supply to provide services in a frontier ecology disappeared. By 1972 the Comuna San Jacinto del Pindo represented a barrier to nationalization, just as the reentry of massive petroleum interests once again represented the possibility of foreign domination of eastern Ecuador. The Puyo Runa now confronted the very real possibility of ethnic annihilation, for with oil companies blanketing the area to the east, encroachment out of Puyo in the north, and the plantation areas to the west and south, they stood to lose immediate and distant refuge zones.

Knowledge and money would be meaningless if the Puyo Runa were left without a viable, life-giving, and life-symbolizing biosphere to which they could return. They were excluded from most services in Puyo because of their dependence on the Quito office of the Ministry of Social Security. The comuna was beset by colonist and plantation strategies of land acquisition, and to make things worse pro tempore transfers of authority to IERAC for resolution of colonist-comunero disputes were frequently made. The new military dictatorship which came to power in 1971 increased the local charter of IERAC, the very agency charged with helping colonists settle land claims, to try to "solve" the problem of the Isla. By the time IERAC was told to settle finally and definitively all colono claims, there were 150 colonists illegally settled along the road from the Brazo Chinimibimi to the Pastaza, and native-colonist conflicts were constant. The Ministry of Social Security itself moved in the early 1970s to preserve its tenuous control of comuna holdings by backing all colonists' claims to the Isla land, its representatives claiming ignorance of comuna holdings in this area.

PUYO RUNA RESPONSE AND ADAPTATION

One adaptation of the Puyo Runa on the Comuna San Jacinto was to replicate in their hamlet structure feasible organizational facets of provincial microcosms. Such microcosms were provided by the growing villages (Madre Tierra, Tarqui, Veracruz) surrounding Puyo. Each of these villages had a committee of parents, the president of which worked with parish, canton, and provincial officials. The Puyo Runa adapted aspects of these microcosm organizations to their own social order, while at the same time modifying their social system to function in new ways.

To articulate more effectively with canton and parish educational structure most caseríos developed a *Comité de Padres de la Familia* modeled on the town system. The president of this PTA-like system carried caserío decisions and statistics on population to the municipal officials and worked directly with a resident schoolteacher, when one was present and willing to help, and with clergy, Peace Corps Volunteers, and anyone else with a "program" for the specific caserío.

Through this comité system the caseríos developed soccer teams and tied their teams into regional and national sports organizations to secure uniforms and arrange games with other teams from the new non-native towns and hamlets off the comuna. The caserío teams extended reciprocal challenges to one another, and soccer games in one or another caserío became fiestas, during which time a great deal of drinking, talking, fighting, politicking, and necessary social readjustment took place. Caserío teams also invited new teams from the Jívaro proper and from the Andes to come and play, endeavoring to use this ritual context as a means to extend their ethnic ties to those also classed as indio. Most of the intra-native games were played on the caserío quadrangle, although a few took place in Puyo. Soccer games also offered good opportunities to assess the qualities of various individuals. Strength, aggression, and skill of particular players and mediating abilities in fistfights were discussed, as the Puyo Runa studied one another in the new ritual contexts.

A large caserío on the Comuna San Jacinto del Pindo, 1970.

Playing soccer in the caserío, 1971.

Minga labor organized to chop out a roadbed between Puerto Santa Ana and Puyo Pungo, 1973.

Another sort of caserío officer was also created as an adaptation of llacta structure to caserío life. A *vocal* (spokesman) for the caserío was selected every year or so to represent llacta affairs to national, provincial, regional, and comuna officials, and to report back to the caserío members the work of these officials. The vocales were chosen not so much for their competence in political or administrative affairs, however, as for some debt which they owed to the dominant segmental ayllu of the llacta. Internally, in the llacta system, the vocal represented in-law relationship to the dominant ayllu segment. The concept of vocal was one of *service* to his llacta. Within the llacta the vocal officially called mingas to clean the caserío, and represented himself as a "leader" to outside non-natives. The vocal system effectively masked the shaman ayllu nodes to outsiders, and those serving as vocal gained opportunities to learn more of the formal political arena.

Articulation of the caserío formal organization with the comuna polity was strengthened by the elaboration of a system of open meetings. An *asemblea general*, a general assembly much like a town meeting in New England, was established to function in a juro-political arena characterized by external encroachment and llacta consolidation and centralization. The asemblea was called by the president of the comuna whenever a clear and present outside threat to formal comuna boundaries occurred. Although the charter for such an assembly is given in the law of communes, what I will describe here is the native mechanism which evolved as both a political and juridical institution in the face of external pressures and internal adjustment strains.

The asemblea general[6] is called by the comuna president. He notifies each of the vocales in writing as to its date and place, during Sunday market day at Puyo. The time announced is always 10:00 A.M., and the place is chosen by invitation extended by one of the caseríos. Secular governmental officials are invited to the asemblea just as the priests and compadres are invited to ayllu ceremonies. There follows about a week of discussion in each of the caseríos, throughout the comuna in other llactas lacking caserío formation, in sacha huasis scattered in the interior of the comuna, and among other Runas related to comuna members who are not residing on the comuna proper but for whom this territory is nonetheless the Runa territory to which they belong. Discussions revolve around three topics: imminent threats to the comuna itself; faults found in the cabildo officers, especially the president; and inequities and breaches which have occurred either within a given llacta or between members of adjacent llactas.

On the morning of the asemblea, huasi members arise, as usual, before dawn. Falsetto shouts rend the air as segmental ayllu representatives, formal caserío spokesmen (vocales), powerful shamans, and whoever else wants to go drink their chicha, eat a hearty breakfast, and start off on foot to the designated site. As people arrive they go immediately to the house of their nearest gumba partner or ayllu member in the caserío, drink chicha, talk, laugh, and share information about outside events. Those who have no gumba partner, ayllu mates, and no masha huasi—household of an in-law to their own ayllu—simply stand near the edge of the quadrangle. Sometimes soccer is played for half an hour or so, and at times an actual soccer game is called by the local Comité de Padres de la Familia (or more recently by a local sports club).

The asemblea begins around 11:00 A.M. It is held in the local school or chapel. The president formally calls the meeting to order in Spanish, and the secretary reads the minutes of the last meeting, also in Spanish. Invited guests normally say a few words. For example, the teniente político of Tarqui may say he is pleased that "civilization" is finally coming to the natives, because without civilization there will be no progress and things will be as they once were, in a backward state. Then, perhaps a visiting agronomist from Quito will warn the people not to cut down all their trees, for then they will have to have a plan of reforestation. He will then offer services to those who wish to understand the establishment of plantations so that "development" can occur on the comuna, just as it has on land adjacent to the comuna. As the comuneros puzzle over how one national agronomist can, in a sentence, both tell them not to destroy the forest and offer them services to do just that, other outsiders rise to speak. Within half an hour, the outsiders succeed in demonstrating how inchoate their system is, and carefully drop sufficient ethnic markers to establish the basic blanco-indio hiatus. Then the asemblea enters a phase of Runa validation of the cabildo.

People object to the minutes of the preceding meeting and begin to question the cabildo as to what it is doing, generally voicing negative sentiments about the cabildo itself. Critical conversation is in Quichua. Minor issues and minor mistakes of the president and other cabildo members are raised; each cabildo member must respond forcefully, verbally correct the mistake, and in all ways possible demonstrate his competence to handle the serious issues that the comuneros will bring up. This part of the asemblea may last from half an hour to two hours. It is a fundamental testing of the qualities of the cabildo. If the president is strong enough, he emerges as asemblea spokesman and judge, a person who will initiate political action, to whom interpersonal breaches will be reported, and whose suggestions on how to resolve the breach will be taken seriously by pivotal figures in ayllu and llacta systems. But if the president does not show sufficient skill in his handling of criticism—that is, if he does not manage to validate his pending political and juridical roles—then the people assembled challenge more strongly another member of the cabildo. Secretary, vice-president, síndico can take on some aspects of the role complex if they demonstrate verbal skill and judgmental wisdom in providing information on past decisions and hypothetical solutions to perceived problems. (On the few occasions when a cabildo member other than the president has emerged as juro-political leader, however, the people have had doubts about the asemblea's success.)

During the crescendo of criticism leveled against the president, increasingly important issues are raised about the comuna, and when the president skillfully handles these issues, the asemblea becomes an agency of political decision. The president endeavors to suggest solutions to immediate problems which affect everyone. Imminent loss of more land, or continuing encroachment of the *mashca pupus*, or even steady harassment of natives on the Isla segment of the comuna by truckers, colonists, and *mashca chapas* (barley-gut guards—the rural police) are typical problems. When the president hits on a feasible solution, such as going to Quito to protest, seeing the provincial governor on Sunday, or even taking the cabildo as a group to the house of a colonist to order him to leave, the asemblea very rapidly joins in unanimous accord, validates the political action, and backs the president in his continuing efforts.

Once such political action vis-à-vis outsiders and the larger political economy has been decided upon, the president assumes a juridical role vis-à-vis the comuneros. He begins to hear minor complaints and petitions from llacta and ayllu members and from officials of the caseríos. The first issues brought to him involve usufructory rights within the comuna. Since the population of the comuna is growing steadily (from about 1,200 in 1968 to 1,600 in 1973), the settled swidden cultivation system described in Chapter 2 has become more land-intensive. Many sons and sons-in-law find that half of the father's, or father-in-law's, land is inadequate, and their families need to "hop over" another huasi's chagra–fallow area into still unclaimed land. In so doing, however, the huasi group may well move onto another llacta, or an area designated by a llacta group for purina chagra within the comuna. Invariably, the president affirms that land is open to all comuneros, and that chagras can be established wherever a comunero can work the land. Such a statement is cast in the national idiom of comuna, but the message to the Puyo Runa carries another meaning. This statement by the president validates the Canelos Quichua strategy of outposting and embedding (see Chapter 4, pp. 126ff.), and the young man seeking a new chagra lot in another llacta (as he invariably does) places himself and his huasi in the strategically ambiguous position of having responsibilities to two llactas. Validation of this strategy gives the younger members of the comuna freedom of maneuver in a system where land is becoming increasingly dear, and encourages their own autonomous establishment of huasi and ayllu segment in alliance with dominant ayllu and residential llacta competitiors. It also increases their responsibilities in interpersonal relations with an expanded network of fellow Runas.

The president hears cases of reported infidelity between spouses, and descriptions of fights between young men. Usually the public statements of these breaches and the snickering they evoke from those assembled are sufficient to deter escalation of interpersonal factionalism arising from minor problems. More serious schismatic conflict over land and over interpersonal breaches is delayed when the president agrees to visit the aggrieved parties in their caserío setting for further juridical functions. A series of such agreements establishes the basis for the president and other members of the cabildo to travel from caserío to caserío before the next asemblea, carrying on the juridical role until it becomes necessary to revalidate the role within the politicized context of boundary encroachment or some other grave problem of comuna-wide concern. Validation of the juridical role is predicated on demonstrated political competence.

The end of the asemblea seems to most outsiders just to dwindle away. Women interrupt to let some of the men know that manioc, plantains, and chicken are cooked, and members of the cabildo invite the outside guests to eat. By this time many comuneros may be playing soccer or volleyball outside the building, and most people are talking about a dozen different subjects. Quickly now small groups of Runa approach the president with what they regard as grave problems which do not yet affect comuna life. The president hears these cases in "closed court" and gives advice. When necessary he agrees to visit the parties in their huasis, which may be well away from the caserío, or he may agree to make a visit with them to the proper office in Puyo. Often he refers people to the appropriate government office for help regarding problems such as wife stealing, or a land deal off the comuna, or a decision as to how to recall a son working under contract for an oil company.

After the asemblea people are fed by gumba partners, ayllu or masha mates, and most leave for their houses, endeavoring to arrive an hour or two after dark. Some travel a circuitous route with other ayllu mates or gumba partners, and spend a night and a day drinking and talking in another caserío, verbally rehashing the events of the asemblea and their processual significance to the enduring, adapting structure of the Puyo Runa.

In succeeding weeks the president or another cabildo member visits the caseríos in an effort to resolve any residual problems which may still exist. He meets with the caserío members after the weekly minga (each caserío has a minga on a specified day). At this meeting the comuna official as mediator assumes the role played earlier by a priest or perhaps a Peace Corps Volunteer, who represented the source of neutral adjudication.

By the late 1960s the Puyo Runa had evolved a juro-political system which articulated to the national system through replication of the feasible aspects of rural non-native microcosms and through participation in all allowable channels of access to national resources. Secularization of the Puyo Runa became complete with the growth of the asemblea general and the articulation of caserío structure and cabildo adjudication. When this occurred the cabildo petitioned the Ministry of Social Security for a change in name from cabildo—which was the church-sponsored organization growing out of the varayo system—to directiva, and the request was granted.

By 1972 the elected directiva represented a completely secular indigenous organization which dealt directly with incredibly complex, anti-comuna machinations by local representatives of the military dictatorship in alliance with national and foreign plantation interests, colonization officers, and commercial concerns. This alliance constantly attempted to seize large sectors of comuna territory and destroy native adaptive potential in the name of a new, imposed "national culture."

In 1972 the directiva took decisive action to establish an absolute ethnic charter to govern specific strategies of territorial defense. It categorically stated, at every asemblea and in writing to IERAC, the Ministry of Social Security, the teniente político of Madre Tierra, the jefe político of Canton Mera, and the governmental office in Puyo, that no more rentals to outsiders would be considered, legally or illegally, and furthermore that all

male blanco spouses of the Puyo Runa were to be denied chagra space on
the comuna unless the father of the native woman gave the outsider half of
his own chagra. All comuneros backed up the directiva, and the rental
strategy completely ceased. There remained the continuing and as yet
unresolved problem of the 150 colonists already settled on the Isla, a
subject briefly discussed in the next chapter.

Shamanism and ayllu rituals, as presented in Chapters 5, 6, and 7,
continue within and beyond comuna boundaries to the present day. The
largest ayllu ceremony of all was held in December, 1972, along the road of
the Isla. As the ayllu rituals are performed in most of the contemporary
caseríos, the reorganization taking place afterward tends to be more
intra-caserío than intra-territorial. These internal Puyo Runa territorial
adjustments are, in turn, brought to the asemblea general for validation
and any necessary adjudication. The consolidation of caserío-llacta structure together with that of comuna structure is not without tension, but the
Puyo Runa management of tension, based on the complex system of
transformable relationships in Canelos Quichua culture, continues.

Grave external threats confront the Puyo Runa, stemming from problems created by nationalization procedures and national demographic
shifts which seek to confine and obliterate native ethnic lifeways. The Puyo
Runa are swelling in numbers and seeking other land bases away from the
Comuna San Jacinto del Pindo, while maintaining and bolstering comuna
structure and endeavoring to multiply its functions.

A new airport has opened at Canelos and a comuna has been established
there; a trickle of colonists promising an imminent invasion has already
begun. A road is under way between Veracruz and the Pastaza River,
running down the Siguin range, ancient zone of the Caninche-Penday
territory. Some of the descendants of the original Caninche-Achuara
intermarried kin group have also just moved there from the Comuna San
Jacinto. They have gone back to the ancient territory to establish another
comuna near the site of more infrastructural expansion. Furthermore, in
the formation of this new comuna they have formed an alliance with Jívaro
proper from the Chiguaza River with whom they hope to hold their
territory while participating in national development. Paca Yacu and Sara
Yacu are also experiencing some of the effects of nationalization following
the oil boom and bust, and the inhabitants of these areas are studying the
adaptive aspects of Puyo Runa organization and modifying them according
to specific ecological niches and outside strategies confronted by these
territorial segments of Canelos Quichua culture.

Today the Pastaza River constantly flows a deep chocolate brown, not
only because of the natural periodic falling and crashing of the montaña

slides, but also due to efforts of a contracting company funded by a loan from the World Bank to establish a paved road between Baños and Puyo. Water-borne soil is joined by steel and human litter as bits and pieces of bus, car, plane, and remains of dozens of dead passengers are carried through the white-water Sungui domain to the Amasanga-Nunghuí spirit power source of the Puyo Runa. But for the dozens who perish in the slides, auto and bus accidents, and plane crashes into the Llanganati Mountains, hundreds upon hundreds of people survive to create the still-swelling human deluge validating the national conquest of this western edge of Upper Amazonia.

NOTES

1. For a photograph of this airport in the 1940s see Blomberg (1956), plate facing p. 16 and its overleaf.

2. Jaime Galarza Zavala (1972:72–99) argues that the Peruvian invasion itself came about due to the competition between Standard Oil of New Jersey and Royal Dutch Shell Oil. On p. 90 he presents a map of the two oil concessions drawn up at the Protocol of Río de Janeiro in which the new boundaries are drawn almost exactly according to the claims of Standard Oil of New Jersey, on the Peruvian side, and Royal Dutch Shell Oil, on the Ecuadorian. He dedicates his work "to the memory of the Ecuadorian soldiers who fell in 1941, in a petroleum war." For his stand on such issues in the current international political economy Galarza Zavala was jailed as a political prisoner (see *El Comercio*, Jan. 22, 1973, in an interview entitled *Famoso escritor Cortázar visitó en el Penal al autor del "Festín del Petróleo"*).

3. The 1967 edition of the *Ministerio de Previsión Social*'s publication, issued by the *Departamento de Asuntos Sociales y Campesinado*, gives the *ley de comunas* as decree no. 679 of the *Junta Militar de Gobierno*. The basis for this publication is governmental decree no. 23, Dec. 7, 1937, published in the *Registro Oficial* as nos. 39 and 40 on Dec. 10 and 11 (*Ministerio de Previsión Social* 1967:8). Art. 1 states: *Todo centro poblado que no tenga la categoría de Parroquia, que exista en la actualidad o que se estableciere en lo futuro, y que sea conocido con el nombre de caserío, anejo, barrio, partido, comunidad, parcialidad, o cualquiera otra designación, llevará el nombre de "Comuna," a más del nombre propio con él que haya existido o se fundare.*

4. The description of the boundaries of the comuna is given on the map prepared by an "engineering aide of the Department of Public Lands and Colonization." I am grateful to Udo Oberem for giving me a blueprint of this original map, which he procured in the mid-1950s in Quito. The boundaries (see Javier Beghin n.d.) were established as

"North: Pindo River for a thousand metres downriver to its southern junction on the Puyo, then the Pindo-Puyo to the junction of the Indillama; South: Pastaza River to the junction of the Llushín downriver to the junction of the Puyo; East: Pindo-Puyo River to the junction of the Indillama, to its junction with the Pastaza; West: Brazo Chinimbimi from the Paz Yacu junction downriver to where it changes to an eastward direction, from this point drop an imaginary north-south line to the Pastaza. Then [make] a line parallel to the existing trail [marking the boundary] that now runs south from the Pindo to the Brazo Chinimbimi for a distance of two thousand metres that will be lots marked off by thirds."

Norte: Río Pindo en una extensión de mil metros, aguas abajo hasta su desembocadura en el Puyo luego el Pindo-Puyo, hasta la desembocadura del Indillama: Sur: Río Pastaza desde la

desembocadura del Llushín, aguas abajo hasta la desembocadura del Puyo; Este: Río Pindo-Puyo desde la desembocadura del Indillama, hasta su desembocadura en el Pastaza; Oeste: Brazo Chinimbimi, desde la desembocadura del Paz Yacu, aguas abajo, hasta cuando cambia su rumbo para dirigirse al este, de este punto se tomará una línea imaginaria con dirección norte-sur, hasta cortar al Pastaza. Además, línea paralela a la trocha existente que ya desde el Pindo hacía el sur hasta el Brazo Chinimbimi distante dos mil metros y que separará de lotes denunciados por terceros.

In the Javier Beghin (n.d.:3) version the last sentence reads: *Además, línea paralela a la trocha existente que va desde Salacara Cocha, en el Pindo Grande, hacia el sur....*

5. The cattle complex was immediately adapted to the Puyo Runa chagra swidden system during the maize-planting phase. When planting maize at the tail end of the chagra, the men also plant grass. The maize and grass grow together, and after the maize is harvested cattle are placed on the new grassland. Thereafter, the grassland remains as a hectare set aside for grazing, and brush and trees are periodically cut down. In many cases caserío members now rent their grazing area to a colonist. The colonist, in turn, puts eight to twelve cattle on the one hectare of land, and within three months the cattle have eaten all the grass down to the roots, churned up the soil, and thoroughly fertilized the resulting mulch-soil complex; then they are moved to another field to repeat the process. The grass, together with many jungle trees and shrubs, returns within three more months; then the trees and shrubs are cut down again, and the process repeated.

6. There is a great deal of variety in the asembleas generales, far more than can be analyzed and discussed in this work. I have attended some asembleas where no outsiders (other than myself) were present, and one in which a governmental official took over the entire meeting and scarcely let the president speak. All told, the members of our research group have attended about twenty asembleas, and at least two every year since 1969. Prior to 1969, data are also available from other outsiders, including Peace Corps Volunteers and missionaries, as to the content, pace, style, and results of these meetings. The asembleas which we attended were held in Puyo Pungo, Puerto Santa Ana, Amazonas, Playas del Pastaza, Río Chico, San Jacinto, Unión Base, Rosario Yacu, and Madre Tierra (a parish seat off the comuna).

9

Internal Colonialism, Ecuadorian Ethnocide, and Indigenous Ethnogenesis

A CASE OF NATIONAL CULTURE AND NATIVE RIGHTS

On September 15, 1972, the president of Ecuador, General Guillermo Rodríguez Lara, flew into the Shell aiport, accompanied by a group of colonels and captains each of whom was the chief officer of a national agency or bureaucracy. The twenty-minute flight from Quito was timed to correspond with sunrise, and the versatile STAL (short takeoff and landing) plane, locally called "the cockroach," touched down on the gravel strip at exactly 6:00 A.M. There the red-beret crack paratroopers, trained in Panama for commando warfare, displayed their virtuosity by flourishing Czechoslovakian automatic rifles at passing busses and cars. Still other troops carrying rifles with fixed bayonets stood at attention along the short path of the group's walk. The governor of the province whisked the president and his entourage into Puyo to meet briefly with civil administrators from all Oriente provinces, and with the committee of prominent Puyo families at the governmental offices. Then the entire group moved directly to the large auditorium in the Red Cross building, where the president began a prolonged, programmatic speech about infrastructural development in the Oriente, the entirety of which was projected outward by loudspeakers and broadcast on Radio Pastaza.

The president's five-hour speech stressed two main aspects of "development." The first of these was the infrastructural expansion through a projected network of roads, bridges, schools, public services, and new administrative division to govern the anticipated population expansion and demographic shifts toward the sites of improved communications and stepped-up commerce. He made it redundantly clear to everyone who

The military on parade in Tena, 1972.

heard him that responsibility for this expansion was centered in his hands, as dynamic administrator of the National Revolutionary Government.[1]

The second aspect of the president's speech stressed the need for acceleration in small-scale commercial production and improved land utilization. The president railed against the prevalence of such critical subsistence crops as manioc and the practice of swidden agriculture. He urged poor colonists to work with IERAC to secure titles to land, loans from banks, and to clear away the jungle and plant such marketable crops as rice, cacao, corn, and grain, and obtain and care for cattle and swine. He promised that modern pesticides and defoliants would be made available through government programs of education aimed at conquest of the forest.

Members of the cabildo of the Comuna San Jacinto had previously prepared a letter to be delivered to President Rodríguez which, in their customary fashion, was in line with the direction of explicit national policy. They said they wished to participate in the processes of nationalization, to sell products, and to educate their children. Then they simply stated that until a means was found to eliminate encroachment and settlement of colonists on their land, they had little time to participate in the nationalist development of the Oriente. They urged him to set up the mechanism leading to a rapid solution to their loss of rights of usufruct on comuna territory, and to direct a small percentage of the budget designated for intrastructural development to provide access roads and improved schools and more teachers for the comuna's current inhabitants and expanding population. The cabildo members were told by a lawyer in the president's entourage that these matters must be taken up with officers of the Ministry of Social Security in Quito. The agency was not represented in the president's party simply because it had no direct relationship to development in the Oriente.

Among themselves, while listening to the radio, the comuneros puzzled over the "production" aspects of the president's speech. Many of the colonists they know either buy manioc and other staples from comuneros, or grow them in the system of swidden horticulture. Other colonists purchase staples trucked down from the sierra. If everyone plants cash crops, the comuneros mused, what will we eat? In semi-jest some of the men who had returned from oil exploration said that "maybe we will be like the gringos and have canned sardines, cheese [which they despise], plantains, and manioc flown in to us from the coast and highlands." But the comuneros knew there was no way to finance such endeavors given the available cash crops. To undertake the ecological destruction suggested by the president would plunge them into the poverty which results from loss of a subsistence base with no means of purchasing essentials. They approached a visiting Dominican bishop, a man who had spent most of his life in the Oriente and was now retiring to his highland province of Loja in southern Ecuador, and asked him to state their case when the time came for questions and answers.

Around noon the president asked for questions, and the bishop arose at about 1:00 P.M. to plead eloquently the case of the Oriente natives. He urged the president to remember that there were 50,000 or more native peoples in the areas designated for colonization. He said that they knew subsistence agriculture and they knew survival techniques that were crucial to national development. He went on to state exactly their problem. On the one hand, if they opt for comuna status they are shunted aside into a ministry with no knowledge of the area or its people and little if any interest in indigenous problems. Furthermore, they are prohibited from establishing a system of individual landholding and usufruct recognized by any governmental agency. On the other hand, "full participation" in development policies is equally destructive, for here one must ask for free land on which to colonize through the IERAC agency, or prove permanent residence on a particular site of land, over a specified period of time, and register this proof with the proper authorities in Quito.

In either case, documentation of the claimant's boundaries requires a surveyor, and ultimately involves the petitioner with IERAC personnel in the eastern frontier areas. If the site claimed is far from the roads and access trails, it is nearly impossible to get a surveyor to the site, but by the time access becomes readily available there are a host of independent IERAC-sponsored colonists, many with legal and financial backing, clamoring for the same parcels of land. Native peoples, the bishop argued, have little chance for survival without formal recognition from the central government in its new development policies.

The president responded to this appeal far differently than when asked other questions about the economy of the Oriente. He did not address himself to economic, political, or legal matters, but rather invoked his own legendary ancestry. He stated that he had always maintained that all Ecuadorians were part Indian, all of them contained some blood of the Inca Atahualpa; that although he did not know where he had acquired such blood, he insisted that he, too, was part Indian. "There is no more Indian problem," he insisted; "we all become white when we accept the goals of the national culture."

The proclamation of national ethnic homogeneity by President Ro-dríguez in response to the bishop's defense of native needs was soon to be codified by the military establishment. Within ten days a new "Law of National Culture" was established by executive decree (see *El Comercio*, September 17, 1972:1). From this point on the process of creating a "national culture" through military bureaucracies dominated much of the publicized national ideology during 1972 and 1973. The text of the "Law of National Culture," published in *El Comercio* on February 24, 1973, is illustrative of the force of this approach. A National Cultural Council was established and charged with "a) Planning the cultural politics of the country, and b) Coordinating the cultural action so as to incorporate distinct regions of the country into the national culture."[2] The idea of a "national culture," merging with that of "cultural politics," had by early 1973 resulted in an ideal national culture established by centralized administrative decree. This ideal became the formal, permissible cultural emphasis for those who would seek to participate in national development under the auspices of the National Revolutionary Government.

The day after the president's visit an asemblea general was held in a hamlet of the Comuna San Jacinto. It began at 10:00 A.M. and continued without a break until 4:00 P.M. The bishop's statement on behalf of native problems was repeatedly discussed, together with the president's answer. Recent events in Puyo and the ubiquitous problems over illegal colonist settlement on the Isla were brought into the discussion as the comuneros used their evolving juro-political system to cope with the nationalist position underlying observable events. Great attention was given to the fact that the east Ecuadorian rainforests and their inhabitants are part of the Ecuadorian republic, and that the human and environmental adaptation for the present and probable future were bound to the success of Ecuadorian nationalization and modernization processes. Equally stressed was the total lack of understanding by governmental officials of the enduring, creative capacity of the Jungle Quichua and other native peoples to adjust their lifeways to modernization processes while at the same time maintaining a viable subsistence base. A fundamental insight which had been mentioned repeatedly in day-to-day conversation was publicly articulated: "The nation once needed our knowledge, then we were wealthy; it now needs our land, and seeks to make us poor."

The president had spoken of the law, and he repeatedly noted that its application would flow through two independent channels: (1) through the agency of his representative in Puyo, the military colonel appointed as governor of both Pastaza and Napo; and (2) through civil agencies and subprovincial units which as yet have no military personnel. The comuneros attending the asemblea decided that they would press a legal case for a final solution to the colonist encroachment problem through both military-provincial and civil-subprovincial-national channels. The former involved them with the governor of the province and his representatives, the latter with two tenientes políticos (since the comuna abuts two parishes) and one jefe político (of Mera Canton), as well as with the Ministry of Social Security in Quito.

Shortly thereafter, some members of the cabildo journeyed by bus to Quito to meet with officials in the Ministry of Social Security; others visited the governor of the province. The governor said he wanted to hear no more comuna problems, and sent the cabildo to the jefe político in Mera, eighteen miles away. In Quito representatives of the Ministry of Social Security said they would send a delegate to Puyo to settle the problem. They did this; but the delegate spent all of his time with colonists whom he knew, and refused to look at a map of the legal boundaries of the comuna. Upon his return to Quito he wrote to the governor of the province and to the jefe político of Mera, stating that the comuneros had "given up" their land, not understanding its worth, to colonists who had now "developed" it. The ministry lawyers said that the comuna would have to buy back its land at an increased price, to which would be added the worth of all of the produce (sugar cane, cacao, bananas) growing on it. But the ministry added that it was illegal to sell comuna land. The comuneros were again placed in a typical bind. To regain usufructory rights they would have to buy land at prohibitive rates; but even if they could afford the rates they still could not buy back their own land, for comuna land cannot be sold. Colonists visited the government office to ask that comuna land on the Isla be opened for sale, and this possibility was rapidly communicated back to the comuneros.

The comuneros were willing to lose some ground, but their understanding of universal intent of juridical precedents was correct in that they justly feared that one legal sale would lead to others. It was quickly decided that any land sales, or transfers of rights of usufruct, on the Isla would have to carry guarantees that no precedent would be set which could be used in future sales of Tierra Negra land.

An additional social factor within the national system controlling their juridical fate became crystal clear: both the jefe político of Mera and the representative of the Ministry of Social Security responsible for comuna affairs enjoyed enduring compadrazgo ties with prominent renters of Isla land. The comuneros confronted, in effect, individuals unified through a network of personal relationships extending from their territory to the canton head to the Ministry of Social Security.

Under ordinary circumstances such a series of personal ties would have little effect on political economic process. But in this inter-ethnic context disputes over land combined with a challenge to blanco supremacy, and the symbolism behind compadrazgo between co-nationals was sufficient to weld the dispersed network built around a few colonists and two officials into a special set of people at least temporarily dedicated to blocking native maneuvers within some local and national offices. Colonists of the Isla (even many with close ties to some comuneros) rallied around the nodal men with the compadrazgo ties; the people responsible to the jefe político stood firmly behind him; and the Quito lawyer used his established official staff in Quito, none of whom had reason to question any move on behalf of a people and land so distant to them.

This set of interlocked personnel in strategic positions prevented comunero access to possible resources within the local political economy and within national bureaucratic structure. Without support from the governor's office in Puyo they would surely lose the entire Isla. But they had confronted many such blocs before, and they set about building temporary alliances beyond the personal network of their adversaries, while needling these adversaries to more open and provocative action which they could denounce before Puyo administrators.

The comuneros intensified their territoriality strategy. In late December a large ayllu ceremony was held on the Isla. No colonists were invited, and the jisteros verbally abused and threatened all colonists passing by. No Ecuadorian nationals were accepted, and curious onlookers were rapidly driven away. Many jokes were also made about invoking the power of Sungui to flood the Isla when land fell into the colonists' hands.

In the elections of January, 1973, four of the five directiva members were chosen from Spanish-Quichua bilingual Puyo Runa living on the Isla. Other Puyo Runa from all over the comuna began verbally threatening the colonists, mentioning in such threats the possibility of razing houses.

Comuneros continuously pointed to colonists' crops and piles of cut wood and carbon, loudly demanding to know who had authorized the work. Every newcomer was told stories of the fierce "Jívaros" living nearby, who the comuneros said (with some justification) still raided occasionally on the Isla. When colonists asked why the Isla was chosen for raids the comuneros replied, "Because there are too many colonists here, and the Jívaros know that you people are weaker than the rest of us in Tierra Negra."

This mixed strategy of territoriality ranging from ritual enactment of ayllu power to skewed cabildo representation through outright harassment of colonists succeeded in again obtaining for the comuneros audiences with representatives of national bureaucracy and local political economy. When colonists continuously complain about uncertain or "unstable" native behavior in their immediate neighborhoods, the governor's staff listens. And the minute the governor acknowledged a "problem" on the comuna, the comuneros began to shout back, "Why are the colonists on our territory?"

The governor appointed his own military lawyer to the "comuna problem" with the charge to settle all issues pertaining to the comuna. His first act was characteristic. He called in prominent colonists and informed them of his decision, setting a time of adjudication of all cases within a couple of days. But word of the meeting quickly spread throughout the comuna.

On the designated day the governor was amazed to encounter not only the directiva but *every powerful shaman, including all llacta founders,* from the comuna. All had quickly set aside antagonisms and joined forces in the face of a clear external threat to the Sacha Runa domain. There ensued a fascinating meeting in the governor's chambers in which the shamans affirmed loyalty to one another's ayllus and to the territory of Tierra Negra, beyond the Isla, while some of their sons and sons-in-laws, many of them current or past members of the directiva, argued the case of usufructory transaction on the Isla. The former conversations were all in Quichua, the latter in Spanish.

Issue after issue, including alleged land transactions made by the Puyo Runa themselves, was presented to this group of powerful ones. In every instance unanimity of response was generated, in Quichua, and conveyed to the governor and his lawyer, in Spanish. In principle, all present agreed to concede rights of usufruct through legal land transfer to the most powerful, wealthy colonists, and to endeavor to regain usufructory rights from the less wealthy through the purchase of products assessed at a labor-market rate by an IERAC team. The governor then ordered his lawyer to proceed to the hearing of cases, for purposes of drawing up a list of specific agreements.

The hearings were held in several sessions in January, 1973, during which time engineers from IERAC began surveying land and assessing property values. Many of the issues of illegality revolved around the jefe político of Mera, and he sought to withdraw from all proceedings, delegating authority to the teniente político of Madre Tierra, himself the son of an old colonist family with a great many co-parent linkages with comuneros. An asemblea general was held in Madre Tierra to communicate the structure of military investigations to the comuneros and colonists. Two hundred comuneros and about three dozen colonists attended. At every turn the colonists' protests were answered point for point by comuneros, and in some cases comuneros either shouted down or verbally threatened the colonists. In the face of such overt and increasing public hostility, members of the governor's staff rapidly moved to effect a final solution. The last hearing was held on January 30, at which time it was agreed that about a dozen colonists would gain permanent rights to their land but that the rest of the colonists would have to leave. Some would sell their products, but others who had not worked the land would simply have to go without recompense.

With this ruling many colonists went to IERAC with new requests. Instead of requesting validation of their illegal property on the comuna, they sought new land in another area. The "winning" colonists, by contrast, went to the Ministry of Social Security in Quito to argue against the military ruling. They pleaded another case on behalf of the poorer colonists, and asked that the ministry reject the governmental ruling. The plight of the powerful colonists was simple, and all comuneros understood it. The strong blanco land controllers would lose their cheap labor supply if the poor colonists were forced to leave, for no native comunero would work for them under any circumstances.

For their part the comuneros saw victory. They had succeeded in isolating the powerful colonists on their own territory and could slowly work at making their lives as miserable as possible. No one was deluded into thinking that all grave problems would disappear, but this solution would allow for continuing adaptive strategies with some regenerated resources. The Ministry of Social Security would not support such a pro-native decision and rejected the military solution. The governor, in turn, told the ministry either to accept the offer or give up its control of the comuna. As supreme commander of the provinces of Napo and Pastaza he had this authority, so the ministry agreed to the solution in principle, again turning rights for actual settlement—surveying land, arranging payments, and securing land title—over to IERAC representatives in the Puyo area. Up to August, 1974, no land had been transferred and the powerful colonists were still in control of their holdings; but some of the poorer colonists had left.

This narration of national and local events presents adequate data to demonstrate the fundamental adaptability of Canelos Quichua culture, as members of the Puyo Runa applied their system of social analysis and juro-political adaptation to nearly overwhelming nationalist constraints in their endeavor to maintain a viable lifeway in a modernizing setting. It is also adequate to show that the modernization processes, as implemented by Ecuadorian officials, continuously excluded native peoples seeking their guaranteed juridical and political rights. Events within this moment of micro-evolutionary time signal the coalescence of interrelated processes which have profound effects on the Republic of Ecuador and upon the dynamic, adapting tropical forest people of its eastern region. We turn now to these processes, all of them well identified cross culturally, to consider their present and potential effects.

INTERNAL COLONIALISM

This concept varies considerably in the literature (cf. Frank 1967, 1969, Gonzáles Casanova 1965, van den Berghe 1967, Stavenhagen 1970, Hoetink 1973) in terms of levels of generality, but draws direct attention to situations "where an independent country has, within its own boundaries, given special legal status to groups that differ culturally from the dominant group, and created a distinct administrative machinery to handle such groups" (Colby and van den Berghe 1969:3).

Twentieth-century Ecuador has been characterized by gradual though stormy and bloody ideological and legal transformation from a system of rigid castes, with Catholic whites on top and pagan Indians on the bottom, to a reticulated class-caste system with pronounced regional differentiation of linked ethnic, linguistic, and cultural systems (see, e.g., Blanksten 1951:13–31, Linke 1960:22–38, 58–86). By the 1970s the ideology of mestizaje dominated the public ideology of Ecuadorian nationalism. We considered this concept in terms of Puyo's development in the previous chapter but must now consider it in a broader perspective, seeking contemporary national sources of pervasive cultural, social, and ideological pluralism.

One critical manifestation of continuing pluralism is the projection of the mestizaje nationalist charter onto Ecuador's culturally diverse peoples. Alfredo Pareja Diezcanseco (1970:89) sums up this prevalent intellectual and military view of his country: "Ecuador is not a country inhabited by white folk, for as an ethnic minority they only add up to scarcely one-tenth of the total population. Neither is it a country of Indians, for in that case its history would be one of regression, or else, of stratification. . . . the nation is *Mestizo*. . . . Once the Indians enter civilized life . . . the Mestizo part of the population will be more homogeneous." No person casually wandering

through any part of Ecuador, talking with its people, listening to their own
conversations, and watching their transactions could ever be so ideologically deluded as to imagine himself in anything resembling an ethnically
homogeneous setting. Joseph B. Casagrande offers a startlingly contrastive
view to that of Pareja. Significantly, his view reflects the results of intensive
participant field research by a number of anthropologists in six highland
Indian communities, "each representative of a distinct ecological type"
(Casagrande 1974:93).

> Like several of its neighbors [Colombia, Peru, Bolivia], Ecuador is
> characterized by a sharply stratified dual society in which there is a castelike
> division between the Indian and non-Indian sectors. Estimates of the Indian
> population of the sierra vary greatly depending upon the criteria of Indianness
> employed, but a figure of one million would probably not fall far off the
> mark. . . . the Indian's situation is aggravated by being relegated to the lowest
> stratum of Ecuadorian society.
> . . . Even the kindliest among the whites tend to look upon the Indian as a
> child perpetually held at a developmental stage lower than that of a full adult
> human being, or they regard him simply as a brute little better than any other
> animal capable of carrying a heavy load. . . . The fact that some Indian groups
> in Ecuador are singled out for special comment or praise—the Otavaleños, for
> example, are said to be proud, clean, industrious, intelligent, and so on—is in
> effect to commend them for having qualities that one is surprised to find
> among Indians and at the same time to damn other Indian groups with the
> implication that these are precisely the qualities they *don't* have. . . .
> In short, racism in Ecuador is institutionalized to a degree that would shock
> even black Americans [Casagrande 1974:94].

On first glance, Pareja's view would seem naive or alarmingly biased.
But his is a statement of Ecuadorianist, intellectual, political nationalism,
while Casagrande's is one of ethnographic description and social analysis.
Pareja's concern seems to be with those who might seek to escape the
racism attendant on being regarded as indio. The gap between indio and
blanco is structurally homologous to the black/white distinction made in
the United States, and which Ecuadorians make as well (Whitten
1974:174–201, Stutzman 1974). The mestizo concept is an ideational
resolution professed by intellectuals and political nationalists, but it is not
an ethnic category to which most Ecuadorians aspire. Those who would
shed Indianness and claim national identity seek to participate as blanco
within an ecological niche devoid of elite, non-mestizo, superordinate
blanco status. As intellectuals and political leaders in Ecuador manifest an
identity of mestizo they seem to clean away the racist mire within specific
sectors of the country, thereby admitting those aspiring to class-based
identity to less stigmatized participation in the "revolutionary" political
economy.

Although not documented by research in Ecuador as in Guatemala (van den Berghe 1974:316–327), I strongly suspect that shedding the stigmata of imputed Indianness by Ecuadorians seeking national acceptance as blanco is dependent upon *geographical mobility and the change of ecological niches*. There is an Ecuadorian concept reflecting such mobility which provides tenuous linkage between elite concepts of mestizaje, on the one hand, and the poor nationals' concepts of *blanqueamiento* (whitening), on the other. The concept often revolves around the term *cholo*.

Cholo is a polysemic construct which suggests Quichua-speaking "racial" heritage, slowness of thought, but clear assimilation into national culture. Ronald Stutzman (1974:46–47), in a recent study of highland ethnicity in northern Ecuador, states:

> The biological heritage of the *cholo* population is said to be predominantly indigenous and their cultural heritage predominantly Hispanic-Ecuadorian including the use of the Spanish language as the native tongue (Hurtado 1969:174, Peñaherrera de Costales and Costales Samaniego 1961, Rubio Orbe 1965). . . . The term cholo is sometimes used interchangeably with the term mestizo. Both connote a mixing or a blending of two biological and cultural streams—the indigenous and the Hispanic (Hurtado 1969:175–66, Terán 1966:25–26). There is an enormous range of diversity among the people categorized, often invidiously, as cholo, and their cultural or ethnic status is still an open question.

People within a highland town or village will employ the term cholo for poor locals whose parents or grandparents spoke Quichua and were thereby excluded from many civil and ecclesiastical practices and activities. But from the standpoint of many people from the capital city or other large towns, *all* people from that rural town may, in some contexts, be regarded as cholo. Even in the corridors of a foreign university I have known Ecuadorian students or other Ecuadorian residents to stigmatize colleagues with the cholo designation, drawing their criteria from known place of origin, body build, and other personal and physical characteristics suggesting stereotypic Indian ancestry.

Any "liberalizing" of Ecuadorian racial ideology includes all cholos in Pareja's "mestizo" part of the country. From the elite standpoint, such inclusion embraces many "Indians," but for those who are stigmatized by the cholo classification, Indianness is far behind them. The nationalist, intellectual, concept of mestizo *incorporates* the notion of Indian descent (remember President Rodríguez's response to the retiring bishop in Puyo) as part of *an ideology of prior mixture.* And the ideology of prior mixture asserts contemporary participation in national (blanco) culture. The conceptual framework, then, for those previously stigmatized to participate as ethnic blancos in a modernizing, military-controlled political economy is to be found in Pareja's representative statement.

The actual mechanism for such national incorporation seems to come primarily through geographic mobility. For highland Ecuadorians, movement down the slopes of the Andes, either toward the coast or Oriente, is the actual demographic mechanism triggering transformation from stigmatized bearers of an unwanted, localized Indian heritage to a nationally exalted, generalized, mixed heritage with a blanco future.

Such a movement into the Oriente pushes the nationalizing population smack into the face of its rainforest inhabitants. This, as we have seen in the preceding chapters, is a profoundly indigenous face, having nothing whatsoever in common with the ideal of blanqueamiento. If acknowledged in their richness and adaptable character, the native cultures of the Oriente would contradict the ideology behind the revolutionary force of nationalistic consolidation.

In the eighteenth and nineteenth centuries the United States of America undertook policies of genocide, and later internal colonialism, to deal with its native populations. In mid-twentieth-century Ecuador a somewhat more humanitarian government is now choosing only internal colonialism and ethnocide as its strategies of political nationalism. Agrarian reform in the Ecuadorian sierra was accompanied by colonization schemes of the Oriente, as we have seen. As colonization stepped up, the process of internal colonialism rapidly evolved and brought the sierran indio/blanco contrast to the eastern rainforest. Everything having to do with "development" and "progress" was equated with IERAC, a dynamic national bureaucracy aimed at opening new land claims for people self-identifying as non-Indian.

The only really viable alternative open to native peoples living within range of governmental control of the Oriente was found in the formation and maintenance of native communes.[3] These were relegated to another sort of national bureaucracy, the Ministry of Social Security, governed by another set of laws and decrees. In every conversation with Ministry of Social Security personnel by members of our research group, and in every meeting on the Comuna San Jacinto participated in by ministry officials, a concept of the indigenous comuna emerged as a reservation complex governed from a distance as a total institution. Local maintenance is supposed to be by a form of primitive democracy where, as one official stated in a formal lecture to the comuneros, "even the most ignorant and backward of you can assume the presidency."

Comuna members have done everything in their power to resist such encapsulation since the founding of the comuna. They have clearly evolved a system based upon the replication of feasible organizational aspects of the small towns bordering the comuna. Because they resist their designated stagnant role in developmental processes, ministry and governmental personnel deplore what they see as the natives' inability to live communally on a comuna. While colonists get technical assistance and a responsive ear to infrastructural development from such agencies as USAID, the Peace Corps, and IERAC, comuneros get courses (in Spanish) on how to better regulate their own lives.

The processes of internal colonialism affect both national developers and native peoples at various levels in the developing republic. The possibility of transformation from comuna system into one of parishes and cantons is extraordinarily difficult, particularly in zones where swidden horticulture is practiced. No provisions for formal land claims can be made prior to re-incorporation as another sort of regional unit, and incorporation as parish or canton opens all land claims to outsiders. Furthermore, appointments to office are made by a system of political favoritism (Blanksten 1951, Whitten 1965) effectively excluding native peoples.

Processes of internal colonialism have their genesis in formal recognition within national systems of cultural differentiation. But the elaboration and evolution of such systems, even under the most enlightened, liberal governments, provide differential and unequal technological and administrative advantage to the dominant cultural sector, to the escalating disadvantage of other sectors.

A step beyond the Ecuadorian case is that of relocation of native peoples and the development of reservations. Both of these processes of course restrict even further the adaptive advantage of peoples by destroying their economic and social capacity to maintain their system of rapid change on their own terms. Few contemporary Ecuadorians favor reservation systems, except for those seeking to control and preserve the most exotic, evangelical mission–dominated groups such as the Huarani Auca. Ecuadorian planners seek to assimilate those who speak Quichua into the cholo way and to extend the blanqueamiento franchise to the expanding mass of national poor. This process is ethnocidal.

ETHNOCIDE AND RACISM

According to Webster's *New World Dictionary,* "Genocide" is a concept "first applied to the attempted extermination of the Jews by Nazi Germany, the systematic killing or extermination of a whole people or nation." The concept of ethnocide is taken from genocide, and refers to the process of exterminating the total lifeway of a people or nation, but in the ethnocidal process many of the people themselves are allowed to continue living.

The current attempts at ethnocide of indigenous people in eastern Ecuador are systematic, large-scale, and planned, as well as random, local, and unintended. Illustrations of ethnocidal policies include monolingual

education in Spanish, proselytizing by Catholics and Protestants, courses
in social organization aimed at altering family, kinship, and other bases of
social cooperation and competition launched by government, church, and
Peace Corps Volunteers, and the steady encapsulation of natives on
eroding territories without infrastructural support. Even in the area of
medicine it is difficult for a native person to buy a physician's services
without being treated to a lecture about the evils of drinking chicha.

From the capital city to the Puyo hinterland a general agreement among
non-Indians exists that the process of ethnocide of Amazonian peoples,
including those residing in the Oriente, is nearly complete. Because the
Canelos Quichua near Puyo, for example, have shed overt signs of the
national stereotype of what Amazonian natives should look like—they wear
Western clothes, eschew face painting and feather wearing in the presence
of mestizos, and speak Quichua, a language which many poor Ecuadorians
understand—local non-Indians attribute differences to disorganization
resulting from rapid change. The double-edged assumption of the passing
of traditional ways, on the one hand, and of the remaining native peoples as
the disorganized residue of modernization, on the other, generates policies
that seek stepped-up destruction. By considering the Canelos Quichua to
be an inadequate variant of imposed Western standards, those who claim to
be "pro-Indian" engage in assimilation activities with the native peoples,
while those who dislike native peoples, or even the idea of their existence,
deplore the effort and make invidious comparisons between comuneros
and colonists, always pointing out the cash value of the latter's labor.

When the might of international petroleum consortiums descended on
eastern Ecuador in the late 1960s, many native peoples witnessed
catastrophic short-run change. Within a few years a subsistence economy
with wide-flung trade networks was saturated with a morass of technological imposition, and in some areas floods of highland colonists were flown
into forest areas where they were totally dependent for their survival on
either imported goods or take-overs of native chagras. Most of those who
witnessed parts of the process, Ecuadorian and foreign, cried "ethnocide!"
(Robinson 1971, Whitten 1975).

Perhaps the response of President Rodríguez, when he told the bishop
that he was descended from Indians rather than saying that Indians had no
place in the government's development plans, is now more understandable. Ethnocide occurred in the Oriente during the time of foreign
exploitation, so the current legend of the revolutionary government goes.
Today the republic should mourn the passing of a native heritage, but in so
doing learn to respect the mestizo all the more, for he is the last living
embodiment of nativeness. The native and his environment have become

nationalized, and in the new blanqueamiento ethnic charter lie both the future and the past of national consolidation.

For the present, natives such as the Canelos Quichua simply *do not exist*, on their own terms, vis-à-vis bearers of national culture and ideology, in any context stressing technological change or infrastructural expansion. The clearly dynamic and puzzlingly non-national cultural adaptation of the Canelos Quichua is viewed as the residue of deplorable ethnocide. Intellectuals point out that, because they speak Quichua, they were either conquered early by the Inca or "tamed" by the Catholic missions. They are sometimes portrayed, in the words of one "sympathetic" priest, as "slaves looking for a master." The ordinary colonist in the Oriente is more bluntly racist; he categorizes all Quichua speakers by the clearly pejorative term indio. His basic contrast is between indio and blanco. The former is categorized as *infrahumano* (subhuman), the latter as *gente* (person). It is common to hear "the Indian is more backward than the animals," "the Indian is lower than the animals," and "the Indian is not a person because he is lower than the animals."

When colonists relegate native peoples to "below animal" status, they refer to the *cultural* adaptation made to the jungle. Indeed, in all such discussions, the ability of native peoples to understand the dynamics of tropical forest ecology dominates. Animals live in the forest; they are conditioned by their natural environment to their present biological adaptation. Native peoples of Amazonia creatively transcend animal ways, not by denying the forest but by elaborating a symbolic, transformational structure of humanity out of its everlasting sound and motion. Moreover, native Quichua speakers of the eastern forests of Ecuador also participate in nationalization processes, seeking to expand their social system to incorporate the new technology and to adapt that technology to their known environment.

Such cultural adaptation is in a deep sense antithetical to the nationally espoused ideology of development and the emergence of national culture. For the mestizo caught up in the nationalistic process of blanqueamiento, the thought of living with the jungle is repugnant. It suggests living like an animal. Some colonists do regard themselves as living such an existence, but they invariably hope for eventual incorporation into national culture. They see Jungle Quichua elaborating another cultural adaptation within a rainforest biosphere, and here they relegate such native people to *alien*, non-human status, no matter how closely other aspects of their lifeways, or actual living conditions, approximate those of the colonists.

Conquest of Amazonia has long been an Ecuadorian dream, one in which frustration and continuous loss to other nations has been an overriding

feature. In a very real sense the Jungle Quichua, both as a people rising to
defend themselves and symbolically, stand in the way of realizing this
dream. And it is on this deeper ideological front that a fundamental
confrontation is now occurring. This is why, I think, no agency in contemporary Ecuador can bring itself to the final solution of a land problem involving native peoples unless that solution involves obliteration
of indigenous adaptability and creative environmental exploitation. Any
current ruling in favor of such peoples would demonstrate national or
agency weakness and open the door to new alliances and dynamics of local
politics and change in which the Canelos Quichua would play an increasingly active, pivotal role. The national bureaucratic apparatus and the agencies
furthering colonization are still too weak to overwhelm 1,600 or more native
peoples living within a refuge zone in one of the country's most rugged
rainforest territories. This combination of factors leads to increasing negotiation over usufructory rights in part of the Puyo hinterland—notably on the
Comuna San Jacinto but elsewhere as well—and creates a situation condu-
cive to the Canelos Quichua knowledge of governmental policy. In the face
of ethnocidal policies seeking to hem them in, deny their existence, and
denigrate their rationality and culture, the Puyo Runa have expanded and
diversified their population, and, as we have seen, effectively maintained
control of their dwindling zone.

Throughout the contemporary world peoples such as the Canelos
Quichua are increasingly placed in separate legal categories, with separate
governmental and international agencies developed to deal with them. In
short, national ideologies of ethnic homogenization spawn processes of
cultural pluralism (see Despres 1975). To advocate such homogenization is
necessarily at the same time to call attention to the cultural differences to
be eradicated, and this heightened attention triggers the elaboration of
ethnic boundaries. In turn, "the persistence of ethnic groups in contact
implies not only criteria and signals for identification, but also a structuring
of interaction which allows the persistence of cultural differences" (Barth
1969:16).

National policies aimed at incorporating "different" ethnic segments also
spawn programs which seek to "help" people assimilate more rapidly. In
countries such as Ecuador, where the political ideology of race mixture
predominates in the public set of nationalization symbols, peoples with
distinctive lifeways are ultimately regarded as engaging in, or disposed to
take, political action, and so they come to justify reprisal. In 1973 the
Canelos Quichua were alternatively regarded as invisible, non-national,
and sometimes politically anti-national by many Puyo administrators.
Whatever the policy of the day within the party of the revolutionary

government, a salient feature of bureaucratic life was that the Puyo Runa would neither disappear nor take the step necessary to justify annihilation.

ETHNOGENESIS

Peoples whose cultures are acknowledged by an application of ethnocidal policies often intensify and adapt ways of doing things which underscore their own implicit, transformable symbolic relationships. The symbolic template, so to speak, provides a manageable cosmogony (Fernandez 1974:126) linking the known and the unknown and provides a set of ethnic markers (Barth 1969:9–38) in the face of inevitable nation-state expansion (Fried 1967). Such adaptive processes, known as ethnogenesis, are taking place everywhere.

The Canelos Quichua have a clear-cut set of reference categories which they transform into an adaptable system of relationships through which they relate known history to mythology, immediate history to the present, and out of which they seek to transform their culture to a future lifeway which improves upon the present. Internal diversification is maintained through both ayllu and huasi systems, and transformable structures allowing for communication and alliance with various tropical forest and Andean peoples are furthered. In the face of the mestizaje ethnic descent rule invoked by political nationalists, the Puyo Runa have repeatedly asserted their own ethnic charter: "We are *people*," they say in Spanish, "natives of this area, descended from the intermarried ancestors in grandparental times." When speaking Spanish they refer to themselves as *gente*, explicitly contrasting their meaning of this word with the ethnic categories *blanco* and *mestizo*.

In addition to the Spanish language reversal in the native-colonist contrast, which the Puyo Runa employ, they have their own rendition of the mestizaje concept; they use the terms *mashca pupu*, barley gut, *saracancha*, corn gut, *guarapurisa*, sugar-beet gut. By developing a set of pejorative categories for the nationals which refer to imputed contents of their "stomachs," the Puyo Runa spread certain implications about these intruders to all Jungle Quichua speakers. The shungu, stomach-throat-heart area, of animals and fish is often examined for special stones. The stones are kept as gifts from Amasanga and Nunghuí, then the shungu is discarded so that its invisible spirit contents can return to the forest or river. The shungu in humans contains inherited and acquired spirit helpers. By typifying outsiders in terms of real or imputed stomachs full of swill—whether of barley powder, toasted corn, or sugar beer—the Puyo Runa make them of lesser status than both humans and animals, and regard

them as devoid of acquired competence. Furthermore, stomachs full of
swill are spiritually impotent, and when the Canelos Quichua make
alliances they invariably base the continuance of alliance on spirit and soul
acquisition. Denial of spirit substance of nationals removes them as a
category from the ethnic charter of the Canelos Quichua. They come to
embody the basic "evil" of life, the *manalli shungu*, bad stomach.

Stress on native intra-ethnic, indigenous intercultural (e.g. Jívaro–Canelos Quichua) intermarriage in Times of the Grandparents is reaffirmed in
periods of external crisis, as in the case of the land inquest discussed above.
When the shamans, each the possessor of an ancient and grandparental
shaman soul, symbolically link themselves together by unanimously
agreeing to courses of political action, many supports are invoked that
reinforce ethnogenesis. First, the llactas are symbolically united through
their founding ayllu nodes against the counterpressure of fission due to
caserío autonomy and individual linkage to the national system. Second,
ayllu fission due to shamanistic duels is glossed over in an intensification of
overlapping membership in discrete ayllus. Third, intensification of
shamanistic power to form a territorial pool is inevitably communicated to
Quichua speakers in other Runa territories, and to Jivaroans of various
zones. So long as the power of the Puyo Runa is massing against
non-natives, some Jivaroan support is usually given. During our field work
a number of entreaties to Jívaro proper and Achuara peoples were made by
the powerful shamans. Such extension of ethnic charter is made by
invoking lines of stipulated descent, and demonstrated intermarriages in
Times of the Grandparents provide the basis for such appeals for support.

In the face of heightened national ethnocide, Alli Runa–Sacha Runa
duality remains adaptable to the sphere of contrasts existing between
brokerage missions and the forest biosphere. The Alli Runa concept has
expanded, though, to incorporate the national distinction between Indian
and non-Indian. Alli Runa becomes a campesino, a rural person manifesting some markers of contemporary Ecuadorian culture (especially in
Spanish speech, Western dress, and some gestures and customs such as
shaking hands, sucking teeth, showing teeth when asking for a favor). For
those self-identifying as Canelos Quichua, the campesino concept embodies both the native notion of Runa, person, and the idea of bicultural,
Quichua-Spanish, adjustment. The Canelos Quichua people capable of
moving about in the rural world of bureaucratized Ecuadorian national
culture clearly self-identify as bicultural, able to compartmentalize the
signals of two cultures and reincorporate them on a deeper level in the
indigenous system described in Chapters 2–6. *Campesino del Oriente,*
then, becomes "rural person of the Oriente [wishing to participate in
nationalization processes]" for the Alli Runa, but also translates exactly as

Sacha Runa (*Runa = Campesino, Sacha = Oriente*), something that the Puyo Runa find hilariously significant.

The Jungle Quichua, as rural campesinos, seek alliances with other Quichua peoples of Andean Ecuador, and use the intermediaries of missionaries, Peace Corps Volunteers, and others seeking to help Indians adjust to nationalization. Opportunities for travel to churches, conferences, governmental and international agencies are sought, particularly with the aim of identifying and gaining an understanding of other indigenous peoples and other non-nationals. The Sacha Runa franchise extends to all native peoples of montaña and Amazonia, known and unknown, who would join with the Canelos Quichua in maintaining their refuge zone and in expanding the adaptive dimensions of tropical forest culture. Through the Alli Runa–Sacha Runa cognitive duality of ethnic patterning, and the strategies played out to maintain it, the Puyo Runa seek to span Andean-Amazonian ecologies, re-incorporating an ancient set of postulated alliances through recourse to modern technology.

The caseríos themselves embody the transformable concepts of Sacha Runa–Alli Runa in their multiple dimensions. Through this set of indigenous-national symbols the Puyo Runa cope with the representatives of the agencies of national and international sponsorship with a specific charge to "help Indians." These include Peace Corps Volunteers, Dominican missionaries, evangelical Protestant missionaries, and most recently Episcopal missionaries. Beginning with discussions of technical problems in either Quichua or Spanish (usually the latter), the Puyo Runa endeavor to lead the outsiders to an appreciation of contemporary Quichua-Spanish biculturalism. For those who will listen and learn, the duality is gradually resolved into a discussion of "Quichua" and "Jívaro" conflict and mixture. Eventually, the basic Sacha Runa system of relationships crucial to continuing adaptation is revealed. But few listen, for understanding of the dynamic symbolic and social foundation of Jungle Quichua culture usually negates the ultimate mission and charter of the "self-helpers." Such representatives seem to feel some compulsion to find floundering remnants of exotic peoples and to help them to live up to the charge given by the revolutionary government, namely, to assimilate to national norms of the "mixed" poor and then to the essential infrastructural support and technical aid so readily granted to colonists. These outsiders are received, fed, treated with courtesy, and asked about their "program." Their support is enlisted to maintain native territorial boundaries and to help with negotiations in Puyo and Quito.

The contemporary Puyo Runa have opted for expansion. There is clear, conscious concern of every adult Runa with increased female fecundity, male fertility, and the health of children and adults. Every conversation with the Puyo Runa over people and land results in the simple assertion that the Canelos Quichua population will again expand to its "ancient" maximum, whatever numbers that may involve. The Puyo Runa are totally aware that this expansion will leave them in a condition of poverty unless they too can participate more fully in the technological development of the Oriente. They make this point to everyone willing to listen. They also point out that the aspects of their existence most deplored by developers— swidden horticulture, extensive use of manioc, chicha as a staple of life, division of labor by sex, classification of the biosphere through metaphors of sentience reflecting rainforest dynamics, and the importance of an enduring forest, fertile soil, and clean water—provide the underlying bases for their adaptability within an environment as yet poorly understood by those who have not encountered Sacha Runa.

Many contemporary Canelos Quichua understandably predict an impending Time of Destruction which they seek to overcome by a judicious combination of ancient and new knowledge. They face the future bravely, with the vision of ultimate survival and cultural integrity. Knowledge of means by which to avoid physical destruction as occurred in their past Times of Destruction is sought. They know how to maintain and expand productivity, provided land is not wrenched away from them or destroyed through nationally or internationally introduced environmental degradation. They require modern medical services to complement their own system, and modern legal services through which to press their just claims. They seek proficiency in Spanish to add to their proficiency in other native languages and so welcome schools, together with programs of medical help and legal counsel.

The plight of the Canelos Quichua facing nationalistic ethnocide and racism is shared with Quichua and Jívaro speakers (among many other native peoples) in other parts of Ecuador, and in Colombia, Peru, and Bolivia. Although by themselves the Canelos Quichua make up a very small part of the Republic of Ecuador with its more than seven and a half million people, they share common experiences and a common language family with well over seven million other Andean and lowland peoples in these adjacent nations. The processes of ethnocide sponsored by new militaristic governments throughout the Andean zone and across Amazonia have set up the potential mechanisms for resuscitation of non-national forces of indigenous ethnogenesis.

But the reader should not leave this book with the hope of a brighter future for Andean and Amazonian natives. Genocide has already occurred repeatedly in the last few decades (see, e.g., World Council of Churches 1972, Indígena and American Friends of Brazil 1974), and many ethnocidal policies have succeeded in destroying native adaptation and adaptability, leaving bare remnants of earlier magnificence. The complementarity of ethnocide and ethnogenesis exists in the most tenuous balance. As contemporary nationalist governments together with international agencies and corporations strive to conquer Amazonia, this balance may once and for all tip in favor of final native obliteration.

NOTES

1. This party seized control of another military-controlled government in May, 1972. The previous government was under the control of President José María Velasco Ibarra, who brought the country under military rule in 1970, pulling a coup on his own elected regime.

2. See Chapter 1, note 2.

3. This analysis does not consider the development of *federaciones* (federations), which seek to integrate indigenous peoples on a pan-comuna, pan-settlement basis. Extant federations have a locus in Catholic missions; nonetheless, there is some possibility of the federation movements offering increased adaptive advantage, particularly when the organization comes to the attention of international agencies.

Appendix:
Project History, Field Situation,
and Rationale for the Book

Research with Ecuadorian Jungle Quichua was originally designed to apply strategy analysis to native ethnicity. Our intent was to examine carefully the parameters of the complex social environment of the native peoples living near the town of Puyo, and their individual group, and collective responses to nationalist expansion during an economic boom period stimulated by foreign-sponsored oil exploration. We were especially interested in the intranational regularities in adaptive response found among northwest Ecuadorian Afro-Americans and east Ecuadorian native groups experiencing similar changes in their comparable environments.

As the field work progressed we were studied with care by individuals and groups of Jungle Quichua, who questioned us a great deal about our findings, methods, and interests. As we explained our intent and plan to an expanding aggregate of native colleagues, friends, and companions, many of them began to provide detailed, accurate analyses of the outer environment and their own techniques of adjustment. Our aid was solicited to help solve some problems, and our effectiveness noted, communicated to others, and fed back to us. As we became collaborators in the process of native adaptation, the people with whom we were working began to let us know that, strategy and adaptation aside, there were aspects of their lifeways which were enduring, and that the adaptable organization inherent in this culture provided the basis for their expansion and change in the face of chaos.

As our knowledge of Jungle Quichua cultures grew, the framework of this book began to emerge. It became clear while we were still in the field in 1973 that publication of an ethnography on the Canelos Quichua, with stress on the system which they regard as enduring, should precede presentation of our complete analysis of strategy, ethnicity, and adaptation. This book is the first of two on the Canelos Quichua, both of which will be complemented by technical articles on the subjects of our original proposal, in addition to other material in such areas as health, nutrition, socialization, and symbolism.

287

Sibby (Dorothea S. Whitten) and I first met some of the Puyo
Runa—native Jungle Quichua–speaking people living near the town of
Puyo—in the summer of 1968. Our trip there was designed to rapidly
survey native peoples living near the sites of national infrastructural
expansion just as foreign-sponsored oil exploration was accelerating. In
addition to visiting three native hamlets several times over a two-week
period, we also familiarized ourselves with Puyo itself, drove on to Puerto
Napo, and took our rented Volkswagen across the Napo and on to Tena and
Archidona, each the site of large Quichua-speaking Indian populations. We
then went downriver by canoe to Ahuano, the largest native Quichua
settlement on the upper Napo. We followed this trip with a flight to the
Summer Institute of Linguistics base at Limoncocha, timing our stay to
coincide with the SIL summer workshop for bilingual teachers. Native
representatives of most east Ecuadorian language groups—Jívaro,
Quichua, Secoya, Siona—were there, together with the linguists working
with these and other (Huarani Auca, Záparo) languages. We flew out of
Limoncocha for a brief visit to a Cofán settlement on the Aguarico River, a
Secoya-Siona settlement on the Cuyabeno River, and also to spend some
time looking at the placement of Texaco-Gulf oil camps and their
penetration into the areas of these native Ecuadorians.

In 1969 Cynthia Gillette spent three months in Puyo as my assistant, and
subsequently wrote her M.A. thesis at Washington University, St. Louis,
on colonization and native adaptation near Puyo. I returned to Puyo in 1970
to begin the exploratory phase of the Jungle Quichua study. During this
first summer I visited most native hamlets in the Puyo area, undertook a
preliminary survey of riverine native hamlets in Quijos and Napo Quichua
territory along the Napo (east to Coca), Payamino, Suno, and Coca rivers in
the north, and flew twice to Montalvo and once to Curaray, spending a
week at each of these Canelos Quichua sites and traveling by canoe and foot
in the areas. I always collected some artifacts on these trips, and discussed
what I had collected and seen with interested members of the Puyo Runa in
many of the outlying hamlets and in Puyo itself. I lived in a cabin at the
Hosteria Turingia, in Puyo, and was so placed near the main road into town
that Puyo Runa could visit me without disturbing other guests, workers, or
management. During this first summer I worked out basic aspects of kin
terms and placed about 400 people on a chart of genealogical and affinal
ties. Michael Waag, a Peace Corps Volunteer working on the large
indigenous territorial comuna south of Puyo, extended aid and good will to
me in a number of ways. Toward the end of the 1970 summer I attended my
first all-comuna political meeting, and then with Mike went over the
problems confronting this formal political-administrative group from
around 1964 or 1965, when the first PCVs began their work.

During the fall and winter of 1970 Margarita Wurfl began working as my assistant at the University of Illinois, her principle task being to assemble the ethnohistorical material and bits and pieces of earlier ethnography on peoples inhabiting the regions which would have to be included in a comprehensive study of the Canelos Quichua. Mike Waag joined the Lowland Quichua Project for the spring, 1971, semester, and, as my assistant, worked on the analysis of materials pertaining to ecology, history, politics, culture, and adaptation of the comuneros and their immediate neighbors.

On the return visit, which both Sibby and I made for the summer in 1971, we concentrated on the political economy, ecology, and social system of the comuneros, and the politics, economics, and social contexts of Puyo within a framework of increasing nationalization, urbanization, and urbanism. We were able to plot the genealogical position of the 1,000 natives living in the Puyo area, plus about 400 others outside the area, together with the relevant information on household and hamlet composition, land-working areas, and fifty cases of recent movements and their effects on alliance systems. Although we continued to live in the same cabin at the Hosteria Turingia, much of our work toward the end of the summer took place with a subterritorial grouping, Puma Llacta, which is not discussed or located geographically in this book. The people of Puma Llacta invited us to return to their hamlet for a year's study. Such an invitation was not lightly given, for the comuna was beset by colonist encroachment. Members of Puma Llacta voiced their intention of having us live with them to other comuneros at open comuna meetings, and individually to all members of the governing cabildo of the comuna. Permission was given by all native officials for our return to Puma Llacta, but it was always stressed that any aid extended to comuna members would have to benefit all of the comuna.

During this summer of field research Margarita Wurfl joined us to gain preliminary field experience in Puyo and made some trips to several of the native hamlets. She also initiated field research in Tena. Marcelo Naranjo, an Ecuadorian law student, joined our research for July and August and began a study of the legal entanglements attendant on colonist encroachment, together with familiarizing himself with cultural and ecological aspects of the Puyo Runa lifeways. Nicanor Jácome, an Ecuadorian history student, also aided us in a reconnaissance of ethnohistorical sources in Quito archives.

Late in the summer I visited Villano and Taisha, and made a week's trip to a new oil camp at Ayuy, on the right bank of the Pastaza River; there I worked for the first time in a neighborhood of Jívaro proper (with those who were bilingual in Spanish) and visited a settlement of Achuara Jivaroans (intermarried with some Canelos Quichua women) on the Capahuari River. Returning to Puma Llacta with tapes and information on the Ayuy and Capahuari Jivaroans led us to a deeper understanding of the intricacies of alliance and conflict among and between Canelos Quichua and Jivaroan groupings, a subject which we were to pursue much more thoroughly in the coming year.

Two graduate students from the University of Illinois, Theodore and Regina Macdonald, the former as my assistant, undertook preliminary field study in Ecuador during the summer of 1972, Ted spending the entire time in research with Canelos and Quijos Quichua groups. In addition to visiting many hamlets south of Puyo and working on subjects pertaining to mythology and shamanism with many Puyo Runa there and in town, he also extended our knowledge of the Canelos Quichua area and Canelos Quichua–Quijos Quichua relationships by visits to Sara Yacu, Canelos, Villano, Chapana, and Arajuno. J. Peter Ekstrom began intensive library research that summer at the University of Illinois on ecology and colonization in eastern Ecuador, preparatory to doctoral research in Puyo and in areas south of Puyo during the 1972–73 year.

Sibby and I overlapped with the departure of the Macdonalds in August, 1973, in Quito, to share information and work out the details for a coördinated year of library and field research. Ted Macdonald was to begin in Urbana a complete reading of the 400 issues of the magazine *El Oriente Dominicano* as well as travelers' and mission accounts of Canelos Quichua territory, while Sibby and I, with the assistance of Marcelo Naranjo and Pete Ekstrom, undertook our field studies.

We drove to Puyo from Quito on September 6, and moved into a house in Puyo (which Joe Brenner, of the Turingia Tropical Gardens, Hosteria Turingia, had found for us) on September 8. On September 11 I went to Puma Llacta and found that Marcelo Santi Simbaña had completed all work on our small native huasi with palm-wood floor and palm-thatch roof. I worked with him and two of his sons for three days, cutting poles for walls, cutting and splitting the bamboo sides, and nailing and tying poles and sides into place. The president of the republic arrived in Puyo on September 15 to announce a whole series of new policies for the Oriente, and the next day there was a five-hour meeting of the comuna in another hamlet, which we attended. From the night of September 14 through September 18 most of the native peoples of the comuna were in Puyo, coming and going from our "town house." On September 19 we moved into the house at Puma Llacta to begin our Puma Llacta–Puyo alternating residence system, around which many of the other activities revolved until mid-August, 1973, when we departed.

The structure of our two-story house in Puyo was very important to our research. The downstairs included our bedroom, bath, living-dining room exiting to a front gate, and kitchen opening onto a stairway going to the second floor. The second floor contained two large rooms and two smaller ones, another bathroom, a hall, and a balcony overlooking the street. Behind the house was a large area completely planted with lowland flora, something unique in Puyo (except for the Turingia Tropical Gardens). The house, among the larger in Puyo, was owned by a woman who had sold native artifacts in her shop; the location was therefore known to many who had come to sell their crafts to her.

We lived downstairs and designated one of the large upstairs rooms which was nearest the bathroom, and very well ventilated by evening breezes, as native property. The second large room was my study-workroom, one smaller room was Marcelo Naranjo's bedroom and the other his study. All of our maps, notes, cassettes, typewriters, note paper, kin diagrams, and so forth were kept in the two offices, available at all times to all native peoples with whom we worked and who watched us work. From the beginning there were always people upstairs, and we spent most of our time there, too, when not cooking, sleeping, or undertaking some urgent written work. We made it clear to all that no native person would ever be denied shelter for the night or a place to rest in town during the day. Sometimes we had people who were enemies of one another staying in the house, and in such cases they simply used my study and Marcelo Naranjo's as extra rooms. Keys were occasionally requested by one or another family so they could lock themselves or their possessions in the rooms, and we always complied. During the Founding of Puyo Day celebration in May between fifty and sixty-five people slept there.

We put two long benches, a table, and a set of shelves in the room reserved for the people native to the area, and it became a site for visiting and a way station for travelers. Often, on Sunday, more than forty people from all over the comuna and down the Bobonaza River would come by to chat, look at pictures, and sometimes request favors. Since Puyo is the site of all national and provincial administration and businesses serving a large frontier hinterland, government offices and all shops are open on weekends. There is also a large outdoor market on Saturday and Sunday. Hundreds of native peoples are in Puyo on the weekends, undertaking a large variety of tasks ranging from intra-native meetings to negotiations between comuna officers and the governor. Until fairly late in our field work we spent most weekends in Puyo, and there gained a great deal of knowledge about the relationships between Puyo Runa and non-native townsmen and officials.

People came and went at all times of the night and morning, whether or not we were in the house, and primarily for this reason we reserved the upstairs as the sleeping-visiting area. The Canelos Quichua are accustomed to arising around 4:00 or 5:00 A.M., and on market days in Puyo many of them talked, or stayed up, until 3:00 A.M. During the week we maintained their schedule, but could not then turn around and have two days and nights of conversation on a weekend and expect to function again by 5:00 A.M. on Monday. We explained this to everyone, and they in turn explained to others, and before long there was a real effort to enter our upstairs and exit from it as quietly as possible. Elaboration of the system we used is revealing in terms of Canelos Quichua consideration and intelligent response to potentially irritating problems. We had an outer iron gate with a bolt latch that squeeked loudly when opened. We also had a cocker spaniel that barked when the latch squeeked. The native peoples rapidly learned to open the bolt without squeeking it (something none of us could ever do), and when the dog barked they spoke to him quietly in Quichua, using his name. By the quietness and the dog's behavior we always knew that native peoples were coming and going, so when he set up a loud barking we would know that a non-native was entering, or trying to, and could quickly get up to check on things. Because of this system, and the near-constant presence of Indians in the house, we had no problem with thieves, even during big annual celebrations when Puyo filled up with outsiders. The people also rapidly learned to use the upstairs bathroom, even though many had never heard of such a contraption, let alone used one.

I began to make a collection of material culture and stored most of the things upstairs, where people coming and going could comment on them. We also bought available magazines, which were serials for encyclopedias with many excellent pictures of flora and fauna of the world, and left them there for people to look through, often discussing animals and plants from other countries, as they told us more about their sources of knowledge. During their visits we brought out books such as the *Handbook of South American Indians*, Karsten's *Headhunters of Western Amazonas*, and Harner's *The Jívaro*. When requested we translated portions of them and discussed with the people similarities, differences, transformations of ideas, and so forth. In turn, they commented on all of the pictures and provided a great deal of interesting and valuable information through the medium of print. Very different people, from distant territories, also visited us there in different sorts of groupings, providing information from other perspectives. Discussions taking place in Puyo were carried back to the visitors' territories, and the subjects were raised again and again during my visits to those areas. We also hung contact prints of all black-and-white photographs upstairs, and gave a 3 x 4 print of each to interested people. Photos of ceremonies, political meetings, work situations, houses, pottery, etc. from the entire field area provided a catalyst for a great deal of conversation in Puyo, and were a very valuable source for checking materials and expanding the information gathered in the Canelos Quichua's own settings. We also played tapes back to anyone interested, and again frequently collected new songs, versions of myths, and the like after playing the original version.

Sibby fed most of the people coming to stay in the house. She would typically cook eight to ten meals in the evening and morning, and a few times she provided over twenty-five people with the simple evening fare of rice, fried eggs, sardines, or, when we had them, beans and a little meat. Breakfast consisted of coffee, boiled eggs, and bread. We were fortunate in that the oil boom had stimulated an overproduction of eggs in Puyo. Many townspeople invested in chickens hoping to get a contract for thousands of eggs per day with the food contractors, but the problem of transportation from Puyo to Shell (eight miles) without excessive breakage was never solved. We could buy eggs for about three U.S. cents each, and Sibby purchased as many as two dozen a day on a normal weekend, spacing her purchases out between various shops so Puyo townspeople wouldn't think she was an "egg freak."

Before explaining more of our in-town research setting, our life in Puma Llacta and beyond must also be considered. To get to Puma Llacta from Puyo we drove for half an hour to a colonist settlement and then walked through a cane field and on into the forest for about thirty to forty-five minutes. Our own house, at one edge of the hamlet, was the smallest native dwelling in the entire area, which befitted our neophyte status. We had a sleeping room enclosed with bamboo sides where we kept two canvas cots and sleeping bags on the split-palm floor, and we hung clothes and some tinned food from the rafters of the thatched roof. We also had a small platform area for visiting with people and another one acjacent to it where we washed, prepared food, and stored some pots, pans, and a single-burner gasoline camp stove. Candles provided our light at night.

Puma Llacta consisted of a dozen households, six of which were located around a cleared, clean quadrangle, and the rest scattered around the llacta neighborhood from ten to thirty minutes' walk away. It also had a small school (split-palm floor, bamboo sides, tin roof), which was without a teacher from about June until December, 1972. Four other hamlets with adjacent outlying houses were within a half-hour's to two hours' hard walk away, and four more were within about three to three and a half hours' walk or canoe trip away. From Puma Llacta, then, we could visit almost any other site and could cross the territory in various ways, connecting with one or another access road to adjacent, bordering plantations and non-native hamlets. In Puma Llacta itself we were in some contact with between 80

At home in Puma Llacta.

and 300 adults over the course of any week, for much walking to and from
other places brought many Puyo Runa through this hamlet.

The caserío was on a hill overlooking a small river and the surrounding
jungle. Water percolated through the base of the hill to provide fresh, cold
drinking water. One of the great joys in living there, beyond the company
of the people themselves, was the majestic view of clouds of mist rising
from the thick canopy of the forest, against the western backdrop of two
great snow-covered mountains, one of them an active volcano. Facing
eastward in the morning we would often feel enveloped in the vastness of
the Amazonian forests as the mists rose and swirled across the caserío.
Evening intensified the immensity of the Andes as a red sunset was
occasionally followed by a flow of red lava on the moonlit snow cone of
Mount Sangay.

Our life in Puma Llacta contrasted totally with that in Puyo. Although we
prepared our own breakfast, and, when possible, ate a brief lunch of bread
and cheese or tinned tuna or sardines carried from Puyo, we were
otherwise dependent upon the hospitality of the people. Faviola Vargas
Aranda de Santi, Marcelo Santi's wife, gave us a hearty dinner of manioc
every night, and we gave her, in turn, tinned sardines or tuna, which she
divided between us and her family. Other people, too, either fed us manioc
or brought us fresh fish and meat, which we sometimes prepared and
sometimes took to Marcelo Santi's huasi to share with his family.

Marcelo Santi worked as my assistant throughout the field research (I will say more about this role below). Other people in Puma Llacta and beyond participated in our work as they wished, and allowed us to work with them when they thought it important for us to do so, or generously allowed us access to their affairs when we thought it important. Everywhere we went we were fed, and when possible we reciprocated with food. Basically, though, our reciprocation of favors given to us in the native settlements was made by us in Puyo.

Within the first couple of days in Puma Llacta we established a kitchen garden around our house, planting all of the basic crops of the area and a few others which were of interest to us. Slowly but surely the variety in the garden grew as I brought plants from areas farther east and as various Puyo Runa peoples brought me special plants. We did not endeavor to establish a chagra, however, for this would have been a very serious encroachment onto the comuna swidden territory. Rather, I worked with Marcelo Santi and his sons in clearing his chagra, and visited other chagras from time to time, either at the invitation of the owners or occasionally on my own when I knew men were working there. Sibby was too occupied with caserío life, as well as with aspects of life in Puyo and Shell, to engage in the dawn-to-near-dusk horticultural tasks of the women working the chagras.

I worked on the Friday minga of the caserío almost without failure, and also participated in huasi mingas to clear new fields for nearly every individual in Puma Llacta and in some other areas as well. Most of my days in Puma Llacta were spent either working or walking to a work or visiting site. Much of the information directly given to me was volunteered while my companions and I were engaged in actual activities; these included hunting, fishing, canoe making, house construction, chagra clearing, repairing trails, gathering and preparing plants for curing or psychedelic healing, ceremonial preparation and enactment, shamanistic healing, shamanistic feuding, marriage negotiation, and the ubiquitous maneuvering vis-à-vis attempts on the part of non-natives to disfranchise the Puyo Runa.

The Canelos Quichua sustain themselves between 7:00 A.M. and late afternoon on chicha mixed with water. I could not always drink the two to three gallons a day necessary for continuous exertion in this rainforest setting, and so carried a few Pillsbury food sticks with me for occasional additional sustenance.

Sibby and I maintained the native division of labor by sex in Puma Llacta. But instead of chagra work Sibby devoted more time to helping people in town, and I carried water from underground streams up the steep hillside to our huasi, though this is normally a woman's task. During all ceremonies and festive occasions in Puma Llacta we participated as separate male and female should. For example, she sat with the women, or helped them

serve, while I sat with the men, served when they did, and participated as
drummer when invited to do so. By learning sex-specific roles for native
dances and ritual styles for self-presentation, we gained very important
data on symbolism behind stylized action and ritual structure. Life in Puma
Llacta was physically exhausting, but the most personally satisfying and
psychically rewarding that either of us has ever experienced.

The Canelos Quichua way stresses the integration of two concepts,
generally expressed by the root verbs *muscuna,* to dream, and *ricsina,* to
know. An individual must learn, *yacha,* to integrate the concepts at various
levels if he is to have proper intracultural perception. People soon realized
that we were randomly mixing the concepts and therefore prone to build a
distortion of the very lifeways we were trying to understand and they were
trying to teach us. For example, we frequently asked what the designs
painted on pottery serving bowls and storage jars represented. For the
Canelos Quichua, this holistic end product is perceived as iconographic
portrayal of visionary experience, understandable only when one's knowledge of its creation is thorough and accurate. In their eyes we were sometimes inattentive to all of the knowledge necessary to understand the design. Such knowledge includes not only temperature for firing to make
the colors come out, slips and clays which also vary according to origin,
treatment by water, heat, and rock paints, but also those people in specific
kin and territorial groupings who can impart such knowledge under
specifiable circumstances. As we gained information and knowledge of the
wide-flung social system of the Canelos Quichua, together with detailed
information on individuals' life histories and personal life situations, much
of the iconographic symbolism was relayed to us, not for its own sake but to
bring us closer to the contemporary and legendary reality which inter-
penetrate in Canelos Quichua daily life.

We were also taught about visionary reality as a complement to our
increasing supply of "knowledge." We initially concerned ourselves with
"knowledge" about the Canelos Quichua world view, improperly trying to
understand their concepts of soul, spirit, and unseen substances. The
people of Puma Llacta let us know that in this realm individual structuring
of vision and self-experience precedes canalized cultural knowledge, and
led us to our own dreams as an important, personal step toward
understanding their complex visionary reality. Slowly but surely the
people educated us, asking about dreams and then interpreting, probing,
finding out more about our personalities, and insistently, insidiously,
giving us relevant segments of myth and relating such segments to daily
events until we finally began to "perceive" the integration possible from
individual personality to culture, and the relationship between the two to
ongoing activities in a flow of human interaction.

Our learning process is far from complete. The people of Puma Llacta undoubtedly know as much about us as we do about them, and they know exactly, we think, the extent of our knowledge and understanding of Canelos Quichua culture. Over 10,000 people know more; but none of them has the requisite skill to write this material down in such a manner as to communicate it to an international audience of Western readers. This information on our involvement is crucial to an understanding of the material in this book. As we learned, our teachers communicated our progress to other people, and they too treated us as maturing natives as we attained various levels of understanding. Quite a while prior to our departure it was widely understood that the book entitled *Sacha Runa* would be written.

Sometimes, when I was typing field notes in Puyo, people would ask me exactly what I had put on paper, and I would translate into Spanish, using Quichua wherever possible. People who had learned to read some Spanish sounded out the Quichua phrases in my notes, for I used a modified Spanish orthography. Corrections or ranges of interpretation would sometimes be offered, but more important, the power of writing was realized and many people mentioned how easy it would be to distort their lifeways if the writer simply made things up. Dozens of native people from the Puyo area and also some from other territories to the east decided to be sure that such distortion did not occur and so helped to clarify everything possible. The resulting intensive informant work was done in Puyo.

In Puma Llacta, and later in other llactas as well, our close friends employed subtle techniques attendant on the complementarity of knowledge and vision, using the personality and psychic makeup of the field workers as their medium for understanding the nature of cross-cultural transmissions of perception.

I return now to the role of Marcelo Santi as field assistant, because without him this book might never have been completed. Marcelo is not fully bilingual in national Spanish and Quichua, but he has several brothers who are, and his father is trilingual in Quichua–Achuara Jivaroan–Spanish and knows the culture of the Jívaro proper. His son-in-law is also trilingual in the same languages, literate in Spanish, and thoroughly knowledgeable about his Achuara relatives. I met Marcelo in 1971 on my second day in the Puyo area. I had begun a walk through the comuna during which I intended to visit every hamlet and, if possible, every single house in the 17,000-hectare area during the first month. I began on a route to take me through Puma Llacta, since the area was the least familiar to me and I wanted to meet as many people as possible on their own territory before renewing associations in Puyo itself. I told Marcelo what I was about when I came upon him, and spent most of a day talking and working with him on a new house he was constructing. He showed me some trails and for several days accompanied me, always taking care to explain things to me in his own perfectly adequate east Ecuadorian trade Spanish.

Unlike many of the Puyo Runa far more fluent in national Spanish, Marcelo always tried to use his Spanish to get across Quichua concepts. When he thought I finally understood something, because I could explain it back to him in Spanish in several different ways, he would always then quickly repeat the explanation in Quichua. I began to write down this Quichua explanation and repeat it back to him, and he would then correct, elaborate, and sometimes give me more information by telling me a myth, giving me genealogical material, or suggesting that we go and talk to someone else or see something else.

As this process went on Marcelo became increasingly reluctant to give me information but more and more interested in helping me understand, in his language and through native concepts, information which I gleaned from other people. I made him my assistant and we worked out a satisfactory means of remuneration which combined several different forms of payment and mutual aid. He accompanied me on many sojourns around the Puyo area, and eastward to Canelos and Sara Yacu on the Bobonaza River. I also worked intensively with a number of other people, and often explained my observations and experiences to Marcelo. These ranged from telling him that X addressed Y as masha but Y responded to X by using his proper name or a nickname, to trying to find out how to keep people from pouring manioc beer on my head and tape recorder during special kinds of ceremonies. No answer was ever simple, for Marcelo always tried to implant in me the various contexts of life through which culture was maintained and transmitted as well as impart to me the sense of interaction in a particular context. We would converse in the common trade Spanish of east Ecuador and then move into Quichua, until I could not only repeat back in Quichua what he was telling me but also find some other applications for the same Quichua phrases and expressions. We would then move to verb tenses, multiple meanings of nouns, and aspects of grammatical structure. Marcelo did his best to give me a generative approach to Canelos Quichua culture, because he was convinced, I now know, that I would be able to use this cultural system in my own life if I could grasp the underlying structure of transformable symbolic relationships. Although I did not learn to speak Quichua well, I was able to elicit the data presented in this book in Quichua, and to analyze texts and follow conversations without recourse to Spanish.

Sometimes in Puma Llacta, and always in our travel (where we slept in the same room or on an open platform), dream analysis was invoked to check my growing awareness of relationships which were emerging in the process of field work. For example, at 4:00 A.M. one morning in Sara Yacu Marcelo softly asked me if I were dreaming. Waking, I said yes; he asked what I dreamed. I told him, he thought about it, discussed its meaning with other companions, and for several days they tried to decide what in my dreams might be an analog to their symbolism. To help me along they gave me more of their common symbols and interpretations and asked me to note what correspondences might exist.

Other people too, especially in Puma Llacta but elsewhere as well, engaged in this same process, not only with me but with other members of our research group. I frequently re-lived these experiences with Marcelo, and he began to re-live many of his experiences with me.

Such introspective, intensive, often intersubjective work with Marcelo Santi took place within a setting of continuous activity. We came and went between Puma Llacta and Puyo accompanied almost constantly by various individuals and groups of native peoples. At the same time our crops planted in Puma Llacta and other jungle plants behind the house in Puyo grew, providing a source for continuous commentary. Children were born, people fell in love and married, some people separated, there were some ceremonies and some fights, a few deaths occurred, and many people fell ill. The ubiquitous specter of complete ethnic disfranchisement hung over the Puyo Runa and involved virtually everyone in political meetings vis-à-vis national, regional, and local officials. We endeavored, with the help of the Puyo Runa, to participate efficiently and effectively in selective aspects of the totality of their existence while trying to immerse ourselves in the microcosm of Puma Llacta life.

Two main kinds of applied anthropological work were carried out in the extension of free legal service to all native peoples and in providing medical services for as low a cost as possible. The first was the primary responsibility of Marcelo Naranjo; the second, that of Sibby Whitten.

The comuna is beset by illegal land-renting schemes which began soon after the founding and are sketched out in Chapter 8 above. At the time of our study the comuneros had no legal counsel in Puyo, although all colonists had a great deal of such support. Marcelo Naranjo examined every contract and quasi-contract (slips of paper with the signatures of people who had no legal rights to transfer land) and advised native peoples of their probable rights. He also worked closely, for a time, with the military governor of Pastaza Province to explain the legal-political actualities of the comuna situation. At one point he was designated as governor's lawyer for the comuna, and he did manage to clarify many legal points and secure a working solution of usufruct transfer acceptable to the military government, to the agency of colonization, and to the native people. But another government bureau, the Ministry of Social Security, is formally responsible for the governing of all comunas; unfortunately, in this case, important members of the ministry were closely tied by friendship and ritual co-parent bonds to the most powerful illegal settlers on native territory. A formal protest against our work was made in Quito, and although we were exonerated of all charges in short order, the governor decided that it was best to order us to stop giving legal assistance, advice, or counsel to native peoples. The comuneros understood that we could no longer extend this needed aid, and the officers of the comuna moved quickly to extend even more formalized permission to work in the area, anticipating (accurately) an attempt on the part of the Ministry of Social Security to bar us from entry into native territory. The comuna officers wrote a letter to the ministry and delivered a copy, in person, to the provincial governor, giving us public, written permission to continue other work on the comuna itself.

The medical program fared somewhat better. The National Science Foundation provided $960 to cover medical expenses for the people of our study. We explained what we had to work with to all the native peoples, individually and in public meetings, for there had been a great deal of interest during the preceding two summers in the possibility of an applied program of medical care. It was essential to find the cheapest and most effective sources for referral, diagnosis, treatment, and follow-up attention. Possibilities included a Protestant evangelical mission hospital in Shell, eight miles from Puyo; among its resources were one or two physicians, a staff of nurses, lab technician, X-ray technician, and pharmacy. There was also a military hospital in Shell with similar facilities. In Puyo there was a Red Cross drugstore, a public health office, malarial station, social security hospital, two independent drugstores, and a Dominican mission with free or inexpensive medicine and services; until spring, 1973, a nurse who was a specialist in obstetrics also worked there. Later, near the time of our departure, this mission acquired a resident lab technician.

It was clear that the funds provided for this program could be expended almost at once with little benefit to anyone. For example, sending a few people to Quito for stomach X-rays or providing a year's treatment for tuberculosis for a half-dozen people could exhaust a good part of them. The entire program cannot possibly be discussed here—an article will be prepared on the project. In brief, however, we worked with medical problems of people ranging from powerful shamans to babes-in-arms. We also came to work closely with the Protestant and Dominican missions, to establish a delivery care system in the native domain wherever possible, and to make rapid, effective use of the hospital and laboratory facilities when necessary. We discussed in detail the economics of this endeavor with the people, and spent considerable time explaining their real needs to the physicians and nurses at the missions. We almost always had people from the comuna, or farther east, with us during our discussions; Marcelo Santi frequently served as go-between, interpreting, explaining, and building on previous observations with us at the missions to present a comprehensive picture of facilities and costs to many people.

During the year we accompanied about 600 people through various diagnoses and treatments in the Protestant and Dominican missions, and followed these up with return visits in their own settings. Equally important were the several hundred people who replicated the aid extended by us, visited the appropriate agency, and followed up this visit with some sort of re-checking with us or native colleagues.

As the medical program grew under Sibby's direction, my own collection of material culture also grew. By November, 1972, the Museum of the Central Bank of Ecuador asked me to deposit there, on my departure, artifacts not needed in my research. I countered with the proposal that I would make them a comprehensive collection of material culture, if they would see to the eventual packing in Puyo and shipping to Quito. In addition to this I decided to make a collection to bring back with me to Urbana.

Not only did we think that Ecuador should have such a collection, but it was becoming apparent that national planners were beginning to regard the whole territory of the Canelos Quichua as devoid of "true" native culture and hence ripe for colonization. We hoped to demonstrate the opposite by donating the colleciton, and the Puyo Runa agreed that a demonstration of their virtuosity with, for example, pottery, had long been ignored by local, regional, and national officials. Furthermore, there was a tuberculosis program run by German volunteers (analogous to the U.S. Peace Corps) working in Jívaro territory, and we understood that the Puyo Runa could benefit from the program if their "nativeness" could be demonstrated. A museum collection seemed to be an appropriate demonstration.

I established a series of prices that I would pay for artifacts, and made it clear that multiple duplicates would be sold and the profits returned to the applied medical program. Over the year I collected about 500 pieces of pottery and around 200 other items of material culture. As the collection grew and we discussed the nature of symbolism to Canelos Quichua culture, on the one hand, and the economic worth of products under various conditions, on the other, the officers of the comuna, together with other interested individuals, asked why we couldn't establish a museum in Puyo or on the comuna. I agreed to help do this, provided a site could be found. My primary role would be to try to make my collection in triplicate instead of duplicate, and to secure the necessary papers in Quito so that the collection in the local museum would be part of the "National Heritage" and thereby not subject to confiscation. The idea was that other artifacts would be sold, but not those specifically collected for the museum.

It was impossible to establish the museum in Puyo—some local merchants dealing with native artifacts blocked all our attempts. But we did have an exhibition there, run by the native people with the aid of Joe Brenner and some other Puyo residents, during Founding Day. A small shop was loaned for the exhibition and Joe Brenner had the interior painted sunshine yellow. He also interspersed plants, a terrarium of reptiles, and a tropical fish aquarium among our exhibition of pottery and other household, chagra, hunting, and fishing paraphernalia. The overall effect pleased most comuna, Puyo, and outside visitors. Just before our departure a group of Puyo Runa established the Sacha Músiu in the hamlet of Río Chico, with all necessary papers and formalities from national, regional, and native governing bodies.

About 200 pieces with adequate documentary information were given to the National Museum in Quito, to be eventually transferred to a new ethnological museum in Guayaquil; 100 artifacts, but proportionately more pottery, went to the Sacha Músiu; and I returned to Urbana with 75 pieces. I gave a few things to people who helped the project; everything else was sold through the Turingia Tropical Gardens or directly by us in our Puyo house, the proceeds going to the Sacha Músiu treasury to serve as a continuing loan system for emergency medical care. Many of the people whom we helped with medical expenses repaid us, or the program, by donating pottery or other products of the highest quality. In fact, it was through the people's preference for this sort of payment that the idea of combining the medical program with the museum-collecting project came together.

Lest the reader at this point feel that we were depleting the material culture of this area let me hasten to add that the pottery forming the bulk of the collection is made to last only a short time, and women prefer to make ten to fifteen decorated serving bowls or figurines at one time. In fact, many of the older women told us that they had almost forgotten the skills involved in making some of the more difficult black serving ware, until it seemed appropriate to produce such works to round out the collection.

I used NSF finances and oil-exploration facilities to travel again by plane to Villano, and on by helicopter to Sara Yacu, Paca Yacu, Canelos, and Chapana on two occasions (three separate trips were made to Paca Yacu on one occasion). In each case I arrived at the site around 6:00 A.M. and departed about twenty minutes before dark. Fortunately I was able to revisit many of the same people and share information about mutual relatives and friends, as well as to collect a good deal of material in this short period. I was also able to visit about thirty-five separate purina chagras in some very remote areas, and in every one of them found people who were relatives of my friends from the Puyo area. This travel was of enormous aid in defining the culture area, in checking basic intra-household symbolism, crops, and gardening techniques, in gathering minimal genealogies, and in clarifying notions of territoriality (upriver, downriver, identification with a specific trade site, and so forth). In all cases a helicopter would simply drop me on a river bank and I would walk up to a strange house and initiate a conversation, usually in Quichua except when bilingual people were around.

On these trips I "filled orders" for many of the comuneros by looking for special products from the areas or making special requests of their relatives living in a distant zone. For example, I got a small tuber of a special shaman's plant for one person, another man's porpoise tooth from his brother, and a third person's chicken left behind six months earlier with his mother-in-law. I also brought back genipa for face painting, chambira for fishnets and net baskets, and other such products, which I gave to friends in the Puyo area. By dealing with such small, personal things over a great distance I was often received as ritual kinsman rather than outside intruder. I also collected material culture and, on my departure from a household, always gave a gift of salt, cigarettes, and sometimes canned sardines. On my third trip some people gave me special gifts with secret significance, which Puma Llacta colleagues helped interpret for me.

Late in the field study, after the departure of the oil-exploration companies, I flew to Sara Yacu for a few days with Marcelo Santi, his trilingual son-in-law, Luis Antonio Vargas Canelos, and Marcelo Naranjo. We stayed in Luis's brother's house and divided into two teams, working intensively from dawn until well into the evening double-checking and cross-checking genealogies, shamanism, pottery manufacture, and many other aspects of life that had been the subject of, by now, about fifteen months of ethnography. We visited most occupied houses within five hours' walk from the house in which we stayed. Returning to this area for the third time with two people well known to the residents contributed greatly to our rapport. Later many of these people visited us in Puyo. After Marcelo Naranjo left Puyo, Marcelo Santi, Luis Vargas, and I made a final trip to Canelos, spending a week in intensive research there, and revisiting Marcelo's wife's family. During this trip work also began before dawn, lasted long into the night, and took us for miles by foot and canoe in all directions. I did find some time on this last sojourn east to work through much of the legible material in the Canelos Dominican archive, copying some portions of documents that seemed particularly relevant to our research.

Sibby, Marcelo Naranjo, Marcelo Santi, and I also made several one- to two-day trips to Puerto Napo, Tena, Archidona, and Misahuallí, stopping here and there along the road to visit other native peoples not identified with Canelos Quichua culture, and visiting distant Quijos Quichua relatives of Marcelo Santi's deceased mother. One of these trips was for the express purpose of carrying out spouse negotiations for one of Marcelo Santi's sons, who had eloped with a girl from near Archidona. By leaving early in the morning in our Volkswagen and frequently stopping to visit, buy things, trade, and chat, we informally gathered a good deal of material on cultural contrasts and sentiments of ethnic differentiation between Canelos and Quijos Quichua cultures. Oral history was often presented during these trips. Marcelo Naranjo also took a longer, more extensive canoe trip up and down the Napo with one of his close companions from the Puyo area, and a second walking trip down the Pastaza with another companion from the same family.

On every trip we brought back plants, some artifacts, and lots of information to share with all of the people with whom we came into contact. In addition to the work mentioned above, Marcelo Naranjo worked closely with people from several other hamlets and became embedded in a distinct, though somewhat overlapping, set of peoples. Sibby, too, in spite of our common residence, developed her own independent network of friends and associates, and collected a great deal of material on life history, kinship, family, socialization, nutrition, and health in her constant work on the medical program.

Superficial though this brief sketch is, it should be adequate to give a general sense of the work which we carried on in a variety of contexts during our research with the Jungle Quichua. I wrote this book, but with constant consultation with Marcelo Naranjo and Sibby Whitten. In some cases I had to write to Marcelo Santi to clarify some issues, and he responded, in both trade Spanish and Quichua, his young sons spelling out the words for him in the modified Spanish orthography which I used in writing my field notes. The experiences from which the material in this book derive, then, represent our collective work; but I alone remain responsible for all errors and faults in presentation.

Ayahuasca mama. See *Ayahuasca.*

Aya rumi. Soul stone.

Aya tullu. Soul bone—right tibia.

Ayllu. Referential kinship system. Includes terminological system, clan, kindred.

Ayudante (Span.). A central ceremonial participant chosen by a prioste.

Bancu. Seat, stool; a powerful shaman who has become a vehicle for spirits.

Barbasco (Span.). Fish poison.

Batea (Span.). Wooden bowl.

Bátia. Wooden bowl.

Biruti. Dart. See also *Supai biruti.*

Blanco (Span.). White.

Blanqueamiento (Span.). "Whitening," assimilating to national culture.

Bunga. Bee, wasp, spirit helper.

Cabildo (Span.). Council.

Cachun. Daughter-in-law, sister-in-law.

Caitu. Bed, sleeping platform.

Caja. Double-skin drum with snare.

Cajonero uyariungui. Sound-making and dream-bringing drummer.

Callana. Pottery eating dish or bowl.

Callari. Ancient time.

Callarina. Beginning.

Camari. Feast.

Campesino (Span.). Rural person.

Candoshi (not Quichua). Language family of eastern Peru. See Murato and Shapra.

Cánua. Canoe.

Carbonero (Span.). Charcoal maker.

Cari. Man, husband.

Cariyuj. Possession of a man.

Caru. Distant.

Casa (Span.). House.

Caserío (Span.). Hamlet.

Cauchero (Span.). Rubber exploiter.

Causan. Lives.

Causana. To live.

Causanchi. We are living.

Causanguichi. You (pl.) live, you (pl.) are living, live on.

Chagra. Cleared field for swiden agriculture.

Chagra mama. Swidden-plot mother. See *Nunghui.*

Challua. Silver sucker-mouth fish.

Chambira. Palm-leaf fiber.

Chapaj. Mire.

Chaqui. Foot.

Charapa. Water turtle.

Chayuj manda. Ceremonial participant. See *Ayudante.*

Chicha (Ec. Span.). Fermented gruel.

Chimbajta. Either side; north, south.

Cholo (Ec. Span.). Polysemic construct suggesting various aspects of *mestizaje.*

Chonta, chontaduro (Span.). *Pejibaye* palm, hard palmwood.

Chuba. Spider monkey, Cebus monkey.

Chunda. Pejibaye palm.

Churana. Decorate, "dress," place pattern on.

Churi. Son.

Cocama (not Quichua). Tupian-speaking Indians of eastern Peru.

Comadre (Span.). Female ritual co-parent.

Compadrazgo (Span.). System of relationship between ritual co-parents.

Compadre (Span.). Male ritual co-parent.

Comuna. Commune, a territory set aside for peoples choosing to incorporate themselves within Ecuador in some manner other than the county-parish system.

Cucha. Lagoon.

Cuchapitiuri biruti. Lagoon toucan dart.

Cuchi. Pig.

Cuillur. Morning star (usually, though morning and evening star—*Cuillur* and *Docero*—can be reversed).

Cunalla. Present time, right now.

Cunan. Present time.

Cunan manda. From or of the present.

Cusca. Straight up.

Cusca yachaj. Shaman who controls his ability to harm others.

Cushma. Indian of northeast Ecuador wearing long robe—Cofán, Secoya, Siona.

Cutana. Whirlpool.

Cuyachina yuyu. See *Simayuca.*

Desarrollo (Span.). Development.

Directiva (Span.). Governing board.

Docero. Evening star (usually; see also *Cuillur*).

Familia (Span.). Family, household.

Gaye, Gae (not Quichua). East Ecuadorian Zaparoan speakers.

Gente (Span.). Person, people.

Guarapo (Span.). Sugar beer.

Guiringu. Gringo.

Gumba. Ritual or mystical co-parents.

Huaccha huahua. Orphan.

Huaccha mama. Widow.

Huaccha mani. I am orphan.

Huachi. Pinduj-cane lance.

Huagra. Cattle.

Huagra puma. Large black jaguar.

Huahua. Child.

Huaira. Wind.

Huairu. Game played at wake in Andes.

Huambishuara (*Huambisa Shuara*). Peruvian Jivaroans with culture and dialect much like that of Ecuadorian Jívaro proper.

Huambra. Youth.

Huanchij. Killer, assassin.

Huanduj. Datura, a hallucinotropic substance of the nightshade family.

Huanduj supai. Datura spirit: *Amasanga, Nunghuí, Juri Juri, Ayahuasca* spirits, *Yaji.*

Huandujta upisha muscuna. Datura-induced vision.

Huangana. White-lipped peccary.

Huangu. Bundle.

Huanushca. Dead body, dead person.

Huarani (not Quichua). East Ecuadorian Indians famous for their missionary spearing of some years ago. Language is not known to be related to other languages.

Huarmi. Wife, woman.

Huarmiyuj. Possession of a woman.

Huasca. Vine.

Huasi. House, household, household symbolism, household economy.

Huasipungu. Household garden.

Huatsalala. Enchanted lagoon.

Huauqui. Brother, male ego.

Huayusa. Ilex species; tea-like brew made from leaves.

Huiduj. Genipa.

Huihuishu pilchi. Calabash piece used to scrape inside of pottery bowls.

Huishina. Round dip net.

Ichilla. Small.

Ichilla huasi. Woman's side of house.

Ihua. Jicama.

Indi. Sun.

Indiaycushca. Sun's twilight domain over Andes.

Indígena (Span.). Indian.

Indio (Span.). Pejorative term for Indian.

Iquitos (not Quichua). Zaparoan language family.

Isha. Squash, cucurbit.

Iwanchi (Jiv.). Demon.

Jachi. Uncle.

Jacu. Let's go.

Jacu huanshigrishu. Assassination.

Jacu huañuna cushun. War.

Jacu macanacushu. Brawl.

Jahuama, jahua. Sky.

Jalinga. Shoulder sling of *chambira*, cotton, and decorations.
Jambi. Medicine, poison.
Janaj. Upriver, up.
Japa (Jiv.). Deer.
Jatun. Big, high.
Jatun huasi. Men's side of house.
Jatun yacu. High river, big river, sky river (certain clouds).
Jatun yana puma. See *Huagra puma.*
Jauya. Relationship established between parents of spouses, with extensions.
Jefe político (Span.). Political official, canton (county) level, over *teniente político,* under provincial governor.
Jilucu. Moon's sister-wife; common potoo bird.
Jista. Ceremony.
Jista huarmi. See *Asua mama.*
Jista puru. Pottery figurine.
Jívaro (Span.). Jivaroan language family including Jívaro proper, *Achuara, Aguaruna, Huambisa.* Pejorative term for east Ecuadorian natives.
Jucha. Blame, sin.
Juí. Greeting, or announcement call.
Juliahuatu. Three-hole transverse flute.
Juri juri. Foreign people's soul master spirit.

Kakaram (Jiv.). Powerful one, killer, assassin.

Lancero. Dancer in ceremony who carries wooden knife.
Lica. Large rectangular fishnet.
Lichi, lichihuái. Rubber sap.
Lumu. Manioc.
Lumucuchi. Collared peccary.
Lumu mama. Manioc mother; black "stone" from stomach of peccary.
Llacta. Intermarried grouping in defensible territory for swidden horticulture.

Llambu. Everyone.
Llautu. Headdress.
Llullucu, llullu. Green, unripe, young, inexperienced.
Llullucu marcashca. Godchild.
Llushti. naked.

Macana. Fighting stick made of hard wood, wooden ceremonial knife.
Máchica. See *Mashca.*
Machin. Monkey.
Mama. Mother, female continuity.
Manalli. Evil.
Manalli shungu. Bad stomach; evil, worthless person.
Manda. From, of.
Manduru. Achiote.
Manduru Chaqui Auca. See *Puca Chaqui Auca.*
Manga. Pot.
Manga allpa mama. Pottery-clay mother. See *Nunghuí.*
Mani. I am.
Marca mama. Godmother.
Marca yaya. Godfather.
Masha. Son-in-law, brother-in-law.
Mashca. From *máchica,* gray barley flour.
Mashca chapa. Police.
Mashca pupu. Barley gut; pejorative ethnic term for national nonindigenous Ecuadorians.
Matiri. Quiver for blowgun darts.
Mestizaje (Span.). Ideology of race mixture.
Mestizo (Span.). Person of stipulated Indian-European descent.
Mindal. Large tree with red wood.
Minga. Labor-exchange system.
Miquia. Aunt.
Misha puru. A pod in which spirit substances are kept.
Misha rumi. A hard ball of hair in the stomach of a tapir or peccary.
Miticushca. Hidden.
Mucahua. Decorated pottery bowl for drinking chicha.

Mucu huasca. See *Ayahuasca.*

Mucuna. To eat.

Mucushca. Masticated.

Muisak (Jiv.). Avenging soul.

Murato (not Quichua). Candoshi-speaking Indians of eastern Peru.

Muscuí. Soul dream, vision.

Muscuna. Dream, vision.

Muscuyu. Vision.

Mushuj. New.

Mutya. A small wild or semi-cultivated nightshade plant.

Naranjilla. A fruit of the nightshade family.

Nunghuí. Pottery-clay and garden-soil master spirit. Wife of *Amasanga.*

Nuspa. Crazy.

Ñaña. Sister, female ego.

Ñuca. My.

Ñucanchi. Our.

Paccha. Waterfall, sometimes cataract.

Paccha supai. Waterfall spirit; Amasanga fear manifestation.

Pacha. Earth (in Andean Quechua).

Pactashca. Pact with a spirit.

Paju. Illness not caused by spirit dart, generalized mystical danger.

Palanda. Plantain, banana.

Pani. Sister, male ego.

Panshi (pansi). Filter for making *vinillu.*

Parihú. Equality, togetherness.

Paspanchu. Small bird that sings just before a storm.

Pasuca. Shamanistic ritual to kill.

Paushi. Curassow.

Pilchi. Calabash.

Pinduj. Tall cane growing along river banks, *caña brava.*

Pingullu. Flute, tibia, soul bone.

Pintashca. Painted.

Piruru, piruruhuá. Stick for spinning *chambira* fiber.

Prioste (Span.). Current Spanish name for ceremonial leader.

Puca. Red.

Puca Chaqui Auca. Red-foot heathen. Unknown group of east Ecuadorian Indians reputedly in Tiputini River area.

Pucuna. Blowgun.

Pucushca. Ripe.

Pugllana. Play.

Puma. All jungle cats—jaguar, cougar, ocelot, etc.

Puma tucuna. Jaguar succession.

Puma yuyu. See *Puma tucuna.*

Puncha. Day.

Pungara. Chicle.

Puñuna. Sleep.

Puñuna huasi. Sleeping part of house (center).

Pupu. Umbilicus, belly button.

Pura llata. Fighting among ourselves.

Purina. To walk, trek.

Puru. Drinking vessel.

Putan. Bee, wasp, spirit helper.

Puyu. Fog.

Quijos, Quijos Quichua (not Quichua). Quichua dialect north of Canelos Quichua territory; probably heterogeneous, and still in need of clarification.

Quilla. Moon.

Quillu. Yellow.

Quipu. Younger.

Quiru. Beak, lower jaw.

Rayu. Thunder and lightning.

Ricsina. Knowledge.

Rima tullu. Talking bone. See also *Aya tullu, pingullu.*

Rucu. Old, older.

Rucu chitus. Permanently rooted tree, tree trunk, petrified wood.

Rucuguna. Old (pl.).

Rumi. Stone.

Runa. Person, indigenous person.

Runa shimi. Human speech.

Ruya. Tree.

Ruya largartu. Tree cayman.

Ruyaj. White.

Sacha. Jungle.

Sacha aicha. Animal meat.

Sami. Like, class of, similar to.

Sara. Maize.

Sarpa manga. Finger-print design on cooking pots.

Shapra (not Quichua). Candoshi-speaking Indians of eastern Peru.

Shigra. Net bag.

Shihuara. Quichua pronunciation of Shuara.

Shimigae. Zaparoan language family of eastern Ecuador and eastern Peru.

Shingui shingu panga. Bundle of curing leaves.

Shinquillu. Resin used in coating decorated pottery; copal, or similar to copal.

Shiquita. Spiny palm aerial root, or "buttress," used to scrape something.

Shitashca. Blown illness sent in the form of a spirit dart; spirit attack.

Shuara, Shuar (Jiv.). Person, indigenous person, in Jívaro proper and in other Jivaroan dialects. Comparable to Runa in Quichua.

Shungu. Stomach-heart-throat.

Shutushca yacu. See Vinillu.

Shuuj. Onomatopoeia for blowing dart.

Sicuanga. Toucan, lance, warrior.

Siluguna. Sky (pl.).

Siluí. Sky.

Simayuca. Mystical substance.

Sinchi. Powerful.

Síndico (Span.). Lawyer.

Sisa. Flower.

Sisa puruhuá. Flower vessel, same as jista puru; pottery figurine used for ceremonial purposes.

Sumi. The ability to change one's own body into that of an animal, usually that of a jaguar.

Sungui. Water spirit master. Corporeal representative is giant anaconda.

Supai. Spirit.

Supai allpa. Spirit earth; brown mold.

Supai biruti. Spirit dart.

Tahuacu. Tobacco.

Tahuashiri. Ridge people. Same as Huarani Auca.

Tambero (Span.). Ferryman.

Tamia. Rain.

Taquina. Shaman's song.

Taraputu. Tarapoto palm. Leaves used for ceremonial arches; heart used as food.

Taruga. Deer.

Taruga puma. Cougar.

Tatanga. Flat turtle-shaped plank used for rolling clay coils in making pottery.

Teniente político (Span.). Political official, parish level.

Tinaja (Span.). Large pottery jar.

Tsalamanga. Palid bowl; non–Canelos Quichua shaman.

Tsantsa (Jiv.). Shrunken head.

Tsentsak (Jiv.). See Tsintsaca.

Tsintsaca. Shaman's spirit dart.

Tslambu. Woven bag to carry hunting paraphernalia.

Tsumú (Jiv.). Downriver, strange.

Tula. Digging stick.

Tulumba, turumba. Large toad with poisonous spine.

Tulús-durúng. Onomatopoeia for walk of paccha supai.

Tundüí (Jiv.). See Tunduli.

Tunduli. Large gong made of hollow log.

Turi. Brother, female ego.

Turmindai. Suffer.

Turu. Mud.

Tuta. Night.

Tuta indi. Celestial body, star.

Tutu. Bud, stone with soul inside.

Uchu. Capsicum.

Ucumu. Straight down.

Ucupachama, ucupacha. Underearth, underworld.

Ucupachama manda huichu. Parakeet.

Ulas (Julas) huarmi. Female Amasanga manifestation existing in river rapids.

Uma. Head.

Unai. Before the beginning, a long time ago, mythic time, mythic structure.

Urai. Downriver, down.

Urcu. Hill.

Urcu supai. See *Juri juri*.

Ushi, ushushi. Daughter.

Vara (Span.). Staff.

Varayo (Ec. Span.). Indigenous staff holders appointed by church.

Varayuj. Staff holder in Catholic system of indigenous authority.

Vinillu. Drippings from fungus chicha served as especially strong drink.

Wakani (Jiv.). Soul.

Yacha. Learning process.

Yachaj. Shaman.

Yachaj rumi. Shaman's stone.

Yachajuí. Ritual circling of drummer.

Yacu. River.

Yacu aicha. Fish.

Yacu mama. Water spirit master in feminine form. See *Sungui*.

Yacu puma. Giant river otter.

Yacu Supai Runa. Water (river) spirit people.

Yacunda. *Huayusa* cooking pot.

Yaji. *Banisteriopsis* or *Psychotria* species; leaves are used in preparing hallucinogenic drink.

Yaji mama. See *Yaji*.

Yajocha (not Quichua). Cocama.

Yakíia (Jiv.). Upriver.

Yami. Trumpeter swan.

Yana. Black, including blue.

Yanga yachaj. Shaman who does not control his ability to harm others.

Yanuna manga. Cooking pot.

Yasa. Conical fish trap.

Yawáa (Jiv.). Jaguar, dog.

Yaya. Father.

Yuca (Span.). Manioc.

Zapára. Hexogonal basket with leaves inserted to make waterproof back pack.

Záparo (from *zapára*). One dialect of Zaparoan; person who speaks Zaparoan language. See also Zaparoan.

Zaparoan (not Quichua). East Ecuadorian and east Peruvian language family.

References Cited

Anderson, Lorrie, and Mary Ruth Wise
    1963 "Contrastive Features of Candoshi Clause Types." In Benjamin F. Elson, ed., *Studies in Peruvian Indian Syntax*. Norman, Okla.: Summer Institute of Linguistics Publication 4:67–102.

Anonymous
    1935 *El Oriente Dominicano* 8(38):99–102.

Anonymous ("Misionero Dominicano")
    1951 "Fundación de San Jacinto del Pindo." *El Oriente Dominicano* 111.

Barth, Fredrik, ed.
    1969 *Ethnic Groups and Boundaries: The Organization of Cultural Difference*. Boston: Little, Brown.

Beckford, George L.
    1972 *Persistent Poverty: Underdevelopment in Plantation Economies of the Third World*. New York: Oxford University Press.

Bemelmans, Ludwig
    1964 *The Donkey Inside*. New York: Dutton. (Reprint of 1937 Viking Press ed.)

Bills, Garland D., Bernardo Vallejo C., and Rudolph C. Troike
    1969 *An Introduction to Spoken Bolivian Quechua*. Austin: University of Texas Press.

Blankston, George I.
    1951 *Ecuador: Constitutions and Caudillos*. University of California Publications in Political Science. Berkeley: University of California Press.

Blomberg, Rolf
    1956 *The Naked Aucas: An Account of the Indians of Ecuador*. London: Allen & Unwin.

Campbell, F. A.
    1912 *Correspondence Reflecting the Treatment of the British Colonial Subjects and Native Indians Employed in the Collection of Rubber in the Putumayo District*. Miscellaneous Publication 8, published by His Majesty's Stationary House. London: Harrison & Sons.

Carneiro, Robert L.
    1970 "A Theory of the Origin of the State." *Science* 169:733–738.

Casagrande, Joseph B.
    1974 "Strategies for Survival: The Indians of Highland Ecuador." In Dwight

Heath, ed., *Contemporary Cultures and Societies of Latin America: A Reader in the Social Anthropology of Middle and South America.* 2nd ed. New York: Random House, 93–107.

Casagrande, Joseph B., Stephen I. Thompson, and Philip D. Young
1964   "Colonization as a Research Frontier: The Ecuadorian Case." In Robert A. Manners, ed., *Process and Pattern in Culture: Essays in Honor of Julian H. Steward.* Chicago: Aldine, 281–325.

Chantre y Herrera, P. José
1901   *Historia de las Misiones de la Compañia de Jesús en el Marañón Español, 1637–1767.* Madrid: Imprenta de A. Avrial.

Colby, Benjamin, and Pierre van den Berghe
1969   *Ixil Country.* Berkeley: University of California Press.

Collier, Richard
1968   *The River That God Forgot: The Story of the Amazon Rubber Boom.* New York: Dutton.

Cooper, John M.
1949   "Games and Gambling." In Julian H. Steward, ed., *Handbook of South American Indians,* vol. 5: *The Comparative Ethnology of South American Indians.* Washington, D.C., Smithsonian Institution: Bureau of American Ethnology Bulletin 143:503–524.

Davenport, William
1959   "Nonunilinear Descent and Descent Groups." *American Anthropologist* 61(4):557–572.

Despres, Leo, ed.
1975   *Ethnicity and Resource Competition in Plural Societies.* World Anthropology series. The Hague: Mouton.

Dobkin de Rios, Marlene
1972   *Visionary Vine: Psychedelic Healing in the Peruvian Amazon.* San Francisco: Chandler.

Eastman, Robert, and Elizabeth Eastman
1963   "Iquito Syntax." In Benjamin F. Elson, ed., *Studies in Peruvian Indian Syntax.* Norman, Okla: Summer Institute of Linguistics Publication 4:145–192.

Eigenmann, Carl H., and William Ray Allen
1942   *Fishes of Western South America.* Lexington: University of Kentucky Press.

Eliot, Elisabeth
1961   *The Savage My Kinsman.* New York: Harper.

Elson, Benjamin, ed.
1962   *Studies in Ecuadorian Indian Languages: I.* Mexico City: Summer Institute of Linguistics Publication 7.

Ferdon, Edwin N.
1950   *Studies in Ecuadorian Geography.* Santa Fe: School of American Research and Museum of New Mexico, Monographs of the School of American Research 15.

Fernandez, James W.

1969 *Microcosmogony and Modernization in African Religious Movements.* Montreal: McGill University Centre for Developing Area Studies, Occasional Paper 3.

1973 "Analysis of Ritual: Metaphoric Correspondences as the Elementary Forms." *Science* 182:1366–1367.

1974 "The Mission of Metaphor in Expressive Culture." *Current Anthropology* 15(2):119–145.

Figueroa, Francisco de

1904 *Relación de las Misiones de la Compañía de Jesús en el País de los Maynas.* Madrid: Librería General de Victoriano Suárez.

Flornoy, Bertrand

1953 *Jivaro: Among the Headshrinkers of the Amazon.* London: Elek.

Fortes, Meyer

1969 *Kinship and the Social Order.* Chicago: Aldine.

Frank, André Gunder

1967 *Capitalism and Underdevelopment in Latin America: Historical Studies of Chile and Brazil.* New York: Monthly Review Press.

1969 *Latin America: Underdevelopment or Revolution.* New York: Modern Reader.

Fried, Morton

1957 "The Classification of Corporate Unilineal Descent Groups." *Journal of the Royal Anthropological Institute* 87(1):1–29.

1967 *The Evolution of Political Society: An Essay in Political Anthropology.* New York: Random House.

Furst, Peter T., ed.

1972 *Flesh of the Gods: The Ritual Use of Hallucinogens.* New York: Praeger.

Galarza Zavala, Jaime

1972 *El Festín del Petróleo.* 2nd ed. Quito: "Cicetronic Cía. Ltda." de Papelería Moderna.

Garces G., Jorge A.

1942 *Plan del Camino de Quito al Río Esmeraldas.* Quito: Publicaciones del Archivo Municipal, vol. 19.

Gill, Richard G.

1940 *White Water and Black Magic.* New York: Holt.

Gillette, Cynthia

1970 "Problems of Colonization in the Ecuadorian Oriente." M.A. thesis, Washington University, St. Louis.

Girard, Rafael

1958 *Indios Selváticos de la Amazonia Peruana.* Mexico City: Libro Mex Editores.

Goldman, Irving

1963 *The Cubeo: Indians of the Northwest Amazon.* Illinois Studies in Anthropology 2. Urbana: University of Illinois Press.

Gonzáles Casanova, Pablo
    1965 "Internal Colonialism and National Development." *Studies in Comparative International Development* 1(4):27–37.
González Suárez, Federico
    1970 *Historia General de la República del Ecuador*, vol. III. Quito: Casa de la Cultura Ecuatoriana. (Reprint of 1901 ed.)
Goodenough, Ward H.
    1962 "Kindred and Hamlet in Lakalai." *Ethnology* 1(1):5–12.
    1970 *Description and Comparison in Cultural Anthropology*. Chicago: Aldine.
Greenberg, Joseph H.
    1960 "The General Classification of Central and South American Languages." In Anthony F. C. Wallace, ed., *Selected Papers of the Fifth International Congress of Anthropological and Ethnological Sciences*. Philadelphia: University of Pennsylvania Press, 791–794.
Grubb, P. J., J. R. Lloyd, and T. D. Pennington
    1963 "I. Comparison of Montane and Lowland Rain Forest in Ecuador." *Journal of Ecology* 51(3):567–601.
Grubb, P. J., and T. C. Whitmore
    1966 "II. The Climate and Its Effects on the Distribution and Physiognomy of the Forests." *Journal of Ecology* 54(2):303–333.
Guevara, Dario
    1972 *El Castellano y el Quichua en el Ecuador*. Quito: Casa de la Cultura Ecuatoriana.
Harner, Michael J.
    1962 "Jívaro Souls." *American Anthropologist* 64(2):258–272.
    1972 *The Jívaro: People of the Sacred Waterfalls*. Garden City, N.Y.: Natural History Press.
Harner, Michael J., ed.
    1973 *Hallucinogens and Shamanism*. New York: Oxford University Press.
Harris, David P.
    1972 "Swidden Systems and Settlement." In Peter J. Ecko, Ruth Tringham, and G. W. Dimbleby, eds., *Man, Settlement, and Urbanism*. Cambridge, Mass.: Schenkman, 245–262.
Hartmann, Roswith, and Udo Oberem
    1968 "Beiträge zum 'Huairu-Spiel.'" *Zeitschrift für Ethnologie* 93, 3(2): 240–259.
Heath, Dwight, ed.
    1974 *Contemporary Cultures and Societies of Latin America: A Reader in the Social Anthropology of Middle and South America*. New York: Random House.
Hegen, Edmund Eduard
    1966 *Highways into the Upper Amazon Basin: Pioneer Lands in Southern Colombia, Ecuador, and Northern Peru*. Gainesville: University of Florida Center for Latin American Studies, Latin American Monograph 2 (2nd ser.).

Helms, Mary J.
 1969 "The Purchase Society: Adaptation to Economic Frontiers." *Anthropological Quarterly* 42(4):325–342.
 1971 *Asang: Adaptations to Culture Contact in a Miskito Community.* Gainesville: University of Florida Press.
Hoetink, H.
 1973 *Slavery and Race Relations in the Americas: An Inquiry into Their Nature and Nexus.* New York: Harper & Row.
Hurtado, Oswaldo
 1973 *Dos Mundos Superpuestos: Ensayo de Diagnóstico de la Realidad Ecuatoriana.* Quito: Instituto Ecuatoriano de Planificación para el Desarrollo Social (INEDES).
Indígena and American Friends of Brazil
 1974 *Supysána, a Documentary Report on the Conditions of Indian Peoples in Brazil.* Berkeley: Indígena and American Friends of Brazil.
Javier Beghin, Francisco
 n.d. *Informe General del Resultado de las Investigaciones y Estudios Realizados sobre la Región Oriental. . . .* Quito: Departamento de Tierras Baldías y Colonización, Ministerio de Obras Públicas.
Jijón y Caamaño, Jacinto
 1951 *Antropología Prehispanica del Ecuador.* Quito: Prensa Católica. (1st ed. 1945.)
Jimenez de la Espada, Marcos
 1897 *Relaciones Geográficas de Indias.* Publicadas el Ministerio de Fomento I–XI. Madrid: Tipografía de los Hijos de M. G. Hernández.
Juanen, José
 1941–43 *Historia de la Compañia de Jesús en la Antigua Provincia de Quito, 1570–1774,* vols. I–II. Quito: Editorial Ecuatoriana.
Jurado R., Waldemar
 1970 *El Puyo: Ciudad Septuagenaria.* Ambato, Ecuador: Editorial "Primicias."
 1971 *Dominicos Involidables.* Ambato, Ecuador: Editorial "Primicias."
Karsten, Rafael
 1935 *The Head-Hunters of Western Amazonas: The Life and Culture of the Jibaro Indians of Eastern Ecuador and Peru.* Helsinki: Societas Scientiarum Fennica, Commentationes Humanarum Litterarum 2(1).
Kroeber, Alfred L.
 1909 "Classificatory Systems of Relationship." *Journal of the Royal Anthropological Institute* 39:77–84.
Kreig, Margaret B.
 1964 *Green Medicine.* New York: Bantam Books.
Kuper, Leo, and M. G. Smith, eds.
 1969 *Pluralism in Africa.* Berkeley: University of California Press.
Lathrap, Donald W.
 1970 *The Upper Amazon.* New York: Praeger.

Leach, Edmund R.

1954 *Political Systems of Highland Burma: A Study of Kachin Social Structure*. London: London School of Economics.

Lehman, F. K.

1963 *The Structure of Chin Society*. Illinois Studies in Anthropology 3. Urbana: University of Illinois Press.

1967 "Burma: Kayah Society." In Julian H. Steward, ed., *Contemporary Change in Traditional Societies*, vol. II: *Asian Rural Societies*. Urbana: University of Illinois Press, 7–104.

Lévi-Strauss, Claude

1963 *Structural Anthropology*. New York: Basic Books.

1969 *The Elementary Structures of Kinship*. Tr. James Harle Bell, John Richard von Sturmer, and Rodney Needham, ed. Boston: Beacon Press.

Linke, Lilo

1960 *Ecuador: Country of Contrasts*. 3rd ed. New York: Oxford University Press.

Loukotka, Čestmír

1968 *Classification of South American Indian Languages*. Los Angeles: Latin American Center of the University of California, Los Angeles.

Magalli de Pred, José María

1890 *Colección de Cartas sobre las Misiones Dominicanas del Oriente*. Segunda edición corregida y aumentada. Quito: Imprenta de Juan Pablo Sanz.

Marin, Fr. Ceslao de J.

1927 "Misión Dominicana." *El Oriente Dominicano* 1(1):4–5.

Matteson, Esther

1972 "Toward Proto Amerindian." In Matteson *et al.*, *Comparative Studies in Amerindian Languages*. The Hague: Mouton, 21–92.

Matteson, Esther, Alva Wheeler, Frances L. Jackson, Nathan E. Waltz, and Diana R. Christian

1972 *Comparative Studies in Amerindian Languages*. The Hague: Mouton.

Maybury-Lewis, David

1974 *Akwẽ-Shavante Society*. New York: Oxford University Press.

Meggers, Betty J.

1966 *Ecuador*. New York: Praeger.

Métraux, Alfred

1948 "Tribes of the Western Amazon Basin." In Julian H. Steward, ed., *Handbook of South American Indians*, vol. 3: *The Tropical Forest Tribes*. Washington: Smithsonian Institution, Bureau of American Ethnology Bulletin 143:657–712.

Meyer de Schauensee, R.

1964 *The Birds of Colombia and Adjacent Areas of South and Central America*. Narbeth, Pa.: Livingston Publishing Co.

Ministerio de Previsión Social

1967 Ley de Organización y Regimen de las Comunas, Estado Juridico de las Comunidades Campesinas. Quito: Misión Andino del Ecuador.

Monteros, Raimundo M.
  1937   *El Oriente Dominicano*. Sept.–Oct., 54–55:167–168.
Morales y Eloy, Juan
  1942   *Ecuador: Atlas Histórico-Geográfico*. Quito: Ministerio de Relaciones
         Exteriores.
Murdock, George P.
  1949   *Social Structure*. New York: Macmillan.
Murra, John
  1946   "The Historic Tribes of Ecuador." In Julian H. Steward, ed., *Handbook
         of South American Indians*, vol. 2: *The Andean Civilizations*.
         Washington, D.C., Bureau of American Ethnology Bulletin 143:785–
         822.
Naranjo, Marcelo F.
  1974   "Etnohistoria de la Zona Central del Alto Amazonas: Siglos 16–17–18."
         M.A. paper, University of Illinois, Urbana.
Nordenskiöld, Erland
  1930   "Huayru Game." *Journal de la Société des Américanistes* 22:211–213.
Oberem, Udo
  1966/67 "Handel und Handelsgüter in der Montaña Ecuadors." *Folk: Dansk
         Ethnografisk Tidsskrift* 8/9:243–258.
  1971   *Los Quijos: Historia de la Transculturación de un Grupo Indígena en el
         Oriente Ecuatoriano (1538–1956)*. 2 vols. Madrid: Facultad de Filosofía
         y Letras de la Universidad de Madrid, Memórias del Departamento de
         Antropología y Etnología de América.
  1974   "Trade and Trade Goods in the Ecuadorian Montaña." In Patricia J.
         Lyon, ed., *Native South Americans: Ethnology of the Least Known
         Continent*. Boston: Little, Brown, 347–357.
  n.d.   "Einige ethnographische Notizen über die Canelo ost-Ecuadors." MS.
Orr, Carolina, and Juan E. Hudleson
  1971   *Cuillurguna: Cuentos de los Quichuas del Oriente Ecuatoriano*. Quito:
         Houser.
Orr, Carolyn
  1962   "Ecuador Quichua Phonology." In Benjamin Elson, ed., *Studies in
         Ecuadorian Indian Languages: I*. Mexico City: Summer Institute of
         Linguistics Publication 7:60–77.
Orr, Carolyn, and Robert E. Longacre
  1968   "Proto-Quechumaran." *Language: Journal of the Linguistic Society of
         America* 44(1):528–555.
Orr, Carolyn, and Betsy Wrisley
  1965   *Vocabulario Quichua del Oriente del Ecuador*. Quito: Instituto
         Lingüístico de Verano, Série de Vocabularios Indígenas 11.
Pareja Diezcanseco, Alfredo
  1970   "Ecuador, from Past to Present." Introduction to Arturo Eichler,
         Ecuador: Nieve y Selva / Snow Peaks and Jungles. Quito: Edición del
         Autor, 7–15, 87–93.
Parker, Gary J.
  1963   "Clasificación Genética de los Dialectos Quechuas." *Revista del Museo
         Nacional* (Lima) 32:241–252.

1969 *Ayacucho Quechua Grammar and Dictionary*. The Hague: Mouton.
1972 "Falacias y Verdades Acerca del Quechua." In Alberto Escobar, ed., *El Reto del Multilingüísmo en el Peru*. Lima: Instituto de Estudios Peruanos 9:111–121.

Peñaherrera de Costales, Piedad, and Alfredo Costales Samaniego
1961 *Llacta Runa*. *Llacta* 12. Quito: Organo de Publicación Semestral del Instituto Ecuatoriano de Antropología y Geografía.

Phelan, John Leddy
1967 *The Kingdom of Quito in the Seventeenth Century: Bureaucratic Politics in the Spanish Empire*. Madison: University of Wisconsin Press.

Porras Garces, P. Pedro I.
1955 *Entre los Yumbos del Napo*. Quito: Editora Santo Domingo.
1961 *Contribución al Estudio de la Arqueología e Historia de los Valles Quijos y Misaguallí (Alto Napo) en la Región Oriental del Ecuador, S.A.* Quito: Editora Fenix.
1973 "Descubrese en Roma Documento Anónimo sobre los Indios Quijos del Alto Napo, al Oriente del Ecuador." Chicago: Ninth International Congress of Anthropological and Ethnological Sciences, Inc.
1974 *Estudios Científicos sobre el Oriente Ecuatoriano*, vol. I: *Historia y Arqueología de Ciudad España Baeza de los Quijos, Siglo XVI*. Quito: Centro de Publicaciones de la Pontificia Universidad Católica.

Reichel-Dolmatoff, Gerardo
1971 *Amazonian Cosmos: The Sexual and Religious Symbolism of the Tukano Indians*. Chicago: University of Chicago Press.
1972 "The Cultural Context of an Aboriginal Hallucinogen: *Banisteriopsis Caapi*." In Peter T. Furst, ed., *Flesh of the Gods: The Ritual Use of Hallucinogens*. New York: Praeger, 85–113.

Robinson, Scott S.
1971 "El Etnocidio Ecuatoriano." Reprint from *La Situación Actual de los Indígenas en America del Sur*. Montevideo: Editorial Tierra Nueva; Mexico City: Universidad Iberoamericana.

Rowe, John Howland
1946 "Inca Culture at the Time of the Spanish Conquest." In Julian H. Steward, ed., *Handbook of South American Indians*, vol. 2: *The Andean Civilizations*. Washington, D.C., Bureau of American Ethnology Bulletin 143:183–330.

Rubio Orbe, Gonzalo
1965 *Aspectos Indígenas*. Quito: Casa de la Cultura Ecuatoriana.

Rumazo González, José
1950 *Documentos para la Historia de la Audiencia de Quito*, vol. 8. Madrid: Afrodisio Aguado.

Savoy, Gene
1970 *Antisuyo: The Search for the Lost Cities of the Amazon*. New York: Simon & Schuster.

Scheffler, Harold W.
1972 "Kinship Semantics." *Annual Review of Anthropology* 1:309–328.
Scheffler, Harold W., and Floyd G. Lounsbury
1971 *A Study in Structural Semantics: The Siriono Kinship System.* Englewood Cliffs, N.J.: Prentice-Hall.
Schultes, Richard Evans
1972 "An Overview of Hallucinogens in the Western Hemisphere." In Peter T. Furst, ed., *Flesh of the Gods: The Ritual Use of Hallucinogens.* New York: Praeger, 3–54.
Simson, Alfred
1886 *Travels in the Wilds of Ecuador and the Exploration of the Putumayo River.* London: Sampson Low, Marston, Searle, and Rivington.
Sorensen, Arthur P., Jr.
1967 "Multilingualism in the Northwest Amazon." *American Anthropologist* 69(6):670–684.
1973 "South American Indian Linguistics at the Turn of the Seventies." In Daniel R. Gross, ed., *Peoples and Cultures of Native South America.* Garden City, N.Y.: Natural History Press, 312–341.
Spruce, Richard
1908 *Notes of a Botanist on the Amazon and Andes.* Ed. and condensed Alfred Russel Wallace. London: Macmillan.
Stark, Louisa A.
1973 "Historia y Distribución de los Dialectos Quichuas en la Sierra Ecuatoriana." Paper presented at the Primer Seminario de la Educación Bilingüe, Quito.
Stavenhagen, Rodolfo
1970 "Classes, Colonialism and Acculturation: A System of Inter-ethnic Relations in Mesoamerica." In Irving L. Horowitz, ed., *Masses in Latin America.* New York: Oxford University Press, 235–288.
Sterba, Günther
1966 *Freshwater Fishes of the World.* Rev. ed. Cooper Square, N.Y.: Pet Library.
Steward, Julian H.
1948 "Tribes of the Montaña and Bolivian East Andes." In Julian H. Steward, ed., *Handbook of South American Indians,* vol. 3: *The Tropical Forest Tribes.* Washington, D.C., Bureau of American Ethnology Bulletin 143:507–534.
Steward, Julian H., and Alfred Métraux
1948 "Tribes of the Ecuadorian and Peruvian Montaña." In Julian H. Steward, ed., *Handbook of South American Indians,* vol. 3: *The Tropical Forest Tribes.* Washington, D.C., Bureau of American Ethnology Bulletin 143:535–656.
Stirling, Matthew W.
1938 *Historical and Ethnographical Material on the Jivaro Indians.* Washington, D.C.: Smithsonian Institution, Bureau of American Ethnology Bulletin 117.

Stutzman, Ronald
  1974 *Black Highlanders: Racism and Ethnic Stratification in the Ecuadorian Sierra.* Ann Arbor, Mich.: University Microfilms. (Ph.D. thesis, Washington University, St. Louis.)
Sweet, David G.
  1969 "The Population of the Upper Amazon Valley, 17th and 18th Centuries." M.A. thesis, University of Wisconsin, Madison.
Tessman, Günter
  1930 *Die Indianer Nordost-Perus.* Hamburg: Cram, de Gruyter and Co.
Tobar Donoso, Julio
  1960 *Historiadores y Cronistas de las Misiones.* Biblioteca Mínima Ecuatoriana. Puebla, Mexico: Editorial J. M. Cajica, Jr.
Torero, Alfredo
  1965 "Los Dialectos Quechuas." *Anales Científicos de la Universidad Agraria* (Lima) 2:446–478.
  1972 "Lingüística e Historia de la Sociedad Andina." In Alberto Escobar, ed., *El Reto del Multilingüismo en el Peru.* Lima: Instituto de Estudios Peruanos 9:51–106.
Tropical Fish Hobbyist
  1971 Vol. 20, 188, no. 2:60.
Tuggy, Juan
  1966 *Vocabulario Candoshi de Loreto.* Peru: Instituto Lingüístico de Verano, Série Lingüística Peruana 2.
Uriarte, P. Manuel J., S.J.
  1952 *Diario de un Misionero de Mainas: Transcripción, Introducción y Notas del P. Constantino Bayle, S.J.* Madrid: Consejo Superior de Investigaciones Científicas, Instituto Santo Toribio de Mongrovejo.
Vacas Galindo, Enrique
  1905 *Arbitraje de Limites entre el Perú y Ecuador.* Madrid: Imprenta de los Hijos de M. G. Hernández.
Valladares, Alvaro
  1912 *Cartas sobre las Misiones Dominicanas del Oriente del Ecuador.* Segunda serie—carta primera. Quito: Imprenta de Santo Domingo.
van den Berghe, Pierre L.
  1967 *Race and Racism: A Comparative Perspective.* New York: Wiley.
  1974 "Ethnic Membership and Cultural Change in Guatemala." In Dwight Heath, ed., *Contemporary Cultures and Societies of Latin America: A Reader in the Social Anthropology of Middle and South America.* 2nd ed. New York: Random House, 316–327.
Velasco, Juan de
  1841 *Historia del Reino de Quito en la América Meridional,* vol. I. Quito: Imprenta del Gobierno.
Villavicencio, Manuel
  1858 *Geografía de la República del Ecuador.* New York: Robert Craighead.
Whitten, Norman E., Jr.
  1965 *Class, Kinship, and Power in an Ecuadorian Town: The Negroes of San Lorenzo.* Stanford, Calif.: Stanford University Press.

1974 *Black Frontiersmen: A South American Case.* New York: Halsted (Wiley).

1975 "Jungle Quechua Ethnicity: An Ecuadorian Case Study." In Leo Despres, ed., *Ethnicity and Resource Competition in Plural Societies.* World Anthropology series. The Hague: Mouton, 41–69.

Wise, Mary Ruth, and Olive A. Shell R.

1971 Grupos Idiomaticos del Peru. 2nd ed. Lima: Instituto Lingüístico de Verano y Universidad Nacional Mayor de San Marcos.

Yepez, Jacinto M.

1927 "Puyo y Sus Costumbres." *El Oriente Dominicano* 1(1):6–7.

World Council of Churches

1972 *The Situation of the Indian in South America.* Geneva: World Council of Churches.

Index

validation in asemblea general, 259;
change in name to directiva, 261. *See also*
Directiva
Callana River, 226
Camari. *See* Feast
Campesino, 282
Candoshi, 47, 217, 234
Canelos, 8, 15, 62, 65, 81, 103, 131, 193, 195,
196, 199, 201, 207, 209, 226, 227, 228,
231, 249, 290, 302, 303; Catholic mission,
5; Dominican mission, 10, 207–208, 211,
214; as Ecuadorian canton, 19th-century
boundaries, 10; culture mix, 16; and
Quichua language, 22; founding, 227;
archdiocese center, 243; comuna, 262;
airport, 262
Canelos mission, 10, 31, 214, 225;
depopulation, 47; subdivision in 18th
century, 207–208; and salt, 211; and trade,
211
Canelos Quichua: contrast with Quijos
Quichua, 3–4; origins, 5; and trade, 5; from
Achuara-Zaparoan merger, 7; and early
colonial experience, 7; culture and
formation, 8; trade with Andean people,
10; cultural markers, 11; culture area, 12;
population and territory, 13; reason for use
of term, 15; cultural hearth, 15;
intermarriage with Achuara, 16;
absorption of Zaparoan speakers, 16;
potential state, 20; articulation to other
systems, 27; bilingualism, 28; chagra and
forest, 37; color symbolism, 38; recent
history, 47; metaphor and ethnicity, 56;
ceremonial life, 59; dietary basis in chicha,
84; kinship system and cultural continuity,
121; culture and kinship dynamics, 135;
model of time and demography, 141;
summary of central role of ayllu ceremony
and Dominican folk Catholicism, 167; and
multi-ethnic core, 198–199; territory and
rubber, 210; and Puyo Runa
reconsolidation, 213; key ethnic marker,
219; ethnic dualism, 219; cultural
adaptation vis-à-vis Catholic Church,
221–222; as national guides, 224; cultural
adaptability, 269–273
Canelos Runa, 14, 20, 47, 140, 146, 206, 209,
218, 224, 231, 232; and Puyo Runa, 205
Caninche, 206, 218, 262

Canoe: symbolism, 140
Canton, 270, 277
Capahuari River, 14, 139, 217, 290
Capital, 252; acquisition, 239
Capitalism, 225
Cardinal points, 44, 60
Carneiro, Robert L., 126
Casagrande, Joseph B., 5, 248, 274
Caserío. *See* Hamlet
Caste, 273
Catholic Church, 202; mission at Canelos, 5;
serfdom, 5; missions and Quichua
language, 21; in Canelos Quichua
ceremony, 188, 189; and prioste selection,
189; and varayo-cabildo system, 200; and
bureaucratic expansion, 207; as broker
institution, 219; authority, 224; and
ethnocide, 278. *See also* Canelos mission;
Clergy; Dominican order
Cattle, 252, 266; in Puyo area, 247; and
chagra swidden system, 264
Caucheros, 47, 217, 234; derivation of term,
211
Caudillo, 237
Caves, 41, 238
Cayapa, 22
Cayman, 37, 38, 41, 67; as "grandmother" in
myth, 53, 55; ayllu, 58
Celestial symbolism, 44–45
Ceremonial enactment, 270
Ceremonial figurines, 172–177
Ceremonial leader. *See* Prioste
Ceremonial structure, 222, 225; hunting,
cross-cutting ties, 171; and lanceros, 180;
ritual enactment in, 180–194; and folk
Catholicism, 216; and intercultural
networks, 236
Ceremonial universe, 173–174, 177
Ceremony, 11, 28, 167–202, 243, 298; and
myth, 51; and visions, 59, 180;
shamanistic, 154–159; killing, 158;
structure of ayllu ceremony, 168; concept
of drummers in, 169; sex roles in, 169;
clergy in, 169, 189; interaction within
structure, 170; routine sequence of
preparation, 171–178; and role of lanceros,
179; and identity, 183; *Banisteriopsis* as
spirit in, 184; Datura as spirit in, 184; and
feast, 188, 191; and terminal ritual, 193;
summary, variations, field situation, 199;

Indi. *See* Sun
Indillama, 211, 231
Indio, 258–259, 274; as blanco construct,
 251–252; as racist construct, 279
Industry, 250; and rubber, 210
Infidelity: adjudication, 260
Inflation, 254
Information: dissemination, 18
Infrastructure, 239, 246, 262, 265, 277, 278,
 279, 283; Ecuador's national strategy, 19th
 and 20th centuries, 212; expansion,
 213–214; and colonization, 233; and
 foreign interests, 236, 247; of Comuna San
 Jacinto, 242; and oil exploration, 252
Inga, 29
Ingano. *See* Inga
Interaction style: chicha serving and
 drinking, 16, 85; household, 70; chagra,
 74; hunting, 79; hunter in household, 95;
 and llacta structure, 126; and marriage
 negotiation, 131; at death, 136–138; in
 shamanistic curing, 154–159; in huasi
 ritual, 166; in preparation for ceremony,
 170; and pottery manufacture, 172–177;
 and hunters' return, 178–180; in
 ceremonial enactment, 181–194; between
 ceremonial partitions, 185; and
 ceremonial feast, 189–194; military, 265
Internal colonialism, 273–277
Invariant structures, 23; summary, 135;
 huasi and ayllu conjoined at death, 137.
 See also Household; Maximal ayllu
Iquitos, 7. *See also* Zaparoan
Iquitos, Peru, 5, 30, 232
Isla (of Comuna San Jacinto), 247, 254, 259,
 262, 268, 269, 270, 271; definition, 245;
 road and effects, 246

Jácome, Nicanor, 289
Jaguar, 36, 41, 59, 80, 156, 170, 194, 201,
 222; and Amasanga, 37; in myth, 55, 56;
 ayllu, 58; and kinship, 105, 110; as
 powerful shaman, 156
Jatun huasi. *See* Household; Houses; Huasi
Jatun Paccha, 15, 249
Jatun Paccha Runa, 15
Jauya: definition, 117; formation as
 spouse-negotiating category, 130–131
Jefe político, 248, 261, 269–270; and illegal
 transcations, 272

Jesuits, 10; Borja mission, 8; and upper
 Amazon, 208; and documentation of
 depopulation, 208
Jilucu, 51, 168, 170, 171, 177, 185, 188; in
 ceremonial partition, 59
Jista. *See* Ceremony
Jisteros: preparation, 168–178
Jívaro: culture and ethnicity, 4; national
 stereotype, 5; contrast with Quichua, 5,
 230; pottery, 17; choice of term, 30
Jivaroan, 4, 5, 13, 16, 21, 22, 23, 30, 47, 135,
 199, 209, 210, 213, 284, 288; contrast with
 Quichua, 5; insolence stereotype, 5, 217;
 language replaced by Quichua, 22; salt
 trade with Canelos Quichua, 211; as
 raiding warriors in Puyo, 214; as Peruvian
 troops, 234; support to Canelos Quichua,
 282
Jívaro proper, 4, 5, 8, 11, 12, 14, 16, 23,
 29, 43, 60, 61, 128, 139, 159, 163, 179,
 193, 198, 202, 206, 207, 215, 217, 218,
 224, 226, 233, 234, 238, 247, 252, 255,
 262, 270, 282, 289, 297; compared to
 Canelos Quichua in concepts of souls and
 spirits, 104, 163; soul beliefs, 201–202; and
 Puyo Runa, 205, 219; attack by Ecuadorian
 military, 234; and Peruvian invasion of
 Ecuador, 234
Joking, 270
Juanjiri Runa. *See* Montalvo Runa
Juridical roles, 259, 260. *See also*
 Adjudication
Juri juri, 151, 157, 174, 178, 183, 238;
 description, 41; in Ancient Times, 47; and
 hunting, 80; and shamanistic killing, 158
Juro-political system: comuna evolution,
 257, 261, 276; adaptation, 273. *See also*
 Asemblea general

Kahuapana, 30
Karsten, Rafael, 5, 22, 31, 60, 61, 103, 136,
 140, 200, 201, 209, 225, 292
Kidnapping, 217
Killing ceremony, 158
Kin classes, 105–110, 111–116, 151;
 consanguineal, 106–107, 112–115; affinal,
 108–109, 113; defined as linked social
 statuses, 111; criteria, 112; primary,
 112–115; first ascending generation,
 115–118, 142; second ascending

218; ethnicity summary, 224, 230;
adaptation, summary, 224; as military
couriers, 232; as guides, 233–234; oil
exploration in 1930s, 233–234; after World
War II, 236; adaptive strategies, 236–238;
and national power, 237; as different from
other Runa territories, 237–238; armed
aggression, 238; disfranchisement, 243;
ethnic charter, 281; opt for expansion, 283
Puyo-Tena road, 248

Quechua. See Proto-Quechua; Quichua
Quichua, 3; contrast with Jívaro, 5, 230; and
formation of Canelos Quichua culture, 7;
as mediating language, 8; origins and
reconstruction, 20–21, 29; pre-Incaic as
trade language, 21; dominance of language
in Oriente, 22, 23; as lingua franca,, 23,
235; adaptive advantage, 23; details about,
29; dialects, Orr and Wrisley labels, 30;
Andean, 216, 226; language of porters,
231; national stereotypes, 279; number of
speakers, 284
Quijos, 5, 23, 135, 206, 207, 213, 218
Quijos Quichua, 3–4, 5, 7, 8, 11, 22, 30, 103,
125, 139, 163, 201, 218, 220, 223, 290, 304;
and Canelos Quichua intermarriage, 120,
128; and Puyo Runa, 205; displacement
from Napo tributaries, 230
Quilla. See Moon
Quito, 10, 24, 240, 245, 246, 247, 252, 258,
265, 267, 269, 270, 290, 300; Dominican
archdiocese, 10
Quito-Baeza road, 249

Racism, 243, 251, 274–275, 279, 284; of
Dominican order, 214; and development,
258–259
Radio, 250
Raiding, 179, 193, 205, 206, 211, 218;
warrior, 214, 219
Railroad: Ambato-Curaray, 212
Rain, 36, 38, 44, 61, 173, 191, 205, 229, 252;
and chicha, 166; ritual enactment, 167. See
also Water
Rainbow, 38; symbolism, 40. See also
Amarun
Rainforest, 279, 282, 284; description, 35;
elevation, 36, 206; symbolism, 37; contrast

with water, 38; in Puyo area, 206; and
ethnicity, 219, 251; ecology, 251, 279; and
development, 251, 266, 268, 276
Rank, 220, 247. See also Stratification
Rebirth, 141
Reciprocal labor exchange. See Minga
Reciprocity, 113–114, 129, 235–236, 245,
255; and marriage, 206; in raiding, 218;
asymmetrical between church and Alli
Runa, 219. See also Dyad
Reconstruction: of Puyo Runa baseline,
205–207
Red Cross, 248, 265, 300
Refuge zone, 135, 215, 216, 219, 280, 283;
and exchange of sons, 129; and Amazonian
rubber boom, 211; Puyo, 217; and
marriage, 234; potential loss, 254
Regionalism, 273
Reservations, 277
Residence: three alternatives, 127–128;
effects on ayllu and llacta, 127–128; and
marriage, 128, 131; relation to huasi and
ayllu continuity, 132. See also Marriage
Revitalization, 127
Rhythm, 165, 193; and waterfall spirit, 61
Ricsina: definition, 59, 296–297. See also
Knowledge
Río Chico, 200, 242, 247, 264; museum, 302
Río Topo, 226
Río Verde, 230
Ritual. See Ceremonial structure;
Ceremony; Ritual context; Ritual
enactment
Ritual context, 60; definition, in huasi, basic
movement, 165; of ceremonial helpers,
172; initiating hunt, 172; and social
readjustment, 195; soccer games, 255
Ritual enactment: of thunder, 165, 167; of
rain, 166, 167; soul in, 166; spirit in, 166; in
ceremonial structure, 180–194; drumming
in, 180–194; in front of church, 193–194; of
descent, 194; adaptive features, 236; as
territorial strategy, 271
Ritual kinship. See Compadrazgo; Gumba
Roads, 239, 248, 252, 262, 265, 267–268;
access, 246, 249; effects on colonist-
plantation-comunero interests and
strategies, 246; construction, 249. See
also Baños-Puyo road; Puyo-Napo road;
Puyo-Tena road; Quito-Baeza road

Yatapi River, 60
Yumbos, 5
Yurimaguas, Peru, 15, 21, 30, 47, 232

Zambo republic, 214
Zaparoan, 8, 10, 11, 12, 13, 21, 22, 23, 30, 43,
47, 128, 135, 139, 163, 199, 201, 202, 206,
207, 208, 210, 213, 217, 218, 224, 226,
228, 288; disease and slavery, 7; and
Canelos Quichua, 7; intermarriage with
Achuara, 13, 17; pottery tradition, 30;
biculturalism, bilingualism, 202
Zulay plantation, 231, 237, 242, 245